AMERICA'S
Wonderful
LITTLE
HOTELS
& INNS
1992

The Midwest

States and Canadian Provinces
Covered in This Edition

Illinois	North Dakota
Indiana	Ohio
Iowa	South Dakota
Kansas	Wisconsin
Michigan	
Minnesota	CANADA
Missouri	Northwest Territories
Nebraska	Ontario

Also in This Series

America's Wonderful Little Hotels & Inns, U.S.A. and Canada
America's Wonderful Little Hotels & Inns, New England
America's Wonderful Little Hotels & Inns, The Middle Atlantic
America's Wonderful Little Hotels & Inns, The South
America's Wonderful Little Hotels & Inns, The Rocky Mountains and The Southwest
America's Wonderful Little Hotels & Inns, The West Coast
Europe's Wonderful Little Hotels & Inns, Great Britain & Ireland
Europe's Wonderful Little Hotels & Inns, The Continent

AMERICA'S
Wonderful
LITTLE
HOTELS
& INNS
1992

The Midwest

Edited by Sandra W. Soule

Associate Editors:
Nancy P. Barker
June C. Horn
Kirstin O'Rielly
Mary Ann Boyle

Contributing Editors:
Suzanne Carmichael, Susan Waller Schwemm,
Linda F. Phillipps, Jennifer Klipstein, Ulla Olofsson

Editorial Assistants:
Neil Horn
Jeffrey Soule

St. Martin's Press
New York

This book is dedicated to the people who take the time and trouble to write about the hotels and inns they've visited, and to my children—Hilary and Jeffrey—my husband, and my parents.

The cover illustration was inspired by Pratt Taber Inn, Red Wing, Minnesota.

ISSN 1057-6436

ISBN 0-312-06282-6

First Edition

10   9   8   7   6   5   4   3   2   1

Maps by David Lindroth © 1992, 1991, 1990, 1989, 1988, 1987 by St. Martin's Press.

Contents

Acknowledgments

I would like again to thank all the people who wrote in such helpful detail about the inns and hotels they visited. To them belong both the dedication and the acknowledgments, for without their support, this guide would not exist. If I have inadvertently misspelled or omitted anyone's name, please accept my sincerest apologies.

I would also like to thank Hilary Rubinstein, who originated the concept for this series. Also thanks to my helpful and supportive editor, Anne Savarese; to my colleagues Nancy Barker, June Horn, Kirstin O'Rielly, and Mary Ann Boyle; to Neil Horn, my invaluable assistant; to Suzanne Carmichael, Susan Schwemm, Nancy Debevoise, Linda Goldberg, and Diane Wolf, my colleagues in the field; to John Blewer, April Burwell, Marjorie Cohen, Dianne Crawford, Arlyne Craighead, Willis Frick, Frank Hepler, Stephen Holman, Keith Jurgens, Dave Kendall, Jim & Tina Kirkpatrick, Zita Knific, Pat and Glen Lush, Betty Norman, Carolyn Mathiasen, Carolyn Myles, Ed Okie, Janet Payne, Mary Louise Rogers, Joe Schmidt, Jeanne Smith, Lee Todd, James and Janice Utt, Wendi Van Exan, Hope Welliver, Gay Whitehead, Diane Wolf, and Rose Wolf and the many others who went far beyond the call of duty in their assistance and support; and to Melania Lanni, for without her help, I'd never get anything done.

Introduction

Each entry generally has three parts: a description of the inn or hotel, quotes from guests who have stayed there, and relevant details about rooms, rates, location, and facilities. Occasionally you may find that no general description is given or that the factual data are incomplete. There are two reasons for this: Either the descriptions supplied by guests made this unnecessary, or the facility failed to supply us with adequate information because of time limitations or other problems.

Please remember that the length of an entry is in no way a reflection of that inn or hotel's quality. Rather, it is an indication of the type of feedback we've received both from guests and from the innkeepers themselves. Some hotel owners are totally unaware of this guide; others take an active role in encouraging their guests to write.

Wherever a location is of particular tourist interest, we've tried to include some information about its attractions. If we have only one listing for a town, this description usually falls within the body of the entry. If there is more than one inn or hotel listed for a town, the description of the town and information about its location precede the individual entries.

In some areas the magnet is not a particular town but rather a compact, distinct region. Travelers choose one place to stay and use it as a base from which to explore the area. But because this guide is organized by town, not by region, the entries are scattered throughout the chapter. When this applies, you will see the name of the region noted under the "Location" heading; check back to the introduction for a description of the region involved. For example, inns and hotels in Bucks County, Pennsylvania, start with Erwinna near the beginning of the chapter and extend to Upper Black Eddy at the end, but the description of the area itself is found at the beginning of the chapter.

The names at the end of the quotations are those who have recommended the hotel or inn. Some entries are entirely or largely quoted from one report; if several names follow the quotation, we have distinguished the writers of the quoted material by putting their names first. Some writers have requested that we not use their names; you will see initials noted instead. *We never print the names of those who have sent us adverse reports, although their contributions are invaluable indeed.*

Although we have tried to make the listings as accurate and complete as possible, mistakes and inaccuracies invariably creep in. The most significant area of inaccuracy applies to the rates charged by each establishment. In preparing this guide, we asked all the hotels and inns

1

to give us their 1992 rates, ranging from the least expensive room in the off-season to the most expensive peak-season price. Some did so, while others just noted the 1991 rate.

Since the process of writing and publishing a book takes nearly a year, please don't rely solely on the figures printed. *You should always double-check the rates when you make your reservations; please don't blame the hotel or this guide if the prices are wrong.* On the other hand, given the current level of inflation, you should not encounter anything more than a 5% increase, unless there has been a substantial improvement in the amenities offered or a change of ownership. Please let us know immediately if you find anything more than that!

If you find any errors of omission or commission in any part of the entries, we urgently request your help in correcting them. We recognize that it takes extra time and effort for readers to write us letters or fill in report forms, but this feedback is essential in keeping this publication totally responsive to consumer needs.

Inngoers' Bill of Rights

We've read through a lot more brochures for inns and hotels than the average bear, and can attest to the fact that not one makes mention of its possible drawbacks, however slight. And rightly so. A brochure is paid advertising, no more obligated to provide the full picture—both pros and cons—than a TV ad for diet soda. Furthermore, unlike this guidebook, *which accepts no fee of any kind for an entry,* most inn guidebooks charge a listing or membership fee of some kind, making them basically paid advertisements. Despite brochure promises and glowing listings in other books, we all know that perfection isn't possible in this world, but we feel that (despite the irate reactions of some innkeepers) complete and honest reporting will give readers *reasonable* expectations, ones that are often surpassed in the best of hostelries.

On the other hand, although perfection may not be on the menu, as guests (and customers), travelers have the right to expect certain minimum standards. These rights are especially important in hotels and inns at the top end of the rate scale; we don't expect as much from more modestly priced places, although it certainly is often received.

So, please use this Bill of Rights as a kind of checklist in deciding how you think a place stacks up on your own personal rating scale. And, whether an establishment fails, reaches, or exceeds these levels, be sure to let us know. These rights are especially important because of the financial penalties levied by most establishments; with the exception of the larger hotels, nearly every establishment listed in this book requires a substantial advance deposit, yet travelers have little or no recourse if facilities prove to be substandard. We would also hope that innkeepers will use this list to help evaluate both the strong points and shortcomings of their own establishments, and are grateful to those who have already done so.

The right to suitable cleanliness. An establishment that looks, feels, and smells clean, with no musty or smoky odors. Not just middle-of-the-room clean, but immaculate in all the nooks and crannies—under the radiators, in the dresser drawers, out on the balconies. Rooms should be immaculate prior to check-in, and kept as close as possible to that standard during your stay. You also have the right to prompt maid service, and should not have to wait until mid-afternoon for your room to be made up.

The right to suitable room furnishings. A comfortable bed with a firm mattress and soft pillows (preferably two per person), fresh clean linens, and blankets is a minimum. On *each* side of a double or larger-size bed should be a reading lamp (minimum 60 watts; ideal are three-way bulbs), along with a night table (or its equivalent) giving you a place to leave the bedtime necessities—a glass of water, a box of tissues, your eyeglasses and watch. Two comfortable chairs with good reading lights are a welcome addition, as is a well-lit mirror and readily accessible electric outlet in a room without a private bath. A well-equipped room also has adequate storage space for clothes, both in drawers and closets, along with extra pillows and blankets and a rack for your luggage.

The right to comfortable, attractive rooms. Guest rooms and common rooms that are not only attractive, but livable as well. Not just a visually handsome museum set piece, but a place where you'd like to spend some time reading, chatting, relaxing. You should be as comfortable as you are at home, without having to do any of the work to make yourself so.

The right to a decent bathroom. Of course, cleanliness heads the list here, followed by reliable plumbing, adequate and even supplies of hot water, decent lighting, an accessible electric outlet with wiring that can take a hair dryer, a fixed or hand-held shower added to old-fashioned tubs, a shelf or table for toiletries, and an ample supply of soft, absorbent towels. At more expensive accommodations, an "amenities kit" is a reasonable expectation.

The right to privacy and discretion. In even the most familial of inns, you are entitled to conduct private conversations in common rooms, and even more private ones in your own room—and you have the right *not* to hear the equally private conversations of your neighbors. The right to discretion precludes prying hosts' questions about one's marital status or sexual preference. A truly offensive intrusion on a guest's privacy is the practice of displaying proselytizing religious brochures, tracts, and signs.

The right to good, healthful food. Fresh nutritious food, ample in quantity, high in quality, attractively presented, and graciously served in enjoyable smoke-free surroundings—whether the offering is a cup of coffee and a roll, a seven-course gourmet dinner, or anything in between. An end to dessert masquerading as breakfast and ample supplies of brewed decaffeinated coffee and herbal teas is applauded. Freedom from pretentious menus written in fractured French menuspeak would be a welcome companion.

The right to comfortable temperatures and noise levels. Rooms should be reasonably cool on the hottest of summer nights and warm on the coldest winter evenings. Windows that open, screens without holes, fans, air conditioners, and heating systems that run quietly are all key; although not always possible, individually controlled thermostats are ideal. In locations where traffic noise is a problem, double- or even triple-glazed windows, drapes, and landscaping should all be in place.

The right to fair value. People don't stay in inns or small hotels because they are cheap, which is good, because very few of them are. What is expected, though, is a good value, with prices that are in reasonable relation to the facilities offered and to the cost of equivalent accommodation in the area. This right extends to the times when things go wrong. Even when the problem is beyond the innkeepers' control, guests have the right to an apology at a minimum, and restitution at maximum, depending on the situation. Guests do not have the right to perfection, but they have the right to innkeepers who are concerned and solicitous when a problem arises.

The right to genuine hospitality. Owners and staff who are sincerely glad you've come, and who make it their business to make your stay pleasant and memorable without being intrusive. Innkeepers who help guests to get to know each other when appropriate and who leave the less sociable to their own thoughts. While resident owners are best, resident staff is often acceptable; someone should be readily available for emergencies around the clock.

The right to a caring environment and little luxuries. Seeing that the little extras have been attended to—asking about pet allergies and dietary restrictions, making dinner reservations, providing inside and accurate information on area activities and events. Offering afternoon or evening refreshments, and welcoming new arrivals with refreshments appropriate to the season. Leaving a personal note, fresh flowers, or candies to greet guests is another way of saying welcome. Being there to provide toothpaste or a toothbrush to guests who have forgotten theirs at home. A good hostelry is more than accommodation. It's an end in itself, not just a means to an end. Amenities are more than imported soaps; innkeepers who are attuned to guests' needs and wants, anticipating them before they're even expressed, are the most important amenity of all.

The right to personal safety. Facilities in large cities need to be located in reasonably safe neighborhoods, with adequate care given to building security. Where caution, especially at night, is advisable, innkeepers have an obligation to share this information with guests.

The right to professionalism. Running an inn or hotel is not a business for amateurs, and guests have the right to receive requested brochures promptly, after one request, and to have their room reservations handled efficiently and responsibly. Check-in and check-out should be smooth, with rooms available as confirmed.

The right to adequate common areas. One of the key distinctions between a motel and an inn is the existence of at least one common room where guests can gather to read, chat, or relax, free of any pressure (implied or otherwise) to buy anything.

The right of people traveling alone to have all the above rights. Those traveling alone usually pay just a few dollars less than a couple, yet the welcome, services, and rooms they receive are often less than equal.

The right to a reasonable cancellation policy. Before booking, get the details. Penalties levied for a cancellation made less than 7–14 days before arrival is relatively standard at most inns; the 2–7 day policy found at many Western inns is preferable. Most inns will refund deposits (minus a processing fee) even after the deadline if the room is rebooked. We feel that all should offer the chance to rebook within a few months as an alternative to cancellation penalties. To be avoided are inns with policies such as this: "On cancellations received less than 45 days in advance, the deposit [approximately 50%] is not refundable, whether the room is re-rented or not."

Of course, there is no "perfect" inn or hotel, even when every provision of the bill of rights is met, since people's tastes and needs vary so greatly. But one key phrase does pop up in the hotel/inn reports over and over again, whether the writer is describing a small hotel in the city or a country inn: "I felt right at home." This is not written in the literal sense—a commercial lodging, no matter how cozy or charming, is never the same as one's home. What is really meant is that guests felt as welcome, as relaxed, as comfortable, as they would in their own home. One writer put it this way: "Where does one start in describing this inn? With mixed feelings. (It's a wonderful place, and I don't want the world to discover and spoil it.) But I'll tell you about this grand hideaway. It's clean, quiet, isolated, warm, and comfortable. The fireplaces work and the owners seem intent on making your stay happy. They describe dinner specials with smiles, remember you from trip to trip, and are willing to help in any way they can. The unique qualities of each room make you want to try them all. It's a wonderful place. Please don't take my room."

What makes for a wonderful stay?

We've tried our best to make sure that all the hotels and inns listed in this guide are as wonderful as our title promises. Inevitably, there will be some disappointments. Sometimes these will be caused by a change in owner-ship or management that has resulted in lowered standards. Other times unusual circumstances, which can arise in the best of establishments, will lead to problems. Quite often, though, problems will occur because there's not a good "fit" between the inn or hotel and the guest. Decide what you're looking for, then find the inn that suits your needs, whether you're looking for a casual environment or a dressy one, a romantic setting or a family-oriented one, a vacation spot or a businessperson's environment, an isolated country retreat or a convenient in-town location.

We've tried to give you as much information as possible on each hotel or inn listed, and have taken care to indicate the atmosphere each inn-keeper is trying to create. After you've read the listing, write, if there is time, for a copy of the establishment's brochure, which will give you more information. Finally, feel free to call any inn or hotel where you're plan-ning to stay, and ask as many questions as necessary.

Inn etiquette

A first-rate inn is a joy indeed, but as guests we need to do our part to respect its special qualities. For starters, you'll need to maintain a higher level of consideration for your fellow guests. Century-old Victorians are noted for their nostalgic charms, not their sound-proofing; if you come in late or get up early, remember that voices and footsteps echo off all those gleaming hardwood floors and doors. If you're going to pick a fight with your roommate, pull the covers up over your head or go out for a walk. If you're sharing a bath, don't dawdle, tidy up after yourself, and dry your hair back in your room. If you've admired the Oriental carpets, antique decor, handmade quilts, and the thick fluffy towels, don't leave wet glasses on the furniture, put suitcases on the bed, or use the towels for wiping the snow off your skis or car. After all, innkeepers have rights too!

Hotels, inns . . . resorts and motels

As the title indicates, this is a guide to exceptional inns and hotels. Generally, the inns have 5 to 25 rooms, although a few have only 2 rooms and some have over 100. The hotels are more often found in the cities and range in size from about 50 to 200 rooms.

The line between an inn or hotel and a resort is often a fine one. There are times when we all want the extra facilities a resort provides, so we've added a number of reader-recommended facilities to this edition.

You'll also find that we've listed a handful of motels. Although they don't strictly fall within the context of this book, we've included them because we received letters strongly endorsing their positive qualities, particularly their concerned and involved owners and friendly atmosphere, two qualities usually lacking in even the best of motels. A number of these recommendations have come for properties in the Best Western chain. Please don't be put off by this; Best Western is a franchise operation, with no architectural unity from one property to the next. Those listed in this guide have substantial architectural or historical appeal, and concerned, professional management.

Although we do not provide full coverage of hotel chains, we do want to point out that the Four Seasons and Ritz-Carlton hotels are almost impossible to beat at the luxury end of the spectrum. Readers consistently rave about their unbeatable combination of unparalleled service and plush accommodation.

Rooms

All hotel and inn rooms are not created equal. Although the rooms at a typical chain motel or hotel may be identical, the owners of most of the establishments described in this book pride themselves on the individuality of each guest room. Some, although not all, of these differences are reflected in the rates charged.

More important, it means that travelers need to express their needs clearly to the innkeepers when making reservations and again when checking in. Some rooms may be quite spacious but may have extremely small private baths or limited closet space. Some antique double beds have rather high footboards—beautiful to look at but torture for people over six feet tall! Many inns are trading their double beds in for queens and kings; if you prefer an oversize bed, say so. If you want twin beds, be sure to specify this when making reservations and again when you check in; many smaller inns have only one or two twin-bedded rooms.

Some rooms may have gorgeous old bathrooms, with tubs the size of small swimming pools, but if you are a hard-core shower person, that room won't be right for you. Many others have showers but no baths, which may be disappointing if you love a long, luxurious soak in the tub. If you are traveling on business and simply must have a working-size desk with good light, speak up. Some rooms look terrific inside but don't look out at anything much; others may have the view but not quite as special a decor. Sometimes the best rooms may look out onto a main road and can be quite noisy. Decide what's important to you. Although the owners and staff of the hotels and inns listed here are incredibly hard-working and dedicated people, they can't read your mind. Let your needs be known, and, within the limits of availability, they will try to accommodate you.

Our most frequent complaints center around beds that are too soft and inadequate reading lights. If these are priorities for you (as they are for us), don't be shy about requesting bedboards or additional lamps to remedy the situation. Similarly, if there are other amenities your room is lacking— extra pillows, blankets, or even an easy chair—speak up. Most innkeepers would rather put in an extra five minutes of work than have an unhappy guest.

If your reservation is contingent upon obtaining a particular room, make this very clear to the innkeeper. Some inns will not accept such reservations, feeling that they are too difficult to guarantee. Those that do accept them have an obligation to meet their guarantee; if circumstances prevent them from following through on the promised room, make it clear that you expect some sort of remuneration—either the return of your deposit or a reduction in the price of another room.

If you really don't like your room, ask for another as soon as possible, preferably before you've unpacked your bags. The sooner you voice your dissatisfaction, the sooner something can be done to improve the situation. If you don't like the food, ask for something else—in other words, you're the guest, make sure you get treated like one. If things go terribly wrong, don't be shy about asking for your money back, and be *sure* to write us about any problems.

What is a single? A double? A suite? A cottage or cabin?

Unlike the proverbial rose, a single is not a single is not a single. Sometimes it is a room with one twin bed, which really can accommodate only one person. Quite often it is described as a room with a standard-size double bed, in contrast to a double, which has two twin beds. Other hotels call both of the preceding doubles, although doubles often have queen- or even king-size beds instead. Many times the only distinction is made by the number of guests occupying the room; a single will pay slightly less, but there's no difference in the room.

There's almost as much variation when it comes to suites. We define a suite as a bedroom with a separate living room area and often a small kitchen, as well. Unfortunately, since suites are now a very popular concept in the hotel business, the word has been stretched to cover other setups, too. Some so-called suites are only one large room, accommodating a table and separate seating area in addition to the bed. If you require a suite that has two separate rooms with a door between them, specify this when you make reservations.

Quite a few of our entries have cabins or cottages in addition to rooms in the main building. In general, a cabin is understood to be a somewhat more rustic residence than a cottage, although there's no hard-and-fast rule. Be sure to inquire for details when making reservations.

What is a B&B anyway?

There are basically two kinds of B&Bs—the B&B homestay, and the B&B inn. The homestay is typically the home of an empty nester, who has a few empty bedrooms to fill, gaining some extra income and pleasant company. B&B inns are run on a more professional basis, independently marketed and subject to state and local licensing. Guests typically have dedicated common areas for their use, and do not share the hosts' living quarters, as in a homestay. We list very few homestays in this guide. Full-service or country inns and lodges are similar to the B&B inn, except that they serve breakfast and dinner on a regular basis, and may be somewhat larger in size; dinner is often offered to the public as well as to house guests. The best of all of these are made special by resident owners bringing the warmth of their personalities to the total experience. A B&B is *not* a motel that serves breakfast.

Making reservations

Unless you are inquiring many months in advance of your visit, it's best to telephone when making reservations. This offers a number of advantages: You will know immediately if space is available on your requested dates; you can find out if that space is suitable to your specific needs. You will have a chance to discuss the pros and cons of the available rooms and will be able to find out about any changes made in recent months—new facilities, recently redecorated rooms, nonsmoking policies, possibly even a change of ownership. It's also a good time to ask the innkeeper about other concerns—Is the neighborhood safe at night? Is any renovation or construction in progress that might be disturbing? Will a wedding reception or other social function be in progress during your visit that might affect your use of the common areas or parking lot? If you're reserving a room at a plantation home that is available for public tours, get specifics about the check-in/out times; in many, rooms are not available before 5 P.M. and must be vacated by 9 A.M. sharp. The savvy traveler will always get the best value for his accommodation dollar.

If you expect to be checking in late at night, *be sure to say so;* many inns give doorkeys to their guests, then lock up by 10 P.M.

We're often asked about the need for making advance reservations. If you'll be traveling in peak periods, in prime tourist areas, and want to be sure of getting a first-rate room at the best-known inns, reserve at least three to six months ahead. This is especially true if you're traveling with friends or family and will need more than one room. On the other hand, if you like a bit of adventure, and don't want to be stuck with cancellation fees when you change your mind, by all means stick our book in the glove compartment and hit the road. If you're traveling in the off-season, or even midweek in season, you'll have a grand time. But look for a room by late afternoon; never wait until after dinner and hope that you'll find something decent.

Payment

Many innkeepers don't like plastic any better for payment than they do for decorating. Some accept credit cards for the initial deposit but prefer cash, traveler's checks, or personal checks for the balance; others offer the reverse policy. Still others have accepted credit cards as a part of modern living. When no credit cards are accepted at all, you can settle your bill with a personal check, traveler's check, or even (!) cash.

When using your credit card to guarantee a reservation, be aware that some inns and hotels will charge your card for the amount of the deposit only, while others will put a "hold" on your card for the full amount of your entire stay, plus the cost of meals and incidentals that you may (or may not) spend. If you're using your card to reserve a fairly extended trip, you may find that you're well over your credit limit without actually having spent a nickel. We'd suggest inquiring; if the latter is the procedure, either send a check for the deposit or go elsewhere.

Rates

All rates quoted are per room, unless otherwise noted as being per person. Rates quoted per person are usually based on double occupancy, unless otherwise stated.

"Room only" rates do not include any meals. In most cases two or three meals a day are served by the hotel restaurant, but are charged separately. Average meal prices are noted when available. In a very few cases no meals are served on the premises at all; rooms in these facilities are usually equipped with kitchenettes.

B&B rates include bed and breakfast. Breakfast, though, can vary from a simple continental breakfast to an expanded continental breakfast to a full breakfast. Afternoon tea and evening refreshments are sometimes included, as well.

MAP (Modified American Plan) rates are often listed per person and include breakfast and dinner. Only a few of the inns listed serve lunch, although many will prepare a picnic on request for an additional charge.

State and local sales taxes are not included in the rates; the percentage varies from state to state and is noted in the introduction to each state chapter or in the individual listing. When budgeting for your trip, remember that taxes can easily add 10–15% to the cost of your travels.

When inquiring about rates, always ask if any off-season or special package rates are available. Sometimes discounted rates are available *only* on request; seniors and AAA members often qualify for substantial discounts. During the week, when making reservations at city hotels or country inns, it's important to ask if any corporate rates are available. Depending on the establishment, you may or may not be asked for some proof of corporate affiliation (a business card is usually all that's needed), but it's well worth inquiring, since the effort can result in a saving of 15 to 20%, plus an upgrade to a substantially better room. Another money-saving trick can be to look for inns in towns a bit off the beaten path. If you stay in a town that neighbors a famous resort or historic community, you will often find that rates are anywhere from $20 to $50 less per night for equivalent accommodation. If you're travelling without reservations, and arrive at a half-empty inn in late afternoon, don't hesitate to ask for a price reduction or free room upgrade. And of course, watch for our ¢ symbol, which indicates places which are a particularly good value.

If an establishment has a specific tipping policy, whether it is "no tipping" or the addition of a set service charge, it is noted under "Rates." When both breakfast and dinner is included in the rates, a 15% service charge is standard; a number of B&Bs are also adding on 10%, a practice which sits poorly with us. When no notation is made, it's generally expected that guests will leave about 5 to 10% for the housekeeping staff and 15% for meal service. A number of inns have taken to leaving little cards or envelopes to remind guests to leave a tip for the housekeepers; this practice is spreading as are reader complaints on the subject. Reported one reader: "An envelope was left out for tips for the chambermaids, a practice I dislike very much. I would much rather they paid their employees a living wage and add a service charge if they must. I don't wish to be told that the maids rely on my generosity to pay their rent." If you welcome a no tipping policy, and object to solicitation, be sure to let the innkeeper know.

A few readers have indicated that they feel some innkeepers have taken advantage of the current popularity of B&Bs with a disproportionate increase in their rates: "I've encountered a few American B&Bs without a private bath and serving only a barely adequate continental breakfast that charge two people as much or more than a good chain motel would. Granted, there's a more personal touch, but given the lack of motel amenities, I think the price should be somewhat lower. Even some B&Bs with private baths and considerable charm are, I fear, suffering delusions of grandeur when pricing themselves in the range of a grand hotel." (AD) We agree; judging from recent feedback, so do many of you. Opinions?

Deposits and cancellations

Nearly all innkeepers print their deposit and cancellation policies clearly on their brochures. Deposits generally range from payment of the first night's stay to 50% of the cost of the entire stay. Some inns repeat the cancellation policy when confirming reservations. In general, guests canceling well in advance of the planned arrival (two to four weeks is typical) receive a full refund minus a cancellation fee. After that date, no refunds are offered unless the room is resold to someone else. A few will not refund *even if the room is resold,* so take careful note. If you're making a credit card booking over the phone, be sure to find out what the cancellation policy is.

We would like to applaud many of the inns of the Northwest, where only two to seven days' notice of cancellation is required, and would love to see other areas follow suit. We also feel that even if you cancel on short notice, you should be given the opportunity to rebook within a reasonable time period rather than losing your entire deposit.

Sometimes the shoe may be on the other foot. Even if you were told earlier that the inn at which you really wanted to stay was full, it may be worthwhile to make a call to see if cancellations have opened up any last-minute vacancies.

Minimum stays

Two- and three-night minimum weekend and holiday stays are the rule at many inns during peak periods. We have noted these when possible, although we suspect that the policy may be more common than is always indicated in print. On the other hand, you may just be hitting a slow period, so it never hurts to ask if a one-night reservation would be accepted. Again, cancellations are always a possibility; you can try calling on a Friday or Saturday morning to see if something is available for that night.

Pets

Very few of the inns and hotels listed accept pets. When they do we've noted it under "Extras." On the other hand, over one-half of the country inns listed in this book have at least one dog or cat, sometimes more. If you are highly allergic to animals, *we strongly urge that you inquire for details before making reservations.*

Children

Some inns are family-style places and welcome children of all ages; we've marked them with our ♦ symbol. Others do not feel that they have facilities for the very young and only allow children over a certain age. Still others cultivate an "adults only" atmosphere and don't even welcome children at dinner. When inns and hotels do not encourage all children, we've noted the age requirement under the heading "Restrictions." If special facilities are available to children, these are noted under "Facilities" and "Extras." If an inn does not exclude children yet does not offer any special amenities or rate reductions for them, we would suggest it only for the best-behaved youngsters.

Whatever the policy, you may want to remind your children to follow the same rules of courtesy toward others that we expect of adults. Be aware that the pitter-patter of little feet on an uncarpeted hardwood floor can sound like a herd of stampeding buffalo to those on the floor below. Children used to the indestructible plastics of contemporary homes will need to be reminded (more than once) to be gentle with furniture that dates back 100 years or more.

For some reason, Southerners seem to be more tolerant of children than are New Englanders. Of the dozens of exquisitely decorated, antique-filled inns in the South, there are very few that exclude kids. In the North, nearly all do! And California innkeepers apparently would prefer it if children never crossed the state borders at all! Most inns there won't take any children under 12, and some are strictly for adults only.

State laws governing discrimination by age are affecting policies at some inns. To our knowledge, both California and Michigan now have such laws on the books, although this was rarely reflected in the brochures sent to us by inns in those states. Some inns get around this by limiting room occupancy to two adults. This discourages families by forcing them to pay for two rooms instead of one. Our own children are very clear on their preferences: although they've been to many inns that don't encourage guests under the age of 12, they find them "really boring"; on the other hand, they've loved every family-oriented place we've ever visited.

11

Porterage and packing

Only the largest of our listings will have personnel whose sole job is to assist guests with baggage. In the casual atmosphere associated with many inns, it is simply assumed that guests will carry their own bags. If you do need assistance with your luggage—because you have a bad back, because your bags are exceptionally heavy, or for any other reason at all—don't hesitate to say so; it should be gladly given. Ideally, innkeepers and their staff should ask you if you need help, but if they forget, don't suffer silently; just say "Could you give us a hand?"

If you're planning an extended trip to a number of small inns, we'd suggest packing as lightly as possible, using two small bags rather than one large suitcase. You'll know why if you've ever tried hauling a 50-pound oversize suitcase up a steep and narrow 18th-century staircase. On the other hand, don't forget about the local climate when assembling your wardrobe. In mountainous and desert regions, day- and nighttime temperatures can vary by as much as 40 degrees. Also, bear in mind that Easterners tend to dress more formally than Westerners; if you'll be traveling in New England or the South, men should pack a tie and jacket, women a skirt or dress.

Meals

If you have particular dietary restrictions—low-salt, vegetarian, or religious—or allergies—to caffeine, nuts, whatever—be sure to mention these when making reservations and again at check-in. If you're allergic to a common breakfast food or beverage, an evening reminder will ensure that you'll be able to enjoy the breakfast that's been prepared for you. Most innkeepers will do their best to accommodate your special needs, although, as one innkeeper noted tartly, "we're not operating a hospital."

In preparing each listing, we asked the owners to give us the cost of prix fixe and à la carte meals when available. An "alc dinner" price at the end of the "Rates" section is the figure we were given when we requested the average cost, in 1992, of a three-course dinner with a half bottle of house wine, including tax and tip. Prices listed for prix fixe meals do not include wine and service. Lunch prices, where noted, do not include the cost of any alcoholic beverage. Hotels and inns which serve meals to the public are noted with the ✕ symbol.

Dinner and lunch reservations are always a courtesy and are often essential. Most B&B owners will offer to make reservations for you; this can be especially helpful in getting you a table at a popular restaurant in peak season and/or on weekends. Some of the establishments we list operate restaurants fully open to the public. Others serve dinner primarily to their overnight guests, but they also will serve meals to outsiders; reservations are essential at such inns, usually eight or more hours in advance.

Quite a number of restaurants require jackets and ties for men at dinner, even in rather isolated areas. Of course, this is more often the case in traditional New England and the Old South than in the West. Unless you're going only to a very casual country lodge, we recommend that men bring them along and that women have corresponding attire.

12

Breakfast: Breakfast is served at nearly every inn or hotel listed in this guide. Those that do not, should. No inn is truly "wonderful" if you have to get in your car and drive somewhere for a cup of coffee and a roll, and early-morning strolls should be the choice of the guest, not the host! Nor do we consider the availability of coffee and tea alone an appropriate substitute.

The vast majority of lodgings listed include breakfast in their rates. Whenever possible we describe a typical breakfast, rather than using the largely meaningless terms "continental" or "full" breakfast.

Continental breakfast ranges from coffee and store-bought pastry to a lavish offering of fresh fruit and juices, yogurt and granola, cereals, even cheese and cold meats, homemade muffins and breads, and a choice of decaffeinated or regular coffee, herbal and regular tea. There's almost as much variety in the full breakfasts, which range from the traditional eggs, bacon, and toast, plus juice and coffee, to three-course gourmet extrava-ganzas.

We've received occasional complaints about the lack of variety in the breakfasts served. No one likes to have pancakes three days in a row, and doctors advise against having eggs every day. Sweet breads and muffins are the only breakfast offering at some establishments, yet many would prefer a roll or slice of toast. As one reader put it: "Bed and breakfast hosts seem to think that in order for a breakfast to be special, it has to be sweet. They should make plain toast or unsweetened rolls available to guests without the guest having to ask for them. People feel funny about making special requests—they don't want to cause trouble. What about diabetics? What about people like my husband who simply don't care much for sweets? There are plenty of good things for breakfast that don't have to be made with sugar." We agree. Do make your preferences known!

Lunch: Very few of the inns and hotels listed here serve lunch. Those that do generally operate a full-service restaurant, and you'll see some mention of it in the listing. Quite a number of B&B inns are happy to make up picnic lunches for an additional fee. We've noted this where we know about it; if we haven't, just ask if they can do one for you.

Dinner: Meals served at the inns listed here vary widely from simple home-style family cooking to gourmet cuisine. We are looking for food that is a good, honest example of the type of cooking involved. Ingredi-ents should be fresh and homemade as far as is possible; service and presentation should be pleasant and straightforward. We are not inter-ested in elaborate and pretentious restaurants where the descriptions found on the menu far exceed the chef's ability to prepare the dishes.

Here's how one of our readers put it, reporting on an inn in Virginia: "The inn had changed owners from our first to our second visit, a few years later. Although the rooms were much improved, the food was not. Dinner was of the type I describe as 'American pretentious,' the sort of ambitious would-be haute (and haughty) cuisine that a regional inn with-out a fine professional chef and kitchen staff is ill-advised to attempt. The innkeepers would have been much better off keeping the old cooks who were still in the kitchen the first time we visited, preparing the same

delicious Southern home cooking they'd been doing for at least 30 years."
(Ann Delugach)

Drinks

With a very few exceptions (noted under "Restrictions" in each listing), alcoholic beverages may be enjoyed in moderation at all of the inns and hotels listed. Most establishments with a full-service restaurant serving the public as well as overnight guests are licensed to serve beer, wine, and liquor to their customers, although "brown-bagging" or BYOB (bring your own bottle) is occasionally permitted, especially in dry counties. Bed & breakfasts, and inns serving meals primarily to overnight guests, do not typically have liquor licenses, although most will provide guests with setups, i.e., glasses, ice, and mixers, at what is often called a BYO (bring your own) bar.

Overseas visitors will be amazed at the hodgepodge of regulations around the country. Liquor laws are determined in general by each state, but individual counties, or even towns, can prohibit or restrict the sale of alcoholic beverages, even beer.

Smoking

Most of the larger inns and hotels do not have any smoking restrictions, except to prohibit cigars and pipes in dining rooms; restrictions at smaller establishments are becoming quite common. Where prohibitions apply we have noted this under "Restrictions." When smoking is prohibited in the guest rooms, this is usually for safety reasons; when it's not allowed in the common rooms, it's because your hosts don't care for the smell. A growing number of inns prohibit indoor smoking entirely. We suggest that confirmed smokers be courteous or make reservations elsewhere. One reader noted with dismay that although smoking was not specifically prohibited at one inn, no ashtrays were in evidence, making her feel very uncomfortable about lighting up. When making reservations at larger hotels, nonsmokers should be sure to ask if nonsmoking rooms are available. Such rooms, which have been set aside and specially cleaned, have become common.

Physical limitations and wheelchair accessibility

We asked every innkeeper if the hotel or inn was suitable for the disabled, and if yes, what facilities were provided. Unfortunately, the answer was often no. A great many inns dating back 80 years or more have far too many steps and narrow doorways to permit wheelchair access. If you do not need a wheelchair but have difficulty with stairs, we urge you to mention this when making reservations; many inns and small hotels have one or two rooms on the ground floor, but very few have elevators. Similarly, if you are visually handicapped, do share this information so that you may be given a room with good lighting and no unexpected steps.

Where the answer was positive, we have noted under "Extras" the facilities offered. In some cases the response was not nearly as complete as we would have liked. Wheelchair access (via ramp) to inn and hotel restaurants tends to be better than guest room accessibility. City hotels often have street-level entrances and, of course, elevators. Some innkeepers noted that ground-floor guest rooms were wheelchair accessible but did not note whether that applied to the bathrooms, as well. Please do inquire for details when making reservations, and please share your findings with us.

Air-conditioning

Heat is a relative condition, and the perceived need for air-conditioning varies tremendously from one individual to the next. If an inn or hotel has air-conditioning, you'll see this listed under "Rooms." If it's important to you, be sure to ask when making reservations. If air-conditioning is not available, check to see if fans are provided. Remember that top-floor rooms in most inns (usually a converted attic) can be uncomfortably warm even in relatively cool climates.

Transportation

A car is more or less essential for visiting most of the inns and hotels listed here, as well as the surrounding sights of interest. Exceptions are those located in the major cities. In some historic towns, a car is the easiest way to get there, but once you've arrived, you'll want to find a place to park the car and forget about it.

If you are traveling by public transportation, check the "Extras" section at the end of each write-up. If the innkeepers are willing to pick you up from the nearest airport, bus, or train station, you'll see it noted here. This service is usually free or available at modest cost. If it's not listed, the innkeeper will direct you to a commercial facility that can help.

Parking

Although not a concern in most cases, parking is a problem in many cities, beach resorts, and historic towns. If you'll be traveling by car, ask the innkeeper for advice when making reservations. If parking is not on-site, stop at the hotel first to drop off your bags, then go park the car. In big cities, if "free parking" is included in the rates, this usually covers only one arrival and departure. Additional "ins and outs" incur substantial extra charges. Be sure to ask.

If on-site parking is available in areas where parking can be a problem, we've noted it under "Facilities." Since it's so rarely a problem in country inns, we haven't included that information in those listings.

Christmas travel

Many people love to travel to a country inn or hotel at Christmas. Quite a number of places do stay open through the holidays, but the extent to which the occasion is celebrated varies widely indeed. We know of many inns that decorate beautifully, serve a fabulous meal, and organize all kinds of traditional Christmas activities. But we also know of others, especially in ski areas, that do nothing more than throw a few token ornaments on a tree. Be sure to inquire.

Is innkeeping for me?

Many of our readers fantasize about running their own inn; for some the fantasy may soon become a reality. Before taking the big plunge, it's vital to find out as much as you can about this very demanding business. Experienced innkeepers all over the country are offering seminars for those who'd like to get in the business. While these can be very helpful, they tend to be limited by the innkeepers' own experience with only one or two inns. (Some examples are the Chanticleer in Ashland, Oregon; the Wildwood Inn in Ware, Massachusetts; the Wedgwood Inn in New Hope, Pennsylvania; the Lord's Proprietors Inn in Edenton, North Carolina; and the Big Spring Inn in Greeneville, Tennessee; see entries for addresses.) For a broader perspective, we'd suggest you contact Bill Oates (P.O. Box 1162, Brattleboro, VT 05301; 802–254–5931) and find out when and where he'll be offering his next seminar entitled "How to Purchase and Operate a Country Inn." Bill is a highly respected pro in this field and has worked with innkeepers facing a wide range of needs and problems; his newsletter, *Innquest*, is written for prospective innkeepers looking to buy property. Another good source is Pat Hardy and Jo Ann Bell, publishers of *Innkeeping Newsletter*, as well as a number of books for would-be innkeepers. They also offer a biannual workshop in Santa Barbara, California, entitled "So, you think you want to be an innkeeper?" For details contact them at P.O. Box 90710 Santa Barbara, CA 93190; 805–965–0707.

For more information

The best sources of travel information in this country and in Canada are absolutely free; in many cases, you don't even have to supply the cost of a stamp or telephone call. They are the state and provincial tourist offices.

For each state you'll be visiting, request a copy of the official state map, which will show you every little highway and byway and will make exploring much more fun; it will also have information on state parks and major attractions in concise form.

Ask also for a calendar of events and for information on topics of particular interest, such as fishing or antiquing, vineyards or crafts; many states have published B&B directories, and some are quite informative. If you're going to an area of particular tourist interest, you might also want to ask the state office to give you the name of the regional tourist board for more detailed information. You'll find the addresses and telephone numbers for all the states and provinces covered in this book in Appendix 4, at the back of this book.

You may also want to contact the local chamber of commerce for information on local sights and events of interest or even an area map.

You can get the necessary addresses and telephone numbers from the inn or hotel where you'll be staying or from the state tourist office.

If you are one of those people who never travel with fewer than three guidebooks (which includes us), you will find the AAA and Mobil regional guides to be helpful references. The Mobil guides can be found in any bookstore, while the AAA guides are distributed free on request to members. Both series cover hotels, restaurants, and sightseeing information, although we find the AAA guides to offer wider coverage and more details. If you're not already a AAA member, *we'd strongly urge you join before your next trip;* in addition to their road service, they offer quality guidebooks and maps, and an excellent discount program at many hotels (including a number listed here).

We'd also like to tell you about a guidebook that makes a delightful companion to our own. *The Traveler's Guide to American Crafts,* by contributing editor Suzanne Carmichael, is divided into eastern and western editions. Suzanne leads readers to the workshops and galleries of outstanding craftspeople in every state.

Guidebooks are published only once a year (or less frequently); if you'd like to have a more frequent update, we'd suggest one of the following:

Uncommon Lodgings (P.O. Box 181329, Dallas, TX 75218; 214–343–9766) $15.95, 11 issues annually, $1.50 single copy. Lots of information on inns all over the country, from a delightfully opinionated editor; an excellent value.

Innsider (821 Wanda, Ferndale, MI 48220; 313–541–6623) $18, 6 issues annually. Country inns, B&Bs, historic lodgings; inn-depth articles and lots of pictures; also recipes, book reviews, misc.

Country Inns/Bed & Breakfasts (P.O. Box 182, South Orange, NJ 07079; 800–435–0715) $15, 6 issues annually. As above. Exceptional photography and paper quality.

Glossary of Architectural and Decorating Terms

We are not architectural experts, and when we started writing *America's Wonderful Little Hotels & Inns,* we didn't know a dentil from a dependency, a tester from a transom. We've learned a bit more since then, and hope that our primer of terms, prepared by associate editor Nancy Barker, will also be helpful to you.

Adam: building style (1780–1840) featuring a classic box design with a dominant front door and fanlight, and accented by an elaborate surround or an entry porch; cornice with decorative moldings incorporating dentil, swag, garland, or stylized geometric design. Three-part Palladian-style windows are common.

antebellum: existing prior to the U.S. Civil War (1861–1865).

Arts and Crafts movement: considered the first phase of the Modern movement that led to the Prairie style (1900–20) of Frank Lloyd Wright in Chicago, and the Craftsman style (1905–30) of the Greene brothers in Southern California. In the Arts and Crafts style, historical precedent for decoration and design was rejected and ornamentation, while not eliminated, was "modernized" to remove any trace of its historic origins. It

17

features low-pitched roofs, wide eave overhangs, and both symmetrical and asymmetrical front facades.

carpenter Gothic: *see* country, folk Victorian.

chinoiserie: imitation of Chinese decorative motifs; i.e., simulated Oriental lacquer covering pine or maple furniture. See also Chinese Chippendale below.

Chippendale: named for English furniture designer, Thomas Chippendale, of the Queen Anne period (1750–1790); the style varies from the Queen Anne style more in ornamentation than overall form, with more angular shapes and heavier carving of shells, leaves, scrolls. Chinese Chippendale furniture employs chiefly straight lines, bamboo turnings, and as decoration, fluting, and fretwork in a variety of lattice patterns.

Colonial Revival: building style (1880–1955) featuring a classic box design with a dominant front door elaborated with pilasters and either a pediment (Georgian-style) or a fanlight (Adam-style); double-hung windows symmetrically balanced, frequently in adjacent pairs.

corbel: an architectural member that projects from a wall to support a weight and is stepped outward and upward from the vertical surface.

Corinthian: column popular in Greek Revival style for support of porch roofs; the capitals are shaped like inverted bells and decorated with acanthus leaves.

cornice: projecting horizontal carving or molding that crowns a wall or roof.

country, folk Victorian: simple house form (1870–1910) with accents of Victorian (usually Queen Anne or Italianate) design in porch spindlework and cornice details. Also known as carpenter Gothic.

Craftsman: building style (1905–1930) with low-pitched, gabled roof and wide, unenclosed eave overhang; decorative beams or braces added under gables; usually one story; porches supported by tapered square columns that frequently extend to ground level.

dentil: exterior or interior molding characterized by a series of small rectangular blocks projecting like teeth.

dependencies: buildings that are subordinate to the main dwelling; i.e., a detached garage or barn. *See* also garçonnière.

Doric: column popular in Greek Revival style for support of porch roofs; the simplest of the three styles, with a fluted column, no base, and a square capital.

Eastlake: architectural detail on Victorian houses, commonly referred to as "gingerbread." Typically has lacy spandrels and knoblike beads, in exterior and interior design, patterned after the style of Charles Eastlake, an English furniture designer. Eastlake also promoted Gothic and Jacobean Revival styles with their strong rectangular lines; quality workmanship instead of machine manufacture; and the use of varnished oak, glazed tiles, and unharmonized color.

Eclectic movement: architectural tradition (1880–1940) which emphasized relatively pure copies of Early American, Mediterranean, or Native American homes. This was an opposing tradition to the free stylistic mixtures of the Victorian era.

faux: literally, French for "false." Refers commonly to woodwork painted to look like marble or another stone.

Federal: *See* Adam.

Franklin stove: metal heating stove which is set out into the room to conserve heat and better distribute it. Named after its inventor, the American statesman Benjamin Franklin; some designs resemble a fireplace when their front doors are open. Commonly called a woodstove today.

four-poster bed: variation on a tester bed but one in which the tall corner posts, of equal height, do not support a canopy. Carving of rice sheaves was a popular design in the Southern states, and signified prosperity.

gambrel roof: a two-slope, barn-style roof, with a lower steeper slope and a flatter upper one.

garçonnière: found on antebellum estates; a dependency housing unmarried male guests and family members.

Georgian: building style (1700–1830) featuring a classic box design with a dominant front door elaborated with pilasters and a pediment, usually with a row of small panes of glass beneath the crown or in a transom; cornices with decorative moldings, usually dentil.

Gothic Revival: building style (1840–1880) with a steeply pitched roof, steep gables with decorated vergeboards, and one-story porch supported by flattened Gothic arches. Windows commonly have pointed-arch shape.

Greek Revival: building style (1825–1860) having a gabled or hipped roof of low pitch; cornice line of main and porch roofs emphasized by a wide band of trim; porches supported by prominent columns (usually Doric).

half-tester bed: a bed with a low footboard and a canopy projecting from the posts at the head of the bed. Pronounced "half tee'-stir."

Ionic: column popular in Greek Revival style for support of porch roofs; the caps of the column resemble the rolled ends of a scroll.

Italianate: building style (1840–1885) with two or three stories and a low-pitched roof with widely overhanging eaves supported by decorative brackets; tall, narrow windows arched or curved above with elaborate crowns. Many have a square cupola or tower.

kiva: stuccoed, corner beehive-shaped fireplace common in adobe homes in Southwestern U.S.

Lincrusta (or Lincrusta-Walton): an embossed, linoleum-like wallcovering made with linseed oil, developed in 1877 in England by Frederick Walton.

lintel: horizontal beam, supported at both ends, that spans an opening.

mansard roof: having two slopes on all sides with the lower slope steeper than the upper one.

Mission: building style (1890–1920) with Spanish mission-style parapet; commonly with widely overhanging red tile roof, open eaves, and smooth stucco finish. In furniture, the Mission style is best represented by the work of designer Gustav Stickley. Using machine manufacture, he utilized simple, rectangular lines and favored quarter-sawn white oak for the rich texture of the graining.

Palladian window: typically a central window with an arched or semicircular head.

Pewabic (tile); glazed tiles made in the Detroit, Michigan, area, in the first half of the 1890s, whose unique manufacturing process has been lost.

Prairie: building style (1900–1920) with low-pitched roof and widely overhanging eaves; two stories with one-story wings or porches; facade detailing that emphasizes horizontal lines; massive, square porch supports.

post and beam: building style based on the Medieval post-and-girt method, where upper loads are supported by heavy corner posts and cross timbers, not the thin internal walls below. In contemporary construction, the posts and beams are left exposed on the interior.

Queen Anne: building style (1880–1910) with a steeply pitched roof of irregular shapes; an asymmetrical facade with one-story porch; patterned shingles, bay windows, single tower. In furniture design the Queen Anne (more accurately known as Baroque) style was prevalent from 1725 to 1750, characterized by graceful, unadorned curve of the leg (known as cabriole) and repeated curve of the top crest and vase-form back (splat) of a chair. Sometimes the foot is carved as a claw grasping a ball. Carved shells or leaves are added as a decorative element.

quoin: wood, stone, or brick materials that form the exterior corner of a building and are distinguishable from the background surface because of texture, color, size, material, or projection from it.

rice-carved bed: *See* four-poster bed.

Richardsonian Romanesque: building style (1880–1900) with masonry walls of rough, squared stonework, and round-topped arches over windows, porch supports, or entrance; round tower with conical roof common.

Second Empire: building style (1855–1885) with mansard roof adorned with dormer windows on lower slope; molded cornices above and below lower roof, and decorative brackets beneath eaves.

Shaker: style of furniture constructed by the religious commune of Shakers that represents their belief in simplicity. The finely crafted pieces are functional, without ornamentation. Chairs have ladder backs, rush seats, and simple turned legs; tables and cabinets are angular, with smooth surfaces.

Sheraton: named for English furniture designer, Thomas Sheraton, of the Federal period (early 1800s); style marked by straight lines, delicate proportions, wood inlays, and spare use of carving; legs characteristically are tapered with reed carving.

Shingle: building style (1880–1900) with walls and roofing of continuous wood shingles; no decorative detailing at doors, windows, corners, or roof overhang. Irregular, steeply pitched roof line and extensive porches common.

spandrel: decorative trim that fits the top corners of doorways, porches, or gables; usually triangular in shape.

Spanish Colonial: building style (1600–1900) of thick masonry walls (either adobe or rubble stone covered with stucco), with low pitched or flat roof, interior wooden shutters covering small window openings, and multiple doorways. Pitched roof style often has half-cylindrical tiles; flat style has massive horizontal beams embedded in walls to support heavy roof of earth or mortar. Internal courtyards or cantilevered second-story porches are common.

Stick: building style (1860–1890) with a steeply pitched, gabled roof, usually with decorative trusses at apex; shingle or board walls interrupted by patterns of boards (stickwork) raised from the surface for emphasis.

tester bed: a bed with a full canopy (the tester), supported at all four corners by tall posts. Pronounced "tee'-stir."

Territorial: a variation of the Spanish Colonial building style found in New Mexico, western Texas, and Arizona. The flat roof and single story are topped by a protective layer of fired brick to form a decorative crown.

transom: usually refers to a window placed above a doorway.

trompe l'oeil: literally, French for "to trick the eye." Commonly refers to wall paintings that create an optical illusion.

Tudor: building style (1890–1940) with steeply pitched roof, usually cross-gabled; decorative half-timbering; tall, narrow, multi-paned windows; massive chimney crowned with decorative chimney pots.

vergeboard: decorative trim extending from the roof overhang of Tudor, Gothic Revival, or Queen Anne-style houses.

vernacular: style of architecture employing the commonest forms, materials, and decorations of a period or place.

viga(s): exposed (interior) and projecting (exterior) rough-hewn wooden roof beams common in adobe homes in Southwestern U.S.

wainscoting: most commonly, narrow wood paneling found on the lower half of a room's walls.

widow's walk: a railed observation platform built above the roof of a coastal house, to permit unobstructed views of the sea. Name derives from the fate of many wives who paced the platform waiting for the return of their husbands from months (or years) at sea. Also called a "captain's walk."

Windsor: style of simple chair, with spindle back, turned legs, and usually a saddle seat. Considered a "country" design, it was popular in 18th and early 19th century towns and rural areas. Often painted to give consistency to the variety of local woods used.

For more information:

A Field Guide to American Houses (Virginia & Lee McAlester, New York: Alfred A. Knopf, 1984; $19.95, paperback) was an invaluable source in preparing this glossary, and is highly recommended. Its 525 pages are lavishly illustrated with photographs and diagrams.

Clues to American Architecture (Marilyn W. Klein and David P. Fogle, Washington, D.C.: Starrhill Press, 1985; $6.95, paperback) is a handy, affordable 64-page pocket guide to over 30 architectural styles, from the Colonial period to contemporary construction. Each is clearly described in easy-to-understand language, and illustrated with numerous detailed sketches. Also in the same style and format is *Clues to American Furniture* (Jean Taylor Federico, Washington, D.C.: Starrhill Press, 1988; $6.95), covering design styles from Pilgrim to Chippendale, Eastlake to Art Deco. If your bookstore doesn't stock these titles, contact Starrhill directly at P.O. Box 32342, Washington, D.C. 20007; 202–686–6703.

Regional itineraries

Contributing editor Suzanne Carmichael has prepared these delightful itineraries to lead you from the best-known towns and cities through beautiful countryside, over less-traveled scenic highways to delightful towns and villages, to places where sights both natural and historic outnumber the modern "attractions" which so often litter the contemporary landscape.

To get a rough idea of where each itinerary will lead you, take a look at the appropriate map at the back of this book. But to really see where you'll be heading, pull out a detailed full-size map or road atlas, and use a highlighter to chart your path. (If you're hopeless when it comes to reading maps, ask the AAA to help you plan the trip with one of their Triptiks). Some of our routes are circular, others are meant to be followed from one end to another; some are fairly short, others cover hundreds of miles. They can be traveled in either direction, or for just a section of the suggested route. You can sample an itinerary for a weekend, a week, or even two, depending on your travel style and the time available. For information on what to see and do along the way, refer to our state and local introductions, and to a good regional guidebook. For a list of places to stay en route, see the list of towns at the end of each itinerary, then refer to the entries in the state chapters for full details.

Lake Michigan Loop   Our Lake Michigan tour follows over 1,200 miles of coastline in four states, providing an introduction to the best the Midwest has to offer: sophisticated cities, small hamlets, scenic bluffs and water, water, water. Begin the trip in Chicago, where you can visit the tumultuous Chicago Mercantile Exchange or seek quieter pleasures at the Art Institute and the Field Museum of Natural History.

Head north on I-94, exiting on Route 41 past Lake Forest, then take Route 31 north of Gurnee to Milwaukee. This route takes you through Racine to Milwaukee, where you can savor the bratwursts at sidewalk cafes and sample beer at local breweries. A recommended side trip is to Eagle (southwest on Route 59) to see Old World Wisconsin, an outdoor museum honoring the state's 19th-century immigrants. Leave Milwaukee on Route 57 going north through Cedarburg, where you can visit one of the state's wineries, then take I-43 past Sheboygan to Manitowoc.

From here Route 42 leads north to the Door Peninsula, which divides Green Bay from Lake Michigan. Explore the Peninsula's rugged shoreline, spectacular dunes, picturesque lighthouses and small fishing villages. Stop at Sturgeon Bay to watch ships being built, then loop the peninsula turning east on Route 57 through Baileys Harbor, going north to Ellison Bay, then returning south on Route 42 through Fish Creek, Egg Harbor, and taking Route 57 to Green Bay. If you want to reach the very tip of Door County, follow Route 42 north of Baileys Harbor to its terminus, take a ferry to Washington Island, then another ferry to rustic Rock Island.

In Green Bay, football buffs will want to stop at the Packer Hall of Fame before going north on Route 41 to Marinette, a busy Lake Michigan port city. Cross over to Michigan on the northern lap of your tour, following Route 35 and 2 along Lake Michigan, past rocky cliffs and waterfalls, inland lakes and forests. Leave your car at St. Ignace and ferry to Mackinac Island, a scenic resort island.

Back at St. Ignace, head south on I-75 across the Mackinac Bridge, taking the second exit (Route 31) south, then turning west at Levering to Cross Village. From here Routes 131 and 31 wind first along a forest-lined road, then next to the Lake Michigan shore, through popular vacation spots like Harbor Springs, Bay View, Petoskey and Charlevoix. At Eastport, follow a road on the east side of Torch Lake, then return to Route 31, continuing to Traverse City, the center of America's cherry-growing industry.

Continue on Route 22 past Leland to the Sleeping Bear Dunes National Lakeshore, then past small villages such as Onekama, to Manistee. From here, Route 31 south goes by Ludington (popular with salmon fishermen), Muskegon (a busy industrial city) and Grand Haven (known for its "singing sand"). At Holland take I-196 to the Route A2 exit. A2 hugs the shore, taking you by Saugatuck (an artists' community), and South Haven (try the local blueberries). In Benton Harbor, hop on I-94 which will take you near Union Pier, Michigan, through Michigan City, Indiana, and back to Chicago.

Recommended overnight accommodations can be found in the followings towns (listed in order of their appearance): Chicago and Lake Forest (Illinois); Milwaukee, Cedarburg, Kohler (just west of Sheboygan), Sturgeon Bay, Baileys Harbor, Ellison Bay, Fish Creek, Egg Harbor, Green Bay, and Marinette (Wisconsin); Mackinac Island, Harbor Springs, Bay View, Petoskey, Ellsworth (south of Charlevoix), Alden (south of Eastport on Torch Lake), Traverse City, Leland, Ludington, Grand Haven, Saugatuck, Fennville (southeast of Saugatuck), South Haven, and Union Pier (Michigan); Michigan City (Indiana).

Where is my favorite inn?

In reading through this book, you may find that your favorite inn is not listed, or that a well-known inn has been dropped from this edition. Why? Two reasons, basically:

—In several cases very well-known hotels and inns have been dropped from this edition because our readers had unsatisfactory experiences. We do not list places that do not measure up to our standards. Feel free to write us for details.

—Others have been dropped without prejudice, because we've had no reader feedback at all. This may mean that readers visiting these hotels and inns had satisfactory experiences but were not sufficiently impressed to write about them, or that readers were pleased but just assumed that someone else would take the trouble. If the latter applies, please, please, do write and let us know of your experiences. We try to visit as many inns as possible ourselves, but it is impossible to visit every place, every year. Nor is the way we are received a fair indication of the way another guest is treated. This system only works because of you. So please, keep those cards, letters, and telephone calls coming! As an added incentive, we will be sending free copies of the next edition of this book to our most helpful respondents.

Little Inns of Horror

We try awfully hard to list only the most worthy establishments, but sometimes the best-laid plans of mice and travel writers do go astray. Please understand that whenever we receive a complaint about an entry in our guide we feel terrible, and do our best to investigate the situation. Readers occasionally send us complaints about establishments listed in *other* guidebooks; these are quite helpful as warning signals.

The most common complaints we receive—and the least forgivable—are on the issue of dirt. Scummy sinks and bathtubs, cobwebbed windows, littered porches, mildewed carpeting, water-stained ceilings, and grimy linens are all stars of this horror show.

Next in line are problems dealing with maintenance, or rather the lack of it: peeling paint and wallpaper; sagging, soft, lumpy mattresses; radiators that don't get hot and those that could be used for cooking dinner; windows that won't open, windows that won't close, windows with no screens, decayed or inoperable window shades; moldy shower curtains, rusty shower stalls, worn-out towels, fluctuating water temperatures, dripping faucets, and showers that only dribble top the list on our sh-t parade.

Food complaints come next on this disaster lineup: poorly prepared canned or frozen food when fresh is readily available; meals served on paper, plastic or, worst of all, styrofoam; and insensitivity to dietary needs. Some complaints are received about unhelpful, abrasive, or abusive innkeepers, with a few more about uncaring, inept, or invisible staff. Innkeeping complaints are most common in full-service inns when the restaurant business can dominate the owners' time, leaving guest rooms and overnight guest to suffer. More tricky are questions of taste—high Victorian might look elegant to you, funereal to me; my collectibles could be your Salvation Army thriftshop donation. In short, there are more than a few inns and hotels that give new meaning to the phrase "having reservations"; fortunately they're many times outnumbered by the many wonderful places listed in this guide.

Criteria for entries

Unlike some other very well-known guidebooks, *we do not collect a membership or listing fee of any kind from the inns and hotels we include.* What matters to us is the feedback we get from you, our readers. This means we are free to write up the negative as well as the positive attributes of each inn listed, and if any given establishment does not measure up, there is no difficulty in dropping it.

Key to Abbreviations and Symbols

For complete information and explanations, please see the Introduction.

¢ Especially good value for overnight accommodation.

♰ Families welcome. Most (but not all) have cribs, baby-sitting, games, play equipment, and reduced rates for children.

✖ Meals served to public; reservations recommended or required.

🎾 Tennis court and swimming pool or lake on the grounds. Golf usually on grounds or nearby.

Rates: Range from least expensive room in low season to most expensive room in peak season.

Room only: No meals included; European Plan (EP).

B&B: Bed and breakfast; includes breakfast, sometimes afternoon/evening refreshment.

MAP: Modified American Plan; includes breakfast and dinner.

Full board: Three meals daily.

Alc lunch: À la carte lunch; average price of entrée plus nonalcoholic drink, tax, tip.

Alc dinner: Average price of three-course dinner, including half bottle of house wine, tax, tip.

Prix fixe dinner: Three- to five-course set dinner, excluding wine, tax, tip unless otherwise noted.

Extras: Noted if available. Always confirm in advance. Pets are not permitted unless specified; if you are allergic, ask for details; *most innkeepers have pets.*

We Want to Hear from You!

As you know, this book is only effective with your help. We really need to know about your experiences and discoveries. If you stayed at an inn or hotel listed here, we want to know how it was. Did it live up to our description? Exceed it? Was it what you expected? Did you like it? Were you disappointed? Delighted? Have you discovered new establishments that we should add to the next edition?

Tear out one of the report forms at the back of this book (or use your own stationery if you prefer) and write today. *Even if you write only "Fully endorse existing entry" you will have been most helpful.*

Thank You!

Illinois

Aldrich Guest House, Galena

Chicago, with its dynamic business and convention activities, outstanding museums, and cultural offerings, is the key attraction of Illinois. Ten miles west is Oak Park, which has the world's largest collection of Frank Lloyd Wright architecture. Southern Illinois is rural and agricultural, home to Springfield, the state capital and hometown of Abraham Lincoln. Other areas of interest lie along the Mississippi, from Galena in the north, to St. Louis, on the Missouri side, in the south. Drive along the river on Rte. 96, the National Great River Road, stopping by Historic Nauvoo, a restored 19th century town. Or visit Bishop Hill, north of Galesburg, formerly a 19th-century Swedish religious communal society known for its fine crafts.

Illinois is a good illustration of the explosive growth of B&Bs during the past decade. When contacted for information on this type of accommodation in 1985, the Illinois Office of Tourism had no information on anything but the standard motel or hotel; by the end of 1988 they had published a delightfully illustrated 24-page booklet covering B&Bs, inns, and historic hotels.

Information please: In southern Illinois, just across the Ohio River from Kentucky, is the sleepy river town of Golconda. **The Mansion of Golconda** (515 Columbus Street, Box 339; 618–683–4400) is a century-old home, restored as a B&B and restaurant in 1981. The four guest rooms are furnished with antiques (some original to the house), and the restaurant serves a variety of local and international specialties.

In south central Illinois, 55 miles east of downtown St. Louis, is the **Country Haus** (1191 Franklin, Corner of Hwy. 50 & Rte. 127, Carlyle 62231; 618–594–8313), a century-old Eastlake-style house recently restored as a B&B. Its four guest rooms have private baths, and the reasonable rates include breakfast and terry robes to wear en route to the inn's hot tub. Carlyle is a summer recreation center, being home to Illinois' largest man-made lake, created by the damming of the Kaskaskia River.

In central Illinois, the **Red Rooster Inn** (On the Square, Hillsboro 62049; 217–532–6332) a handsome brick building constructed in 1902, offers inexpensive rooms for B&B, each with private bath. Its restaurant offers American favorites at lunch and dinner.

Southeastern Illinois, about an hour southwest of Terre Haute, is the unlikely location for a lavish country estate, built for a local doctor during the Depression. **The Bertram Arms** (P.O. Box 243, Robinson 62454; 618–546–1122) is an English sandstone mansion, renovated as a B&B by Don and Sue Bertram, and offering four spacious guest rooms, overlooking the lake or 12-acre grounds. Guests can relax in the walnut-paneled great room, complete with winding staircase and balcony, or visit the adjacent country club for golf, tennis, and swimming. Rates include a continental breakfast and range from $70–90.

Chicagoans looking for a relaxing weekend away can also head west to Oregon—Illinois, that is—just 90 miles west of the city via Route 64. One of many homes listed on the National Register of Historic Places is the **Pinehill B&B** (400 Mix Street, 61061; 815–732–2061), a brick Italianate mansion with white trim built in 1874. Bought by Sharon Burdick in 1989, the rooms are furnished with some antiques, and rates include a full breakfast and afternoon tea. About the same distance from Chicago is the **Colonial Inn** (8230 South Green Street, Grand Detour, Dixon 61021; 815–652–4422). Despite its name, it is an Italianate 23-room mansion built in 1850, furnished with period antiques and the owner's clock collection. The modest rates include a light continental breakfast.

Also west of Chicago is the **Stratford Inn** (355 West State Street, Sycamore 60178; 815–895–6789), an English Tudor-style hotel and restaurant, recently restored to offer 39 rooms with modern amenities and period decor.

CHICAGO

Set along the banks of Lake Michigan, Chicago has much to offer business traveler and tourist alike. The list of must-see attractions is a long one, but the following rank high on any list: the Art Institute, the Field Museum of Natural History, and the Museum of Science and Industry. And a trip to the top of the Sears Tower or the John Hancock Center for wide-ranging views is a must. Those with more time to spare will enjoy the city's many ethnic and special-interest attractions, ranging from institutions devoted to Lithuanian culture to free tours of the world's largest post office facility. For all the details, contact the Chicago Convention & Visitor Bureau, McCormick Place-on-the-Lake, 60616; 312–225–5000.

As is the case in most major cities, weekend rates at Chicago's hotels offer substantial savings over midweek rates. Always inquire if any promotional rates are in effect when making reservations.

Also recommended: Although an immutable deadline made a full entry impossible, we received a rave review for the **Mayfair Regent** (181 East Lake Shore Drive, 60611; 312–787–8500 or 800–545–4000). "A wonderful elegant hotel with exceptional service. The lobby is beautiful, with Louis XVI furnishings and fresh flowers. Uniformed staff members greet you, handle check-in, and escort you to your room. Our junior corner suite had a living room with TV, bedroom with TV and honor bar, kitchenette with refrigerator, and a lovely marble tiled bathroom with robes, telephone and scale. We had a view of Oak Street beach and a wonderful breeze—through windows that actually opened; surprisingly, traffic noise was not bothersome. Complimentary tea and fruit were brought up upon check-in, and strawberries and cream and cookies that evening. Furnishings were in good shape, well-coordinated. Breakfast was delicious, and the entire staff was helpful, cheerful, and very fast. We got our car within five minutes of each request, and taxis were quickly summoned when needed." *(LG)*

Although we rarely list big-chain hotels, several readers praised the exceptionally high level of service and luxury (with prices to match) at the **Park Hyatt**: "A 255-room hotel, beautifully furnished, with an elegant and excellent restaurant, La Tour. The ultimate in pampering." *(SHW)* The Park Hyatt is one of only four such hotels in the entire Hyatt chain, and offers such luxuries as complimentary car washes, thrice daily maid service, exercise equipment, and Villeroy & Boch tiled baths. The hotel is located on Water Tower Square, at 800 North Michigan Avenue, 60611; 302–280–2220 or 800–228–9000.

Similarly the 412-room **Ritz-Carlton** (East Pearson Street at Water Tower Place, 60611; 312–266–1000 or 800–621–6906) is highly recommended by some as being Chicago's best hotel, worth every penny of its expensive tariffs. Since this is pretty much true of all hotels in this outstanding luxury chain, we didn't feel a full entry was either necessary or appropriate.

Information please, in Chicago: Business travelers will appreciate the Printer's Row location of the **Omni Morton** (500 South Dearborn, 60605; 312–663–3200 or 800–THE–OMNI), in the city's financial district. Its small size (160 rooms) combined with an attentive staff results in a reputation for good service. Also of interest is its excellent restaurant, The Prairie. Rooms are equipped with two phones, TVs, and VCR, and double rates range from $175–350, with lower weekend rates available.

A good budget possibility is the **Lenox House** (616 North Rush Street, 60611; 312–337–1000 or 800–44–LENOX) located just one block west of Michigan Avenue. All rooms have a fully equipped kitchenette/wet bar, well-lighted work surface with convenient telephone, and sleeper sofa. The executive suites have a Murphy bed; the one-bedrooms have a separate living room. Rates range from $95–170, with substantial savings on weekends.

For those who prefer a more traditional ambience, we'd suggest the 223-room **Whitehall** (105 East Delaware Place, 60611; 312–944–6300 or 800–621–8133), about a block from Michigan Avenue, near Rush Street. Its lobby and sitting area have a clubby English feel, while the dining room continues this motif with its wood paneling, sporting prints and oils, and fireplace. Guest rooms vary in size and shape, but all have chintz flowered fabrics for bedspreads and drapes, and framed botanical prints on the walls. Your opinions please.

Information please, Chicago environs: Bordering Chicago to the north, along Lake Michigan, is the college town of Evanston, home of Northwestern University. **The Margarita Inn** (1566 Oak Avenue, Evanston 60201; 708–869–2273) is a Georgian-style inn in the heart of town. A parlor, library, and den provide ample common areas, and a Northern Italian restaurant is open for lunch and dinner. The 24 guest rooms have period furnishings, high ceilings, and leaded windows. Reports appreciated.

Another elegant inn in the Chicago metro area is the **Wheaton Inn** (301 West Roosevelt Avenue, Wheaton 60187; 708–690–2600), about an hour's drive west of the Loop. Built in 1987, this Williamsburg-style red brick building has 16 luxurious guest rooms, combining period decor with such amenities as Jacuzzi tubs and fireplaces.

Located in another Chicago suburb is **The Deer Path Inn** (255 East Illinois Road, Lake Forest, 60045; 708–234–2280) constructed in 1930, in a traditional English Tudor style, with period detailing and accessories. The decorating theme is definitely English, from the reproduction antique furniture to the artwork. The inn has three separate eating areas, popular with locals as well as visitors.

Just 20 minutes from O'Hare and Midway Airports is **Toad Hall** (301 North Scoville Avenue, Oak Park 60302; 708–386–8623) with three guest rooms renting for $55–65 double, including a full breakfast. Built in 1909, this English-style B&B is furnished with Victorian antiques, Oriental rugs, and Laura Ashley wallpapers, and is located in the Frank Lloyd Wright Historic District.

About 35 miles west of Chicago is **The Oscar Swan Country Inn** (1800 West State Street, Rte. 38, Geneva, 60134; 708–232–0173) which was built by Jessie and Oscar Swan in 1902 and owned by them until the 1950s. It was then sold to Frank and Mary Jo Harding, who added many unusual touches, which remain part of the decor today. The decor is eclectic but features some fine 1920s Art Deco pieces as well as collectibles ranging from carved swans to American Indian artifacts. Comments?

Ambassador West ¢ ✕   *Tel:* 312–787–7900
1300 North State Parkway, 60610   800–621–8090

"This 60-year-old hotel has recently undergone a multi-million-dollar restoration, combining its traditional decor with new carpeting, fabrics, and paint. It's clean and well-kept, with a pleasant staff, a small peaceful lobby, and windows that actually open! Room service is quite good, and the bathroom amenities—from toiletries to towels—are ample. The location is quiet for a big city, and the 'L' is just a couple blocks away. The weekend packages are an excellent value. " *(Laura Scott)*

Open All year.
Rooms 218 suites & doubles—all with telephone, radio, TV, air-conditioning, refrigerator. 2 with kitchen.
Facilities Restaurant, lobby. Pay valet parking.
Location Gold Coast at corner of Goethe.

Credit cards Amex, CB, Discover, MC, Visa.
Rates Room only, $149–169 double. Weekend packages, $99–325.

The Barclay Chicago 🏃 ✕
166 East Superior Street, 60611

Tel: 312–787–6000
800–621–8004

Located in the heart of Chicago's Magnificent Mile, the Barclay is an intimate all-suite hotel, with only six suites per floor.

"Great location, just off Michigan Avenue. Redecorated in 1989–90, the rooms are decorator perfect, yet very comfortable. The lobby is lovely with oak paneling, pillars, fireplace, a massive crystal chandelier suspended over a spiral staircase that leads down to the Bookmark Bar, and camel leather chairs and sofas. Elegant marble halls are intermittently covered with carpet; the paneling is cream with rust suede panels, for a lavish feeling.

"The weekday rates include a complimentary breakfast buffet of fruit, granola, fruit breads, croissants, muffins, hard-boiled eggs, and juices, along with evening turndown. The smallest rooms are the mini-suites, done in green and teal, with a king- or queen-sized bed and a double hideaway bed, with natural wood finish French Provincial furnishings; these are much larger than typical hotel rooms, and represent a good value. The executive parlor suites are the next largest, with lots of closets and three phones, huge windows, dining table and chairs, stocked honor bar, and a dressing area in addition to the bathroom. The one-bedroom suites feel significantly more roomy because the separate living room is so large, well worth the slightly extra cost over the middle-size suite. The staff was pleasant and well-informed." *(SHW)*

And another opinion: "From check-in to check-out, we encountered one service glitch after the next. When we wrote to complain, the hotel manager responded effectively, but it would have been better if the problems had never arisen in the first place."

Open All year.
Rooms 120 suites—all with telephone, radio, TV, desk, air-conditioning, refrigerator, wet bar. Most with kitchen.
Facilities Restaurant, lobby, guest bar/lounge, outdoor rooftop swimming pool. 2 blocks to Lake Michigan. Concierge service. Valet parking.
Location Downtown. Magnificent Mile. 1 block E of Michigan Ave., at corner of St. Clair Ave.
Restrictions Street noise on lower floors.
Credit cards Amex, CB, DC, Discover, MC, Visa.
Rates Room only, $175–440 suite, $155 double. Extra person, $20. No charge for children under 12 in parents' room. Weekend rate/packages, $99–139. Alc breakfast, $5–10; alc lunch, $30; alc dinner, $60.
Extras Crib, babysitting. Spanish spoken. Member, Preferred Hotels Worldwide.

Claridge Hotel ¢ ✕
1244 North Dearborn Parkway, 60610

Tel: 312–787–4980
800–245–1258

Built over 60 years ago, the Claridge (formerly the Tuscany) was completely gutted in 1986, reopening $10 million later in the spring of 1987.

"The Claridge is located a few blocks north and west of where Michigan Avenue intersects Lake Shore Drive and Lake Michigan, in a solid upper middle class/luxury neighborhood, yet just a short walk from the shops of Michigan Avenue and the nightclubs of Rush Street.

"The hotel's facade is unobtrusive, with two large plate glass windows facing twin sitting rooms on either side of the entry hall. These sitting areas are modest in size, with fern-green carpets and average furniture grouping. The lobby area is done in polished mahogany and brushed chrome, in Art Deco style. The staff was friendly and seemed to love the hotel; turnover is very low.

"The dining room is at the rear of the first floor, with no windows and dim lighting. Decor was in the style of the '40s, with dusty rose carpet and rose-padded wood-frame chairs. The complimentary breakfast consisted of a muffin or croissant, orange juice and coffee; a reasonably priced full breakfast menu was also available.

"Recent remodeling and expansion has eliminated the smallest rooms, replacing them with fireplace suites and deluxe king-size rooms, decorated in distinctive colors of burgundy, lilac, cobalt blue, and jade green. The regular rooms have pale blue carpet, blue spreads and drapes with a fan shell pattern, and cream wallpaper. The furnishings are dark wood and blue formica (sounds worse than it looks), with an Art Deco accent. The standard rooms are on the lower floors, and are medium in size, with armoires rather than closets." (Bob Schwemm)

"This hotel is perfectly located for Chicago night life, with several famous Rush Street bars just around the corner. Friendly staff and doorman, nice bar." (Brad & Patty Elliot) "Unbeatable Gold Coast location and good weekend rates; weekday rate is too high considering small size of rooms." (JM)

Areas for improvement: "Noisy automatic venting fan that goes on when the bathroom light is turned on; slow elevators."

Open All year.
Rooms 3 suites, 169 doubles—all with full private bath, telephone, radio, TV, desk, air-conditioning, refrigerator.
Facilities Restaurant, café, bar/lounge with entertainment. Guest privileges at health club. 2 blocks to Lake Michigan, Dearborn beach. Portable exercise equipment. Business services, meeting rooms. Concierge, limousine service. Valet parking, $16.
Location Gold Coast, 1 m to Loop, 3 blocks to Magnificent Mile. From I-90/94 (Kennedy Expressway), exit at North Ave. E to Dearborn, then S 3½ blocks.
Restrictions Traffic noise might disturb light sleepers. No smoking on some guest floors.
Credit cards Amex, CB, DC, MC, Visa.
Rates B&B, $89–150 suite or double, $79–120 single. Extra person, $15. Children under 18 free in parents' room. $68–80 weekend packages. Corporate rates. Alc lunch, $15; alc dinner, $30.
Extras Wheelchair access. Small, well-behaved pets permitted. Crib, babysitting. Spanish, German, Japanese spoken. Complimentary limo to Mich. Ave. Loop. Member, Golden Tulip International (KLM Airlines).

The Knickerbocker ✖   Tel: 312–751–8100
163 East Walton Place, 60611   800–621–8140

Built in 1927, the Knickerbocker is under the same ownership as the Barclay, noted above. It offers a traditional lobby with wood-paneled walls, coffered ceiling, seating clusters, and marble floors. Guest rooms are decorated with period decor; some rooms have canopied beds and double bathrooms. Rates include daily newspapers and nightly turndown service, and the small number of guest rooms per floor enhances privacy and security.

"Charming older small hotel. It has a European ambiance. The service was uniformly excellent and friendly. The furniture was old but well cared for. The location is convenient for business or pleasure in downtown Chicago. Breakfast was fine." *(Harold Weinberg)*

Open All year.
Rooms 256 suites & doubles—all with telephone, radio, TV, air-conditioning. Some with refrigerator, wet bar, 2 bathrooms.
Facilities Restaurant, bar/lounge with entertainment, coffee shop, lobby. Valet parking.
Location Downtown, ½ block W of Mich. Ave.
Credit cards Amex, DC, Discover, MC, Visa.
Rates Room only, $235–345 suite, $157–207 double, $135–185 single. Extra person, $22. Weekend rate/packages, $99–159. Weekly rates. Alc dinner, $50.

Le Meridian ✖

21 East Bellevue Place, 60611

Tel: 312–266–2100
800–543–4300

"Hotel 21 East opened in June 1988, and became a Meridian Hotel in 1990 with no change in decor. The hotel's exterior is smoked glass and brown marble, and is situated so that pedestrians really can see the entire building, unlike most city hotels. Theme colors of mushroom, plum, peach, and turquoise, and a piano key motif are used throughout the Art Deco interior design. The lobby is dark brown marble and smoked glass, with a four-story mirrored atrium. Laurent, the hotel restaurant, is on the mezzanine, and is known for its fine new American and French nouvelle cuisine.

"The standard bedroom is medium large in size and has three two-line speaker phones, a stocked mini-bar, desk and chair, and huge dresser with TV, video, and CD player built in. The furnishings continue the Art Deco motif, with cleanly designed wooden furniture with black glass tops, white globe lights, and black and white covers for the down comforters.

"The bathrooms are high-tech and truly marvelous—among the most unusual and special bathrooms I've ever seen in a standard hotel room. They have black and white tile, black marble sinks with white faucet fixtures, a deep soaking tub with white fixtures, plus separate clear glass-walled shower stalls with thermostatic controls to adjust temperature before you enter the shower. Toiletries are packaged in black to match the decor. The staff was really helpful and professional." *(Sue Waller)*

Open All year.
Rooms —41 suites, 201 doubles, all with soaking tub, shower, telephones, radio, TV/VCR, CD player, air-conditioning, mini-bar.
Facilities Restaurant, lobby, bar/lounge, video/CD library, valet parking.
Location 2 blocks W of the N end of Michigan Ave., at junction of Rush St.
Credit cards All major accepted.
Rates Room only, $255–500 suite, $215 double, $195 single. Weekend rates, $109–169.
Extras BMW limo service.

The Raphael ¢ ✕ *Tel:* 312–943–5000
201 East Delaware Place, 60611 800–821–5343

The Raphael is one-third of a chain of "Raphaels" (the two others are in California and Missouri) owned and managed by Raphael Hotel Group, Ltd.

"Exceptionally spacious rooms, and a great location. The Spanish baroque decor is somewhat out-of-date, but the hotel is immaculately clean, and the windows can be opened. Etched glass doors lead to the tiny lobby. The ceiling is high, and the windows, chandelier, and furniture have a Mediterranean feel. The good-sized standard room has a king-size bed with a butterfly pattern spread and an elaborate gilt headboard, with bamboo nightstands and chairs. The bathroom was small, with green bamboo paper and teal carpeting. The one-bedroom suite has an interesting beamed ceiling; its spacious living room had Mediterranean furniture, including a safe, long chest, upholstered chair, and two tall chairs with upholstered seats. There are two TVs and two phones in all the suites. The deluxe one-bedroom suite is larger than most apartments, with a huge corner living room, handsome king-size half-canopied bed, and a square shower/tub arrangement big enough for two.

"The staff is exceptionally friendly and loyal, going out of their way to make your stay a success; many have been here since the building was converted from apartments into a hotel." *(SHW)* "The food is always good and the small dining room and bar are cozy. The spacious rooms are clean and the staff accommodating." *(Kay Schuler)*

Open All year.
Rooms 75 suites, 100 doubles—all with full private bath and/or shower, telephone, radio, TV, desk, air-conditioning, honor bar, refrigerator, safe.
Facilities Restaurant, lounge with piano bar, lobby. Health club privileges. Valet parking, $18.50.
Location Downtown. 1 block E of Mich. Ave., 2 blocks from Lake Michigan. Between N. Seneca & DeWitt Sts., adjacent to John Hancock Center.
Restrictions No smoking on 16th floor.
Credit cards Amex, MC, Visa.
Rates Room only, $150–165 suite, $130 double, $110 single. Extra person, $20. Weekend, $95–105. Holiday rate.
Extras Wheelchair access. Crib. Spanish, French, Polish spoken.

Richmont Hotel ¢ ✕ *Tel:* 312–387–7580
162 East Ontario Street, 60611 800–621–8055

The Richmont continues to maintain its reputation as a pleasant small hotel with a friendly staff, and is a long-standing favorite of many—but not all—readers. Weekend rates include a continental breakfast and are a good value. The Richmont's restaurant, the Rue St. Clair, has an eclectic menu of American, French, and Italian dishes and a good reputation, as well as an attractive little café.

"The Richmont is right off Michigan Avenue in the heart of the shopping district and is very accessible to everything you'd ever need in Chicago." *(EH)* "Our room was relatively small, but perfectly adequate, nicely decorated with wallpaper and print spread and drapes. Breakfast in the hotel restaurant was good and the atmosphere pleasant. The location is wonderful—you can walk everywhere." *(Pamela Young)*

"The hotel has a French atmosphere, with French art posters prints in all the public areas. The continental breakfast buffet included croissants, a variety of muffins, jams, jellies, orange juice, and coffee. The food was fine, and additional items were available from the menu. My room had French provincial decor, a peach and celadon color scheme, a triple-sheeted bed, and feather pillows. The staff is very friendly, nice, and helpful." *(SHW)*

Areas for improvement: "Hopefully, refurbishing is planned, since both the wallpaper and carpeting in the halls had seen better days. Overall, I thought that housekeeping in this hotel was below par."

And a word to the wise: About a ⅓ of the standard rooms are tiny; try to get confirmation for a larger one when booking.

Open All year.
Rooms 13 suites, 180 doubles and singles—all with full private bath, telephone, radio, TV, air-conditioning, mini-bar.
Facilities Restaurant with jazz entertainment 6 nights per week, bar. Valet parking. Parking garage 1 block away. Guest discount at Grand Ohio health club ½ block away. 2 blocks to McClurg Court sports facility. 5 blocks to Oak St. Beach.
Restrictions Traffic noise in front rooms.
Location Downtown. N of Loop, 1 block E of Michigan Ave.
Credit cards Amex, CB, DC, Discover, MC, Visa.
Rates B&B, $100–157 suite, $85–146 double, $85–134 single. Extra person, $12. Children free in parents' room. Prix fixe dinner, $20–25. Alc lunch, $8–15; alc dinner, $25–35. Weekend rate, $85. Packages. Senior discount.
Extras Wheelchair access. Crib. French, Spanish, German spoken.

DU QUOIN

Francie's B&B Inn ¢   *Tel: 618–542–6686*
104 South Line Street, 62832

If you want to find a B&B that's really far from the beaten tourist path, you'll be intrigued by Francie's. Built of limestone in 1908, this sturdy structure served as an orphanage for 39 years. Long-time Du Quoin resident Frances Morgan grew up in the neighborhood, and played with kids from the Children's Home when she was a child. The home was eventually abandoned, and was in total disrepair when the Morgans bought it in 1986. Now restored, the inn's guest rooms are decorated with antiques, brass, and wicker, with Laura Ashley linens and fluffy comforters. Rates include a full breakfast, and Francie notes that "we offer small-town friendliness and charm and a desire to pamper our guests!"

"Attractive turn-of-the-century decor, congenial innkeepers, and delicious breakfast. My room was very quiet, with plenty of light, a comfortable bed and excellent bathroom facilities. The air-conditioning kept us cool in hot sticky weather, and Francie's brunch was delightful." *(Bob & June Paulsen, also Dwight Baker)* More comments welcome.

Note: There's no sign for this B&B, so watch the street numbers and houses carefully.

Open All year.
Rooms 1 suite, 4 doubles—3 with full private bath, 2 with a maximum of 4

people sharing bath. All with desk, air-conditioning, fan. Suite with TV, refrigerator. Some with radio.
Facilities Tea room, dining room with stereo, living room, club room with piano, gift shop, balcony. 3 acres with lawn games. Tennis, 6 golf courses within 30 miles. 3 blocks to state fairground.
Location S central IL. 80 m SE of St. Louis, MO; 20 m N of Carbondale. 5 blocks from center of town.
Restrictions No smoking in guest rooms. "Well-behaved children."
Credit cards MC, Visa.
Rates B&B, $75 suite, $50–60 double, $40 single. Extra person, $10. Minimum stay required during special events. Holiday weekend dinners, $15–20; brunches; special occasion teas.
Extras Station pickups.

ELDRED

Hobson's Bluffdale ¢ 👫   *Tel: 217–983–2854*
Eldred Road, RR #1, 62027

If you're looking for a relaxing family getaway—one that won't require a second mortgage on your house—pay a visit to Bill and Lindy Hobson, who've owned this working farm since 1955. They've modernized their 1828 stone farmhouse, adding extra buildings to accommodate their guests. Horseback riding begins after breakfast every morning for children nine and over; younger kids can ride in the corral. Afternoon activities include one or more of the following: a trip to an archaeological dig; a motorboat or canoe trip down the nearby Illinois River; a pontoon boat trip past the Mississippi Palisades; fishing; and swimming in the pool or soaking in the hot tub. There's always an optional chore run which consists of feeding the pigs and horses, bottle feeding the calf, gathering eggs, and moving the geese. A square dance, ice cream social and hayride, a ball game, cookout picnic at Greenfield Lake with canoeing, paddle boating and fishing, a water park visit, and a bonfire and singalong are among the typical weekly evening activities. All of the above, plus room and board, are included in the rates. Overachievers can use the maps available for do-it-yourself trips to area attractions, auctions, and antique shops. Accommodations are clean and comfortable, though basic, and the food is plentiful home-style American cooking. Many families stay for a full week, returning each year at the same time to friends they've made at the farm.

"The Hobson family has occupied this property for more than 100 years and each acre of land has real history and character behind it. The Hobsons are extremely warm and honest people. I come to Hobson's to forget about work and get back to nature. It's a place where you can learn to ride horses, care for animals of all types, and more importantly, to respect nature." *(Ted Kornblum)*

Open All year.
Rooms 3 2-bedroom suites, 3 family rooms with 1 double bed & 1 set of bunks, 3 doubles—all with private shower, air-conditioning.
Facilities Dining room, living/family room with fireplace, TV. 320 acres, square

dancing, cookout, hayride, horseback riding, heated swimming pool, hot tub, children's play equipment, boats, 250 bluffs, trails, pond. Golf nearby.

Location SW IL. 40 m N of Alton, 60 m N of St. Louis. 4 m N of Eldred on Eldred Road. Eldred Rd. is 1 m N of intersection of Rtes. 100 & 16.

Restrictions No smoking in main house.

Credit cards None accepted.

Rates Full board, $55 per person, per day. Children under 14, $23–38. Weekly rate. 2–3 holiday/weekend minimum.

Extras Crib, babysitting.

ELSAH

For a welcome break from the big-city bustle of St. Louis, head upriver to Elsah for a relaxing return to the nineteenth century. This entire village, little changed since its founding in 1853, is listed on the National Register of Historic Places and is known for its New England–style architecture. The village is right on the Mississippi River, surrounded by towering limestone bluffs. Antiquers will head for the dozens of shops in nearby Alton, while cyclists will pedal straight for the 14-mile Vadalabene Bike Trail, which goes right through Elsah, following along the base of the limestone bluffs that line the river.

Elsah is located in southwestern Illinois, on the Great River Road. It's 40 minutes north St. Louis, 8 miles west of Alton, and 5½ hours southwest of Chicago.

Information please: Another possibility is the **Corner Nest B&B** (3 Elm Street, P.O. Box 22, 62028; 618–374–1892), a waterfront B&B, bordered by limestone bluffs, built in 1883 and furnished in antiques. Its reasonable rates include a full breakfast weekends, continental on weekdays. Comments?

Maple Leaf Cottage Inn ¢ ✗   *Tel:* 618–374–1684
12 Selma/40 LaSalle, P.O. Box 156, 62028

Four separate cottages make up the Maple Leaf, occupying a full village block in historic Elsah. The Garden House contains the inn's common areas and one of the guest rooms; the other guest rooms are found in the Wash House, originally a summer kitchen; the Maples, whose decor incorporates the picket fence that originally encircled the property; and the Gables, which takes its name from the carpenter Gothic gable trim taken from historic area houses, cleverly utilized here as headboards. Although some may find it a bit cluttered, the inn is furnished with a delightful array of antiques and collectibles, creating a warm and cozy atmosphere. The Maple Leaf was established in 1949, and has been owned by Patty and Gerald Taetz since 1985. Rates include a breakfast of banana waffles, blueberry hot cakes or extra thick French toast, served with fresh juice and coffee; seven-course dinners are served promptly at 7 P.M. on weekends.

We are, of course, appreciative of every report we receive, but among our favorites are those from innkeepers, since they tend to be hardest to please. *Crescent Dragonwagon*, of the Dairy Hollow House in Eureka Springs, Arkansas, had this to say about the Maple Leaf:

GALENA

"We were enchanted by this river town, with its doll house-sized stone buildings. Set into carefully landscaped gardens with brick and stone walkways, the main house contains the cheeriest dining room you can imagine. Upstairs is Grandma's Attic, a guest room where Patty has just ladled on the details. Stencils, careful use of color and texture, antique furniture, lacy bed linens, mementos galore, and lots of extras—from fruit by your bed to sweets and music with turndown service. It all adds up to a romantic, old-fashioned experience. With such abundance one might expect a little dust here and there, but every corner, every object, is as immaculately clean as it is in good taste. Like Grandmas' attic, with its trunks overflowing with antique toys, games, linens, and lace, each room has a theme. We also loved the Wash House, with a fat featherbed, and its laundry theme carried out with antique soap boxes, clotheslines, and old washboards hung on the walls. These common objects and simple themes transcend themselves, becoming sophisticated without being cold, sweet without being cloying.

"Breakfast looks as good as it tastes. The orange juice was fresh-squeezed, the cranberry frappe delectable, the French toast angelically light, and the coffee fresh-ground."

"In a place where time stands still, you feel truly pampered as a guest of Patty & Jerry Taetz." *(Joan Busta)* "A fairyland. The mood created at this inn is incomparable, and the food is excellent." *(Deborah Cortopassi)*

Open All year.
Rooms 6 doubles—all with private bath, radio, TV, desk, air-conditioning. Rooms in 4 cottages.
Facilities Breakfast room, sitting room, screened porch, patio.
Location SW IL. From town, go N on Mill St. to Selma and turn left to inn.
Restrictions No smoking. No children under 13.
Credit cards MC, Visa.
Rates B&B, $75 double. Extra person, $20. Prix fixe lunch, $12; prix fixe dinner, $25. Monthly rates.
Extras Airport/station pickups, $5–20. French, Spanish spoken.

GALENA

A handsome river town, Galena boasts such sights as Grant's Home, Grant Park, and the Belvedere Mansion, plus many craft and antique shops. The town's original fortune (and even its name) came from the local lead mines and later from the steamboat business on the river. When the mines were depleted and the railroads came through in the 1850s, prosperity ended and construction stopped. As a result, nearly 85 percent of the town's buildings are listed in the National Register of Historic Places.

In addition to seeing the sights and shops of the town, area activities include canoeing, fishing, boating, and steamboat rides on the Mississippi and Galena rivers, along with swimming, tennis, golf, horseback riding, and downhill and cross-country skiing in season.

Galena is located in the northwest corner of Illinois, 150 miles west of Chicago and 15 miles south of Dubuque, Iowa. For another area entry, see listing for the **Wisconsin House Inn** in Hazel Green, Wisconsin, nine miles to the north.

Information please: The town's ample supply of Victorian buildings may account for the fact that Galena and the surrounding area are now home to 30 B&Bs and country inns. We'd love to have more feedback on any places you'd like to see added.

Reader tip: "Galena is understandably popular as a weekend getaway for Chicago folks. If you're on a tight budget, try to visit midweek, when rates are about a third less."

Aldrich Guest House   *Tel:* 815–777–3323
900 Third Street, 61036

Aldrich House was built in 1845 as a one-room house. A major Greek Revival–style addition was constructed in 1853, and in the 1880s the house was further enlarged with Italianate ornamentation. The house was restored in 1984 and is owned by Judy Green, who left the New York publishing world to become a B&B innkeeper.

"From the moment Judy answers the doorbell and you enter the foyer with its carved stairway, you know you're going to have a special stay. She escorts you upstairs to your comfortable room, perhaps with a big brass bed or a white wrought iron one. After settling in, you head down to the parlor or porch, where can you relax with wine or a soft drink and look across the lawn to the mansion where U.S. Grant waited to learn the results of the presidential election. One afternoon I curled up in the front parlor with a scrapbook from 1860–1880. As I read the newspaper clippings, I could imagine having a meal with Grant in the dining room, the fashionable musicales held in the parlor, even the tears shed at a family funeral." *(Mary Ann Jensen)*

"The inn is located on a very quiet side street, within walking distance of town; guests are able to park right in front. The decor is a mix of antiques and reproductions, and the guest rooms are fairly large; mattresses are new and firm, and extra pillows and blankets are available. There is a lovely large screened porch on the side of the house, ideal for lounging on summer afternoons. The grounds are spacious and nicely landscaped. Breakfast is a more formal affair. Judy serves each guest individually; plates are arranged in the kitchen. There is always coffee and orange juice, a breakfast bread, a fruit compote and main course which varies from an egg and cheese casserole to pancakes with warmed syrup. Judy serves unobtrusively, while guests socialize among themselves. The table is set with very nice china and silverware, and everything is homemade and hot." *(Lauren & Anthony Zeller, and others)*

"Judy Green is a wonderful innkeeper who makes all the work look so easy." *(MW)* "This house is decorated in greens, mauves, and ivory, with marvelous antiques. The rooms, especially the bathrooms, are meticulously clean; towels are changed daily, and there's plenty of hot water." *(Joan & Denis Bohm)* "Our room had antique oak Victorian furnishings and 'Laura Ashley' style prints and lace; its two large windows, one of them a bay, made it bright and airy. Our private bath had an old-fashioned raised tank toilet and claw foot tub. We shared many lively evening conversations on the screened porch with our fellow guests, enveloped by soft breezes and cricket serenades." *(Jan Wilcox)*

Open Closed during month of January.
Rooms 5 doubles—3 with private bath and/or shower, 2 with a maximum of 4

people sharing bath (bath on 1st floor). 2 rooms with adjoining bath may be booked as suite. All with air-conditioning.

Facilities Dining room; living room with grand piano, fireplace, stereo; library; screened porch. Yard games. 8 m to downhill, cross-country skiing.

Location Just off Rte. 20. 5–10-min. walk to center.

Restrictions Smoking in living room, screened porch only. No children under 6.

Credit cards Amex, Discover, MC, Visa.

Rates B&B, $135–155 suite (for 4), $65–95 double, $60–90 single, plus 9% tax. Senior rate same as single rate. Extra person, $15. 2-night minimum most weekends.

Extras Airport/station pickups.

DeSoto House ✗

230 South Main Street, 61036

Tel: 815–777–0090
800–343–6562

When it first opened in 1855, the DeSoto House was called the best and largest hotel west of New York. It remained in continuous operation as a hotel until 1978. Restored at a cost of nearly $8 million and reopened in 1986, the hotel retains many of its original features. The hotel restaurant occupies a sunny, plant-filled atrium, and offers such entrées as rock Cornish game hen, prime rib of beef, and veal Marsala; guest rooms are decorated with period reproductions. When you're there, be sure to read the fascinating booklet describing the hotel's history.

Unfortunately, the construction costs were overwhelming for a hotel of this size, and the original developer went bankrupt. The hotel re-opened in the spring of 1989 on a financially sound basis, and current reader reports are good.

"The Victorian elegance of the lobby and our spacious, high-ceilinged room with comfortable king-sized bed, complimentary toiletries in the bath, and excellent drinks and breakfast made for a most romantic stay." *(Sylvia O'Connor)* "Our comfortable suite had just been redone with brand-new wallpapering and furnishings, yet retained its historic charm. Friendly staff." *(Kimberly Hawthorne)*

Although we're hopeful that staffing problems have been sorted out by now, readers noted some areas for improvement: "Our room needed an extra mirror besides the small one in the bathroom, and our room was not made up until late afternoon." And: "Off-hours staff could have used more training." Additional comments please.

Open All year.

Rooms 2 suites, 53 doubles—all with full private bath, telephone, radio, TV, desk, air-conditioning. Suites with fireplace.

Facilities 2 restaurants, 2 bars, lobby, sitting parlor, meeting rooms, shops.

Location In town. On Main, between Washington and Green Sts.

Credit cards Amex, Discover, MC, Visa.

Rates Room only, $95–150 suite or double. Extra person, $8. Children's rates. Package rates. Alc lunch, $7, alc dinner, $40.

Extras Wheelchair access. Crib.

Farmers' Home Hotel ✗

Route 20, 334 Spring Street, 61036

Tel: 815–777–3456
800–373–3456

In 1845, the Vogel brothers left their home in Germany for New Orleans, then ventured upriver to Galena, where they built a bakery and, in 1867, a hotel. It became an in-town residence for farmers and a gathering place for others in town on business. The hotel stayed in the Vogel family until recently, when it was bought by Thomas and Bonnie Ogie-Kristianson and restored as an inn; Elissa Gunning is the innkeeper. The hotel is one of Galena's best examples of commercial vernacular architecture; rooms combine Victorian decor and handmade quilts with modern amenities; rates include a full breakfast.

The hotel's restaurant is open for breakfast and dinner, and overnight guests can take their pick from the extensive breakfast menu; a favorite is hobo hash—a mixture of ham or spicy chorizo sausage with potatoes, broccoli, onion, and melted cheddar cheese, topped with sour cream. Dinners include such entrées as beef filet with roasted shallots, red wine, and herbs; grilled salmon with basil fettuccine; and duck breast with fresh cranberries; lighter fare is offered in the hotel's Spring Street Tavern. Much of the food comes from the proprietors' farm, where "we raise our own pigs in a humane and chemical-free environment."

"After a warm welcome, we were given coupons for free drinks in the bar, then were shown to our room at the end of the hall. It was warm, comfortable, authentic, and lovely. The food was excellent, and the candlelit setting at dinner was most romantic. The staff went out of their way to be friendly." *(Marge & Jim Scanlan)*

Open All year.
Rooms 2 suites, 9 doubles—all with private bath, telephone, TV. Some with desk, balcony. Suites with fireplace; 2 doubles in "Cabin in the Woods."
Facilities Parlor, restaurant, bar with piano, conference room, laundry. Hot tub, picnic table, hammock. 8–10 m to downhill, cross-country skiing.
Location On Rte. 20, 1 block W of Galena River bridge.
Restrictions Smoking restricted in some areas. No children under 10 on weekends.
Credit cards All major credit cards accepted.
Rates B&B, $85–125 suite, $65–95 double, $55–85 single. Extra person, $10. Family, children's rate. Commercial rates midweek. Midwinter, midweek, ski packages. Alc dinner, $30.
Extras Airport/station pickup. Crib; babysitting by prior arrangement.

Hellman Guest House
318 Hill Street, 61036

Tel: 815–777–3638

A Queen Anne brick mansion built in 1898, the Hellman House is a testament to the rewards of Victorian entrepreneurship. Originally constructed for John Hellman, a wealthy merchant, and his wife, Wenona, daughter of a shipping magnate, the house still reflects the splendor of the times—complete with turret, stained glass windows, and fine oak paneling. It is decorated with a mixture of period and contemporary furnishings, and comfortable overstuffed couches in the parlor; the large windows throughout give it a light, airy look. Guest rooms have country Victorian appeal, with antique-painted iron bedsteads, wicker furniture, and light floral fabrics and wallcoverings. Rates include a breakfast of fresh fruit, muffins and bread, juice, and coffee.

"Merilyn Tommaro is the non-resident owner who purchased the Hellman House in 1986. She spared no expense when she renovated it as a B&B, adding private baths with ceramic tiled showers to all guest rooms. The magnificent old woodwork in all the upstairs bedrooms has been refinished to its original turn-of-the-century grandeur, complemented by an inspired selection of wallpaper patterns and fabrics. Rachel Stetson is the resident manager and she is as personable and friendly as any owner could be. She knows Galena very well and filled us in on all the good places to visit in town. Rachel's home-baked muffins and her special blend of freshly ground coffee were wonderful at breakfast." *(Jim & Krisha Pennino)*

One area for improvement, hopefully remedied by now: "The lack of both night stands next to our bed and bedside lighting made it virtually impossible to enjoy a few minutes of reading before going to sleep." More reports appreciated.

Open All year.
Rooms 4 doubles—each with private bath and/or shower, air-conditioning.
Facilities Parlor with fireplace, library with fireplace, dining room, porch, patio. Off-street parking.
Location Quality Hill district. If approaching on Rte. 20 from E, go 2 blocks past bridge. Turn right onto High St. (up steep hill) and continue to the corner of High and Hill Sts. to inn.
Restrictions Smoking restricted to library. No children under 12.
Credit cards Amex, MC, Visa.
Rates B&B, $69–89 double, $64–84 single. Winter midweek rates available. 2-night weekend, holiday minimum.

Log Cabin Guest House ¢ 👫
11661 West Chetlain Lane, 61036

Tel: 815–777–2845

If you've always wanted to stay in one of those primitive, *Little House on the Prairie*–type cabins without forfeiting those modern conveniences we've all come to depend on, then one of Scott and Linda Ettleman's four country cabins may be just the thing. The Ettlemans live in a farmhouse dating back to 1826 and have converted the original servants' quarters into a guest house. They have also brought three cabins, dating from the 1860s, to their property, and have decorated them with rustic antiques. There's plenty of room in the cabins for kids, and one even has an antique iron crib; children also enjoy the farm atmosphere, complete with chickens, ducks, and cows in the nearby fields. Rates include a light breakfast of rolls, juice, and coffee.

"Comfortable clean cabins in the peaceful countryside. Friendly owners." *(Philip Wolf)* "Rustic atmosphere. Clean, well-maintained facilities." *(Majorie Jensen)* Additional reports appreciated.

Open All year.
Rooms 5 cabins—all with private bath and/or shower, radio, TV, desk, air-conditioning, fan. 3 with whirlpool tubs, fireplaces; 1 with kitchenette (no utensils provided).
Facilities 3 acres, surrounded by 40 acre farm with animals. $\frac{1}{2}$ m to golf.
Location 1 m from town. From Hwy. 20, go S on Chetlain Lane $\frac{1}{4}$ m to driveway for inn.
Restrictions Smoking not encouraged.
Credit cards Discover, MC, Visa.

Rates B&B, $50–90 cabin for 2 people. Extra adult, $10; extra child, $5. 2-night weekend minimum.
Extras Wheelchair access. Station pickup. Crib, babysitting.

GENEVA

The Oscar Swan Country Inn ¢   *Tel: 708–232–0173*
1800 West State Street (Route 38), 60134

Jessie and Oscar Swan built this colonial revival home in 1902 and owned it until the 1950s, when it was sold to Frank and Mary Jo Harding. Mrs. Harding, an interior designer, added many unusual touches, which remain part of the decor today. Hans and Nina Heymann bought the estate in 1985, thus beginning its new life as a bed & breakfast inn. The decor is eclectic but features some fine 1920s art deco pieces as well as collectibles ranging from carved swans to American Indian artifacts.

"An island of tranquility in a rapidly developing area. Owner Nina Heymann greeted us on arrival, showed to us to our room, and went out of her way to make us feel welcome. We woke up to a lovely view of the gardens and the sound of birds singing. Breakfast consisted of an assortment of breads and muffins, fresh fruit, coffee, tea, and juice." *(Karen Graef)* More comments please.

Open All year.
Rooms 2 suites, 6 doubles—4 with private bath and/or shower, 4 with maximum of 4 people sharing bath. All with radio, TV, desk, air-conditioning, fan. 1 with kitchen, sauna; 1 with fireplace; 1 with waterbed.
Facilities Garden/breakfast room, parlor with fireplace, library, porches. 7 acres with terrace, gardens, swimming pool, gazebo, playhouse, picnic area, cross-country skiing. Tennis, fishing, bicycling nearby.
Location NE IL. 37 m W of Chicago. 1 m from town. From Chicago, follow Rte. 38 W to Geneva; becomes State St. in Geneva. Inn on left near I-88 exit for Farnsworth Ave. North.
Credit cards Amex, MC, Visa.
Rates B&B, $60–110 suite, $50–99 double, $50–89 single. Extra person, $15. Children's rate. Prix fixe lunch, $15; dinner, $32. Alc lunch, $9–15; dinner, $29.
Extras Wheelchair access. Pets permitted by prior arrangement. Station pickup. Crib, babysitting. German, Polish spoken.

GURNEE

Sweet Basil Hill Farm   *Tel: 708–244–3333*
15937 West Washington Street, 60031   800–228–HERB

Following the flower-lined path to the front door of Sweet Basil Hill Farm, visitors come to a handsome old-fashioned school bell and rope with a sign: "Visitors please ring bell." It sets a tone for the B&B experience to follow: handsome, distinctive, no-nonsense. Owners Teri & Bob Jones have combined their artistic talents (she's a photographer, he's a jazz musician and actor) to renovate this 1950s Cape Cod-style house as a delightful getaway. While not large, guest rooms are carefully furnished with antiques, feather comforters, reading chairs, and good reading lights (on both sides of the bed). Extra touches in each room include good books, a candy dish, and the soft scent of potpourri, much of it grown in Teri's garden. The Basil Room has a queen-sized pencil post canopy bed with an Amish quilt and stenciled walls, while the Burgundy Room is painted to match its name, with a four-poster queen-sized Shaker bed, an English pine corner washstand, and stenciled curtains. Throughout the house, the country look remains warm and welcoming, never cute or overdone.

Teri reports that "we try to provide a place for people to relax in a country-like setting. Rooms are furnished with guests' comfort in mind, with feather and foam pillows, luggage racks, good hangers and closet space, and more. We try to see that our guests have what they need without being intrusive. We are familiar with Milwaukee and Chicago and can plan day trips to either one, though there's lots of choices for dining and recreation locally."

Breakfast varies daily, but might include mountain cherry juice, fresh fruit, cheese, muffins, scones, and cinnamon rolls; or raspberry juice, croissants with chicken, broccoli, and cheese, fresh fruit, pumpkin bread, lemon muffins, and a freshly baked pie. Coffee and tea (regular and decaf), apples, and hard candies are always available in the common room. Guest enjoy walking the paths the Joneses have laid out through the grounds, but can also visit nearby Six Flags Great America, a family theme park, for a change of pace.

"Each B&B experience is so unique that comparisons are often not possible. The feeling as you approach, then enter each facility is always one of expectation. When the visit concludes, those expectations have either been met, or exceeded. Even a mediocre facility has often had such a charming host that the skimpy towels or creaky bed were soon forgotten. But Sweet Basil Farm is a complete experience—from wonderfully decorated and thoughtfully appointed rooms to the delightful hostess and the delicious breakfast. Teri and her husband have though of every comfort and provided them with style." (Marilyn Kunz, also Michele Mallin)

Open All year.
Rooms 3 suites—all with full private bath, telephone, radio, TV, desk, air-conditioning, ceiling fan.
Facilities Breakfast room, common room with fireplace, stereo, games. VCR available. 7½ acres with nature trails, sheep, llamas, rabbits, roosters, herb garden, picnic grove, hammock, swing, blackberry picking. Cross-country skiing. Tennis, golf nearby. Boating, swimming nearby. ½ hr. to downhill skiing.
Location NE IL, Lake County. 48 m N of Chicago, 45 m S of Milwaukee. Exit I-94 at Rte. 132 (Grand Ave.). Go E, then turn right on Rte. 21 S, then right (W) onto Washington St. to inn on left (crossing back under I-94).
Restrictions No smoking.
Credit cards MC, Visa.
Rates B&B, $65–115 double. Extra person, $15. Senior, AAA discount.
Extras Airport pickups, $15; free station pickups. French spoken.

NAUVOO

Mississippi Memories ¢   *Tel: 217–453–2771*
RR 1, Box 291, 62354

If the phrase "lazin' on the river" appeals to you, then Mississippi Memories is the place to experience it. A five-level contemporary brick home owned by Marge and Dean Starr, this B&B sits right on the banks of an open stretch of the mighty Mississippi; large decks provide uninterrupted views. There's more than barges and tugs to see, too—bald eagles winter over on this part of the river. Guest rooms are furnished with antiques, country collectibles, and colorful quilts. Rates include a breakfast of fresh breads and pastries, ham and eggs, juice, fresh fruit, cereal and coffee.

The Starrs also own a large grain and livestock farm nearby which they are pleased to share with their guests if time permits; the property is an excellent geode hunting area. Nauvoo was established in 1839 by Mormon founder Joseph Smith, and later became the home of a French utopian community; much of the town's historic district has been restored and is available to tour.

"A quiet, welcoming place with fresh fruit, flowers, and hearty breakfasts. Clean and friendly." *(Terry & Nancy Senn-Kerbs)* Additional comments required.

Open All year. Closed Dec. 25.
Rooms 1 suite, 4 doubles—3 with private bath and/or shower, 2 with a maximum of 4 people sharing bath. All with radio, air-conditioning. Some with desk, fan; 1 with fireplace. Telephone, TV on request.
Facilities Living room with fireplace, library with TV, games, fireplace, piano; dining room, 3 decks. 1 acre overlooking Mississippi River. Boating, fishing, golf nearby.
Location W central IL. 245 m SW of Chicago; 110 m SW of Davenport, IA; 115 m W of Peoria; 65 m N of Hannibal, MO. 2.4 m S of town on Rte. 96.
Restrictions No smoking. No alcohol permitted.
Credit cards None accepted.
Rates B&B, $58–65 suite, $45–55 double, $43–50 single. Extra person, $7. Extra child, $5.
Extras Crib.

OAKLAND

Inn on the Square ¢ ✗   *Tel: 217–346–2289*
3 Montgomery Square, 61943

Innkeepers Max and Caroline Coon invite travelers to relax and enjoy the country pleasures of the area—historic homes, outdoor recreation, and visits to a nearby Amish settlement. Their inn, set right in the heart of this little town, is an imposing white building with a two-story portico running along the front. Rooms are decorated with some antiques, and rates include a full breakfast.

"Our room was large, cheerful, and homey. The bathroom was very clean, with plenty of hot water, towels, and extras. The food was delicious and plentiful; the tea room is quaint, with lots of country charm. The location is quiet and parking is abundant." *(Jackie Karle)*

"Rooms are immaculate and comfortable for sleeping; a three-way bulb is an unexpected bonus. Well-appointed shops in the inn are fun for browsing and buying. Max and Carolyn always offer an after-dinner snack or beverage." *(Mrs. George Rutkoskie)* More reports needed.

Open All year. Inn, restaurant closed major holidays.
Rooms 4 doubles—3 with private bath and/or shower, 1 with a maximum of 4 sharing bath "only when booked to capacity and if sharing with family members." All with radio, air-conditioning, fan.
Facilities Restaurant, tea room, TV/game room, library; gift, antique, apparel shops. Tennis, swimming pool, golf, boating, fishing nearby.
Location E central IL. 45 m S of Champaign/Urbana, 20 m N of Lincoln Log Cabin State Park. On Rte. 133, 15 m E of I-57.
Restrictions No smoking in guest rooms.
Credit cards MC, Visa.
Rates B&B, $45 double, $40 single. Extra person, $10. Alc lunch, $6–9.

ROCK ISLAND

The Potter House ¢ ♠♦   *Tel: 309–788–1906*
1906 Seven Avenue, 61201

Nancy and Gary Pheiffer were fortunate when they decided to restore the Potter House as a B&B in 1989; this Colonial Revival home, built in 1907 and now listed on the National Register of Historic Places, had stayed in the Potter family from its construction until Mrs. Potter died in 1981, and was never "K-Marted" or trashed as a boarding house. Nancy is an interior designer, and she put her talents to good use during the six-month restoration. The leaded glass windows, edged in brass, not lead, sparkle again, as do the many stained glass windows, possibly attributed to Tiffany; the original embossed Arts and Crafts–style leather wallcovering still extends from the entry foyer to the third floor. Although Mrs. Potter's furniture was removed after she died, Nancy has furnished the rooms in period, with Oriental rugs, swagged draperies, lace curtains, period wallpapers, and brass and four-poster beds. Unusual in an era where most houses were lucky to have a single bathroom, five bathrooms are original to Potter House; one has a curved ceramic tiled shower, with original nickel-plated hardware and mahogany toilet seat; another bathroom is faced in marble.

Breakfast is different each day, with fresh fruit and juice, and a hot entrée—perhaps a German oven pancake drizzled with honey and topped with kiwi, strawberries, and orange slices, accompanied by bacon; or a sausage puff casserole with Monterey jack cheese and banana nut bread.

"Nancy Pheiffer welcomed us with tea and desserts, and provided delicious breakfasts. Beds were exceptionally comfortable, and lots of thoughtful touches made me feel relaxed and at home. The location is excellent for visiting Rock Island and the Riverboat casino in Davenport. Unusual in a Mississippi River town, there was no railroad noise." *(Pat Middleton)* "The Potter House was built by my grandfather, and much is still the same as I remember from my childhood; the rest has been lovingly and faithfully restored. Everything is provided to assure guests' comfort, and Nancy is happy to accommodate dietary needs." *(Mary Hambacher)* "An ideal combination of the homey warmth of a B&B with a room that provided complete privacy." *(Janice & Dan Torrence)* "Potter House is easy to find, parking is on the property, the neighborhood is relatively quiet and is home to a number of interesting turn-of-the-century houses. Potter House is furnished with antique and near-antique furnishings. Breakfast and the owner's morning cheeriness are memorable. The Pheiffers are well acquainted with local history and area attractions." *(Alan Olsson)*

Open All year.
Rooms 1 2-bedroom cottage, 1 suite, 3 doubles—all with private bath and/or shower, telephone, radio, TV, desk, air-conditioning. 2 with ceiling fan.
Facilities Dining room with gas fireplace, solarium with TV; living room with fireplace, grand piano. Off-street parking. Swimming pool, golf, boating nearby.
Location NW IL. Across Mississippi River bridge from Davenport, IA. Broadway Historic area; 3 blocks to downtown.
Restrictions No smoking.
Credit cards Amex, CB, DC, MC, Visa.
Rates B&B, $79–100 suite, $55–69 double, $49–69 single. Extra person, $10. Reduced rates for families. 2-night weekend, holiday, special event minimum.
Extras Airport/station pickups. Crib.

STOCKTON

Maple Lane Country Inn ¢
3114 South Rush Creek Road, 61085

Tel: 815–947–3773

After 23 years of farming, Carson and Elizabeth Herring are making this inn their retirement career. The Maple Lane is run as a B&B on weekends, while during the week a "New Start" weight- and stress-reduction program is offered. This program runs from Sunday to Friday, and includes the individual attention of a fitness instructor, nutritionist, medical doctor, and nurse. Elizabeth reports that as of 1991, all guest rooms have been equipped with "brand-new queen-sized firm mattress sets, at a cost of thousands. But we did feel it was important, and now it's done!"

"This inn is on a working farm on the eastern edge of beautiful hilly northwest Illinois. I stayed in the Rose Suite, which was very cheerful and clean, with a comfortable bed." *(Susan Jacques)* "The inn is neat, clean, and comfortable, the grounds well maintained. Clean linens and towels are provided daily; lighting and plumbing are in good order. The area is beautiful and quiet—well off the beaten path—not at all touristy or gimmicky. The Herrings give tips on local points of interest and restaurants, and provide brochures and a large map of the area." *(Janet Brendel)*

"Spectacular breakfast of coffee cake, sausage, ham, bacon, pancakes or French toast, eggs, melon, grapefruit, juices—all prepared to order. The

Herrings are warm, friendly people and their guests reflect this warmth. We swam in the pool, hiked the country roads, picked wildflowers, luxuriated in the Jacuzzi, then shopped, ate and danced in nearby Galena." *(Steve and Christine Kois)*

Open All year.
Rooms 7 suites, 2 doubles—all with private bath and/or shower, TV, desk, air-conditioning. Some suites with kitchenette. 5 rooms in annex.
Facilities Dining room, living room with grand piano, family room with TV, books. 6 acres with lawn games, heated swimming pool, whirlpool/sauna, coin laundry, creek fishing, bicycles.
Location NW IL. 136 m W of Chicago, 22 m E of Galena. 5 m to town. From Chicago, take Rte. 20 W to Stockton. Continue on Rte. 20 W 4 m to Hatton Rd. (look for big red barn and pine trees) and turn left. Go S to intersection of Hatton and Center Rd. and turn left; watch for inn driveway on right.
Credit cards None accepted.
Rates B&B, $55 suite, $50 double, $45 single. Extra person over age 9, $10. Family rates. 10% discount on 2nd night. Prix fixe lunch, $7.
Extras Station pickups by prior arrangement.

WOODSTOCK

Bundling Board Inn   *Tel:* 815–338–7054
220 East South Street, 60098

Deriving its name from a colonial-era courting practice, Rich and Barb Helm have owned the Bundling Board since 1986, and will be glad to steer you to this historic town's most interesting events. Rates include a breakfast of oatmeal, bananas, yogurt, English muffins, bagels, and raisin toast.

"A nicely decorated Queen Anne home, the inn is close to downtown Woodstock, with its lovely town square and nice shops. The old opera house has been rehabilitated, and now hosts plays and concerts. The Helms are congenial and outgoing. The big front porch has a swing where it's fun to sit and watch the passing parade. Plumbing is modern, and parking is adequate." *(Susan Jacques)* "Our room was clean and comfortable, with pretty lace curtains and crocheted bedspread, and beveled, leaded glass upper panels on the windows. The hostess was pleasant but unobtrusive." *(Mr.& Mrs. N.B. Ritchey)*

Open All year.
Rooms 6 doubles—3 with private bath and/or shower, 3 with a maximum of 6 people sharing bath.
Facilities Parlor, kitchen/breakfast room.
Location 60 m NW of Chicago. From Chicago, take the Kennedy Expwy. NW to Rte. 47 N. Go into Woodstock and at 2nd light, go left onto Lake Ave. At first stop sign, go straight (road becomes E. South St.). Inn is at 1st driveway on left.
Restrictions Possible noise in some rooms. No smoking. Children over 14 preferred.
Credit cards Amex, DC, MC, Visa, Discover.
Rates B&B, $35–48 double, $30–43 single. Extra person, $5. Senior discount.
Extras 1 room with wheelchair access. Station pickup. Well-behaved pets permitted by prior arrangement. Crib. Some Spanish spoken.

Indiana

Main Street B&B, Madison

While few travelers plan a trip just to see Indiana, many come on business, or to visit friends, relatives, or kids at college; plenty of others pass through on cross-country trips. Those who like to explore will discover that the state has much more to offer than most people realize. From the Lake Michigan beaches in the north to the wooded hill country along the Ohio River at the Kentucky border, there are a surprising number of places worth visiting. You've told us about some exceptional places to stay, but we could certainly make room for some more!

Information please: Just 20 miles west of the Ohio border, in east central Indiana, is **The Teetor House** (300 West Main Street, Hagerstown 47346; 317–489–4422). This historic mansion on 10 landscaped acres has four guest rooms, each with private bath. The decor is traditional, complemented by hand-crafted woodwork and stained glass windows. Central air-conditioning provides relief from the dog days of summer; rates range from $55–85, including full breakfast and use of a nearby pool and fitness center.

In north central Indiana, near the Michigan border, is the **Queen Anne Inn**, a 1893 Victorian home just three blocks from the Convention Center in South Bend; its five guest rooms are furnished with antiques and reproductions (420 West Washington Street; South Bend 46601; 219–234–5959). For a real change try the **Beiger Mansion Inn** (317 Lincoln Way East, Mishawaka 46544; 219–256–0365) just east of South Bend, and ten minutes from the Indiana toll road. Built in 1903, this four-level neo-classical limestone mansion is an incredible 22,000 square feet, and is now home to a ten-guest room B&B, art gallery, and luncheon restaurant.

CHESTERTON

Another possibility in northeastern Indiana, near the Ohio border about 30 miles south of Fort Wayne, is the **Schug House Inn** (706 West Main Street, Berne 46711; 219–589–2448). A turn-of-the-century Queen Anne Victorian, it features unusual twin towers, inlaid floors, and an open staircase. Each of its five guest rooms have private baths, and the $40 double rate includes a breakfast of fresh-baked muffins, croissants, juice, and coffee. Berne was settled in the 1850s by Swiss Mennonites; their Amish descendants prosper in the area today, and many Amish crafts are sold in local shops. Consider visiting in late July when the town celebrates its heritage with an annual Swiss Days festival. "The house is clean and quiet; furnishings include a few antiques. A friendly woman came in to fix us breakfast, but otherwise we had the entire three-story house to ourselves, and weren't totally comfortable with that." *(AC)*

At the opposite end of the state, in southwestern Indiana, is **Mimi's House** (101 West Maple Street, Washington, 47501; 812–254–5562), about a two-hour drive from either Indianapolis or Louisville. An excellent example of Prairie-style architecture, it was built in 1913, and has beautiful mahogany, walnut, and oak woodwork, as well as unusual murals and tiling. Families will enjoy the common area, equipped with ping pong, pool table, TV, and fireplace, and all will enjoy the special omelets served at breakfast. Rates range from $40–65.

Also recommended: Although they are not quite right for full entries, a frequent contributor recommends Indiana's five state park inns as being ideal for families. Located in the northeast corner and the south central part of the state, they offer meals and clean, comfortable accommodation (both inn and cabin) at very reasonable rates. Recreational opportunities are plentiful year-round, and frequently include outdoor and indoor swimming pools, stream and lake water sports, and cross-country skiing. Call the state tourist office at 800–2–WANDER for more information.

Rates do not include 5% state sales tax, and local lodging taxes where applicable.

CHESTERTON

Gray Goose Inn ₵   *Tel:* 219–926–5781
350 Indian Boundary Road, 46304

Freeways and interstates may be efficient for high-speed travel, but they leave you with little feeling for the territory you're passing through. You'd never guess that less than half a mile from two major highways is a setting as peaceful as that of the Gray Goose Inn. Century-old oaks surround an English-country style home overlooking Lake Palomara. Rooms are furnished eclectically, with English, country and traditional touches and rates include a full breakfast and afternoon refreshments. Breakfast entrées vary daily, and favorites include blueberry pancakes, orange brandied French toast made with croissants, and baked eggs with salsa. The inn has been owned by Tim Wilk and Chuck Ramsey since 1986.

Chesterton is a gateway to the Indiana Dunes National Lakeshore, a sizable memento of the last ice age. Stop by the visitor center for information on this geological phenomenon, hike the many trails that follow Lake Michigan, then cool off with a swim.

"Behind this beautiful white frame house is a pond where geese and mallards gather, in a relaxing, peaceful setting. The rooms are scrupulously clean and have the feeling of a lovingly prepared guest room at home. While not all bathrooms are new, all are freshly decorated and totally adequate. Lovely towels, tasteful decor, interesting antiques and accessories abound." *(Betty Baker)* "I rose early to spend a couple of serene hours on my adjoining wicker-furnished porch, reading and looking out at the lake. We were served a delicious breakfast in the dining room, overlooking the water, and returned in the evening for a superb candlelit dinner." *(Evelyn Thomas)*

"We were a bit alarmed to see Burger King, Dairy Belle, Kentucky Fried Chicken, and then suddenly notice the inn's sign sitting at the end of a tree-lined lane. We were amazed to find it become so peaceful and isolated, once we left the main road. We used the inn's bikes to pedal around the lake and had a grand time exploring the hiking paths." *(Arlyne & Collette Craighead)*

Minor niggle: "Both Tim and Chuck work at outside jobs, and we were disappointed that we saw them only briefly during our two-day midweek stay."

Open All year.
Rooms 2 suites, 3 doubles—all with private bath and/or shower, telephone, radio, air-conditioning. Some with desk, fan. 2 with fireplace. TV on request.
Facilities Dining room, living room with TV. 100 acres with hiking, private lake for swimming, boating. 3 min. to Lake Michigan & dunes.
Location NW IN, Lake Michigan shore, Porter County, dunes country. 55 m E of Chicago, 115 m N of Indianapolis. 1 m from town. From I-94 exit at Chesterton and go S on Rte. 49. Turn right at 1st stop light on Indian Boundary Rd. Go ¼ m to driveway on left.
Restrictions Trains 1 mile away might disturb light sleepers. No smoking in guest rooms. No children under 12.
Credit cards Amex, Discover, MC, Visa.
Rates B&B, $75–85 suite, $62–72 double, $62 single. Extra person, $10. 10% senior, AAA discount. Midweek corporate rate for 3-night stay. 2-night weekend minimum. Prix fixe lunch, $9; prix fixe dinner, $18–25.
Extras Station pickups.

COLUMBUS

Reader tip: "This town is a gold mine of contemporary architecture. Pick up a copy of the self-guiding tour map at the welcome center and spend several hours visiting the sites shown." *(Joe & Sheila Schmidt)*

For additional area entries, see Nashville.

The Columbus Inn 🏃   *Tel:* 812–378–4289
445 Fifth Street at Franklin, 47201

In what surely must be one of the most creative architectural recycling jobs in the country, the old Columbus City Hall, built in 1895, was converted in 1985 into a luxurious bed & breakfast inn by Paul Staublin. Of course, architectural innovation is no stranger to this small city of 30,000. For the past thirty years, the Cummins Foundation has maintained a program sponsoring internationally known architects, from Eero Saarinen to I. M. Pei to Henry Moore, to design major public buildings in Columbus. Rates include a full buffet breakfast, with everything from fresh fruit and juice to egg casseroles, bagels, and quick breads, and afternoon tea and cookies.

Although the inn is ideal for business travelers, vacationers may choose to make Columbus their headquarters for explorations of nearby Brown County, known as the "Bucks County of the Midwest," and for visits to the area's innumerable antique shops.

"The public areas are spacious, and well appointed with formal Victorian furniture and artificial flower arrangements. Desk personnel were friendly and helpful. Guest rooms are spacious, with plenty of floor space and wall-to-wall carpeting. Rooms on the third floor have pressed tin ceilings. The furniture is reproduction American Empire, and the decorative painting on walls and moldings is skillfully done. Rooms without sleigh beds had patterned wallpaper and handmade log cabin quilts, rather than the more formal solid color Empire treatment. My room was very clean, with a lamp for the desk and another lamp at my bedside; it had four or five windows that stretched from the floor almost to the ceiling. The bathroom was modern, with Revlon amenities, medium-weight white hotel towels, a long marble counter, fiberglass tub, and antique replica floor tiles, one inch square. There was no noise from traffic (this town of 33,000 shuts down early) or other rooms. Even though my room was next to the elevator, I did not hear it operating." *(S. Lee Fellows)* "The breakfast buffet included an egg and vegetable casserole, served with oat bread and sunflower seed bread; both it and afternoon tea were delicious." *(Charles & Elizabeth M. Harbit)* "Found your existing entry to be extremely accurate in describing this great hotel." *(Jim King)* "Friendly innkeepers, pleasant rooms." *(JS)* "Beautiful dining room with great breakfasts; hotel-style atmosphere, rather than an inn." *(DMS)*

Open All year.
Rooms 5 suites, 20 doubles, 9 singles—all with private bath and/or shower, telephone, radio, TV, desk, air-conditioning. 3 suites with kitchenette.
Facilities Dining room, lobby/library, game room/lounge area, 2 meeting rooms. 1 acre with flower gardens. Tennis, golf, fishing, swimming, playground, skiing, skating nearby.
Location S central IN. 85 m N of Louisville, KY, 35 m S of Indianapolis, 80 m W of Cincinnati, OH. On 5th St., in between Washington and Franklin Sts.
Restrictions Smoking not encouraged.
Credit cards All major cards accepted.
Rates B&B, $105–225 suite, $79–89 double. Extra adult, $10; no charge for children under 13. Rollaway bed, $10; crib, $5. Senior discount; weekend packages.
Extras Wheelchair access; baths equipped for disabled. Airport/station pickups. Crib, babysitting. Spanish spoken.

CORYDON

The Kintner House Inn   *Tel:* 812–738–2020
101 South Capitol Street, 47112

Indiana's first state capital, Corydon is so close to the Kentucky border
that Confederate General John Hunt Morgan made the original Kintner
House his headquarters during the Civil War, after he had captured the
town on July 9, 1863. After an 1871 fire destroyed an entire block of
buildings, a new Kintner House was constructed as a three-story brick
hotel, with elaborate Victorian furnishings. Restored in 1986, each lavishly decorated guest room is named after a significant person from
Corydon's past (President William Henry Harrison is remembered, along
with the "infamous" General Morgan). The decor includes flowered wallpapers, period lighting fixtures, coordinating bedspreads and draperies,
and plentiful Victorian antiques. Rates include a breakfast of homemade
bread, an egg casserole, fresh fruit, coffee and juice.

"Kintner House is located in the beautiful hills of southern Indiana in
the historic community of Corydon. The inn is an antique lovers' delight,
ranging from country primitives to Victorian, all meticulously restored.
Wallcoverings are Victorian reproductions, giving the rooms a special
brilliance. Rooms are spacious and bright. Baths have either showers or
elegant claw-footed tubs. Every need is cared for, from evening popcorn
and Coke to folding chairs for the Friday night band concert on the green,
a short distance from the inn. The breakfast, from grits to sausage casseroles, is elegantly prepared in a homey atmosphere. Despite its downtown location, the inn is quiet and restful. Parking is convenient, and the
inn is within walking distance of delightful restaurants, gift and antique
shops." *(William Hopper, also Diane Baker)*

"The inn is always clean and beautiful with special decorations for the
holidays or seasons. Homemade cookies in the kitchen and hot cider in the
fall all give you a wonderful feeling of welcome. The staff works breakfast
around my business schedule, and accommodates my needs with an extra
table or whatever. It's fun to take a walking tour of the historic area, but
I especially like the Zimmerman Glass Work, where you can watch the
two Zimmerman brothers make their wares. There are a variety of places
for dinner, but remember this is a small town which closes up early."
(Sandy Tope, also Claudia & Jim Bennett)

"The staff are all friendly, helpful and like to make you feel special. The
innkeeper seems more like a friend and deserves much credit for the inn's
success." *(Mary Hunt)* "Each room contains a description of Corydon's
history, with details on how each guest room was named." *(Juanita &
Albert Zeller)* "Beautiful rooms, large and well decorated. Warm host took
the time to introduce all the guests to one another at the breakfast table."
(Debbie Mishkin & Michael Swiatek)

And an oft-heard lament: "Better lighting would be helpful for reading
at both the desks and in bed."

Open All year.
Rooms 16 doubles—all with private bath and/or shower, telephone, air-conditioning. Some with desk. 2 rooms in annex.

Facilities Dining room, parlor with TV, porch with swings. Guest privileges at nearby club for swimming, tennis, golf. Fishing, boating, spelunking nearby.
Location S IN, 20 m E of Louisville, KY. Center of town. From I-64, take Exit 105 (S.R. 135) to Rte. 62 (2 m). Go E on Rte. 62 to inn on corner of Capitol Ave. and Chestnut St.
Restrictions Light sleepers should request rooms away from street. No smoking.
Credit cards All major cards accepted.
Rates B&B, $62–95 double. Senior, AAA, corporate, group discounts. Rollaway beds, $15; cots, $7.
Extras Cot, rollaway bed.

CRAWFORDSVILLE

Wabash College, one of the first colleges west of the Alleghenies, was founded in Crawsfordsville in 1832; the town was also home to several noted writers, including General Lew Wallace, author of the novel *Ben-Hur*. In addition to this activity, which earned it the nickname the "Hoosier Athens," the region supported a woolen mill, employing up to 300 people in the complete process of weaving fabric, tailoring garments, and pressing the finished clothing. Among the historic buildings open to the public is the old city jail with its circular cell block that enabled the sheriff to check on prisoners with a turn of his crank.

Information please: The Davis House (1010 West Wabash Avenue, 47933; 317–364–0461), located in a residential neighborhood not far from downtown, was a country mansion when it was built in 1870, of brick manufactured right on the site. Substantially renovated in 1940, and owned by Janice Stearns since 1986, Davis House has a colonial look, with high ceilings and decorative woodwork; the four guest rooms have antique, reproduction, and wicker furnishings. Rates include a continental breakfast.

Yount's Mill Inn ¢   *Tel:* 317–362–5864
3729 Old State Route 32 West, 47933

In 1851, Dan Yount built a two-story brick home, just north of his mill on Sugar Creek, to provide room and board for the young women employed there. Listed—along with the old mill—on the National Register of Historic Places, the Yount's Mill Inn is owned by Pat and John Hardwick. Furnished with both antiques and country pieces, each guest room has a distinct decor: the Primitive Room has a chicken crate table, and the Green Room features its Victorian-style paisley wallpaper and antique double bed. Rates include a breakfast of fruit bread, cereal, yogurt, fruit and juice, muffins or coffee cake, and coffee.

"Pat graciously gave us a complete tour while giving a history of the building. Each room is distinctive and inviting. The setting is very peaceful with the creek flowing by the property, ideal for canoeing or rafting. This area of Indiana is lovely with its covered bridges, broad fields, and handsome parks. Crawfordsville has some fun things to see—which evoke its more prosperous and lively past—such as the old city jail, now a museum, and other historic buildings." *(Shelly McDonald)* More reports welcome.

Open All year.
Rooms 4 doubles—1 with private bath and/or shower, 3 with a maximum of 6 people sharing bath.
Facilities Dining room, library, porches. Lawn, woodlands for hiking, bird watching, croquet, horseshoes. Sugar Creek for wading, fishing, rafting. Rubber raft available. Canoe rental in town.
Location W central IN. 35 m NW of Indianapolis. 4 m from town. Go W on SR 32 and cross bridge over Sugar Creek. Just after bridge turn left on next driveway and go to top of hill. Inn is well off the road to the left.
Restrictions No smoking. No children under 13.
Credit cards MC, Visa.
Rates B&B, $35–55 double. Extra person, $10.

GOSHEN

The Checkerberry Inn ✕   *Tel: 219–642–4445*
62644 County Route 37, 46526

If you'd like to combine a visit to Indiana's Amish Country with elegant accommodations that may remind you of a French country hotel, then the Checkerberry Inn will be of interest. Owned and managed by John and Susan Graff, this new inn, opened in 1987, offers comfortable contemporary decor and is set amid 100 acres of rolling farmland; guests are unanimous in their praise of the Graff's exceptional hospitality. Under the supervision of chef Doug Morgan, guests can select from a small but carefully chosen French-accented menu, with such dishes as sliced duck breast served over onions and topped with spiced pear sauce, beef tenderloin with wild mushroom peppercorn sauce, or herbed rack of lamb with garlic mint sauce. The Checkerberry also boasts the distinction of having Indiana's only professional-quality croquet court.

"Impeccably clean and well managed. Service is courteous and efficient." *(Donald Risser)* "Charming, delightful spot. The Graffs made us feel most welcome and took special interest in making sure we enjoyed our visit." *(Mrs. Halbert Law)* "One can enjoy the view of the countryside from the large veranda, enjoy a game of croquet on the neatly manicured court, play a game of tennis, or relax at the swimming pool. Our room was decorated with country French decor, with all the conveniences of home." *(Roy Nussbaum)*

"Beautifully decorated and furnished inn, with well-landscaped, attractive grounds. The view in all directions is pastoral. The inn is fairly large, with a sophisticated ambience." *(BG)* "Room are spacious, well lighted for reading, with pleasing decor. The inn is a quiet, refined oasis in the midst of a heavily touristed countryside of elbow-to-elbow sightseers. At dinner an appetizer of Brie en croûte was average, but the rack of lamb and breast of duck entrées were very good. Breakfast was a tasty buffet of granola, fruit, hot muffins and breads, with juices and coffee." *(John Blewer)*

An area for improvement: "Perhaps it was an exception, but the day we visited, breakfast was unattended by staff or owners, so guests interfaced with each other in a haphazard manner."

Open Feb. through Dec. Restaurant closed Sun., Mon.

Rooms 2 suites (1 with whirlpool tub), 10 doubles—all with private shower and/or bath, telephone, clock-radio, TV, desk, air-conditioning, coffee-maker.

Facilities Dining room, library with fireplace, TV; porch. 100 acres with swimming pool, tennis, croquet green, bicycling, hiking. Golf nearby.

Location N central IN. Amish country. 120 m E of Chicago, 150 m N of Indianapolis, 30 m E of South Bend. 6 m from Goshen, 16 m S of I-80/90. From I-80/90, take Exit 107 (Middlebury); go S (left) on S.R. 13, W (right) on Rte. 4, S (left) on C.R. 37 to inn on right.

Restrictions Smoking permitted on 3rd floor, library, foyer only.

Credit cards Amex, MC, Visa.

Rates B&B, $140–175 suite, $96–120 double, $72–90 single. Extra person, $25. Prix fixe lunch, $10; dinner, $25. 2-night minimum on Notre Dame football weekends.

Extras Wheelchair access.

GREENCASTLE

Walden Inn ¢ ♦ ✕   *Tel:* 317–653–2761
2 Seminary Square, P.O. Box 490, 46135

Built in 1986 on land leased from DePauw University, and owned by local businessmen, the Walden Inn serves the needs of visitors to the university and to the area. Guests have access to all of DePauw's athletic facilities and cultural events.

Reservations for parents' weekend and other special university events must be made long in advance; at other times, there's usually no problem. Rooms are furnished with hand-crafted local and Amish furniture; public rooms are decorated in a "country look" with antiques and original art. The inn's restaurant, the Different Drummer, serves three meals a day. Dinners include daily and seasonal specials; a typically creative dinner might include a salad of avocado, smoked salmon, and melon; lamb grilled with olive oil, garlic, and rosemary, sliced on a bed of pan fried red potatoes and onions, and raspberry cheesecake for dessert.

"One of the best chefs in the Midwest, Matthew O'Neill, an Irishman, was lured to Greencastle (population 8,000) to be chef and general manager. The inn is small and full of archival material from DePauw and central Indiana. Worth the nine-mile side trip from I-70. On a return trip, I wasn't in the room five minutes before the manager called to welcome me back. He later showed me a marvelous route past lovely covered bridges." *(Norval Stephens)*

"Brand-new, beautifully done, long needed in the town of Greencastle; just on the edge of campus. Staff are more than willing to please." *(T. E. Aschenbrener)* More comments required.

Open All year. Restaurant closed Dec. 25.

Rooms 5 suites, 45 doubles—all with private bath and/or shower, telephone, radio, TV, desk, air-conditioning, fan. 1 with fireplace.

Facilities Restaurant, bar with entertainment, library with fireplace, TV/VCR, books, games, cards; veranda with rockers. Indoor swimming pool at DPU, tennis court. Fishing, boating, swimming at 3 nearby state parks. Golf nearby.

Location Central IN. 45 m W of Indianapolis. 40 min. from Indianapolis airport. 3 blocks to Courthouse Square. Take Hwy. 231 to Greencastle. Turn E on Seminary St. and go 3 blocks.
Credit cards DC, Discover, MC, Visa.
Rates Room only, $98–150 suite, $77–125 double, $72 single. Extra person, $8. B&B, $85–150 suite, $55–125 double. Children under 13, free. 5% Senior, AAA discount. Alc lunch, $7; alc dinner, $22. Weekend packages.
Extras Wheelchair access. Crib.

INDIANAPOLIS

Indianapolis dates back to 1820, when it was selected as the site for the state's capital because of its location at the geographical center of the state. Streets were laid out in a wheel pattern similar to Washington, D.C.

Sights of interest include, of course, the Indianapolis Speedway and Hall of Fame. Hotel rates skyrocket on Memorial Day Weekend, when the famous "Indy 500" is held. Cultural attractions include the Museum of Art, with collections of Medieval, Renaissance, and 19th-century arts; the Children's Museum, with carousel, Egyptian mummies, and limestone cave; and the Museum of Indian Heritage.

Information please: Built in 1929, the newly renovated **Renaissance Tower Inn** (230 East 9th Street, 46204; 317–269–2589 or 800–676–7786) offers 81 suites with fully equipped kitchens, furnished with Queen Anne cherry reproduction furnishings, including four-poster beds. The hotel is a project of Robert Borns, who restored Union Station; rates are a reasonable $50 daily. In Union Station itself, now a bustling marketplace area, is the **Holiday Inn at Union Station** (123 West Louisiana Street, 46206–2186; 317–631–2221). Although the 250 hotel rooms are generic Holiday inn, we're intrigued by the 26 Pullman train cars which can now be booked at suites for $130 a night, double; less on weekends. Comments please.

The Canterbury Hotel ✕
123 South Illinois Street, 46225

Tel: 317–634–3000
800–538–8186

A small, full-service establishment, the Canterbury caters to business travelers during the week, and is arguably the state's smallest luxurious hotel. Guest rooms, furnished with Chippendale four-poster beds and Queen Anne furniture, include such amenities as refrigerators, televisions, telephones in the bedroom and bath, bathrobes, and the morning paper. Rates include the morning paper and a continental breakfast, served in the parlor; airport transfers are provided in a stretch limo previously owned by Frank Sinatra. A special treat is afternoon tea, with such treats as salmon and cream cheese sandwiches, chocolate mousse in miniature pastry shells, and scones with strawberry preserves.

"The Canterbury Hotel is a remodeling of an old faded downtown hotel. The lobby has a subdued, expensive-but-tasteful look, sort of British, with thick, deep-green carpeting, lots of shining brass, and hunting prints. The dining room is also clubby looking, with fine wood paneling and more hunt prints—very low-key. The food certainly ranks among the city's best, if not the best. The service is slow but attentive; the idea, I guess, is to make the meal your entire evening. Not a bad approach, considering the tab." *(Cynthia Snowden)*

"Gracious welcoming staff. Our room was decorated with handsome dark woods and deep colors. Although it was one of the less expensive ones, it was good-sized, with two chairs and a reading lamp, and a reasonably sized bathroom. The hotel is convenient to many restaurants and other downtown activities. The continental breakfast was adequate— juice, fruit, pastries, and coffee. It is served in a lovely parlor, and we carried our breakfast up to the mezzanine level, where we were able to eat in a semi-private alcove overlooking the parlor. Valet parking is available, and the attendants were most gracious even through we arrived in rain and left in a snowstorm. In all, we found the atmosphere far more personal and gracious than in any of the city's chain hotels." *(Linda Bamber)* More comments please.

Open All year.
Rooms 15 suites, 84 doubles—all with full private bath, telephone, radio, TV, desk, air-conditioning, refrigerator. Suites with whirlpool tub, wet bar.
Facilities Restaurant, 3 parlors, bar/lounge, atrium with pianist. Meeting rooms, business services. Concierge service. Valet parking. 5 min. to swimming pool. Golf nearby.
Location Downtown. On Illinois between Maryland and Georgia Sts.
Restrictions Some non-smoking rooms.
Credit cards All major cards accepted.
Rates B&B, $220–1,000 suite, $170–210 double, $105–210 single, plus 10% tax. Extra person, $25. Corporate rates, weekend rates and packages. Alc lunch, $12–20; alc dinner, $65.
Extras Wheelchair access. Airport/station pickups. Crib, babysitting. Spanish, French, Norwegian, Japanese, Chinese spoken. Member, Preferred Hotels.

MADISON

Set on the Ohio River, Madison reached its zenith in the 1850s with the rapid growth of river traffic. Much of its downtown area, now listed on the National Register of Historic Places, dates from this period. Architecture buffs will enjoy the variety of styles of its restored buildings, including Gothic Revival, Classic Revival, Federal, and Italianate.

Madison is located in southeast Indiana, near the Kentucky and Ohio borders, about a 1½-hour drive from Louisville, Cincinnati, and Indianapolis.

Information please: One block from the river is the **Elderberry Inn** (411 West First Street, 47250; 812–265–6856), a century-old home in the historic district. Rooms are furnished with a blend of antique and contemporary decor, and the reasonable rates include full breakfast. Another nearby possibility is the **Heritage House** (705 West Second Street, 47250; 812–265–2393) an Italianate Victorian home. Rates include an early morning wake-up tray and an English-style breakfast served by candlelight. Reports?

Cliff House ¢ ♔   *Tel: 812–265–5272*
122 Fairmont Drive, 47250

The Cliff House is a century-old Victorian built on a cliff overlooking Madison and the Ohio River. Jae and Thomas Breitweiser have spent years restoring it. Four guest rooms have river views. A doll museum occupies the third floor of the house. Rates include a breakfast of fruit, homemade breakfast cake, and croissants, served on 100-year-old Haviland china, and an evening snack of fruit and homemade cookies.

"All the rooms are filled with antiques, some of them massive pieces in keeping with the size and style of the house. Our favorite place was the widow's walk, with a panoramic view of the river and Kentucky on the river side—*the* place to be on the Fourth of July. Our reception was very warm, the rooms comfortable and the breakfast, served in the dining room, was pleasant." *(Cynthia Snowden)* "The rooms are bright and cheerful. The evening cookies were sinfully delicious, and the morning pastries, baked in the house, were equally tasty. Our host graciously provided a supply of cookies for the road." *(Joe & Sheila Schmidt)*

Open All year.
Rooms 1 suite, 5 doubles—all with private bath and/or shower, air-conditioning. Some with canopy bed.
Facilities Dining room, parlor, music room, porches, widow's walk.
Location Near center. From Main St., turn N on West St., then left on Michigan St. Turn right on Fairmont St., 1st driveway on right.
Restrictions Smoking in parlor only.
Credit cards MC, Visa.
Rates B&B, $75–150 suite, $75 double, $50 single. Extra adult, $25; extra child, $15; baby, $10. Family rates for suite.
Extras Crib, babysitting.

Clifty Inn ¢ ♔   *Tel: 812–265–4135*
Clifty Falls State Park, Box 387, 47250

"A stay at Clifty Falls makes a nice balance with a tour of historic Madison. After a rainy day spent visiting the town's many historic buildings, the next morning was clear and sunny, perfect for hiking the park's beautiful trails. We hiked past deep gorges and saw the beautiful waterfalls for which the park is named. Our motel-style room was basic, but clean and well equipped, and had a balcony with a view of the Ohio. The food is nothing fancy, but neither are the prices. Our kids adored the curving, bumpy waterslide which feeds into their huge pool, and must have zoomed down a dozen times." *(MW)* More comments required.

Open All year.
Rooms 62 doubles, 10 singles—all with private shower and/or bath, telephone, radio, TV, desk, air-conditioning.
Facilities Restaurant. 100 acres with 2 swimming pools, hiking trails, tennis, nature center. Golf nearby. Guided hikes, nature talks in summer.
Location 1 m to town.
Credit cards Amex, MC, Visa.
Rates Room only, $46–49 double. Rollaway, $5; crib, $3. State park daily entry fee, $2 per car. Alc breakfast, $3–6; alc lunch, $4–7; alc dinner, $6–12.
Extras Wheelchair access. Crib.

Main Street B&B 👫   *Tel: 812–265–3539*
739 West Main Street, 47250

In 1987, Sally and Ken McWilliams decided that the Washington, D.C., area was not where they wanted to raise their children, Carrie and Kevin. They had visited family in the Madison area for years, and were delighted to find a Federal-style home built in 1843 in remarkably good condition. Decorating with a light touch, appropriate to the period, they've furnished the house with 18th century antiques and reproductions, and beautiful quilts made by Sally's grandmother.

"Within walking distance of Madison's shops and historic sites, this B&B has a warm, homey atmosphere. Sally's greeting was so friendly that I felt I had known her for years. There's convenient parking right in front of the house, and street lighting is good. Since the McWilliams live in a separate wing of the house, Sally gives you a house key upon arriving so you can come and go as you please. Each guest room is different, but all have comfortable seating and lots of extras to make you feel at home. The big front bedroom has a large dressing-shower area with great lighting, and is very clean. At five P.M. cheese and crackers are served in the parlor before the large fireplace, and the guests enjoy visiting and reading. Before going to bed we filled out a form to let Sally know what time we'd like to have coffee, tea or cocoa brought to our room. Breakfast is served with fine china and crystal between 8 A.M. and 10 A.M., and included yogurt, fruit, juice, and homemade peach jam, coffee cake, and muffins. Sally is a great baker and her jam even won a blue ribbon at the state fair!" *(Melonie Yates)* "Sally McWilliams has a wonderful personality and was very helpful with information about the area." *(Joe & Sheila Schmidt)*

Open All year.
Rooms 1 suite, 2 doubles—all with private bath and/or shower, radio, desk, air-conditioning, fan.
Facilities Dining room with fireplace, parlor with fireplace, piano, stereo, books; sun room. Golf nearby. Boating, swimming, fishing nearby.
Location Historic district. On Hwy. 56 (Main St.)
Restrictions No smoking in guest rooms. No off-street parking.
Credit cards MC, Visa.
Rates B&B, $93–120 suite, $73–100 double, $50–75 single. Extra person, $20. Children under 6, free; 7–15, $15; 16 or over, $20.
Extras Crib.

MICHIGAN CITY

Creekwood Inn ✕   *Tel: 219–872–8357*
Route 20-35 at I-94, 46360

The Creekwood was built in the 1930s by Dr. Lawrence Robrock, as an English Cotswold-style manor house. Mary Lou Linnen and Peggie Wall refurbished the house and built a guest wing in 1986. Rooms are individually decorated in a variety of styles, with coordinated fabrics, wall coverings, and window treatments, and quality reproduction furniture. Rates include breakfast of homemade breads, fresh fruit, and coffee. Mary Lou reports that in 1991, they planted over 3,000 perennials for an English garden for guests to enjoy.

"The Creekwood has a casual but elegant atmosphere. The lounge and dining area are in the original house, with some marvelous hand-hewn beams and leaded windows, looking out on the woods. The guest rooms are in a new wing that is architecturally compatible with the original home but also modern in every sense." *(Jackson Sloan)*

"Aptly named, the Creekwood Inn is nestled in a lovely wooded area with a creek running through the property. There are winding trails through the woods as well as a patio, screened porch, and large lawn area for enjoying the outdoors. Although the Creekwood is only two blocks off the expressway, it seems much removed from the hustle and bustle. Mary Lou, Peggie, and their staff are pleasant and helpful and go out of their way to accommodate their guests. The rooms are large and appointed with attention to detail—from the ice-maker refrigerator to the fresh fruit in every room. Housekeeping throughout the inn is first-rate. The continental breakfast includes fruit, juice, coffee, and delicious home-made croissants, breads, and muffins. Our Saturday night dinner had a real home-cooked freshness." *(Patricia Snyder and others)*

"The Creekwood is attractive and comfortable, welcoming but not cutesy. Our room was large, with sliding doors onto a patio. The grounds are wooded, nice for short walks." *(Cynthia Snowden)* "Outstanding hospitality. The staff does everything they can to make you happy and comfortable. The food is a real treat; it's worth the extra money to have the full breakfast and enjoy the dinner, and the classical music played during meals enhanced the mood." *(Betsie Frank, and others)*

Open All year. Closed March 4–15.
Rooms 1 suite, 12 doubles—all with private bath and/or shower, telephone, radio, TV, desk or table, air-conditioning, fan, refrigerator/ice maker. Some with fireplace, private terrace.
Facilities Parlor with piano, fireplace, TV/VCR, radio, books, dining room, sun porch, game/library area, conference room/facilities, screened porch, patio. 33 acres with perennial garden, woods, creeks, small fishing pond, trails for cross-country skiing, walking. Lawn games, bicycles. Golf, tennis, horseback riding, charter boat fishing nearby.
Location NW IN, near Lake Michigan. LaPorte County. 30 m W of South Bend; 60 m SE of Chicago, IL. Willow Creek; 3 m from town. From I-94, take Exit 40 B. Take first street on left, then turn left to inn.
Credit cards Amex, DC, MC, Visa.
Rates B&B, $144–150 suite, $99–120 double, $93–114 single, plus 10% tax. Extra person, $15. 5% senior discount. Reduced rates for children under 2. Full breakfast, $5; afternoon tea, $8; prix fixe dinner, $50, Fri/Sat. Alc lunch, $8. 2–3 night holiday weekend minimum. Weekend packages, corporate rates.
Extras Wheelchair access. Airport/station pickups. Crib. German spoken.

MIDDLEBURY

Northern Indiana's Crystal Valley, just south of the Indiana Toll Road, is best known for its large Amish population, and for the famous Shipshewana Auction and flea market. Middlebury is located in northeastern Indiana, 15 miles east of Elkhart and 10 miles west of Shipshewana. It's approximately three hours' drive from both Detroit and Indianapolis.

Reader tips: "We thought the Menno-Hof's visitor center across the street from the Shipshewana auction house was excellent, with informative exhibits and displays to tell the story of the Anabaptist Mennonite movement. On the other hand, we found the much-vaunted Shipshewana Auction House and Flea Market to be a mob scene of people suffocating in pursuit of the trivial and mundane." *(John Blewer)*

Information please: We'd like reports on the **Patchwork Quilt B&B** (11748 County Road 2, 46540; 219–825–2417), known best for its delicious all-you-can-eat Amish dinners. Three rooms sharing one bath are available for B&B in the original century-old farmhouse, and rates are reasonable. "Interesting backroads tours, very good food, small but pleasant room. Atmosphere is a bit more business-like than most B&Bs." *(PB)*

Current feedback on the nearby **Green Meadow Ranch** (R 2, Box 592, Shipshewana, 46565; 219–768–4221) would also be helpful. This working ranch offers seven rooms with shared baths for B&B and the modest rates include a breakfast of raisin bran muffins and jam, locally made cheese and sausage served on the wicker-filled back porch; the house is furnished with antiques and folk art, all of which are for sale. Innkeeper Ruth Miller is friendly and knowledgeable about all area activities, and will happily arrange local tours.

Essenhaus Country Inn ¢ ✗ ♦   Tel: 219–825–9447
240 U.S. Route 20, 46540

"Opened in 1986, the inn is beautifully decorated and situated in a lovely quiet country setting. The restaurant on the grounds, Das Dutchman Essenhaus, has been an Indiana institution for years. The place is huge but the food is superb and the prices low. After you eat, visit the inn's shops: craft, clothing, furniture stores, and bakery. Since it is in Amish country, there are no bars or liquor stores and the restaurant is closed on Sunday.

"Our room was done in deep green and light mauve. The furniture—hand-crafted by local Amish craftsmen—was bleached pine and very plain, yet classy. There was a handsome armoire in lieu of a closet and another, smaller cupboard housing the TV. We also had a small couch, a desk, and several comfortable chairs. We paid a small extra fee for a room with a whirlpool tub, which was really great. The towels were luxurious, and the bath was supplied with attractive soaps and other amenities." *(Virginia Reidy)* "For a new inn, we found it charming and comfortable. The rooms were large but cozy, and the well-planned hallways and decor made our stay fun." *(Jim & Tina Kirkpatrick)*

And another opinion: "We didn't see the rooms, but found the restaurant to be an overwhelming mob scene during our June visit."

Open All year. Restaurant, shops closed Sun. and major holidays.
Rooms 5 suites, 27 doubles—all with telephone, radio, TV, desk, air-conditioning. Some suites with whirlpool tubs.
Facilities Restaurant, living room with antique stove, atrium, shops, game room, sun porch. 40 acres with small lake, landscaping, playground. Amish Country Tours, June–Oct. Swimming, golf, fishing, cross-country skiing within 10 m.

Location N IN. Elkhart County. 15 m E of Elkhart, 10 m W of Shipshewana. 1 m E of Middlebury. 4 m S of I-80/90. On Rte. 20, 1 m W of intersection with Indiana SR 13.
Restrictions No smoking in dining room. No alcohol.
Credit cards Amex, MC, Visa.
Rates Room only, $85–115 suite, $75 double, $60 single. Extra person, $10. No charge for children under 12 in parents' room. Rollaway, $5; crib, $2. Alc breakfast, $3–5; alc lunch, $11. Continental breakfast included on Sunday only.
Extras Wheelchair access. Crib.

Varns Guest House ¢

Tel: 219–825–9666

205 South Main Street, P.O. Box 125, 46540

Carl and Diane Eash report that the Varns House was built by Diane's great-grandparents in 1898 and has been in the Varns family ever since. "My mother and my aunt were born and married in this house. My husband and I bought it in 1988, and restored it as a B&B. My parents live next door, and my mother serves a continental breakfast of wonderful homemade goodies. Our guests enjoy the quaintness of the area, the country shops, the good food, the warm hospitality, the history of the house, and the relaxed atmosphere." The restoration of the house went beyond fresh paint and wallpaper, lovely antiques and refinished wood-work: Diane notes that "although we're on the main street, the house was very well insulated when restored. All you hear is the clip-clop of the horses pulling Amish buggies."

"Varns is a jewel—beautifully restored. Clean as can be, great hospital-ity. The owner's mom even invited us to come next door for a swim. We stayed in the exquisite China Rose Room on the first floor. Had a delicious dinner at the Patchwork and loved the beautiful quilts." *(Kit Carter Wei-lage)* "Fully endorse existing entry. Even though we did not meet Diane, her mom greeted us and made us feel so welcome. She is a sweet dear lady. We stayed in the Nancy Jane room upstairs, and can't wait to return." *(Arlyne & Colette Craighead)*

Open All year.
Rooms 5 doubles—all with private bath and/or shower, radio, air-conditioning. 1 with whirlpool tub.
Facilities Living room with fireplace, dining room, breakfast room, wraparound porch. 1 acre with lawn.
Location N IN. 2 hrs. E of Chicago, 3 hrs N of Indianapolis. Center of town.
Restrictions No smoking. "Rooms comfortably sleep only 2 people."
Credit cards MC, Visa.
Rates B&B, $65 double, $60 single. Extra person, $10.

NASHVILLE

Popular with artists since the turn of the century, this heavily forested area explodes with color each October. Craft studios and galleries abound in the Nashville area, and musical and theatrical productions thrive all sum-mer.

Also recommended: Although received too late to complete full entries, two recommended Bloomington B&Bs of interest are the **Grant Street Inn** (310 North Grant Street, Bloomington 47401; 812–334–2353, two Queen Anne Victorian homes joined together with gardens to create 14 large guest rooms with private baths; and the **Little Peddler Inn** (321 North Lincoln Street, Bloomington 47408; 812–334–2353) a 1870s home with three guest rooms with private baths, located within walking distance of Indiana University. Rates at both are $75 daily, $95–125 weekends. *(LG)*

Information please: The Allison House Inn (90 South Jefferson Street, P.O. Box 546, Nashville 47448; 812–988–0814) is a restored Victorian home within walking distance of many craft shops; each of its five bedrooms have modern private baths, and the $85 rate includes a breakfast of cereal, fresh fruit, and home-baked bran muffins and cinnamon cake. The overall look is light and airy country, accented by handmade quilts, antiques, and bird prints by a local artist.

A short drive from town is the **Wraylyn Knoll** (P.O. Box 481, Nashville, 47448; 812–988–0733), a contemporary home with five guest rooms, each with private bath. The $50–80 rates include a continental breakfast on weekdays; on weekends, cooked apples, eggs and sausage, and biscuits might make up a typical meal. Owners Larry and Marcia Wray invite their guests to enjoy the inn's ample common areas, as well as the swimming pool, fishing pond, and creek found on the inn's 12 acres.

A very intriguing Brown County possibility is the **Rock House** (380 West Washington Street, Morgantown 46160; 812–597–5100), just 11 miles north of Nashville and 30 miles south of Indianapolis. It was built in 1894 of handmade concrete blocks; the owner/builder embedded rocks, marbles, jewelry, seashells, glass bottles, dishes, and even an animal skull into the drying concrete. This homestay B&B is gradually being restored by owners Marcia and Doug Norton; rooms have some antique furnishings, and the reasonable rates include a full breakfast. Reports please!

For an additional area entry, see Columbus.

Story Inn ¢ 🛉 ✕   *Tel:* 812–988–2273
Rte. 2, Box 166-A, P.O. Box 64, 47448

Built in 1850 as a general store, and now a well-known country restaurant with rooms available for B&B, the Story Inn has been owned and operated since 1978 by resident innkeepers Benjamin and Cynthia Schultz, and Susan Barret. Behind its weather-beaten corrugated tin façade and "antique" gas pumps is a well-known restaurant of unexpected sophistication for such a rural setting, with all dishes made from scratch. Menus change twice a month, and a recent dinner included such entrées as raspberry chicken with three-berry sauce; rack of lamb with carrots, onions, and new potatoes; and swordfish with pepperonata relish. With desserts such as turtle cheesecake, blueberry pie, and chocolate custard cake, it's worth saving room. Rates include a breakfast of homemade bread with apple butter, and such specialities as gravy and biscuits, Story fries (grated potatoes grilled with cheese), and banana walnut hot cakes. Guest rooms are located on the second floor of the old store, and in adjacent cottages; all are furnished with period antiques. *(CF, also LG)*

"We were made to feel very comfortable immediately upon our arrival, both in the restaurant and in our room. The owners and staff were extremely friendly and helpful with information and advice about attractions, roads, directions. The food in the restaurant was excellent—fresh and innovative." *(Paula Jenkins)* "Staying here is like spending the night with friends—good food, good conversation, a peaceful setting." *(Kathy Merriman)*

Open All year. Restaurant closed Mondays.
Rooms 4 suites, 3 doubles, 6 cottages—all with private shower and/or bath, desk, air-conditioning. Some with radio, deck. Cottages with TV, refrigerator. 2 suites in annex.
Facilities Restaurant, screened dining porch, common room with TV, games, bar/lounge. 3 acres with childrens' play equipment, picnic area, carriage rides. Borders state park for hiking, cross-country skiing, swimming, horseback riding, tennis, golf.
Location S central IN. 30 m SE of Bloomington, 21 m SW of Columbus, IN. From Bloomington, take Rte. 46 E 22 m through Nashville, then go right onto Rte. 135 S 9.5 m to Story.
Restrictions No smoking.
Credit cards Discover, MC, Visa.
Rates Room only, $65 suite, $55 double, $45 single. B&B, $85 cottage, $75 suite, $65 double, $55 single. Extra person, $10. No charge for children under 12. Mystery weekends. Prix fixe lunch, $8–10; prix fixe dinner, $18–20. Alc dinner, $18–20; 15–20% service additional.
Extras Crib. Pets permitted by prior arrangement in cottages. French, German, Spanish spoken.

NEW HARMONY

The New Harmony Inn ¢ 🛏 ✖   *Tel:* 812–682–4491
North Street, P.O. Box 581, 47631

The town of New Harmony was founded in 1814 by a group of Harmonists, who were persecuted in their native Germany and came to the fertile Wabash valley to start anew. After eleven years of hard work they moved to Pennsylvania, leaving many sturdy and ingeniously constructed buildings behind. They sold the town to the British social reformer Robert Owen, who arrived in 1825 with many distinguished scholars to start an experiment in communal living. Although the experiment failed, much of its intellectual heritage lives on. Many of the historic buildings have been restored, contrasting modern ones have been built, and a variety of music, art, and drama programs is offered.

The inn is a simply designed contemporary structure, spare, yet very handsome in decor, blending well with the clear lines of the original Harmonist structures. Two restaurants are connected with the inn, the Red Geranium and the Bayou Grill.

"Just as you described it. Food at the Red Geranium was excellent, as were the service and wine selection. The Shaker lemon pie was good and properly tart; the buffet breakfast at the Bayou Grill included very good bread pudding, plentiful fruit and juice, tasty corned beef hash and bacon.

As often happens in a buffet, the scrambled eggs and sausage didn't look too appetizing, but they happily fixed eggs to order." *(Al & Jeanine Muller)*

"The New Harmony Inn is a quaint, down-to-earth inn. Each room is original and some have their own fireplace—very cozy, especially in the fall. The whole town is historically significant, so a two- or three-day stay is rewarding." *(Stephen Tucker)* "Grounds were lovely. Our room faced the river. The lobby was peaceful, with rocking chairs, a fireplace, books." *(KLH)*

"Very nice, but 'stark,' as it should be, considering the background of New Harmony. Our room had bare wooden floors, although some of the others have small scatter rugs. The bath was very clean but merely functional. Although the inn has expanded in recent years, and has added a conference center, this did not detract from the wonderful atmosphere. We enjoyed good service, food, and accommodations in a peaceful, historic setting." *(Carolyn Snyder)* More reports welcome.

Open All year.
Rooms 90 doubles—all with full private bath and/or shower, telephone, radio, TV, desk. Some with kitchenette, balcony, fireplace.
Facilities Family room, lobby, bar, restaurant, TV/game room. Rose garden and pond, indoor/outdoor heated swimming pool, hot tub, sauna, health club, tennis court, chapel. Golf nearby.
Location SE corner of IN. 25 m W of Evansville.
Credit cards Amex, CB, DC, MC, Visa.
Rates Room only, $65 double, $55 single. Extra person, $10. No charge for children under 12. 15% winter discount. Corporate rates. 10% AARP discount. Alc lunch, $6–9; alc dinner, $16–21.
Extras Wheelchair access. Airport/station pickups.

ROCKPORT

The Rockport Inn ¢ ✗   *Tel:* 812–649–2664
Third at Walnut, 47635

Built around 1855, the Rockport Inn was one of the first buildings in the area to have glass windows; a number of the original panes are still in place. Although the inn has been renovated several times over the years, much of the 1855 structure is still intact, including the hand-hewn logs and beams, held together with square-shaped iron nails.

"In the small town of Rockport, set on the beautiful Ohio River bluffs, is the Rockport Inn, just across from the courthouse. For some years, it has been operated by Emil Ahnell, a college professor from Owensboro, KY. An old boardinghouse, it serves very good food served to the general public. Spencer County is where Abraham Lincoln spent his boyhood years." *(Edith Wells)* "Since it was a holiday, the restaurant was closed for dinner, but we had juice, coffee, and rolls in the morning and had a lovely chat with the innkeeper. Our room was charming, as were several others which I saw." *(Ruth McBride)*

Areas for improvement: "The hallway rugs could use a good cleaning; I would have appreciated tissues in the bathroom since I don't usually travel with my own supply."

Open All year. Restaurant closed Mon., major holidays.
Rooms 6 doubles—all with private bath and/or shower, telephone, TV, desk, air-conditioning.
Facilities Restaurant, lobby.
Location SE IN. 30 m E of Evansville. In center, by courthouse.
Credit cards None accepted.
Rates B&B, $35–45 double, $30–35 single. Family discount. Alc lunch, $6; alc dinner, $15–23.
Extras German, Swedish spoken. Crib, babysitting.

WARSAW

A small town in north central Indiana, Warsaw is located 50 minutes south of South Bend, and the same distance west of Fort Wayne. It's two hours east of Chicago, and four hours southwest of Detroit. Local attractions include the 101 lakes of Kosciusko County—two with public beaches and playgrounds—a summer theater, golf course, along with antique shops, the Warsaw cut glass factory, and Amish crafts and foods. The county is both an industrial center (orthopedics are a specialty) and a top producer agriculturally.

Candlelight Inn   *Tel:* 219–267–2906
503 East Fort Wayne Street, 46580

Although their 1860s Victorian home is a long way from the south, Debi and Bill Hambright feel that it evokes the mood of *Gone With the Wind*. They've furnished the inn, established in 1985, with period antiques, restoring its handsome woodwork and covering the walls with documented reproduction wallpapers. With one exception, guest rooms are named for Scarlett O'Hara, Rhett Butler, and Tara, and have been decorated to subtly evoke their namesakes. Rates include a full breakfast, afternoon refreshments, and evening turndown. Favorite breakfast treats include New England popovers, orange French toast, fluffy omelets, and crêpes, accompanied by hot or cold fruits, coffee and herbal teas.

"The Candlelight's antique decor gives it a turn-of-the-century atmosphere, yet the plumbing, electricity, and in-room telephones offer everything the modern traveler expects. The Hambrights are exceptionally warm hosts and the town's location between two lakes makes it ideal for the both the business and vacation traveler." *(George Kempsell)* More comments welcome.

Open All year.
Rooms 4 doubles—all with private bath and/or shower, telephone, radio, TV, desk, air-conditioning, ceiling fan, fireplace, refrigerator. 1 with Jacuzzi.
Facilities Dining room, parlor with TV, games; porch. 3 lakes within walking distance for swimming. Tennis, golf nearby.
Location N IN. 40 m W of Fort Wayne, 40 m SE of South Bend. 4 blocks from center of town. From SR 30, turn S on SR 15 and go 3 m to inn.
Restrictions Train passes once during the night. No smoking. No children under 10.
Credit cards Amex, MC, Visa.

Rates B&B, $69–76 double, $58–70 single. Extra person, $6. Group rates. 10% senior discount. Weekend, anniversary packages.
Extras Airport/station pickups.

White Hill Manor   *Tel: 219–269–6933*
2513 East Center Street, 46580

Warsaw claims to be the world capital of the orthopedics industry, and one of its most successful entrepreneurs built himself a magnificent 4,500-square-foot English Tudor manor in 1934, in the depths of the Depression. Once an isolated hilltop mansion, it became surrounded by commercial projects as Warsaw developed. The inn was restored in 1988, and is managed by Gladys Deloe; rates include the morning papers, full breakfast (perhaps crab-filled crèpes or cinnamon French toast) and afternoon tea. Although all are welcome, the inn has particular appeal to the business traveler who wants the warmth of an inn setting, without sacrificing professional necessities: breakfast available at 6:30 A.M. on weekdays, copying and FAX service, and so on. Hand-hewn oak beams, arched doorways, mullioned and stained glass windows are complemented by the clubby English decor, with wing chairs and leather sofas in the parlor, and reproduction mahogany and brass furnishings in the bedrooms. Ivory, soft sea greens, and shades ranging from mauve to maroon key the color scheme.

"Rooms are impeccably clean, handsomely decorated with antiques. Service is warm, accommodating, and friendly." *(Elizabeth Kamano)* "Breakfast consists of quiche, fresh fruit, muffins, juice, and coffee, and is served in a glass-enclosed porch. Parking is ample and the inn is close to shopping and restaurants." *(Steve & Diana Main)* "We had a king-sized bed in the original library. Although there was no room for a separate reading area, the room was comfortable and quiet. The master bedroom, the Windsor Suite, is wonderfully large and perfect for anyone who needs space and comfort, but book well in advance as the inn is very popular with business interests. Despite its location on a busy highway, not far from a major intersection, it is a lovely inn, definitely recommended." *(John Blewer)*

Note: At press time we learned that the inn was for sale; inquire further when booking.

Open All year.
Rooms 1 suite, 7 doubles—all with private bath and/or shower, telephone, TV, desk, air-conditioning.
Facilities Breakfast room, living room with fireplace, stereo, books; guest refrigerator, microwave, parlor, conference room. 1 acre with courtyard. Fishing, boating, swimming nearby.
Location N IN. 40 m E of Fort Wayne, 40 m W of South Bend. 10 blocks from center of town. Next to Wagon Wheel Restaurant and Theater.
Restrictions No smoking in guest rooms.
Credit cards Amex, MC, Visa.
Rates B&B, $110–117 suite, $75–105 double, $70–100 single. Extra person, $7. No tipping. 10% corporate discount.
Extras Wheelchair access. Airport/station pickups, $.25/mile. Crib.

Iowa

Die Heimat Country Inn, Homestead

Since you've turned to this chapter, we assume you know better than to think of Iowa as an endless cornfield. There's a lot to do here. Many of the historic towns along the Mississippi and Missouri rivers sponsor summertime events and river excursions, while other towns proudly display their ethnic heritage—Dutch, German, Czech, and Native American. The Amana Colonies, in eastern Iowa, offer a fascinating glimpse into a religious communal society dating back to the mid-1800s. Several historic reconstructions will appeal to visitors, from the Living History Farms and the Boone & Scenic Valley Railroad near Des Moines, to the Fort Museum at Fort Dodge. Iowans love fairs, and you'll find them sponsored by towns around the state from April through October. Highlights include the Iowa State Fair in Des Moines and the National Hot Air Balloon Championships at Indianola.

Information please: In eastern Iowa, roughly halfway between Davenport and Iowa City, just nine miles north of I-80, is the **Victorian House of Tipton** (508 East 4th Street, Tipton 52772; 319–886–2633), a striking example of the Eastlake style, decorated in period with handsome antiques, Vermont marble fireplaces, and stained glass windows. Another possibility is **Wellington Place** (4th & Wellington, Waterloo 50701; 319–234–2993), about 80 miles west of Dubuque. A turn-of-the-century Colonial Revival home, it offers three suites; a full breakfast is served in the room, and is included in the $75 room rate.

Those looking for a small B&B in the Omaha, Nebraska, area might do well to check out the **Robin's Nest Inn,** a three-guest-room B&B, built in 1881 (327 Ninth Avenue, Council Bluffs 51501; 712–323–1649).

Rates do not include 4% sales tax.

ADEL

Walden Acres B&B ¢   *Tel: 515—987—1338*
2965 340th Trail, RR 1, Box 30, 50003   515—987—1567

Legendary Cleveland Indians pitcher Bob Feller built this English-style country home for his parents in 1940; true baseball history fans will want to see the 100-year-old barn where he practiced pitching with his father. Phyllis and Dale Briley have lived here for a dozen years; as their children grew up and left home, they made two rooms available for B&B.

"The house is very clean; our room had ample closet space and a comfortable bed. Both a fan and extra blankets were available if needed. The bathroom had everything we could possibly need in the way of toiletries. Dale and Phyllis Briley are gracious people who seem to have thought of everything." *(Karen Burkhart)*

"We had a great hike through the wooded pastures by the lake. Deer were in the woods and a herd of horses were playfully running in the pasture. The grounds are immaculately kept and the brick porch with white wicker furniture and lots of flowers was a nostalgic place to sit. The family has lots of pets, kept near or far at guests' request. We stayed in the bright Sunrise room, with its homey quilts. Phyllis is a friendly and gracious hostess, very helpful with all requests and directions to local attractions and restaurants." *(Bonnie & Ken Ellis)*

"The Brileys combined Midwestern hospitality with our need for privacy. Fresh-baked chocolate chip cookies awaited us on arrival, and Phyllis served us a tray of hot tea after we walked through snowy fields. In the morning she brought up hot coffee and orange spice muffins with the Sunday paper an hour before breakfast." *(Elizabeth Baum-Ferrer)* "The Walden Pond theme is found throughout the house, and our room had a number of beautiful books illustrating Thoreau's masterpiece. Dale is a semi-retired veterinarian, and his office is in a tiny cottage outside the house. Included among the house's inhabitants is a lovable one-eyed cat he rescued. She gets cheddar cheese every night when the Brileys have wine and cheese, but will eat only medium—not mild or sharp! Just below the house is a lovely lake, surrounded by oak trees and delightful for fishing. In the morning, we enjoyed a breakfast of pumpkin bread, apple cider, apple jelly, ham and eggs, and orange butter—all homemade by Phyllis." *(Timothy Amsden, also Jim Ferrer)*

Open All year.
Rooms 2 doubles sharing 1 bath. Both with radio, TV, desk, air-conditioning, ceiling fan.
Facilities Dining room, living room with fireplace, country kitchen, game room with piano, TV, books, games; solarium, patio, antique shop. Yard with trampoline, volleyball, badminton. 40 acres with hiking, fishing, cross-country skiing.
Location Central IA. 15 min. W of Des Moines. Take Exit 117, Waukee/Booneville, off I-80. Go S 1 m; turn right (W) 1 m to farm.
Restrictions Smoking in game room or kitchen only.
Credit cards None accepted.

Rates B&B, $55–60 double, $45–50 single. Extra person, $10. Children under 13, $5.
Extras Airport/station pickups. Pets permitted (in veterinary kennel on property).

DAVENPORT

Also recommended: A landmark Italianate mansion, the **Bishop's House Inn** (1597 Brady Street, 52803–4622; 319–324–2454) is listed on the National Register of Historic Places. Its six guest rooms are highlighted by stained glass windows and antique decor; some with fireplaces and whirlpool tubs. *(Richard Goodson)*

River Oaks Inn ¢ 🏃
1234 East River Drive, 52803

Tel: 319–326–2629
319–324–6843

Davenport first prospered because of its location on the Mississippi River, then continued to grow when the railroad bridged the river to Illinois in 1856. Shipping by river and rail continues to support the economy today. For entertainment, visitors can choose from riverboat cruises, harness racing, a Civil War muster, and blues and jazz festivals.

Just five minutes from the Mississippi is the River Oaks Inn, an 1850s Italianate Victorian listed in the National Register of Historic Places. Owned since 1986 by Mary Jo Pohl, the inn offers comfortably furnished rooms and a full breakfast served either in the formal dining room, on the deck, or in your own room. An ornate gazebo (also a historic landmark) graces the front lawn and is the perfect spot for coffee while enjoying the view. "Nice place. I especially like the big upstairs room with a sun porch." *(Richard Goodson)* More comments please.

Open All year.
Rooms 1 cottage, 1 suite, 3 doubles—all with private bath and/or shower, telephone, radio, TV, desk, air-conditioning, fan. Suite with fireplace. Cottage with VCR, piano, stereo.
Facilities Dining room, living room with organ, deck. 4 acres, hot tub, children's play equipment, gazebo, picnic area. Walk to boating, fishing.
Location E central IA, 167 m E of Des Moines, 79 m SE of Cedar Rapids, 160 m W of Chicago. From Hwy 67, turn N on College Ave., or Bridge Ave. Turn into first alley halfway up the hill to inn.
Restrictions No smoking in guest rooms.
Credit cards MC, Visa.
Rates B&B, $69–75 suite, $49–65 double, $39–49 single. Extra person, $10. No tipping. Senior, AAA discount.
Extras Wheelchair access. Airport/station pickup. Crib; babysitting by prior arrangement. Italian, Spanish spoken.

DUBUQUE

Iowa's oldest city, Dubuque grew prosperous in the 19th century, first from lead mining, later from the lumber, meat packing, and other industries. The city's many handsome Victorian buildings are a legacy of this prosperity, and many have been restored as art galleries, B&Bs, and theaters. If you have just a short time for sightseeing, take a ride up the Fenelon Place Elevator, billed as the country's "shortest, steepest railway" for a three-state view of the Mississippi and beyond. If you've a little more time, we'd suggest a visit to the Woodward Riverboat Museum, and a ride on a Mississippi River sternwheeler. Exercise enthusiasts will enjoy the 26-mile-long Heritage Trail, a railroad track now converted for hiking and bicycling.

Also recommended: Received just as we were going to press was an enthusiastic report on the **Squiers Manor B&B** (418 West Pleasant, Maquoketa 52060; 319–652–6961) located about halfway between Dubuque and Davenport. Built in 1882, the inn features walnut, cherry, oak and butternut woods throughout, and combines Victorian antique decor with such modern conveniences as in-room telephone and TV. "We stayed in the Jennie Mitchell Suite, furnished with beautiful antiques and spotlessly clean. The spacious bathroom had a whirlpool tub and a separate shower. Virl and Kathy Banowetz were our hosts and they are friendly and proud to share their home with guests; they also own Banowetz Antiques, with 30,000 square feet of quality antiques in 3 buildings. Breakfast included seafood quiche, bagels, toast, banana bread and strawberries. Four of the six guest rooms have whirlpool tubs, and cost $55–75 for a double, and $95 for the suite, including breakfast." *(Jennifer Coder)*

Information please: Just over the hill from the Sundown Ski Area, and eight miles out of town, is the **Juniper Hill Farm** (15325 Budd Road, 52001; 319–582–4405), a B&B with three guest rooms. Owners Ruth and Bill McEllhiney renovated this farmhouse as a retirement project, enabling them to be near the ski area which they founded years ago. 40 acres of woods and walking trails provide ample opportunity for appreciating Iowa's natural beauty; hearty breakfasts include egg casserole or entrée, homemade muffins, and fruit smoothies.

We need current feedback on the **Burgundy Inn**, previously known as the Little Switzerland Inn (126 Main Street, Box 195, McGregor 52157; 319–873–3670) on the Mississippi River, 60 miles north of Dubuque. Recently purchased by John and Sherry Auten, the inn was built in 1862 as the home for Iowa's oldest weekly newspaper, the *North Iowa Times*. Today the building houses a bakery downstairs and the B&B upstairs; a balcony, original to the building, provides a handsome view of the Mississippi, less than a block away. Just next door is a log cabin, built in 1848 and moved to this location by the previous owners. Rates are reasonable, and McGregor makes a good base from which to explore the cliff-lined beauty of the upper Mississippi and its many antique and craft shops.

Redstone Inn ¢   *Tel: 319–582–1894*
504 Bluff Street, 52001

The Redstone was built in 1894 by A. A. Cooper as a wedding present for his daughter. Mr. Cooper owned the Cooper Wagon Works, the company that manufactured many of the prairie schooners that made their way to the West. When Henry Ford proposed converting one of Cooper's factories for the building of horseless carriages, Cooper turned him down, saying it was a fad that would never last.

In 1984 a group of local businessmen purchased the Redstone and, at considerable expense, converted it into an elegant small hotel. Now listed on the National Register of Historic Places, it combines Victorian furnishings and styles with modern baths, air-conditioning, private telephones, and television.

"Beautiful decor, gourmet treats, delicious breakfasts. The staff was cheerful and very accommodating." *(JP, also Charles Hillstad)* "We stayed in the Governors Room, complete with a four poster bed, fireplace, an antique couch, and a whirlpool bath. Every detail was meticulously tended to, from the bourbon and snifters on the cocktail table in the room, to the candle on the ledge by the whirlpool." *(Debbie Mishkin & Michael Swiatek)*

Open All year.
Rooms 6 suites, 9 doubles—all with private bath and/or shower, telephone, radio, TV, air-conditioning. 6 with whirlpool tub, 3 with desk, 2 with fireplace.
Facilities Dining room, parlor, bar/lounge with games. Fishing, riverboat rides, casino excursions, greyhound racing, skiing nearby.
Location E central IA, 186 m NW of Chicago. In center of town, 1 block from Civic Center and cable car.
Restrictions Traffic noise could disturb light sleepers.
Credit cards Amex, DC, MC, Visa.
Rates Room only, $110–165 suite, $65–88 double, plus 9% tax. Extra person, $10. Children under 12 free in parents' room. Rollaway bed, $5. 2-night weekend minimum for some rooms, May 1–Nov. 15. Alc breakfast, $2–6.
Extras Crib available, $5 daily.

Richards House ¢
1492 Locust Street, 52001

Tel: 319–557–1492

The Richards House is a magnificent Stick style Victorian mansion built in 1884, and is considered one of Dubuque's finest and most original homes of the period. Over 80 dazzling stained glass windows shed light on the woodwork made of seven varieties, including ash, butternut, and cherry. One room boasts fireplace tiles painted by children's illustrator Kate Greenaway, and all have Victorian antique or reproduction lighting, wallcoverings, and furnishings, although the queen-size mattresses are to 20th century specifications. Guest bathrooms were added by converting dressing rooms and large closets, and appropriate reproduction fixtures were used. Owner David Stuart has been working on the home for three years, and has done an incredible job of restoration. He warns guests that while the interior renovation is complete, the exterior may look shabby, "as the concrete-based paint which was used in the '60s is keeping progress slow." Eventually it will be completed in its original 'painted lady' color scheme of chocolate brown, rust, pumpkin, and moss green.

Rates include a full breakfast of fruit, muffins, bacon or sausage, and egg dish or French toast, juice and coffee, served in the elegant dining room. Complimentary beverages are always available in the guest refrigerator, and a snack of perhaps cheesecake or banana bread is served nightly.

"Friendly, welcoming, down-to-earth owners. Their talents for cooking

72

and personal attention really made our stay memorable. The guest rooms are clean, full of wonderful antiques and individual character. It will be even more charming when they can finish their renovation dream for the exterior." *(Mary Engel)* "David explained the history of the house, and told us about other points of local interest." *(Shelby & Roy Raschein)*

Open All year.
Rooms 5 doubles—3 with private bath, 2 with a maximum of 4 sharing bath. All with telephone, radio, TV, air-conditioning. Some with desk, fireplace, balcony, whirlpool tubs.
Facilities Dining room, living room, both with fireplace; library; music room with fireplace, pianos, TV/VCR; guest laundry; porch. Off-street parking. Riverboat cruises nearby. 10 m to downhill skiing.
Location Jackson Park National Historic District.
Restrictions Smoking restricted to kitchen.
Credit cards Amex, MC, Visa.
Rates B&B, $75–125 suite, $35–85 double. Extra person, $10. Mid-week rate.
Extras Airport/station pickup. Pets permitted by prior arrangement. Crib.

Stout House   *Tel: 319–582–1890*
1105 Locust Street, 52001
Mailing address: 504 Bluff Street, 52001

Under the same ownership as the Redstone is the nearby Stout House, a red sandstone mansion built in 1890 in the Richardson Romanesque style. Its interior, carefully preserved during 75 years of ownership by the Archdiocese of Dubuque, displays an exceptionally lavish decor, with elaborate wood carvings using four kinds of wood, marble fireplaces, mosaics, and stained glass in nearly every room. Reservations should be made through the Redstone Inn (see above entry).

When well-traveled and highly critical innkeepers rave about an inn, a detour is probably in order. Here's what *Jim & Krisha Pennino* had to say about the Stout House:

"This grand mansion will keep every visitor in awe from the moment they walk in the front door. The home was built a century ago by a prominent Dubuque lumber baron and construction magnate as what might be called a 'designer showcase' home today. Every feature, element, treatment and design was purposefully built to show prospective home-owners of the period what was available and how it would actually look. The different but complementary use of woods, textures, fabrics, paint, and lights make for a magnificent B&B. Our room was marvelous, huge with a comfortable sitting area, a firm bed, and a beautiful crystal chandelier. The opulent bath, though shared, was adjoining so we didn't have to leave our room. It had highly polished red marble wainscoting all around, plenty of built-in glass shelves for toilet articles and a uniquely angled built-in shower." More comments appreciated.

Open All year.
Rooms 6 doubles—2 with private bath and/or shower, 4 with a maximum of 4 people sharing bath. All with air-conditioning. 2 with TV.
Facilities Lobby, library with fireplace, dining room, parlor, guest lounge with telephone, TV.
Location E central IA. Center of town. Between Loras & University Sts.

Restrictions Light sleepers should request rooms away from street.
Credit cards Amex, DC, MC, Visa.
Rates B&B, $75–100 double. Extra person, $10. Children under 12 free in parents' room. Rollaway bed, $5. 2-night weekend minimum in some rooms, May 1–Nov. 15.

HOMESTEAD

To escape religious persecution in Germany, the ancestors of the Amana colonists came to the U.S. in 1844. They pooled their money and resources and established a communal religious society that built seven villages and acquired thousands of acres of farm and timberland. The colonies prospered and became well known for their delicious food and wine and their quality craft and industrial products. In 1932 the membership voted to end communal ownership, and all property reverted to private hands. The colonists purchased the town of Homestead because it was on the railroad line to Iowa City.

One common point of confusion among visitors: There is no connection between the Amana colonists and the Amish, except for a coincidental similarity in their names and the fact that both sects originated in Germany. Although both are devout peoples, the Amana colonists are not opposed to 20th-century innovation, as evidenced by the Amana Refrigeration company, manufacturers of refrigerators, stoves, and microwave ovens, once owned by the Amana's communal society.

For an additional listing in the Amana Colonies, see the entry for the **Rettig House** in Middle Amana.

Die Heimat Country Inn ¢   *Tel: 319–622–3937*
Main Street, Amana Colonies, 52236

"Amid thousands of acres of rolling Iowa landscape is the Amana complex of seven colonies and Homestead. These pleasant, kindly people make this an ideal place to enjoy pure relaxation in a serene atmosphere." *(Alfred Chione)* "The feeling of welcome and homecoming is the first thing you notice as you enter the lobby of Die Heimat. Soft zither music is playing, and the lobby is furnished with Amana furniture and an antique chiming clock. As for the noise level, all we heard were the comfortable sounds of cattle in some of the nearby fields and the sound of a train once a day. The large, well-kept lawn surrounding Die Heimat has lawn chairs and old-fashioned wooden lawn swings. The well-lit parking lot is immediately behind the home." *(Elizabeth Young)* "The friendly staff helped to arrange our weekend of visiting the colonies—sights, attractions, and restaurant reservations." *(Terri & Jeff Patwell)*

"When we had a dilemma of arriving too late and leaving too early to purchase some of the sauerkraut bread for which the Amanas are well known, we had only to mention it to Mr. Janda and he had some ready at the desk for us. The service is exceptional, rooms well furnished and well kept."*(Mrs. Dennis Johnson)* "Breakfast portions were generous, with ample *hot* coffee. We found the living room well laid out for playing bridge, without disturbing the guests. The atmosphere is conducive to meeting other guests." *(Betty & Dick Thomas)*

"Added on to many times over the years, Die Heimat has a bit of the feel of a motel. Rooms are comfortably furnished, and ours was one of three with a canopy bed crafted by an Amana furniture maker; reading lights were adequate. The inn's parlor shared the lobby and check-in desk. Mid-week in November it was a pleasant place to sit in the traditional Amana furniture and read about the area, but probably gets quite busy weekends in season. Don Janda took time to fill us in on some of the history of the inn and area, and let us try some Amana fruit wine. The collection of menus from local restaurants help us decide where to have dinner. The light, self-service breakfast included juice, coffee and sweet rolls." *(Jim & Krisha Pennino)*

Open All year.
Rooms 19 doubles—all with full private bath, TV, desk, air-conditioning. 5 with radio.
Facilities Lobby/sitting room, meeting room. 1-acre grounds with lawn swings and benches.
Location E central IA. 18 m S of Cedar Rapids, 18 m W of Iowa City. Take Exit 225 off I-80, go N on Rte. 151 to Rte. 6 E to Homestead. Inn is at end of Main St.
Restrictions No smoking in public areas or some guest rooms.
Credit cards Discover, MC, Visa.
Rates B&B, $36–60 double, $36 single. Extra person, $5; children under 6, $2. Cribs, rollaway cot, $3; babysitting. Winter weekend specials. Midweek winter rates.
Extras Local airport pickups. Pets permitted by prior arrangement, $5. Crib, babysitting. German spoken.

MIDDLE AMANA

For more information about the Amana Colonies, see entry for Homestead above.

The Rettig House ¢   *Tel:* 319–622–3386
Box 5, 52307

The Rettig House was built in 1893 from bricks made of native clay, fired in the Middle Amana brickyard. As one of the original community-kitchen houses of old Amana, the Rettig House's kitchen was used to prepare meals for 40 people three times a day. After the "Great Change" in 1932, its ownership passed to Lina Rettig and eventually to the current owners, Ray and Marge Rettig. Rooms are furnished with family heirlooms and authentic Amana antiques. The Rettigs note that they "like visitors who appreciate the history of the Amanas. Our yard is beautifully landscaped and offers a quiet and relaxing atmosphere."

"Mrs. Rettig, a charming, wholesome lady, welcomed us to her immaculate home, located in the center of the block, away from the street, with convenient, private parking. Middle Amana is about two miles from Main Amana, where most of the shops are located. (Shops are closed in the evening anyway.) Our bedroom was cozy, comfortable, and well ventilated; the bathroom had new fixtures and fresh wallpaper. A small sitting room nestled between three bedrooms had magazines and inspirational reading material available. Breakfast consisted of juice, garden-fresh strawberries, homemade coffee cake, and plenty of coffee. A freshly picked rose adorned the table, which was set with old-fashioned dishes. The large yard was meticulously kept with vegetables and beautiful flower gardens, large trees, and a marvelous four-person glider swing. A lovely evening was spent in the yard with Mr. and Mrs. Rettig, the other guests, and seemingly hundreds of singing birds." *(Janet Jessup)* "Absolutely spotless. Not a speck of dirt or chip of paint missing." *(Darrell & Betty Frohrib)* "Our gracious hosts gave us the chance to learn firsthand the history of the Amana Colonies." *(Neil Schroeder)* "Homey, warm, quiet—we felt a part of the residential atmosphere of the Amana Colonies. The house is squeaky clean, the lawn manicured." *(Carolyn Schenk & Diane Blake)*

Open All year.
Rooms 5 doubles—3 with private bath and/or shower, 2 with a maximum of 4 people sharing bath. All with air-conditioning. 2 with TV. Telephone, radio, desk, fan on request.
Facilities Dining room, living room, sitting room. 1 acre with gardens, swing. Fishing, indoor swimming pool, tennis, golf nearby.
Location E central IA. 20 m SW of Cedar Rapids, 20 m NW of Iowa City. From Des Moines or Iowa City, take exit 225 off of I-80. Go N on Rte. 151 to Rte. 220. Go W on Rte. 220 to Middle Amana. Inn is behind print shop and old school.
Restrictions No smoking, no alcohol. No children under 13.
Credit cards None accepted.
Rates B&B, $45 double or single.
Extras Airport pickups. German spoken.

NEWTON

LaCorsette Maison Inn ¢ ✗
629 First Avenue East, 50208

Tel: 515–792–6833

Cognoscenti in the laundry business may know Newton as the home of the Maytag Company, but few would think of this town as the place to go for a leisurely gourmet dinner, served by tuxedoed waiters to the accompaniment of a pianist playing a baby grand. Kay Owen has always enjoyed cooking, and in 1984 she opened LaCorsette as a restaurant and inn. There's no choice of menu at dinner; the entrée of the evening is determined by the first caller to make reservations—perhaps broccoli-stuffed game hen with Mornay sauce, pork medallions with mushrooms in cognac cream sauce, or beef tenderloin in tarragon butter. The rest of the six-course meal is decided by Kay and what's fresh in her garden. Dinner is preceded by a ½ hour tour of the inn, a 1909 Mission-style mansion built in 1909 and listed on the National Register of Historic Places. The original Mission oak woodwork, Art Nouveau stained and beveled glass windows, and brass light fixtures highlight the decor; guest rooms are eclectically furnished with French country motifs, with down comforters and pillows.

"This Mission-style home has been brought to life by Kay Owen— great care has been taken to preserve and enhance its architecture and style. We stayed in the penthouse suite, and awoke to a dazzling display of rainbows emanating from the cut glass windows. The food is exquisite, and the care and charm of the surroundings match it." *(Mark Sherman)* "We loved our visit from the pre-dinner tour of the house to the full dinner (stuffed Cornish hen with Mornay sauce), with excellent wines, and piano accompaniment. Our room was a spacious converted billiard room with adjoining sitting room and fireplace." *(Brian Lynner)*

Open All year. Restaurant open "several nights a week by reservation only."
Rooms 2 suites, 2 doubles—all with private bath and/or shower, telephone, air-conditioning. TV available.
Facilities Restaurant with pianist, living room with fireplace, den with fireplace, atrium. 20 miles to lake for swimming, fishing, boating.
Location 23 m E of Des Moines. 7 blocks from center of town. From Des Moines, go E on I-80 and exit at Newton. Go E on Hwy. 6 (First Ave.) to inn.
Restrictions No smoking. No facilities for infants.
Credit cards MC, Visa.
Rates B&B, $75–115 suite, $55–65 double. Extra person, $20. Prix fixe dinner, $29–33 plus 15% service, 4% tax.
Extras Some pets permitted by prior arrangement. Airport/station pickups, $10.

PELLA

Strawtown Inn ¢ ✕
1111 Washington Street, 50219   *Tel:* 515–628–2681

The town of Pella, settled by Dutch refugees in 1847 who built their first houses of sod, with a roof of woven straw, received its original name "Strawtown" from this unusual variation of prairie construction. Rebuilt in wood and brick on the same plot of land, these homes are now part of the Strawtown Inn and are listed in the National Register of Historic Places. Priding itself on its heritage, much of the town has been renovated to look like a town in Holland, with tulips blooming everywhere in May, the annual festival time. The inn, with its steeply pitched stairs, and restaurant, wine and gift shops, is similarly styled with an Old World atmosphere of lace curtains and quaintly painted wood detailing.

Guest rooms, with modern amenities discretely installed, are individually decorated and uniquely named; the Bedstee Kamer has Dutch bunk beds built into the wall, while the Hindeloopen Kamer is decorated in the style of the Frisian painters. Of particular honor is the Juliana Kamer, named in honor of the visit of Princess Juliana of the Netherlands to Pella in 1942.

The restaurant, with its café painted in Delft blue, Rembrandt dining room, and Tuin Kamer (or garden room), provides meals with a flavor of Holland. A true Dutch breakfast is served daily to inn guests, which includes cold meats and cheeses, homemade raspberry jam, and assorted breads and sweet rolls. Authentic ethnic entrées include Hollandse Rollade (Dutch spiced beef) and Gevulde Karbonade (stuffed pork chop with apple dressing and mushroom wine sauce), served with traditional side dishes of barbecued meatballs and apple bread; the selection of homemade ice cream includes, of course, Dutch chocolate.

"Pella is a tiny Dutch enclave, and this inn has much the feeling of the small inns I've enjoyed in Holland." *(Arthur Fink)* "The inn is housed in several old buildings; despite the small-town setting, it's an efficient, quality operation, although somewhat impersonal. The food (both Dutch and American cooking) was good, and service excellent. Rooms were spacious, with individual heat and cooling, and furnished mostly with traditional, high quality furniture." *(Barry Gardner)*

Open All year.
Rooms 17 suites and doubles—all with private shower and/or bath, telephone, TV, air-conditioning. 1 with whirlpool.
Facilities Restaurant, bar/lounge, sun room, gift shop, wine shop.
Location SE IA. Approx. 30 m SE of Des Moines, on State Route 163.
Credit cards Amex, MC, Visa.
Rates Room only, $85 suite, $60–70 double.

SPENCER

Hannah Marie Country Inn ¢ 🚸 ✕ — *Tel:* 712–262–1286
Highway 71 S, RR #1, 51301 — 712–332–7719

Inngoing requires traveling, usually on the part of guests. But in 1990, it was a vintage 1907 building which travelled five miles from the center of town, coming to rest 40 feet away from the existing Hannah Marie Country Inn. Connected with a covered walkway, the new building (named the Carl Gustav), will house additional dining rooms, an expanded kitchen, and eventually, more guest rooms.

The Hannah Marie is named after innkeeper Mary Nichols' mother, "one of the most hospitable people I've ever known. After all, hospitality is what innkeeping is all about." Mary also named the three guest rooms at her B&B after her mother's sisters, decorating them with handmade quilts and teddy bears, along with extra touches that echo their personalities—tomboyish, romantic, and delicate. The inn, a restored farmhouse built in 1910, has Victorian furnishings, with Iowa antiques, brass and laces. Mary runs the inn with the help of her husband Ray and son Dave, who also keep busy farming the surrounding 200 acres of land. Rates include a full breakfast, afternoon tea, and bedtime chocolates. Breakfast menus vary daily, but might include juice, poached pears with almonds, frittata, poppy seed muffins, and sticky buns.

The Hannah Marie is best known for its theme teas, including Alice in Wonderland teas hosted by the Queen of Hearts and the Mad Hatter, as well as Irish, English, Victorian, and chocolate teas. A recent addition to the menu is the European-style lunch, by reservation, with open-face sandwiches, cappuccino, and espresso served.

"Breakfasts are outstanding, afternoon teas elegant, with Mary serving in a long skirt and lace-trimmed blouse. Handmade chocolates on your pillow plus fresh fruit in your room are the perfect ending to the day." *(Rita & Robert Bowsher)*

"An early 1800s farmhouse so delightfully furnished and decorated that you feel like you're coming home as you go up the walk to the large front porch. Cleanliness and attention to details are a specialty here. While there is traffic on the highway nearby, it keeps on moving so it isn't noticeable. Breakfast is enjoyable, either eating with the other guests or if you want, alone." *(Mrs. Doris Soderquist)* "Each guest room has its own style and charm. Mary gives every meal the special touch of being individually prepared." *(Ron & Cindy Pingel)*

Open April to mid-Dec.
Rooms 3 doubles—all with private bath and/or shower, telephone, radio, TV, desk, air-conditioning, fan, fireplace.
Facilities Dining room, breakfast room, parlor with fireplace, library, lounge, porch. 5 acres surrounded by 200 acre farm. Garden, swings, hammock, raspberry patch, croquet "in the Wonderland Manner." Near Iowa Great Lakes for boating, swimming, fishing. Cross-country skiing nearby.
Location NE IA. 100 m NE of Sioux City. 5 m from town. From Spencer, take Hwy. 71 S to inn.
Restrictions No smoking.
Credit cards Amex, MC, Visa.
Rates B&B, $50–60 double. Extra person, $10. Children's rate. Alc lunch, $6–9; tea, $5–6.
Extras Local airport pickup, $5. Crib, babysitting. Basic Sign Language spoken.

We Want to Hear from You!

As you know, this book is only effective with your help. We really need to know about your experiences and discoveries. If you stayed at an inn or hotel listed here, we want to know how it was. Did it live up to our description? Exceed it? Was it what you expected? Did you like it? Were you disappointed? Delighted? Have you discovered new establishments that we should add to the next edition?

Tear out one of the report forms at the back of this book (or use your own stationery if you prefer) and write today. *Even if you write only "Fully endorse existing entry" you will have been most helpful.*
Thank You!

Kansas

Heritage House, Topeka

Set right at the center of the continental U.S., Kansas has a history far more complex than most people realize. From 1492 to 1845 six nations claimed all or part of what is now Kansas. Although included as part of the U.S. with the Louisiana Purchase, it became part of the Republic of Texas until that state was admitted to the Union in 1845. Kansas's own admission to the Union was delayed until 1861 by intense and bloody feuding between the territory's pro- and anti-slavery factions.

Although Kansas is known as one of the country's leading wheat producers, its farmers have never had it easy, from the hardships faced by the first settlers of the early 1800s, through the "dust bowl" period of the 1930s, to the present day. Industry now plays an important role in the state's economy, with meat packing and aviation among the leading fields.

While it is by no means a tourist mecca, Kansas does have many towns of interest, including Wichita, center of the state's aircraft industry; Lawrence, home of the University of Kansas; and Dodge City, once known as the Wickedest City in America, with a saloon for every 50 citizens. Many towns sponsor fairs and festivals during the warmer months; ask the tourist office for a calendar of events.

Information please: We have more questions than answers when it comes to Kansas B&Bs. Though the state B&B association numbers over 30 members, most don't seem quite right for these pages. We've noted a few below (in no particular order) that sound worth investigating.

The **Halcyon House** (1000 Ohio, Lawrence 66044; 913–841–0314) is located in the lovely college town of Lawrence, about 40 miles west of

Kansas City. A century-old Victorian home, this eight-guest-room B&B has been totally restored with such contemporary touches as floor-to-ceiling glass windows in the vaulted kitchen. Also in Lawrence is the **Eldridge Hotel** (7th & Massachusetts, Lawrence 66044; 913–749–5011), built in 1926 and the fourth hotel to occupy this site. A historic landmark now restored as an all-suite hotel, the spacious rooms are equipped with wet bars, refrigerators, and coffee makers; the $75 rates include complimentary limo service in the hotel's restored 1938 Buick.

The Cottage House Hotel (25 North Neosho, Council Grove 66846; 316–767–6828 or 800–727–7903) dates back to 1867, and offers 26 rooms decorated with Victorian antiques, including lace curtains and stained glass windows. Guests enjoy relaxing on the hotel's gazebo-style verandas after a hearty made-from-scratch meal at the Hays House, just around the corner. Council Grove was the last outfitting point on the Santa Fe trail, and is about 50 miles southwest of Topeka. About 30 miles south of Topeka is the **Schoolhouse Inn** (106 East Beck, Melvern 66510; 913–3473), a two-story limestone building constructed in 1870. Its three guest rooms have private baths, and the $40 rate include a breakfast of homemade muffins. Heading south another 25 miles is the **Victorian Memories B&B** (314 North Fourth, Burlington 66830; 316–364–5752), a century-old home with fancy woodwork, stained glass windows, and period decor.

Northwestern Kansas is home to a friendly place called the **Pomeroy Inn** (224 West Main, Hill City 67642; 913–674–2098), a massive limestone hotel built in 1886 and recently restored as an inn. Its nine guest rooms are simply furnished, though all have a hand-made quilt or comforter. Freshly baked cinnamon rolls and wheat bread is served with plenty of hot coffee each morning in the spacious lobby, where locally made crafts are also sold. B&B rates are only $25.

Rates do not include 5% state tax plus local taxes.

CIMARRON

Cimarron Hotel ¢ 👫   *Tel:* 316–855–2244
203 North Main Street, P.O. Box 633, 67835

One of the town's first brick structures, the Cimarron is listed on the National Register of Historic Places. It was built in 1887 as the New West Hotel, and was restored as the Cimarron in 1977. "Housed in a lovely old brick building, the Cimarron's rooms are simply decorated with antiques and period wallpaper; guests share clean and spacious baths at the end of the hall. The atmosphere is a cross between going back 100 years in time and staying with the family next door. But, if you want to get away from it all, the third floor, where the guest rooms are located, is quiet and off-limits to the family. The choice is yours." *(Lynne Wagner)* "We were quite pleased with the accommodations, cleanliness, and historic ambience of the Cimarron. Kathi's breakfast was outstanding, and she is an excellent hostess. The hotel is convenient for a visit to Dodge City, and we thought

it several cuts above the motels and hotels in that area." *(Robert Bizal)*
More reports appreciated.

Open All year. Restaurant open Sun. only.
Rooms 9 doubles, 1 single—most with sink in room and a maximum of 5 people
sharing baths. Radio, air-conditioning. 2 rooms with desk. TV on request.
Facilities Dining/breakfast room, family room with fireplace, games. Gazebo.
Swimming pool, tennis courts, playground, golf nearby.
Location SW KS. 20 m W of Dodge City, on Hwy. 50.
Credit cards None accepted.
Rates B&B, $30–40 double. Reduced rates for families, seniors. Prix fixe dinner
($10–15) served Sun. noon; other days on request for groups. Mystery weekends,
$150 double.
Extras Airport/station pickups available at moderate cost. Pets permitted. Baby-
sitting available.

CONCORDIA

Concordia is located in north central Kansas, on Route 81, about 50 miles
north of Salina.

Crystle's B&B ¢   *Tel:* 913–243–2192
508 West 7th Street, 66901

Built in 1880, Crystle's B&B has been owned by the Warren family since
1920; Carrie Warren-Gully and Jim Gully have restored the family home
and opened it as a B&B in 1989. Rates include a continental breakfast on
weekdays, with a heartier meal on weekends—perhaps strawberry puffs
hot from the oven with strawberry syrup, or baked egg-stuffed tomatoes
with cheese and home-baked muffins, in addition to juice, coffee, and tea.

"This Victorian house has an inviting front porch swing. We were
shown to our room by Jim and were offered cool refreshing drinks. Our
room, 'The Nutcracker Suite,' had a beautiful hardwood floor, beveled
glass windows with lace curtains, and a queen-size bed with a lace tier that
rose to the ceiling. The colors were soothing and the room had a very airy
feeling. Jim and Carrie made a special bed just for our 2-year old son.
Breakfast was served in the dining room, and included scrambled eggs
with shredded cheese, fresh fruit and fresh muffins, accompanied by
delightful conversation with the other guests." *(Mark & Sandy Stump)*
"Carrie and Jim have preserved Carrie's grandmother's homestead with
such love and warmth that you almost expect Grandma Crystle to sit
down to breakfast with you. The delicious breakfast was presented with
an arrangement of fresh fruit almost too pretty to disturb. The homemade
muffins were warm and tasty. Our bedroom was decorated in a rich
combination of reds and greens—with unusually painted walls—contrasting with Crystle's *Gone With the Wind* plate collection. The adjacent
bathroom was huge and beautifully decorated, with a footed tub on a
raised floor, a separate shower, an unusual sink set into a piece of furniture,
and a stained glass window. Concordia is an appealing town, with a
restored theater, a history museum, and a delightful restaurant, Kelher

House, in a renovated 19th century home." *(Winnie & Noel Smith, and others)*

Area for improvement: "Bedside lamps and tables."

Open All year.
Rooms 1 suite, 4 doubles—1 with private bath, 4 with a maximum of 4 sharing bath. All with desk, air-conditioning. 1 with fan, deck.
Facilities Parlor with TV, piano, books, games; dining room with stereo; porch. Tennis, golf nearby.
Location N central KS. 52 m N of Salina. 1 block from downtown.
Restrictions No smoking.
Credit cards Discover, MC, Visa.
Rates B&B, $35–45 double. Extra person, $4.
Extras Pets permitted by prior arrangement.

LINDSBORG

Reader tip: About 25 miles northwest of Lindsborg and 14 miles west of Salina is the **Brookville Hotel** (Brookville 67425; 913–225–6666), famous since 1915 for its chicken dinners. "Reserve your table for a wonderful old-fashioned fried chicken dinner with creamy coleslaw, cottage cheese and relishes, mashed potatoes and chicken gravy, cream-style corn, baking powder biscuits, and home-style ice cream. You can tour the antique-filled bedrooms and parlor, but no accommodations are available."

Swedish Country Inn ¢   *Tel:* 913–227–2985
112 West Lincoln, 67456

The Smoky River Valley was homesteaded in the 1860s by Swedish immigrants, and its Swedish heritage has been well preserved. Lindsborg, known as Little Sweden, is the area's hub and offers a number of Swedish-style restaurants and shops selling Scandinavian imports. The Swedish Country Inn, built in the early 1900s as a feed store, was later used as a Studebaker showroom and was converted into a hotel in 1929. In 1985 Quintin and Florence Applequist remodeled it into a country inn; Virginia Brunsell is the long-time innkeeper.

Rooms are decorated with natural hard-pine furniture and lamps imported from Sweden or made by local craftsmen, handmade American quilts, and lace curtains from Holland. Most rooms are done in blue or rose and white, and the effect is light, airy, and very inviting. The Swedish buffet breakfast includes fruit, juice, cereal, specialty breads, pastries, cheeses, two kinds of eggs, meat, and herring.

"Our room was clean, spacious, and comfortable, with the added charm of pleated cloth bonnet-type lamp shades and shuttered windows. The restaurant has a similar decor; at breakfast, the tables were set with flowers, and cloth place mats and napkins. The rooms are color-coordinated, with handmade quilts." *(Mr. & Mrs. William Harford)*

"The ladies who greeted us were very kind and made our dinner reservations before we even unpacked. They were also very helpful with suggestions on shops and museums we might want to visit." *(Doug &*

Linda Kirmer) "Our room had colorful wallpaper and a modern but modest bathroom. We borrowed the tandem bike and explored Lindsborg's many shops, eateries, and sites of interest." *(James Doyle)*

"Downtown, with its shops featuring Swedish crafts and furniture, is just around the corner. The Swedish Crown Restaurant, well known for its Swedish and American menu, is also nearby. Residents of Lindsborg also pride themselves on the Old Mill Museum and the Messiah Festival, sponsored by Bethany College and held annually during Easter Week." *(Carolyn Ward)* "The inn is very Swedish, from the furnishings to the breakfast. The rooms are spotless, the facilities modern. The hosts are very friendly and helpful, and they make a visit to Lindsborg a beautiful taste of Sweden in the middle of Kansas." *(Timothy Amsden, also Dennis & Beth Johnson)*

"A charming and unexpected find. This small, Swedish-settled Kansas town is attractive and interesting, fortunately *not* redone into a touristy travesty as so many ethnic towns have been. The innkeeper, Virginia Brunsell, is not the owner, but you'd never know it from the way she runs the inn. The Swedish buffet breakfast was good." *(Barry Gardner)* "Fully endorse existing entry." *(LeAnn Binford & Kim Campbell, and others)*

Open All year.
Rooms 1 suite, 18 doubles—all with private shower and/or bath, TV, air-conditioning, telephone.
Facilities Dining room, lobby with TV, game table; gift shop; sauna; bicycles. Fishing, swimming pool nearby.
Location Central KS. 60 m N of Wichita. Approx. 20 m S of Salina, 12 m N of McPherson. From I-135S take Exit 78, from I-135N take Exit 72. ½ block W of Main St.
Restrictions No smoking.
Credit cards MC, Visa.
Rates B&B, $60–70 suite, $50–60 double, $40 single, plus 7% tax. Buffet breakfast, $4.50 (outside guests).
Extras Bus station pickups. Crib. Some German, Swedish spoken.

TOPEKA

Heritage House ✗   *Tel:* 913–233–3800
3535 Southwest Sixth Street, 66606

Once home of the famous Menninger Clinic, Heritage House was transformed into a B&B by a 1988 designer showcase, and is owned by Betty and Don Rich. Now listed on the National Register of Historic Places, its individually decorated guest rooms are equipped for business and pleasure travelers alike; because each room was done by a different designer, the furnishings run the gamut from contemporary to period, formal to country casual. Rates include a continental breakfast.

"Beautifully and thoughtfully decorated, pristinely maintained and helpfully staffed with eager-to-serve, clean-cut students, it works extremely well as either a simple overnight business stop or as a romantic destination. Although we've found some other midwestern B&Bs which

ivaled Heritage House for looks, what sets it a country mile apart from
he others is its incredible restaurant. To our view, it offers the finest
dining in Kansas." *(Charles Hillestad)*

"The dining area is cozy but not crowded. The ambitious menu features
fish, and our waiter was exceptionally congenial and helpful, without
being intrusive. Our entire meal was excellent, and the portions generous,
from the crabcake appetizer, to the Oriental vegetable salad, to the
Alaskan halibut with fettucini, to the triple chocolate torte." *(Virginia
Wulfkuhle)*

Open All year.
Rooms 2 suites, 11 doubles—all with private shower and/or bath, telephone,
radio, TV, air-conditioning. Some with desk, 1 with whirlpool tub.
Facilities Restaurant, 2 living rooms, sun room, meeting room, patio. Gage Park
(home of Topeka Zoo) across street.
Location E KS. 60 m W of Kansas City. ½ m from I-70. From Rte. 40 W, take
Exit 357B. Go S on Gage St., E on 6th St. to inn on right. From I-70 E, take Rte.
4/40 to Exit 357A. Go E on 6th St. to inn on right.
Restrictions No smoking in guest rooms.
Credit cards Amex, CB, DC, Discover, MC, Visa.
Rates B&B, $60–135 double. Prix fixe lunch, $26; prix fixe dinner, $40–48. Alc
lunch, $29; alc dinner, $70.
Extras Wheelchair access. Crib. Italian, German, Spanish spoken.

WICHITA

A bustling and prosperous city, Wichita was for years a wide-open "cow
town;" later grain and oil became key sources of income, and today
Wichita is also known as a center for the manufacture of small aircraft.
Sights of note include the Old Cow Town Museum, the zoo and botanical
gardens, and the outdoor sculptures at Wichita State University.

Inn at the Park   *Tel: 316–652–0500*
1751 East Douglas Avenue, 67218

Some of the most handsome B&Bs in this guide were created by designer
showcases, and the Inn at the Park is no exception. Built in 1909 by Cyrus
Beachy, this three-story brick Colonial Revival mansion remained in family hands until 1955. The building then passed through many uses and
owners until 1989, when it was purchased by Kevin Daves and Greg
Johnson, a local architect and contractor, respectively. Working with 27
area designers, the partners showcased the house as a fund-raiser for the
Wichita Symphony Orchestra, and the results are as striking as they are
eclectic. The decor ranges from English Victorian to French country to
Oriental, from Neoclassic to Art Nouveau. Rates include a continental
breakfast, served on the enclosed dining porch, and afternoon wine and
tea.

"My suite in the Carriage House was beautifully decorated, the personnel friendly and efficient, and the setting quiet and restful. I used the hot
tub outside my door morning and night. Breakfast consisted of fresh

baked muffins and breads, and plenty of fresh fruit." *(Ted Relihan)* Mor comments welcome.

Minor niggle: "Better bathroom lighting for putting on makeup."

Open All year.
Rooms 5 suites, 7 doubles—all with private bath and/or shower, telephone radio, TV, desk, air-conditioning. 7 with fireplace, 1 with whirlpool tub. 1 suit with refrigerator, wet bar; 1 suite with kitchen. 2 rooms in Carriage House wit private courtyard, hot tub.
Facilities Living room with fireplace, dining room, breakfast room, guest refresh ment area. Business services, conference room. Off-street parking. Adjacent t College Hill Park for walking.
Location S central KS. 5 min. from downtown. From I-35, turn E on Hwy. 5 (Kellogg St.) and go 2 blocks to Clifton St. and turn left to inn at corner of Clifto & E. Douglas Sts.
Restrictions No smoking. No children.
Credit cards Amex, MC, Visa.
Rates B&B, $95–135 suite, $85–120 double, $75–110 single. 10% senior di count.
Extras Limited wheelchair access.

The Inn at Willowbend
4130 Tara Circle, 67226

Tel: 316–636–403

Those new to inngoing, especially business travelers, are often reluctar to sacrifice hotel comforts for the warmth of an inn. A newly constructe inn, such as the Inn at Willowbend, is an ideal compromise. Built in 199 by Gary and Bernice Adamson, it overlooks the Willowbend golf cours designed by Tom Weiskopf and Jay Morrish; museum-quality sculpture are displayed near the tee on each hole. Guest rooms are named fo famous golf courses, and are traditionally furnished, highlighted by go memorabilia and art. Rates include a breakfast of juice, cereals, toas English muffins, and bagels, plus a hot entrée—egg and cheese strat biscuits and gravy, French toast and bacon, or pancakes and sausage—an a night-time sweet.

"Gary and Bernice Adamson provided a welcome change from th faceless chain hotels I usually stay at. Never did I expect to meet suc caring, service-oriented innkeepers on a business trip. The inn is somewha off the beaten path, but nothing is very far away in Wichita. The in combines beautiful decor and excellent food with all modern amenities *(Daniel Arkins)* "Exceptional hospitality, impeccable maintenance. Gary i a super cook and the food is first-rate. No expense was spared in the inn' fixtures and finishing work; the furniture is plush and comfortable, with Scottish flavor. The inn overlooks the second fairway of one of the mos distinctive and enjoyable golf courses I've ever played." *(Robert Hoeffne*

Open All year.
Rooms 7 suites, 15 doubles—all with telephones, radio, TV/VCR, desk, ai conditioning, fan, coffee-maker. Suites with fireplace, wet bar, whirlpool tub; 1 wit kitchenette.
Facilities Breakfast room with fireplaces, common room with fireplace, TV/VC library. Computer, fax services. Deck, putting green. On 18-hole golf course.
Location 10 m from center of town.

Credit cards Amex, DC, MC, Visa.
Rates B&B, $120–130 suite, $79–99 double, $69–89 single. Extra person, $10.
Golf packages.
Extras Wheelchair access. Airport/station pickups. Crib.

Max Paul Inn ¢   Tel: 316–689–8101
3910 East Kellogg, 67218

Opened in 1984, the Max Paul is a luxury B&B inn, housed in three side-by-side, 50-year-old English Tudor cottages. It caters to business travelers on weekdays and to couples on weekends. Rooms are lavishly and imaginatively decorated in a country Victorian mood, with European antiques, English chintzes, and memorable featherbeds. Rates include a continental breakfast of fresh-squeezed juice, fresh fruit, and home-baked muffins, croissants, bagels, or turnovers stuffed with ham and cheese, served in the breakfast room on weekdays and brought to your room on weekends. Conscientious innkeepers Roberta and Jill Eaton have added extra insulation, storm doors and windows, a fence and plantings to further insulate the front rooms from possible traffic noises.

"Although all that is claimed in the inn's brochure (illustrated by Jill) is accurate, what doesn't show up are the warm, friendly, almost bubbly personalities of innkeepers Jill and Roberta Eaton, making this place a true oasis of warmth and friendship." *(Jeff Lee)* "My room had a small crystal chandelier with a well lit working area." *(Louis Barr)* "The Rob Roy Suite was perfect with a fireplace, king-size feather bed, and cozy sitting area." *(Dr. Ted Delhotal)*

"Our favorite for special occasions, with its European antiques, fireplaces, and 'tubs for two.' The light breakfast is always superb and fresh, served on antique dishes and trays coordinated to the rooms' decor. Private balconies overlooking the beautiful gardens add to the feeling of privacy." *(Rob & Debbie Robbins)* "One of our favorites. Beautifully decorated, ideal for a romantic weekend getaway. Creative and delicious breakfasts are delivered to your door in charming and whimsical antique dishes." *(Jim & Tina Kirkpatrick)*

Open All year. Closed several days near Christmas.
Rooms 8 suites, 6 doubles, in 3 adjacent cottages. All with full private bath and/or shower, telephone, radio, TV, desk, air-conditioning. Some with working fireplaces, balconies, fan.
Facilities Breakfast room, library with fireplace, gallery, conference rooms, exercise room and deck with Jacuzzi. ½ acre with garden, pond. College Hill Park several blocks away for tennis, swimming, jogging, picnicking.
Location S central KS. On the edge of College Hill. From U.S. 54 (Kellogg): westbound, turn right into inn just west of Bluff; eastbound, turn right off Kellogg just after exit 135 onto Roosevelt; continue left on Lakeview and turn left at Bluff; turn left onto Kellogg westbound as above.
Restrictions Traffic noise might disturb light sleepers. Children "discouraged, but please inquire." Those allergic to cats should ask for a room not in the main cottage.
Credit cards Amex, CB, DC, Discover, MC, Visa.
Rates B&B, $90–115 suite, $65–75 double, $50–95 single. Extra person, $15.

Michigan

The Kingsley House, Fennville

Taking its name from the Indian words for "the great water" *(Michi gami)*, Michigan is made up of the mitten-shaped Lower Peninsula, and the rugged terrain of the isolated Upper Peninsula; they meet at the Straits of Mackinac. A recommended drive follows Routes 31 and 22, south from the Mackinac Bridge along Lake Michigan through Petoskey (scour the beach here for fossilized coral), Charlevoix (balanced on a narrow strip of land between lakes Michigan and Charlevoix), around Grand Traverse Bay and through the Sleeping Bear Dunes National Lakeshore (scenic detritus left by the last glaciers).

The state's economy is diverse, with heavy industry—most notably cars and cereals—based in the south, substantial agriculture, and a prosperous tourist business throughout. Bordered by four of the Great Lakes, and with 11,000 inland lakes, water sports are of course a key attraction on both peninsulas, along with hunting and skiing.

Information please: We'd like reports on the **Atchison House** (501 West Dunlap Street, Northville 48167; 313–349–3340), an Italianate Victorian B&B, built in 1882. It's located in Northville's historic district, 20 miles northwest of Detroit, and its five guest rooms are decorated in period with Eastlake, Victorian walnut, and wicker furnishings. Innkeeper Sally Lapine offers a breakfast of granola, yogurt, cheese, fruit, and home-baked breads and muffins; double rates range from $70–85.

Note to families: Recent state anti-discrimination legislation has caused Michigan's B&Bs to become nervous about prohibiting young children as guests, and a number asked us to drop the line in their write-up which read "No children under 12" or words to that effect. But, if you're looking for a place where your family will be welcomed—not just tolerated—look for entries with our family symbol: 👫

Rates do not include 4% state sales tax.

ALDEN

Torch Lake B&B ¢   *Tel: 616–331–6424*
10601 Coy Street, 49612

A compact pink "painted lady," the Torch Lake is highlighted by its original gingerbread trim and stained glass windows. Jack and Patti Findlay, who've owned this B&B since 1986, have decorated it with period furniture and Irish lace.

"We toured this beautiful inn, and what a gem it is. Its owner, Patti Findlay, is equally charming. It's clean and welcoming, with a view of Torch Lake (one of the world's loveliest, according to *National Geographic*); ask about five-color days, when the lake sparkles with five distinct shades of blue. Alden is within an easy drive of Harbor Springs, Traverse City, Petoskey, and Charlevoix." *(Sue Gradel)* "We stayed in the Violet Room, with white walls, white lace curtains, a white iron and brass queen-sized bed, and violet accents. The windows look out onto the lake, and have stained glass borders, which glow at sunset." *(MW)* More reports needed.

Open Late May to Sept 1.
Rooms 3 doubles—1 with private bath, 2 sharing 1 bath. All with ceiling fan.
Facilities Living room, dining room, porch, garden, croquet. Lake for swimming, boating, fishing. Golf, bicycling, walking, skiing nearby.
Location NW MI. Approx. 22 m NE of Traverse City. Take M-72 E to Rapid City turnoff (Cty. Road 597); turn N to Alden. Inn is on NE corner of Coy and Alden Street, just S of downtown. 2 min. walk to downtown.
Restrictions Children discouraged. No smoking.
Credit cards None accepted.
Rates B&B, $55–65. 2-night weekend minimum.
Extras French, Spanish spoken

BATTLE CREEK

The Old Lamplighter's Homestay   *Tel: 616–963–2603*
276 Capital Avenue NE, 49017

Built in the Arts and Crafts style in 1912, and listed on the National Register of Historic Places, it boasts many original features, including hand-painted murals, mahogany beams and trim, and beveled and stained glass windows. Rooms are decorated with period furnishings; Oriental carpets highlight the restored hardwood floors. Opened as a B&B in 1987, the inn was recently acquired by Perry and Joyce Warner; the reports below precede their ownership, and reports are hereby requested! Rates include a full breakfast.

"The Old Lamplighter's Inn is a very big Tudor-style brick mansion, located in a prosperous, early Battle Creek neighborhood. Many of the fine old homes lining Capital Avenue have been put to commercial use, and some restored to their original elegance. This house is fun to explore, with all its many nooks and crannies, from the 'drying room' in the basement to the butler's pantry and library on the first floor, the elegant bathrooms on the second, and the servants' sitting room on the third. My favorite room has a four-poster bed with a beautiful handmade quilt, a velvet Victorian love seat in the window alcove, a marble-topped table on little wheels, and an old-fashioned rocker. The whole house is scrupulously clean and very nicely appointed. Towels are trimmed with lace borders, and each room has fresh flowers.

"Adequate lighting and parking, convenient location. The main bathroom is almost decadent—with a large marble shower, long and deep antique tub, two sinks, and beveled glass windows." *(Frederick Fellers)* "Beds are good, and bathrooms have all been remodeled, consistent with the Arts and Crafts style." *(James Oswald)* Comments required.

Open All year.
Rooms 2 suites, 7 doubles—all with private shower and/or bath, air-conditioning. TV, telephone, refrigerator available.
Facilities Lobby with fireplace, dining room, library with fireplace, parlor, music room, pantry with guest refrigerator, microwave, porch. Lakes, cross-country skiing nearby.
Location Walking distance to downtown.
Restrictions No smoking. Traffic noise in front rooms.
Credit cards Amex, MC, Visa.
Rates B&B, $75 suite, $55 double, $48 single. Weekly and corporate rates. Golfing, skiing packages available.
Extras Crib.

BAY VIEW

Bay View was founded as a Chautauqua summer campground and hosted, among other notables, Helen Keller and William Jennings Bryan. Because of its four hundred Victorian summer homes, Bay View is listed on the National Register of Historic Places. The town offers a wide variety of recreational activities, as well as chamber music concerts, drama, and musical theater productions. Little Traverse Bay and Lake Michigan are available for all water sports, and nearby Boyne Mountain offers excellent golf in summer and downhill skiing in winter. Cross-country skiing is available right in town.

Technically a part of the town of Petoskey (1 mile away), Bay View is located on Little Traverse Bay, near the northeastern end of Lake Michigan, about 30 miles southwest of the Straits of Mackinac. To get there from I-75, take Rte. 31 south from Mackinac, or take Route 68 west from Indian River to Rte. 31.

Reader tip: "In our search for new taste experiences, we found ourselves in Cross Village, about 30 miles up the coast (via Route 119) from the Petoskey area. There we discovered the Legs Inn, a dance hall, bar, arcade, gift shop, and restaurant. Only the last was open for lunch, and after a serious discussion about the extensive menu with the waitress, who undoubtedly recognized our uneducated palates, we ordered *pierogi* and Polish beer (of a choice of Krakus and Zywiec). Unaccustomed as we are to Polish food, we found this meal to be a treat, and urge adventurous souls to opt for an ethnic lunch. Although not a dessert eater, I determined to expand my horizons with a *nalesnik* (cheese blintz) and was not disappointed." *(Nancy & John Blewer)*

Also recommended: Although it is not appropriate for a full entry, *Karen White* suggests the **Comfort Inn** (Routes 31 & 119; 616–347–3220 or 800–228–5150), a 64-unit motel set in a wooded area. "My suite was immaculate and attractive, with a double Jacuzzi. Helpful staff, wonderful location for skiing." Rates range from $55–85.

Information please: The Perry Hotel (Bay and Lewis streets, Petoskey 49770; 616–347–2516 or in MI 800–654–2608) was built as a resort hotel in 1899. A half-dozen years ago, under new ownership, it underwent a multi-million-dollar renovation and expansion, which increased the hotel's size by 54 rooms. The views remained as lovely as ever, and readers noted that the food improved dramatically. In 1989 the hotel changed hands again, and was bought by Stafford Smith. Initial reports indicate that the rooms vary widely in appeal—some are indeed quite lovely, others less so—but that the lack of sound-proofing is a significant annoyance. Good reports have been received on the food, service, and restful veranda.

The **Terrace Inn** (216 Fairview, P.O. Box 1478, 49770; 616–347–2410), a four-story Victorian hotel built in 1911 to host "overflow" guests from private cottages, was restored by owners Patrick and Mary Lou Barbour in 1986. In addition to Michigan hemlock paneling in the lobby and dining room, furnishings include many oak chairs and dressers original to the hotel, and white wicker rockers on the wide porch. Rates include a continental breakfast. Although reports on the rooms and the food at dinner have been good, we need more feedback on the staffing and housekeeping.

Stafford's Bay View Inn 🏃 ✕   *Tel: 616–347–2771*
613 Woodland Avenue (Route 31), P.O. Box 3, 49770

When it was built in 1886, the Bay View Inn had fifty tiny rooms, many large enough to hold only a single twin bed; none had a private bath. One hundred years later, longtime owner Stafford "Duff" Smith renovated all the rooms of this small hotel, adding private baths and increasing the guest rooms in size by decreasing the total to thirty. Rooms are decorated with period antiques and reproductions, and lots of wicker. Rates include a full breakfast.

"Bay View is a summer village of huge Victorian homes, gracious lawns, and a quiet pace of life. The inn fits in well with the old-fashioned charm of the village, sitting up a little from the lake with a huge porch and wicker furniture. Inside is a small lobby, and off to the side, a large airy room filled with more white wicker chairs, pretty blue walls, and striped curtains and pillows—a very cool, relaxing place to read or attempt a game of skittles. Guest rooms vary widely in decor, size and amenities. I liked #1 because of its double sleigh bed; #10 which had a small sofa and painted rocking chairs; #31 and 32, both suites, one with a lake view, the other with a canopied bed. Bathrooms are all small but clean and adequate. A short stroll takes you to the lake and a beach where you can look for Petoskey stones—white fossilized coral." *(SC)*

"Set in a quiet part of town, just a block from the bay, the inn offers lovely rooms, friendly service, and wonderful food. We dined on spicy pumpkin bread, a creamy vegetable soup, mixed salad with cherry-vinaigrette dressing, whitefish with almonds, fresh squash and tiny round potatoes. For dessert we had real strawberry shortcake and a cream puff with rich fudge sauce." *(Paul & Elizabeth Lasley)* "The ample breakfast was tasty and featured cherry muffins and cherry sauces—apparently a local speciality." *(Constance Trowbridge)*

"We were delighted with our large and extravagantly decorated room, with its wild floral paper above the chair rail and its coordinating striped design below. The unoccupied rooms were open to view; all had dried flower wreaths on the doors, and a complimentary bottle of wine, handsome glasses, and an ice bucket, matching, of course. Staff was helpful about making reservations and such extras as bringing you coffee on the porch. The breakfast was solid and satisfying, elegantly served." *(Zita Knific)* "We couldn't get a room reservation, but were delighted with the best dinner of our short trip. The dining room personnel were quick, courteous, and helpful." *(Nick Mumford)* "Food good but not exceptional; friendly attentive staff." *(John Blewer)*

Areas for improvement: "Ask for a room on the second floor facing the lake; ventilation on the third floor didn't seem as good." Also: "Our attractive room was poorly lighted. We brought in a standing lamp from the sitting area in the third floor foyer. We never received a long-distance telephone message." And: "A bit overpriced for off season, we thought."

Open May 1 to Nov. 1; Dec. 26 to March 17. Restaurant closed midweek during Jan. 1 to March 17.
Rooms 6 suites, 24 doubles—all with full private bath, radio, desk, air-conditioning, fan.
Facilities Guest lobby with books, fireplace, restaurant with piano, parlor, sunroom with TV, VCR, games. Children's play equipment, tennis. 100 feet from Bay. Off-street parking. Golf, beach, cross-country & downhill skiing nearby.
Location 180 m N of Grand Rapids. 1 m from Petoskey on Rte. 31.
Restrictions Street noise in front rooms; light sleepers should ask for lakeside rooms. No smoking in dining room. No cocktail or wine service with meals; BYOB.
Credit cards Amex, MC, Visa.
Rates B&B, $88–160 suite, $56–128 double, $46–88 single. Extra person, $18. No charge for children under 3. Family rates. Packages available. Alc lunch, $7; alc dinner, $18.
Extras Free airport/station pickups with prior notice. Wheelchair access. Crib, babysitting.

BIG BAY

Big Bay Point Lighthouse   *Tel: 906–345–9957*
3 Lighthouse Road, 49808

Lighthouses and islands, either separately or in combination, are probably our most favorite places for an inn. At Big Bay, all the guest rooms are in the lighthouse, set on a wooded point 120 feet above Lake Superior with magnificent views of the water and the Huron mountains beyond. Keepers of both the lighthouse and inn are Buck and Marilyn Gotschall. Buck reports that "we are near the end of the world, so bring your compass, your camera and film, and a pair of warm slippers." He also notes that "Big Bay is a small village composed of many spirited individualists and craftsmen. Its citizens do not necessarily go along with accepted modes and are ingenious in their substitutions." The lighthouse is surrounded by miles of forest, and is ideal for hiking and cross-country skiing.

"The lighthouse sits on a peninsula, poking into the south shore of Lake Superior. There is access to the light tower and its splendid view. On a clear day one can see miles of shoreline; on foggy ones, you can hear the sound of the water gently slapping the coast. Breakfast includes whole grain bread, sourdough pancakes, and fruit. Folklore and lighthouse history are part of the on-going conversation, and there is even a quiz to make certain you pay attention! Keep in mind this is Upper Michigan, where many interesting and beautiful sights are at the end of a trail or logging road. Buck provides maps to guide you. Take advantage of Jeff's tours; he's a well known local guide with a four-wheel drive vehicle that is not easily discouraged by water, ruts, or snow. For evening meals, several residents are available to act as 'rent-a-chefs.' Meals are prepared and served at their homes or the lighthouse. Lake Superior whitefish is often the entrée." *(Richard & Mary Hertel)*

"The route from Marquette is poorly marked, so be sure both driver and navigator keep a sharp eye for occasional small signs in red script with the sole word, 'lighthouse.' You'll find it at the end of at least a mile of dirt road that will convince you that you have lost the scent and are hopelessly lost—but persevere. The guest rooms are small but adequate. The Sunset Room is the largest—two double beds and a private bath. But the rooms are not the reason for staying here. After all, it is a lighthouse, and it is fascinating. There is a wonderful family room with a working fireplace and a tape deck with a vast selection of classics and lighter fare; an extensive library covers a wide area of interests. Our catered dinner included smoked whitefish sausage and smoked herring appetizers, lake trout glazed with orange, red potatoes with sour cream, baby carrots, salad with raspberry vinaigrette, and a fruit tart, served with a light California jug wine." *(John Blewer)* Less favorably: "No one seemed in charge when we were there—as far as we could tell, Buck's wife was in Rome for a month, and Buck was in Detroit or Chicago getting supplies and watching a basketball game. None of our towels or bed linens matched, the mattress smelled like it had been in a fire, and our room had an envelope with a hand-written message: "My name is so-and-so and I clean your room.' Well, she missed. Nor, at $85 a night, did we care for the typed message requesting occupants to strip the beds on the last day of their stay. The inn was for sale when we were there; my personal opinion is that he may have lost interest in this project."

Open All year.
Rooms 1 suite, 5 doubles—all with private bath and/or shower.
Facilities Dining room, living room with fireplace, kitchen, game room with potbelly stove, lighthouse tower. 100 acres, lawns, 1 m of shoreline. ½ million acre forest for public use. Hiking, swimming, fishing, cross-country skiing. Downhill skiing, marina nearby.
Location Upper peninsula, on Lake Superior. 26 m N of Marquette, MI. From Marquette take Rte. 550 to Big Bay. Go right on Rte. 352, then left on Lighthouse Rd. to Big Bay Point.
Restrictions No smoking. No children.
Credit cards None accepted.
Rates B&B, $130–160 suite, $95–135 double, $65–75 single. 20% 2nd-day discount. 2-night weekend minimum. Prix fixe "rent-a-chef" dinner, $25–30 by 24-hour advance notice.
Extras Limited wheelchair access. Airport pickups, $40.

BIRMINGHAM

The Townsend Hotel　　　　　　　　*Tel:* 313–642–7900
100 Townsend Street, 48009　　　　Outside MI: 800–548–4172

The Townsend is a new luxury hotel, lavishly furnished in traditional decor, from the wood-paneled lobby to the elegant guest rooms; rich shades of blue, red, and ivory key the color scheme. Guest room amenities include marbled baths with robes and French soaps, Belgian linens and down pillows. Specializing in American cuisine, the hotel restaurants turn out everything from "power breakfasts" to romantic dinners.

"Truly a small, first-class hotel with impeccable furnishings, rooms, and service. The location is suburban with dozens of shops within walking distance." *(Sheryl Gill)*

Open All year.
Rooms 87 suites & doubles—all with full private bath, telephone, radio, TV, air-conditioning, refrigerator, personal computer. Most with desk, balcony. Some with VCR.
Facilities Lobby with fireplace, restaurants, bar/lounge. Concierge, room service. Meeting rooms.
Location Detroit metro area; approx. 20 m NW of downtown. Turn W off Woodward Ave. on Merrill or Brown Sts. and go 1 block to hotel at corner of Pierce and Townsend.
Credit cards Amex, DC, Discover, MC, Visa.
Rates Room only, $205–475 suite, $165–190 double, $150–180 single. Extra person, $25. Weekend, theater packages.
Extras Airport pickups. 9 foreign languages spoken.

CHESANING

Bonnymill Inn ¢ 🛏 ✗   *Tel:* 517–845–7780
710 Broad Street, P.O. Box 36, 48616

Built in the 1920s, the Chesaning Farmers Coop Grain Elevator is enjoying a new life as the Bonnymill Inn. It was purchased by the Ebenhoeh
family in 1988, and underwent an eight-month transformation into an
inviting small hotel. The Ebenhoehs also own the Chesaning Heritage
House restaurant across the street, a 1908 southern-style mansion offering
lunch and dinner daily.

"The Bonnymill welcomed us with mini-lights that cover the entire
length and width of the inn. The main lobby and living room are filled with
Victorian furniture, Oriental rugs, a grand piano, lace curtains, bouquets of
fresh flowers, attractive ceiling fans, and an elegant wooden staircase. For
breakfast, we enjoyed a sausage omelet, choice of tea breads, croissants and
muffins, fresh fruit cup, orange juice, and piping hot regular or decaf coffee.
The food was attractively presented on a buffet table with ornate silver
serving trays and coffee urns. Our second floor room was spacious, clean,
and attractively decorated with country touches. Its double beds had white
bedspreads with a pattern of blue ribbons and pink roses that matched the
headboard and drapes, and extra firm mattresses. White wicker furnishings
and a cedar chest with extra blankets at the foot of the bed completed the
decor. The in-room thermostat provided heat in an instant. The spotless
bathroom was spacious with shower and clawfoot tub, and had excellent
lighting, a good supply of white fluffy towels, and a basket of toiletries.
From our warm welcome by one young fellow, to our conversations with
the desk clerks, to an encounter with owner Barbara Ebenhoeh, we found the
Bonnymill to be very cordial and friendly, not stuffy or posh." *(Arlyne &
Collette Craighead)* "Just as delightful on a return visit as it was the first time."
(AC) "We arrived in mid-afternoon, and were greeted with ice-cold lemonade, cheese and crackers. We ate across the street at the Heritage House—
you can have an elegant meal upstairs, or a casual one in the Ratskellar.
Coffee is available at any time, so we helped ourselves to a cup and looked
through the photo albums which depict the inn's restoration. Charming and
friendly, with window boxes of well-kept flowers, and a wraparound porch
with old-fashioned rockers and white wicker chairs for watching the
activities of small-town U.S.A." *(Donna Bocks)*

Open All year.
Rooms 24 suites & doubles—all with private bath, telephone, TV. Some with
Jacuzzi, fireplace, balcony, wet bar.
Facilities Lobby, living room with grand piano, conference room, porch, atrium.
Off-street parking.
Location Central MI. Approx. 30 m SW of Saginaw, 50 m NW of Lansing. 18 W
of I-75; 22 m E of Rte. 27. On Rte. 57, across from Heritage House.
Credit cards Amex, MC, Visa.
Rates B&B, $125 suite, $65–85 double. Corporate rates. Alc lunch, $4–8; alc
dinner, $15–20.
Extras Free crib.

COLDWATER

Chicago Pike Inn   *Tel: 517–279–8744*
215 East Chicago Street, 49036

Named for its location on what was once the major road to Chicago, the Chicago Pike Inn is a Colonial Reform mansion built in 1903. It's been owned since 1989 by Jane and Harold Schultz, with daughter Becky as innkeeper. Set in a historic residential neighborhood, the inn's original stained glass windows, parquet floors, and gas chandeliers are complemented by Victorian antiques and collectibles. Rates include a fruit appetizer, juice, bread or muffins, and a hot meat and egg dish—perhaps homemade peach sorbet and caramel French toast. Those on sugar-restricted diets will need to alert the innkeepers in advance. The inn's ample common areas include a reception room with an Oriental rug, a cherry double-mantle fireplace with the original brown tile, comfortable chairs, cherry paneling and ceiling beams. The library is a guest favorite with its white-painted woodwork and bright floral wallpaper in greens, mauves, wines, and pinks, while the dining room has cherry paneling, wide plate rails, a built-in mirrored buffet, and a large carved walnut table with seating for all guests.

Guest rooms are named and decorated around the theme of their original inhabitants. Clarke's Room, on the first floor, has a queen-sized carved lace-covered canopy bed and fainting couch; the Grandchildren's Room is a fantasy of pink florals, lace, and ginghams with white wicker chairs and white iron and brass twin beds; and the Hired Girl's Suite is more restrained with black-and-white ticking fabric, red plaid wall covering, and braided rag rugs. Thoughtful touches include the two pillows—one hard, one soft—for each guest, lace curtains supplemented by room-darkening shades, in-room thermostats, and comfortable seating areas with good reading lamps.

"Becky made us feel like family; it is obvious that the Schultz family enjoys hosting guests. The food tastes as good as it looks, and Jane is happy to share recipes." *(Jerry & Johanna Hippensteel)* "Friendly, helpful staff. Delicious breakfast served on lovely china and crystal. Decor is beautiful, welcoming, and homey." *(GR)* "We stayed in Clarke's Room and loved it. The flickering 'candle' bulbs made a beautiful night light. The soaps and amenities made us feel well cared for. It made me feel so special to be surrounded by beautiful things, from the soap dish to the candy dish in the library, to the butter knife with a mother-of-pearl handle. Jane is very approachable and made us feel that she really wanted to serve our needs." *(LN)*

Open All year.
Rooms 2 suites, 4 doubles—all with private bath and/or shower, telephone, radio, TV, ceiling fan. 1 with fireplace.
Facilities Dining room, living room, library—all with fireplace; library with TV/VCR, books, porch. 1 acre with gazebo, off-street parking spots; bicycles. Fishing, boating, swimming, cross-country skiing nearby.
Location S central MI. 100 m W of Detroit, 120 m E of Chicago, 35 m SE of Battle Creek. On U.S. 12, 1 m W of Coldwater exit of I-69.

Restrictions No smoking in guest rooms. No children under 12. Daytime traffic noise in front rooms.
Credit cards Amex, MC, Visa.
Rates B&B, $140 suites, $85–105 double. Extra person, $20. 2-night special weekend minimum.
Extras Wheelchair access. Airport/station pickups, $20.

COPPER HARBOR

Keweenaw Mountain Lodge ¢ ⛹ ✗ 🏹   *Tel:* 906–289–4403
Copper Harbor, 49918

If you *really* want to get away from it all, head for the Keweenaw Peninsula, which juts out into Lake Superior, forming the northernmost point of the Upper Peninsula. Built by the WPA during the early thirties, the Keweenaw Mountain Lodge has all the flavor of a true wilderness lodge. "Lunch was thoroughly enjoyed in front of a roaring fire in the natural stone fireplace. Unfortunately accommodations in the log cabins were remodeled in generic motel furnishings, and do not have the rustic charm of the main lodge. The lodge is owned and operated by the county, so it lacks a certain personal flavor; on the plus side, rates are very reasonable." *(Joe Schmidt)* More comments required.

Open Mid-May–mid-Oct.
Rooms 34 1- and 2-bedroom cottages, 8 doubles in motel section—all with private bath. Most cottages with fireplace.
Facilities Restaurant, bar/lounge, pro shop, souvenir shop. Tennis court, shuffleboard, 9-hole golf course.
Location Upper peninsula, Keweenaw Peninsula.
Credit cards MC, Visa.
Rates Room only, $50–60 cottage, $48 double. Extra person, $5.

DETROIT

Although hardly a tourist mecca, the Motor City is also a major port and industrial center. Of interest to visitors are the shops and restaurants of Greektown, and the Detroit Institute of Arts, one of America's finest art museums. In nearby Dearborn, the Henry Ford Museum and Greenfield Village are home to outstanding collections that highlight the history of transportation and technology in the U.S.

   Reader tip: "Be sure to eat at least one meal in Greektown. The Greek food is especially good, and the prices are reasonable. You can get there easily on foot or take the People Mover from downtown."

   Also recommended: As a chain hotel with 308 rooms, the **Ritz-Carlton, Dearborn** (300 Town Center Drive, Dearborn, 48126; 313–441–2000 or 800–241–3333) does not qualify for a full entry. However, *Susan Schwemm* reports, "Readers should know about the Dearborn Ritz, because being treated as an individual is a big part of the 'wonderful little' experience, and on that score this hotel rates a perfect 10." Although a new building, the Ritz creates the impression of an old, luxury hotel through antique furnishings like Oriental rugs, Spanish chandeliers, English porcelain, and original 18th and 19th-century artwork. Guest rooms come with mahogany antique reproduction furniture, plus all the modern amenities and lots of little extras. The weekend rates are a terrific value at $95 per double."

Information please: Now run by Marriott, **The Dearborn Inn** was Henry Ford's vision of the ideal inn. It's set on 23 acres with 94 rooms in the Georgian style, with an additional 85 rooms in five colonial-reproduction homes and a motor lodge (20301 Oakwood Boulevard 48124; 800–228–9290 or 313–271–2700).

The Blanche House Inn ¢
506 Parkview, 48214

Tel: 313–822–7090

We know that B&B inns in big cities are growing in popularity, and are delighted to add the Blanche House to the list. Mary Jean Shannon and her son Sean restored this 1905 Greek Revival mansion in 1987, along with its sister mansion, the Castle, built in 1898. Known locally as the "Little White House" for reasons that become obvious when you combine the inn's name with its appearance, the inn has twenty-foot Corinthian porch pillars and ten-foot entrance doors of etched glass. Interior features include ornate plaster moldings and medallions, beautiful oak woodwork, and Pewabic tiling. Guest rooms combine period charm with all the amenities a business traveler might need, and those at the back of the inn have views of the Stanton Canal, Waterworks Park, the Detroit River, and a working boathouse. Rates include a full breakfast, with fresh fruit and home-baked goods.

"Immaculately clean. Charming decor, with an eclectic combination of period antiques and not-so-antiques. Closets were converted to provide a private bath for every room, so some are a very tight fit. The Shannons are delightfully warm and friendly, anxious to assure their guests of a pleasant stay. The attic suite has a separate room with a private hot tub; its creative decor and paint job (done by some artists friends) will be enjoyed by some but not all guests. The Castle was still under renovation when we visited, but judging from the magnificent woodwork, will be gorgeous when completed. Detroit's famous Pewabic Pottery is within walking distance, and is well worth a trip." *(Diane Wolf)* More reports welcome.

Open All year.
Rooms 1 suite, 7 doubles—all with private bath and/or shower, telephone, TV, desk, air-conditioning. Most with desk. Suite with hot tub. 3 doubles with porch, 1 with fireplace. Tennis, swimming nearby. Off-street parking.
Facilities Dining room, parlor with TV/VCR, video library, books.
Location Downtown; 3 m from center of town. Approx. 1 m from Belle Isle ridge. ½ block to River, Mayor's Residence. From Jefferson Ave. turn S on Parkview to inn on left.
Restrictions No smoking.
Credit cards Amex, MC, Visa.
Rates B&B, $115 suite, $65–85 double, $60–80 single. Extra person, $5. 10% senior discount. Discount for 7-night stay. Special event packages. Corporate packages.
Extras Airport/station pickups, $3–10; van service to downtown.

ELLSWORTH

The House on the Hill ¢   *Tel:* 616–588–6304
Lake Street, Box 206, 49729

A common complaint made of B&Bs in lovely rural settings is that there's no place to go for a good dinner. Julie and Buster Arnim kept that in mind when they sold their business in Texas and began an eight-state hunt for the perfect spot. One of the reasons they chose to transform this hilltop farmhouse into a B&B is because two of the state's best restaurants, the Rowe Inn and Tapawingo, are within walking distance. The inn's setting overlooking St. Clair Lake, and its location in the Chain of Lakes resort area were additional pluses. In renovating the house, they added a family room with fieldstone fireplace, and a marvelously inviting porch filled with pink geraniums and white wicker rockers, overlooking the lake and the wooded hills beyond. Guest rooms are decorated in country Victorian decor, with touches of Texas, and rates include a very full breakfast of eggs and sausages, oven French toast, or perhaps apple puff pancakes, accompanied by sour cream walnut coffee cake or another home-baked treat.

"A gorgeous area filled with galleries, beaches and antique shops. The hosts make it all so wonderful—they combine Texas warmth with the beauty of their Michigan inn." *(Linda Griffith)* "Especially delightful in spring for the flowers, and in fall for the foliage colors. The rooms have lovely antiques and gorgeous quilts, but we are partial to the ones overlooking the river opposite the house. An added plus is the proximity to our all-time favorite restaurant—Tapawingo. Best of all are the Arnims themsleves, who graciously make us feel like part of an extended family. To sit down to one of Julie and Buster's delicious breakfasts is a delight, but great company is an even bigger one." *(Mary Porter)*

Open April 15 to Jan. 15.
Rooms 5 doubles—2 with private shower, 3 sharing 2 baths. All with radio, ceiling fan.
Facilities Dining room, living room with fireplace, TV, veranda. 53 acres overlooking lake, with woods, fields, cross-country skiing. Swimming, boating, fishing, tennis, golf nearby. 17 m to downhill skiing.
Location N part of Lower Peninsula. 42 m N of Traverse City. 8 m S of Charlevoix. 2 m from center of town. From Traverse City, go N on Rte. 31 to Ellsworth. Turn E on Rte. 48 to inn.
Restrictions No smoking. No children under 12.
Credit cards MC, Visa.
Rates B&B, $75–95 double. Tipping allowed.
Extras Airport pickups, $10 one way. Babysitting.

ESCANABA

Escanaba was founded as a port, first for lumber, later for iron ore shipped from its deep-water harbor. It makes a good stopover if you're traveling scenic Route 2 along Lake Michigan on your way to or from Mackinac.

Information please: We'd like reports on **Celibeth House** (Route 1, Box 58A, Blaney Park 49836; 906–283–3409) roughly halfway between Escanaba and Mackinac, and about 40 miles south of Grand Marais, on Lake Superior. A thriving resort at the turn of the century, the entire town eventually became a ghost town, and was auctioned a few years ago. Elsa Strom has fixed up one of these homes as a B&B, and has cut hiking trails through her 85 acres. Reports?

The House of Ludington ¢ ✕

223 Ludington Street, 49829

Tel: 906–786–4000

Although the original hotel dates back to 1865, the current House of Ludington was built in 1883, with a wing added in 1910. Unusual and impressive in appearance, it's a cream stucco building, with medieval turrets and green window awnings. Pat Hynes bought the hotel in 1939 and did much to establish its reputation with his eccentric personality and such innovations as a glass-walled elevator, installed in 1959. Gerald and Vernice Lancour bought the Ludington in 1982; Carey Lancour is the manager. They restored and expanded the rooms, decorating them simply but comfortably with period antiques and reproductions. Meals are hearty and portions generous; the menus feature a selection of both steaks and such German-style dishes as schnitzel and smoked pork tenderloin with sauerkraut.

"Charming, friendly and well-run place, right across the street from Lake Michigan and a lovely park. Our room was decorated in Spanish style—inviting and clean. We liked the fact that the rooms are decorated in a variety of themes, and the glass elevator is charming. The dinner was great and so was the service." *(Kimberly Hawthorne)* "Good service, interesting historic background. Rooms were quiet, well-furnished, and comfortable—like a bedroom in a home. The bar area was quite relaxing and featured good quality live music on Saturday night." *(Pat & Glen Lush)* "Very good food and adequate rooms in an area where interesting accommodations are hard to find." *(Sheila & Joe Schmidt)*

Open All year. Restaurant closed Jan. 1, Dec. 25.
Rooms 4 suites, 21 doubles—all with private shower and/or bath, telephone, TV, air-conditioning. Some with desk.
Facilities Dining rooms, bar/lounge with weekend dancing, beauty salon, garden, gazebo. Room service. Valet parking. Lake nearby for swimming, fishing, boating. Golf nearby.
Location Upper Peninsula, near WI border. 100 m N of Green Bay, WI. On Little Bay de Noc near Yacht Harbor; across from Ludington Park.
Credit cards Amex, DC, Discover, MC, Visa.
Rates Room only, $57–72 suite, $46–58 double, $27–53 single. Extra person, $10. Tipping encouraged. Alc breakfast, $4; alc lunch, $6; alc dinner, $25. Crib, $4. Golf packages.
Extras Limited wheelchair access. Pets permitted by prior arrangement. Crib.

FENNVILLE

The little town of Fennville is known as the "gateway to the Allegan Forest," with miles of hiking and cross-country ski trails. It's also part of Michigan's fruit basket, with acres of fruit orchards covering its rolling farmland. Fennville is located in southwestern Michican, about 15 minutes southeast of Saugatuck, and about 15 minutes east of Lake Michigan.

The Crane House   *Tel: 616–561–6931*
6051 124th Avenue, 49408

Dating back to 1870, Crane Orchards now includes a 300-acre fruit farm, a cider mill, and the Pie Pantry restaurant, known for its great fruit pies, homemade soups and sandwiches, and fresh fruit. Visitors can also pick their own fruit starting with raspberries in July and ending with apples in September. The B&B is located in the family homestead, built in early 1870's, and restored as a B&B in 1988. The rooms are decorated with primitive antiques, hand-stitched quilts and fascinating collectibles, highlighted by hand-stenciling throughout. One room has an antique rope bed, with trundle underneath, while another has a brass and iron bed with a log-cabin patterned quilt.

Nancy Crane McFarland reports that "we are a family-run business on a working fruit farm. My parents really enjoy talking with guests in the evening. There is a lot of history in our family, and we enjoy sharing it. City people who want to get away from it all enjoy the relaxing atmosphere here; many have never been on a farm before and are pleasantly surprised." Rates include a full breakfast, perhaps fresh fruit with French toast, sausage quiche and cherry preserves, or apple pancakes; most guests try at least one meal at the Pie Pantry across the street as well.

"Lue and Bob Crane, and their daughter Nancy, are excellent innkeepers who provide lovingly restored rooms, with stenciling done by Lue and luxurious feather beds, a wonderful country breakfast, and outstanding hospitality. Wonderful lunches and dinners are available across the street at the Cider Mill, also owned by Crane Orchards—don't miss the peach pie." *(Elisabeth & Lloyd Grant)* "Delightful extra touches included the handmade quilts and needlework in each room. The Cranes are exceptionally nice people who were willing to share their time and stories with us, as well as take our kids for a ride in the antique truck. Their daughter Nancy is a good cook and we enjoyed each meal, served on pretty china or antique stoneware." *(Carol & John Eckman)*

"The location in a working orchard is special. From our room we could walk out into acres of apple, cherry, and pear trees. It's close to the attractions of Saugatuck, Douglas, and Holland, yet far enough away to retain its country charm." *(Andrew Neu)* "We snowshoed through the orchard, then sat by the parlor stove and drank hot cider and talked with the Cranes about apple farming. We especially enjoyed reading through a 1920s Sears Catalog." *(William Palmer)* "In the parlor is an antique stove with plenty of reading material nearby. We picked apples in the orchard to take home." *(Diane & Bill Patrick)*

101

An area for improvement: One otherwise delighted guest noted that better reading lights would have been welcomed in both her bedroom and in the sitting room.

Open All year.
Rooms 5 doubles—3 with private bath and/or shower, 2 with a maximum of 4 people sharing 1 bath. All with fan. 2 with desk.
Facilities Breakfast room, parlor with woodstove, TV room, porch. 1 1/2 acres surrounded by 300 acre orchard with restaurant, gift shop. 15 min. to Lake Michigan for water sports. 10 min. to cross-country skiing.
Location SW MI. 50 m SW of Grand Rapids, 50 m N of Benton Harbor. From I-196, take Exit 34 and go E on Rte M-89. 4 1/2 m to inn on left.
Restrictions Light sleepers should request room away from street. No smoking. Families with children under 8 must stay in downstairs room.
Credit cards Discover, MC, Visa.
Rates B&B, $60–80 double or single. Extra person, $10. Children under 2 free in parents' room.
Extras 1 room with wheelchair access and equipped for the disabled. Playpen.

The Kingsley House
626 West Main Street, 49408

Tel: 616–561–6425

After operating a B&B in Holland, Michigan, for several years, David and Shirley Witt moved to Fennville and restored the turreted Kingsley House as a B&B; the house was designed by a New York architect and built in the Queen Anne style in 1886. The Kingsleys introduced apples to this part of Michigan over a century ago. The Witts have appropriately named the guest rooms after locally grown apples: Dutchess, Jonathan, Golden Delicious, McIntosh, and Granny Smith. Rooms are charmingly decorated with Victorian antiques, and rates include a full breakfast of ham and eggs, homemade breads and muffins, juice and coffee. Guests are welcomed with afternoon tea or a cold drink and a sweet treat.

"Warm and friendly atmosphere with owners that will do everything to make your stay pleasant. Our room was very romantic and elegant, and a delicious family-style breakfast is served every morning." *(Kirk & Tina North)* "Immaculate inn, gracious hosts, careful restoration." *(Marietta Reid)* "Shirley and Dave told us about area restaurants, activites and points of interest." *(Hazel & Galen Hodge)* "Decorated with imagination, eye-appeal, and comfort in mind." *(Patricia Hough)*

Open All year.
Rooms 1 suite, 5 doubles—all with private bath and/or shower, telephone, radio, desk, air-conditioning, ceiling fan. Suite with fireplace. TV on request.
Facilities Breakfast room, dining room, living room with piano, fireplace, games; porch. 1 acre with lily pond, swing, bicycles, softball equipment. Boat, trailer parking. Cross-country skiing nearby.
Location 2 blocks from center of town. From I-196 take Exit 34 and go E 5 m on M-89 to inn.
Restrictions No smoking. Children over age 5 preferred.
Credit cards MC, Visa.
Rates B&B, $125–150 suite, $65–80 double, $50 single. Extra person, $15. 1/2 price for 4th night. Free room for children off season. 10% senior, AAA discount midweek. 2-night weekend minimum May–Oct. Holiday dinner packages.
Extras Limited wheelchair access. Airport/station pickups, $.30/mi. Dutch, Friesian spoken.

GLEN ARBOR

The Sylvan Inn ¢   *Tel:* 616–334–4333
6680 Western Avenue (M-109), P.O. Box 648, 49636

The Sylvan Inn was constructed as a private home in 1885, but was converted to an inn in the early 1900s when timber cutting and seafaring trade helped boost the local economy. Jenny and Bill Olson have owned the recently renovated structure since 1987. Rates include a continental breakfast.

"The inn is very attractive with well-maintained grounds, plenty of parking, well-lit areas, and a nice porch for rocking. The spotless guest-rooms upstairs contain brass and iron beds, a mini-corner sink, oodles of authentic antiques, and a private bath down the hall. Downstairs guests find a cozy sitting room where they serve a tasty continental breakfast of fresh fruit, muffins, juice, and coffee." *(Arlyne Craighead)* More reports appreciated.

Open 10 month; closed April and November.
Rooms 1 suite, 13 doubles—8 with private shower and/or bath, 7 rooms with sink sharing 3 bathrooms. All with telephone, fan; some with TV, desk, deck.
Facilities Common room with TV, porch. Hot tub, sauna. Lake Michigan and Glen Lake for swimming, boating, fishing. Close to downhill and cross-country skiing.
Location NW Lower Peninsula, Leelanau Peninsula. 26 m NW of Traverse City. In town.
Restrictions No smoking.
Credit cards MC, Visa.
Rates B&B, $85–110 suite, $50–60 double. Extra person, $12.
Extras Station pickups. Pets by special arrangement. Crib.

GRAND HAVEN

Although originally developed as a port where the Grand River emptied into Lake Michigan, Grand Haven is now best known as a resort. Visitors enjoy the two-mile boardwalk along the lake, the farmers' market and shops in Harbourfront Place, and of course, the sandy beaches and dunes along the lake.

Grand Haven is located in southwestern Michigan, on Lake Michigan.

Also recommended: Built in 1874, **Boyden House** (301 South Fifth, 49417; 616–846–3538) was the property of the owner of a shingle mill, Charles Boyden; his pride in his wares shows in the abundance of shingles and variety of woods used in the home's construction. The $75 rate includes a full breakfast. "Once a beauty, then a dilapidated apartment building, Boyden House was totally rebuilt over 18 months as a handsome B&B by Corrie and Bernie Snoeyer. Delicious breakfast with fresh-ground coffee; cordial, interesting hosts." *(Donna Bocks)*

Roughly 50 miles north of Grand Haven, in Pentwater, is the newly restored **Nickerson Inn** (262 West Lowell, P.O. Box 102, Pentwater 49449; 616–869–8241). "Although the exterior was still unrestored when

103

we visited, the inside had been totally renovated with great charm and comfort. Breakfast was good, and dinner here is a clear choice over other local options." *(John Blewer)*

Information please: The original turn-of-the-century **Highland Park Hotel** (1414 Lake Street; 616–842–6483) was destroyed by fire about twenty years ago. Only the annex built in 1923 escaped the blaze, and this building has been restored as a B&B by Terry Postmus. Set on a bluff overlooking the lake, the inn has been furnished with period antiques; rates include a continental breakfast and afternoon refreshments.

Harbor House Inn
Corner of Harbor and Clinton, 49417

Tel: 616–846–0610

"Innkeeper Carolyn Gray showed me five rooms and all the common areas of this beautiful inn. Each bedroom is different and lovely. The harbor view from most rooms is wonderful. Grand Haven is a busy resort town on Lake Michigan, but this must be the nicest place in town. The atmosphere is light, airy, comfortable, and clean, clean, clean." *(Elizabeth L. Church, also MN)* More reports necessary.

Open All year.
Rooms 15 doubles—all with private bath and/or shower, radio, air-conditioning. 9 rooms with desk, whirlpool tub, fireplace.
Facilities Living/dining room with fireplace, library, wraparound porch. Guest refrigerator, icemaker. Lake beaches, cross-country skiing nearby.
Location From US Rte. 31 N turn left on Washington St., then left again on Harbor. Go 1 block to Clinton St. to inn on corner.
Restrictions No smoking in bedrooms. No children under 12.
Credit cards MC, Visa.
Rates B&B, $65–125 double. Extra person, $25. Corporate rates, weekend packages off-season. 2-night weekend/holiday/special events minimum.
Extras Wheelchair access.

The Washington Street Inn ¢ ♣
608 Washington Street, 49417

Tel: 616–842–1075

An American four-square style house built as a private home in 1902, The Washington Street Inn has been owned by Anthony and Michelle Ciccantelli since 1986. The Ciccantellis are only its third owners, and were able to restore the original leaded glass windows, oak woodwork, and hardwood floors. The guest rooms are named for the owners' grandmothers of Italian and German descent, as well as the original owners. Each has its own style and color scheme, from the peach and green colors and white iron bed of Bettina's Room to the blue tones and brass bed of Mary's room.

"Tony and Michelle are warm and friendly, making us feel right at home. Our room was beautifully furnished with antiques, and the bed was cozy and inviting with soft flannel sheets, down pillows and comforter. The delicious breakfast included fresh fruit, quiche, apple dumplings with lots of cinnamon, and light, buttery croissants. Beautiful woodwork. Their young daughter Gina is a delight." *(Carol Alexander)* "A beautiful and meticulously furnished inn with gracious hosts and marvelous breakfasts." *(Lizabeth Leeson)*

Open All year.
Rooms 5 doubles—3 with private shower, 2 with sink in room & maximum of 4 people sharing bath.
Facilities Dining room, living room with books, stereo, games; sun room. Telephone in common room. Bicycle rentals. 1/2 m to beach, public fishing. Golf nearby. Off-street parking.
Location SW MI, on Lake Michigan. 30 m W of Grand Rapids, 20 m N of Holland. 1 1/2 blocks W of U.S. 31, between 6th & 7th Streets. From the S, take Rte. 31 N to sign for Downtown/Waterfront. Turn left (W) onto Franklin St. & go 1 block. At light turn left (W) onto Washington St. to inn on left.
Restrictions No smoking.
Credit cards MC, Visa.
Rates B&B, $65–75 double, $55–65 single. Extra person, $15. Senior discount. Children under 2 free. 10% discount for families if whole house is rented. 2-night weekend minimum during summer.
Extras Crib.

HARBOR SPRINGS

Popular for water sports in summer and skiing in winter, Harbor Springs is located at the northeastern tip of the Lower Peninsula, on Little Traverse Bay, across the bay from Petoskey.

Kimberly Country Estate
2287 Bester Road, 49740

Tel: 616–526–7646
616–526–9502

Kimberly Country Estate is a luxurious B&B inn opened in 1989 by Ronn and Billie Kimberly. Set on a hill overlooking Wequetonsing Golf Course and a duck pond, this plantation-style home features a columned portico entrance and cut fieldstone walls. Floral chintz designs mix with more masculine plaids and stripes to create an elegant yet comfortable atmosphere. A country English theme keys the decor with overstuffed furniture, European antiques, hardwood paneling, and cornice moldings found throughout the house. From the large step-down living room, French doors open onto an inviting terrace and pool area. Most of the bedrooms have high, four-poster beds or canopy beds with lace bedspreads. Rates include a buffet breakfast, afternoon tea, and lemonade.

"A beautiful place. Everything is spanking new—a very good value." *(ELC)* "Not only is this place gorgeous and set in beautiful Harbor Springs, but Billie and Ronn are as nice as can be. Billie serves a delicious breakfast of homemade rolls and muffins, eggs, fruit trays, cereals, etc. Also, since the Kimberlys used to be florists, there are beautiful flower arrangements all around the house." *(Karen Graef)*

Open All year.
Rooms 3 suites, 4 doubles—all with private bath. Some with fireplace, fan. 1 suite with Jacuzzi. Telephone on request.
Facilities Foyer, dining room, library with fireplace, TV; den with fireplace, TV; veranda, terrace. 7 acres with swimming pool. 5–10 min. to golf, skiing nearby.
Location Take Rte. M-119 S from downtown Harbor Springs. Turn left on Hoyt St., then right on Bester Rd. to inn on right.

Restrictions No smoking. "Not suitable for small children."
Credit cards Amex, MC, Visa.
Rates B&B, $200–225 suite, $85–200 double. 2-3 night weekend, holiday minimum.
Extras Airport/station pickups.

Main Street B&B ¢
403 East Main Street, 49740

Tel: 616–526–7782

"Since 1988, Donna and Jerry Karson have owned this 180-year-old transplanted hotel, brought to its current location across the frozen bay about 80 years ago. Their enthusiasm and delight in meeting people is contagious. Our room was lovely in wicker, with peach and ivory colors, and the shared bath was immaculate. Breakfast was served on the wraparound screened-in porch decorated in wicker with blue accents. Breakfast was decaf coffee (by request), bacon and eggs, homemade muffins with honey butter and fresh sliced strawberries and bananas. The pier, restaurants and shops are just a ten-minute walk away." *(Zita Knific)* And Donna adds: "We offer a cozy, comfortable home, right on Main Street—small town America. Our wraparound porch is a wonderful place to savor our breakfasts, and to return to relax and enjoy the view of Lake Michigan at day's end. Jerry and I enjoy not only our work, but the pleasure of meeting so many interesting people. We take pride in our B&B and do our best to keep it immaculately clean, cheerful, and fun!"

Open All year.
Rooms 4 doubles—all with private bath, desk, fan, deck.
Facilities Dining room, gathering room, wraparound sun porch, deck. 1 block from tennis, beaches, golf.
Location Downtown. On Rte. 119, 9 m N of Petoskey.
Restrictions No smoking.
Credit cards MC, Visa.
Rates B&B, $60–85 double. Extra person, $25. 2-night weekend (June–Aug.), holiday minimum.
Extras Airport/bus pickups.

HARRISVILLE

Big Paw Resort 🏃 🎿
818 North Lake Huron Shore, P.O. Box 187, 48740

Tel: 517–724–6326

Big Paw is a small but complete family resort set on the Lake Huron side of the northern Lower Peninsula, with a four-diamond AAA rating. It was started by Chuck and Emily Yokom in 1938, when they bought the property and built a cabin for their own use. Over the next ten years, they constructed all the remaining buildings, cutting the trees from their own forests to make the log structures. The resort is now run by son Ron and daughter-in-law Nancy, with help from their children.

The Yokoms' spring newsletter to former guests is filled with chatter about their children's baseball teams and girlfriends/boyfriends—Big *aw is a homey kind of place. One somewhat unusual feature: both the ive motel units and the secluded cabins are connected to the main odge and to the beach by a series of smooth paths, a real boon to hose with limited vision or mobility. The Yokoms note that they "try ıot to change the atmosphere at Big Paw. It seems much of the world ıas been changing so fast, and not always for the better. We want to :eep Big Paw as quiet, serene, and restful as it has been for the past 46 rears."

"Big Paw is utter relaxation, peace, quiet—a place to read, commune with nature, walk, and, for those inclined, tour Michigan and play golf. Cabins are spotlessly clean; food is simple but good and homemade." *(Lola Rothman, also Mark Slen)* "Flowers abound around every unit, especially he main lodge/dining room, where we all gather twice a day for meals. Ron and Nancy Yokom are what all visitors hope to find in their innkeepers, but seldom do. They are warm and friendly, always available, helpful, and never too busy to stop for a chat.

"The Yokoms share the cooking chores, with Ron doing the steaks on 'steak night,' and the delicious fish for the outdoor cookout on Wednesday. The Sunday hot dog roast on the beach is always a high point—huge fire, hand-cut green branches shaved to a point, homemade hot dog rolls, with lemonade and brownies for dessert. Although lunch is not served, fresh homemade cookies are always left out around noontime. While you are at breakfast, your cabin is cleaned and beds made." *(Betty & Harry Morley, also Howard King & Liz Sayer-King)*

Open May 21 to Oct. 31.
Rooms 4 cottages with 1- to 3-bedrooms, 5 doubles—all with full private bath, radio, TV, desk, working fireplaces.
Facilities Dining room, game room with library, Ping-Pong, pool, puzzles, magazines, games. 60 acres with 1,300-foot sandy beach, swimming, motor & rowboats, shuffleboard, lawn games, hiking trails, flower gardens, tennis court. Charter fishing for lake trout, salmon. Golf, horseback riding nearby.
Location NE Lower Peninsula. Alcona County. 30 m S of Alpena. 100 m N of Saginaw, 200 m N of Detroit. 1½ m from town. Turn right off Rte. 23, N of town, at sign.
Restrictions No smoking in dining room.
Credit cards MC, Visa.
Rates MAP, $150–190 double, plus 10% service. Reduced rate for children, families. Midweek packages off-season (mid-Sept. to mid-June).
Extras Paved walks to 2 cottages for wheelchair access. Airport/station pickups. Crib, babysitting.

HOLLAND

Dutch Colonial Inn ¢   *Tel: 616–396–3664*
560 Central Avenue, 49423

In selecting the name of the B&B they've owned since 1987, Bob and Pat Elenbaas have described both the architecture of the Dutch Colonial Inn and the well-known Dutch heritage and traditions of their town. Pat notes that "our B&B is beautiful all the time, but it's especially lovely at Christmas when the outside is decorated with 4,000 miniature white lights outlining the inn, with candles in each of the windows."

Each room of their B&B has a different style: The Jenny Lind Room is a romantic pink fantasy, with lots of ruffles and flowers and a king-size bed; the Country Room has a sleigh bed with an old-fashioned quilt and hand-stenciled wall borders; and the attic Hideaway Suite has simple cozy charm with a sloping wall, white eyelet comforter on the king-sized bed and double whirlpool tub. Breakfasts are served in the dining room, with its crystal chandelier and mahogany furnishings from the 1930s. Although Pat is happy to serve a continental breakfast of juice, fresh fruit with vanilla yogurt, and home-baked muffins to the many business travelers that stay here, she loves to pamper her guests with baked French toast and sausage and her own pastry—perhaps Swedish kringle or cherry coffee cake, accompanied by hazelnut-flavored coffee.

"Congenial innkeepers, exceptional breakfasts; impeccably clean, comfortable accommodations." (Elaine & Dave De Lange) "Warm, friendly atmosphere—yet privacy is respected." (Carol Vammings) "The exceptional breakfasts are served on elegant china by candlelight. The whirlpool tubs are an ideal way to end a long day." (Sharon Rumohr)

Open All year.
Rooms 1 suite, 4 doubles—all with private bath and/or shower, telephone, radio, desk, air-conditioning, fan. 1 with TV. 3 with double whirlpool tub.
Facilities Dining room, living room with fireplace, sun porch with TV/VCR, deck.
Location SW MI. 30 m W of Grand Rapids. 15 blocks from center. From I-196, take Exit 52 (Adams St.) to Central Ave. Go S on Central to inn, which is #560.
Restrictions No smoking or alcohol. Infants, children over 10 preferred.
Credit cards Amex, MC, Visa.
Rates B&B, $75–95 suite, $60–80 double. Extra person, $15.
Extras Airport/station pickups.

KALAMAZOO

Information please: *Glenn Roehrig* reports that he toured two attractive Kalamazoo inns, the **Stuart Avenue Inn** (405 Stuart Avenue, 49007; 616–342–0230) and the **Kalamazoo House** (447 West South Street, 49007; 616–343–5426). The Stuart Avenue Inn is actually a collection of five nearby Victorian homes, handsomely restored and decorated in period; the Kalamazoo House offers 11 guest rooms decorated individually with formal or country Victorian decor; rates range from $55–100, including a continental breakfast.

Hall House ¢   *Tel:* 616–343–2500
106 Thompson Street, 49007

More and more business travelers are discovering B&Bs and loving them. Pam and Terry O'Connor, who've owned Hall House since 1985, explain why: "Our business travelers return again and again, because we are such a welcome change from the places they normally stay. We have fluffy pillows, comfortable mattresses, and large rooms with space for them to spread their things out and work in the evenings. They love to see the same welcoming faces each time they visit, a real comfort when you're away from home."

Hall House is a Georgian Revival home built in 1923, and highlighted by Pewabic tile and mahogany woodwork. Although decorated largely with traditional furnishings, there's a spareness to the decor which is refreshingly contemporary. For example, one guest room has a white iron bed, with blue-and-white striped fabric used for the comforter, bedside table, and café curtains; on one wall, set off by the old-fashioned wall molding, are a few simple objects arranged to great effect: a straw hat, a wooden pineapple cutout, a wicker basket, and a cane carpet beater.

Breakfasts change daily, but might include apple juice; oranges with sliced bananas and pomegranate; raisin scones and blueberry muffins; and hazelnut coffee (freshly roasted and ground) or herbal tea.

"Pat and Terry take care of every detail and are helpful in a very personal way. Delicious breakfast, immaculately clean home." *(Connie Heard)* "Ideal location. Cheery light-filled room." *(Grace Mihi Bahng)* "The O'Connors are friendly, caring people who never intrude on your privacy." *(Catherine Stimpson)* "The innkeepers were well informed about Kalamazoo, and able to put us in touch with others in the community who could help us." *(Melissa Barlow)* "They clearly think personally about each guest—I arrived to find a magazine article relevant to my personal interests lying on the bed." *(Janet Bennett)* "My room, the Borgman, was a delight, attractive yet functional. It included a brass bed, a bathroom with a large shower, and a sitting room with a study area and second TV. In the evening, guests often gather in the living room in front of the fireplace to chat with each other and with their hosts. Typical of their thoughtfulness is the way Terry had already swept the snow from my car when I went to leave early on a winter morning." *(George Lavrosky)* "My favorite is the spacious Vander Horst Room with a gas-burning fireplace and a 10-jet shower. Breakfast is always light, healthy, varied, and presented with Pam's sense of élan." *(Charles Heach)*

Note: At press time we learned that the inn is for sale; check further when calling for a reservation; Pam notes that she'll be returning to school full-time eventually, but that "to be honest, it will be hard to give the inn up!"

Open All year. Closed Dec. 21–Jan 2.
Rooms 2 suites, 2 doubles—all with private bath and/or shower, radio, TV, desk, air-conditioning, fan. 1 with fireplace.
Facilities Breakfast room, living room with fireplace, piano, TV, books; porch. Off-street parking.
Location SW MI. Halfway between Detroit & Chicago. 5 blocks from business district, ½ block N of Kalamazoo College, 4 blocks from Western Mich. Univ. From I-94, take Rte. 131 N (Exit 74). Go 4½ m on Rte. 131 to Exit 38, W. Main St. (M-43). Go E on W. Main 3 m to inn on right, at corner of Thompson St.
Restrictions No smoking.
Credit cards Amex, Discover, MC, Visa.
Rates B&B, $75 suite/double. Extra person, $10. 2-night weekend minimum on local events.
Extras Some German spoken.

LAKESIDE

The Pebble House   *Tel:* 616–469–1416
15093 Lakeshore Road, 49116

Built in 1912 as a vacation retreat, Pebble House consists of the main house and several guest buildings, and takes its name from the beach stones from which the fence posts and much of the main house is built. Long-time owners Jean and Ed Lawrence have decorated primarily in the American Arts and Crafts style, also known as the Mission style. This movement started in England in a reaction to the machine age; this movement (1895–1920) spread to the U.S., and expressed the desire to return to the simple angular lines of handcrafted furnishings made from natural materials. Jean notes: "We are actively involved in spreading the word about the Arts and Crafts Movement. I teach seminars on the topic, and am pleased to share our knowledge with interested guests."

Rates include a Scandinavian buffet breakfast of juice, cereal, yogurt, European-style breads, cheeses, meats, coffee cakes, herring, and a daily hot dish—quiche, baked eggs, pancakes, or French toast. Afternoon coffee and cookies are also available. After a day walking along the beach and dunes, guests like to select a book from the Lawrence's library of art, architecture, and travel books, and curl up before the woodstove with one of the inn's cats for company. *(MA)* More comments please.

Open All year.
Rooms 4 suites, 3 doubles—all with private bath and/or shower, desk, air-conditioning. 2 with fireplace. 4 rooms in cottages. Some with balcony, deck, kitchen.
Facilities Breakfast room, living room with fireplace, library with fireplace; guest kitchen, porches, deck. 1⅓ acre with gazebo, picnic area, hammock, garden, tennis court. Beach across the road.
Location SW MI. 1½ h E of Chicago, 4 hrs. W of Detroit. From I-94, take Exit 6 and turn left at stop sign. go through Lakeside to Lakeshore Rd., turn left and go to inn.
Restrictions Smoking only on decks, balconies, screenhouse. No children under 12.
Credit cards MC, Visa.
Rates B&B, $96–140 suites, $90–96 doubles, $80–86 single. No tipping. 10% senior, AAA discount. 2-night weekend minimum. Weekly rate. Arts & Crafts theme weekends.
Extras Wheelchair access. Station pickups.

LAWRENCE

Oak Cove Resort ¢ 👫 ✕   *Tel:* 616–674–8228
58881 46th Street, 49064   708–983–8025

One of Michigan's oldest and smallest resorts, Oak Cove dates back to the turn of the century, and has been owned by Susan and Bob Wojcik since 1973. Over the past few years, the Wojciks have redecorated rooms in turn-of-the-century style. The staff includes local high school students, as well as college interns from the hotel management program at Michigan State.

"The comfortable cabins and lodge rooms are clean and well lit, with good plumbing. The food surpasses the quality of most area restaurants; in fact, many locals come just for lunch or dinner. Be prepared for fresh fruit and vegetables, delicious main dishes, and superb desserts—all in large quantities. Any special food needs are easily accommodated. The grounds are beautiful, quiet, and exceptionally peaceful. The lake and pool are as clean as can be. The most wonderful part about Oak Cove is the people who operate it: Susan and Bob, along with their adult children, and the high school girls who work there, spread warmth and cheer and comfort. They always make a special effort to know everyone's name, and spend time visiting with guests. This family-type warmth and caring cannot be matched." (R. Paul)

"A rustic family resort, nestled in the trees. We come to sail, swim and snorkle, and walk the country trails. Our room in the lodge was clean and refurbished with new curtains and linens. The owners are always warm and friendly, and we have formed lasting friendships with the other returning guests." (John & Margo Rannells) "The staff was helpful with our kids, always willing to prepare special meals or snacks." (Debra LaPlante) "Homey atmosphere. All ages seem to enjoy Oak Cove, from infants to senior citizens." (Nancy & Jim Smetana)

Open May 25 to Sept. 15.
Rooms 7 doubles in main lodge share 3 baths. 7 1- to 2-bedroom cottages with shower and porch.
Facilities Living room with TV/VCR; "Fun House" with pinball, jukebox, pool table, books, games, bar. 13 acres with heated swimming pool, fitness trail, lake with 500 ft. sand beach, boats, canoes, fishing, children's play equipment. Free golfing. Bicycling, hiking, snowmobiling, cross-country skiing nearby.
Location SW MI. 3 hrs. W of Detroit, 2 hrs. E of Chicago, 5 m from Paw Paw. Take Exit 56 off I-94. Go N ½ m on Rte. 51 to Red Arrow Hwy. Go W 1 m to fork; bear left and follow signs.
Restrictions No smoking in lodge guest rooms.
Credit cards None accepted.
Rates Weekly, full board, $490 lodge double, $550 cottage. Daily, full board, $125 double, $85 single. Children, $60–215 weekly; $20–45 daily, depending on age. Extra adult, $55. 15% service additional. Prix fixe lunch, $6; prix fixe dinner, $13. Special packages: "Women only" spa weeks, golfing weekends.
Extras Airport/station pickups. Crib, babysitting.

LELAND

Leland Lodge ✗   *Tel: 616–256–9848*
565 Pearl Street, P.O. Box 344, 49654

Leland (originally Leeland) received its name because of its lee position on the shore of a lake, a hard place for sailors to reach. The French added their word *eau*, for "water," giving Lake Leelanau its name. The town is situated between Lake Leelanau and Lake Michigan and abounds in recreational activities. In addition to a full range of sports (see below), Leland offers numerous antique and craft shops and five vineyards to tour.

Rooms at Leland Lodge are furnished with reproductions and some antiques; the bar has an interesting collection of photographs of Leland and Fishtown at the turn of the century. The lodge serves breakfast, lunch, dinner, and Sunday brunch. Food is fresh and locally produced, desserts are homemade.

"A most charming hotel/motel . . . warm and clean, with delightful decor both in the lobby and guest rooms." *(Eve Berland, Elizabeth Church)* More comments please.

Open Late May through Oct.

Rooms 4 suites, 18 doubles and singles, all with full private bath, telephone, radio, TV, desk, air-conditioning.

Facilities Restaurant, bar/lounge, living room with fireplace, books, TV/game room, bar, deck, conference center. 2.5 acres with gardens. Bicycling, tennis, beaches, sailing, windsurfing, canoeing, horseback riding, fishing charters, Manitou Island cruises, golf nearby.

Location NW Lower Peninsula, Leelanau Peninsula. 20 m N of Traverse City. 3 blocks from Main Street.

Credit cards Amex, MC, Visa.

Rates B&B, $90–160 suite, $70–135 double. Extra person, $10. No charge for children under 10. Weekly rates. Alc lunch, $7–10; alc dinner, $27–30. Suites in annexes do not include breakfast.

Extras Barrier-free room/ramp entrance for wheelchair access. Crib. Airport/station pickups.

LEWISTON

Lake View Hills Country Inn ✕   *Tel:* 517–786–2000
One Lakeview Drive, P.O. Box 365, 49756

On a forested hilltop, its natural wood exterior blending with the forest, is the Lake View Hills Country Inn, built in 1989 by owner Shirley Chapoton. The inn has four levels: at the top is the observatory; then the guest rooms; next the great room and kitchen; and at the lowest level are the game and exercise rooms with two less expensive guest rooms. A 165-foot porch runs the length of the inn. Each of its guest rooms represent places in the history of Northern Michigan, from the pink and white colors of the country Victorian Goldie Wheeler Room to the rustic bunk beds and lumber camp mood of the Mitchelson-Hanson Bunkhouse. The Otsego Room has Deco-style furnishings while the rich green and dark woods of the Chapoton Suite give it an English Tudor flavor.

"The Lake View enjoys a secluded setting, off the highway and down a tree-shaded lane. It's quiet and relaxing—a real getaway. Shirley is a charming, attractive lady who is an antiques auctioneer, which helps explains why every nook and cranny has marvelous decorator touches and beautiful antiques. There's an observatory tower with views of the lake and the surrounding countryside. There's even a certified Class A sanctioned (bent grass cut daily) six-wicket English croquet court, with a croquet master on the premises. Trails (easy, medium, and difficult) offer hiking in warm weather and cross-country skiing in winter. The rooms are charming, and the wall treatments and handmade quilts and coverlets are exceptional. A substantial breakfast of cereal, muffins, quiche is all homemade. The kitchen is open to guests for making popcorn, nibbling just-baked cookies, or to placing their own libation in the guest refrigerators. Two casual restaurants are nearby for dinner. Beautifully landscaped, spotless housekeeping." *(Patricia Evans)*

Open All year.
Rooms 1 suite, 14 doubles—all with private bath, TV.
Facilities Restaurant, great room with fireplace, guest kitchen, library, observatory; porch. Fitness center with sauna, whirlpool, exercise equipment. 355 acres with tournament caliber croquet court, hiking, cross-country ski trails, ski rentals, bicycle tours. Golf, fishing nearby.
Location N central MI. From Lewiston, go S on Cty. Rd. 491, W on Old 612 Fleming Rd. to inn on left.
Restrictions Smoking in designated area only.
Credit cards Amex, MC, Visa.
Rates B&B $135 suite, $75–105 double. Picnic lunches.
Extras Wheelchair access; 1 room equipped for disabled.

MACKINAC ISLAND

The Upper and Lower Peninsulas are connected at the Straits of Mackinac by the Mackinac Bridge, at five miles one of the longest suspension bridges in the world—a twentieth-century achievement that forms a pleasant contrast with the nineteenth-century charms of Mackinac Island. A trip to Mackinac (pronounced *Mackinaw*) Island is a trip back to another era. Cars were banned from the island in the thirties; you drive to either Mackinaw City (Lower Peninsula) or St. Ignace (Upper Peninsula) and park at the ferry. The dock porters meet all boats as they arrive at Mackinac, and help transfer luggage to the hotels. You can get around the island on foot, hire a horse-drawn carriage, or rent a bike from one of the many rental shops.

"It's not difficult to see why Mackinac Island has become such a popular summer resort. As you approach by ferry or hydroplane, you see high cliffs rising from the shoreline change to wooded bluffs dotted with some remarkable houses. Then, rounding a bend, you see a charming village nestled around the harbor. The sheer number of tourists milling about the village, along with the inevitable fudge and T-shirt 'shoppes,' may cause you momentary panic, but don't let it deter you from exploring the island's natural beauty. About 3 miles long and 2 miles wide (four-fifths of the island is a state park), Mackinac is basically a limestone outcrop with ravines, natural bridges, caves, and interesting rock formations. Rent a bicycle and explore the beach road and the cliffs—it doesn't take long to get away from the crowd. Be sure to spend some time at Old Fort Mackinac, built in 1780, and now preserved as a museum, with interpretive exhibits. The tearoom offers nice lunches and views of the bustling town below and the Straits of Mackinac." *(Maria & Carl Schmidt)*

Although with 275 rooms and plenty of convention business, the **Grand Hotel** is not right for this guide, it is a splendid century-old establishment, and well worth seeing. You can pay $3 to tour the grounds, or dress up in your finest and come for dinner (call 906–847–3331 for reservations).

Information please: Originally built as employee housing, the **Inn on Mackinac** (Main St. and Bogan La., P.O. Box 476, 49757; 906-847-3361) is decorated with 12 beautifully coordinated colors of paint on the exterior; this 44-room establishment may qualify as the most colorful on Mackinac. This is one of the island's newest hostelries; rates range from $69 to $150 and include a continental breakfast. Reports please.

Haan's 1830 Inn ¢ ♠♦

Huron Street, P.O. Box 123, 49757
Winter address: 1134 Geneva Street, Lake Geneva, WI 53147

Tel: 906–847–6244
Winter: 414–248–9244

Among Mackinac's oldest buildings, Haan's Inn sits on the foundations of a log cabin built in the late 1700s. The present structure, a pillared Greek Revival cottage, dates back to 1830. In the early 1900's, the house served as the residence of Colonel William Preston, an officer at Fort Mackinac and the mayor of the island. The Haan family bought the inn in 1976, and restored it as a bed and breakfast, furnishing it with period antiques. As Vernon Haan puts it: "This is our summer home and we enjoy sharing it with our guests." Breakfast includes fruit, juice, and fresh-baked breads, muffins, and coffee cakes.

"Our room was fairly small, but beautifully decorated and furnished with antiques. We enjoyed a tasty breakfast while talking with the other guests at one big table. The innkeepers, Joyce and Vernon Haan, are very congenial and went out of their way to make our stay pleasant." *(Pat & Glen Lush)*

"Due to a fortuitous circumstance, we were upgraded to the well decorated and spacious suite. The inn is away from the downtown crush, with a beautiful setting next to St. Ann's Church. The front yard is highlighted by huge ferns, which give the setting a woodsy look. The hosts were very outgoing and friendly and kept the conversation flowing at breakfast." *(John Blewer)* "Fully endorse existing entry." *(Mrs. DeWayne Farrar)*

Open Late May to mid-Oct.
Rooms 2 suites, 5 doubles—5 with private bath and/or shower, 2 sharing 1 bathroom. All with fan, desk. Some with deck.
Facilities Dining room with fireplace, living room with books, games. 2 open porches, 1 screened porch. Large yard adjacent to garden of church. Four blocks from historic fort and village. Near ferry dock and charter fishing. Bike, horse, carriage rentals, golf, tennis nearby.
Location Four blocks E of ferry docks on Huron Street. From MI Lower Peninsula, go N on I-75 to Mackinaw City, then 7½ m ferry trip. From WI and MI Upper Peninsula, take Rte. 2 to St. Ignace, then 3½ m ferry trip.
Restrictions No smoking.
Credit cards None accepted.

Rates B&B $105 suite, $60–95 double. Extra person, $10. Child's discount. No tipping.
Extras Crib, games.

Hotel Iroquois on the Beach 👫 ✖

298 Main Street, P.O. Box 456, 49757

Tel: 906–847–3321
906–847–6511

The Hotel Iroquois is a rambling Victorian structure, with plenty of turrets and gables. It's been owned and operated by Sam and Margaret McIntire for the last thirty years, and is managed by their daughter Mary McIntire. Rooms overlook the beautiful Straits of Mackinac. Rates vary with room size, location, and view. Continental breakfast is served in the rooms, and lunch, dinner, and drinks are available in the hotel's Carriage House restaurant.

"We first visited Mackinac and the Iroquois in 1978 as starry-eyed newlyweds and loved it. Now we visit with three children, who are always made welcome. The hotel staff is well trained and personable. The dining room is glass-enclosed, and it is truly relaxing to watch the freighter traffic pass through the Straits of Mackinac right before your eyes. The island is filled with sports activities and history; it was a major Great Lakes center of the fur industry until the 1830s." *(Rebecca Barnwell, also Arlyne & Collette Craighead)* "Charming old-style decor with wicker furniture, yet neat and comfortable. Our spacious room had a king-size bed, coordinating fabrics for the wallpaper, bedspread, and window shutters; it overlooked the fort and harbor. The hotel staff were helpful and polite—altogether a lovely stay." *(Nick Mumford)*

"A truly memorable dining experience. The large, cheerful and well appointed dining room has a marvelous harbor view; try to reserve a window table if possible. For starters we had a richly flavored French onion soup, followed by an exquisite salad with a generous blue cheese vinaigrette. Our entrée was fork-tender veal piccata with butter, lemon, and capers, accompanied by tri-color fettucini. An adequate wine list provided a 1986 St. Emilion which added enormously to the enjoyment of our dinner. Peanut butter pie was an exquisite dessert. Service was attentive and professional throughout. Toward the end of our meal, a squall passed through the harbor. When the sun emerged a marvelous, intense rainbow pronounced the finale to our evening." *(John Blewer)*

Open Mid-May to mid-Oct. Restaurant opens in June.
Rooms 6 suites, 41 doubles—all with private bath and/or shower, desk, fan. All suites with TV.
Facilities Lounge, veranda, patio by water, family room, TV room. Right on beach. Golf and tennis nearby.
Location N Michigan, 290 m N of Detroit. Island in Lake Huron, at Straits of Mackinac, between Upper and Lower Peninsula. 1 block from center of town; 2 blocks from ferry docks. SW end of Main Street on Windemere Point.
Credit cards Discover, MC, Visa at checkout; check required for deposit.
Rates Room only, $260–305 suite, $60–230 double. Extra person, $10. Reduced rates for 2-night stays after Labor Day. No charge for children in off-season. $1.50 baggage charge (from ferry dock). Alc breakfast, $7–13; lunch, $10–15; alc dinner, $45–50. 2-night weekend minimum, July–Aug.
Extras Wheelchair access. French, Spanish, German spoken. Crib, babysitting.

Island House 👥 ✕   *Tel:* 906–847–334?
Main Street, P.O. Box 1410, 49757   800–626–630◀
Off-season: 31181 Kendall Drive,
Fraser, MI 48026   Off-season: 313–293–060(

A registered historic site and the oldest hotel on Mackinac, the Islanc
House dates back to 1852. Rooms are decorated with traditional furnish
ings as well as some Victorian-style fabrics and decorative touches. Majoı
renovations were completed in 1990, including remodeling of the gues'
rooms, dining room, lobby, and lounge; the addition of an elevator, anc
gift shop; the installation of a new spinkler and smoke detection system
and the addition of air-conditioning on the top floor. To supplement
the Governor's Dining Room where breakfast and dinner are served, the
Garden Grill is now open for lunch on the front lawn, overlooking the
harbor. Guest rooms are priced according to three categories: moderate
standard, and deluxe; the difference is in the size of the room and its view
(or lack of one). Rates include the full-service buffet breakfast and dinner
soup or salad, choice of entrée, dessert and beverage.

"Despite the hotel's size, the staff really tries to personalize the Islanc
House; they are more than willing to assist guests and answer questions
One can relax on the huge porch, watching the boats coming in and the
horse-drawn carriages rolling past. The restaurant has a fine selection oı
entrées, and the rooms are nicely decorated." *(Jeff & Terri Patwell)* More
comments required.

Open May 1 to Oct. 31.
Rooms 94 doubles—all with private bath, radio, fan. 22 with air-conditioning, 35
with desk. 22 rooms in annex.
Facilities Restaurant, lounge with TV, piano entertainment nightly; lobby with
fireplace, games; porches. 4 acres with lawn.
Location Across from State Yacht Marina. 2 blocks from Ft. Mackinac. Next tc
Marquette Park, 5-min. walk from village.
Restrictions Light sleepers should request quiet rooms.
Credit cards MC, Visa.
Rates Room only, $106–134 double. MAP, $162–194 double. Extra adult, $15–
45. Children under 14 free (room only); $15–20 (MAP). Midweek, spring/fall
weekend packages. Full breakfast, $8. Alc dinner, $25.
Extras Crib, babysitting.

Metivier Inn 👥   *Tel:* 906–847–6234
Market Street, P.O. Box 285, 49757   Off-season: 616–627–2055

Built by Louis Metivier in 1877, this turreted Victorian home stayed in the
Metivier family until 1984, when it was bought by Mike and Jane Bacon
and Ken and Diane Neyer, who restored it as a bed & breakfast inn.
Rooms are decorated with antiques and reproductions, some with four
poster or brass beds. Rates include a buffet breakfast of fresh fruit and
juice, coffee cake and croissants.

"Everything at the Metivier Inn appears clean, efficient, and new, yet
it has the pleasant aura of a much older establishment. Two rooms are
done with antique decor, while the rest feature white wicker or brass
furnishings. The porch is a great spot for sitting and watching the parade

f carriages, bicycles, and pedestrians. The stable across the street takes
bit of getting used to, but don't let it deter you from a wonderful stay."
Pat & Glen Lush) "Fresh, crisp, and clean. Very good breakfasts. Not
heap, but you get what you pay for." *(Pat Borysiewicz)* "Convenient
ocation; not as noisy since it's a block from the main drag. The owners
ere very accommodating, and found a great babysitter for our two-year-
lds. They even listened for calling children while we relaxed on the porch
te at night." *(Juli Robbins Greenwald)*

)pen May through October.
ooms 2 suites, 19 doubles—all with private bath and/or shower, fan.
acilities Living room with fireplace, porch.
ocation 1 block from ferry dock.
estrictions No smoking in common rooms.
redit cards MC, Visa.
ates B&B, $145–160 suite, $88–135 double. Extra person, $20.
xtras Crib, babysitting.

MARSHALL

Marshall was founded in 1830 by northeastern settlers who fully expected
he town to become the state capital. They built beautiful Victorian homes
f many different styles; the houses have all been recently restored.
Marshall is located in south central Michigan, halfway between Detroit
nd Chicago, at the juncture of interstates 94 and 69. In addition to
istoric home visits, area activities include lakes for swimming and fishing,
olf, and cross-country skiing. Sunday night specials are available at inns
nd restaurants. Inquire for details.

McCarthy's Bear Creek Inn ₵ 🕴   *Tel: 616–781–8383*
5230 "C" Drive North, 49068

ear Creek Inn, built in the 1940s, is a cream-painted brick home, set on
knoll overlooking Bear Creek; it's encircled with fieldstone fences built
y the original owners. Mike and Beth McCarthy purchased the inn in
985, and say that they "welcome all kinds of travelers, but those looking
ɔ slow down the pace and relax are particularly well served by what we
ffer." First-floor highlights include an intricate fieldstone floor, wide bay
windows, and oak staircases, while the country-style guest rooms feature
rass or four-poster beds and flowered wallpapers. During 1988, the
McCarthys completed reconstruction of the original barn, now called the
Creek House. Decorated with furniture built by Mike, it's highlighted by
ntiques and balconies overlooking the creek. Beth serves a tasty breakfast
f fresh fruit, eggs, baked goods, cheese, cereals, and juice, coffee, and tea.
   "The atmosphere is so relaxing, and the inn beautiful. The McCarthys
nd their staff treated us like part of the family during our entire stay."
anice Stafford) "Our delightful room had a beautiful bed made of cherry
vood, handcrafted in the inn's own workshop. The McCarthys are gra-
ious and hospitable, breakfast is generous and tasty, and we loved
vatching all the ducks in the creek." *(DK)*

Open All year. Closed Dec. 23–25.
Rooms 14 doubles—all with private bath and/or shower, radio, desk, and air conditioning. 7 rooms in Creek House with balcony.
Facilities Breakfast room; living room with fireplace, books, games; porch. 1 acres with cross-country skiing, stream for trout fishing, children's play equipment
Location 1½ m from town. From I-69/I-94 juncture, take I-69 S 1 exit t Michigan Ave. Go W on Michigan Ave., turn left on 15-mile Rd. Turn right c "C" Dr. N to inn on left.
Restrictions No smoking in breakfast room.
Credit cards Amex, MC, Visa.
Rates B&B, $54–93 double. Extra person, $5.
Extras Local airport pickups. Crib.

The National House Inn ¢   *Tel:* 616–781–737
102 South Parkview, 49068

Built in 1835 as a stagecoach stop, this Greek Revival structure is th oldest operating inn in Michigan, and is listed on the National Registe of Historic Places.

"The public and guest rooms are authentically furnished in 19th centur style. The inn has been extensively renovated with a modern heating an air-conditioning system, using designs and fixtures in keeping with th early American decor." *(Walter Willey, also KJ)* "Our room was delight fully done in wicker and looked out onto a little garden with a lighte fountain." *(Dr. & Mrs. Kurt Neumann)* More reports required.

Open All year. Closed Christmas.
Rooms 1 suite, 15 doubles—14 with private bath and/or shower, 2 with hal bath, shared shower. All with TV, air-conditioning. 2 with desk.
Facilities Dining room, sitting rooms with fireplaces, games; family room, gi shop. Garden. Racquet club privileges, including sauna, whirlpool tub. Lake, swim ming pools, fishing, cross-country skiing, golf nearby.
Location On the village circle.
Credit cards Amex, MC, Visa.
Rates B&B, $99–110 suite, $62–88 double; $58 Sunday night.
Extras Crib, babysitting.

MENDON

Information please: Fourteen miles south of Sturgis is the **Christmen House** (110 Pleasant Street, Sturgis, MI 49091; 616–651–8303), a 188 brick Queen Anne mansion restored as an inn in 1984. Its ten guest room are individually decorated in period, and range in from from $62–8. including a full breakfast and afternoon tea, served on the veranda in goo weather.

Mendon Country Inn ¢   *Tel:* 616–496–813
440 West Main Street, 49072

Dating back to the 1840s, the Mendon was rebuilt in 1873 by Adam Wakeman, who added the 8-foot windows, the high ceilings, and th winding walnut spiral staircase. Dick and Dolly Buerkle bought the inn i

1987 and have added two fireplaces, private baths for all rooms, and built the new Creekside Lodge and the cottage suites.

The inn is a collector's paradise—the rooms are decorated with wonderful old quilts, baskets and Native American art. Guests enjoy antiquing, visiting the Amish settlement, and exploring the river.

"Dick greeted us warmly, and Dolly always had delicious smells wafting from the kitchen, which emerged as homemade soups, apple crisp, brownies, cookies, and more. She also invited us to make use of the kitchen at our convenience. The rooms are lovely, with Amish themes, and with fresh fruit always in the nightstand." *(Patricia Vodry)*

"We found we could be as busy or relaxed as we wanted. The inn offers bicycles for a spin around quiet little Mendon, and a canoe livery for paddling down the calm and picturesque St. Joe River." *(Kim Sanwald-Reimanis)* "The handsome quilts, grandmothers' trunks, high-button shoes and dried flower arrangements all transport you to a more gentle time, yet there is modern plumbing, lots of hot water, good reading lights, and ample parking spaces." *(Jack & Betty Fitzpatrick)*

"The grounds are extensive and private, and guests are encouraged to wander along the creek, complete with a covered bridge, small island, gurgling rapids, and an adult tree house. If you wish to go antiquing, shopping, visiting with the Amish or sightseeing, Dick will give you the directions you need. Inside the inn, guests may help themselves to teas, coffee, cookies, and malted milk balls from the kitchen. Open guest rooms may be explored, and there are board games to play, and photo albums to leaf through. The rooms are very clean, and it is obvious that attention is spent on the details. Each is very different, from the Victorian to the western style Sundance Room, complete with saddle, sliding barn door, and 'rain barrel.' If you feel there is anything lacking in your room, you need only mention it to Dick, Dolly, or the friendly young ladies who help, and it is taken care of graciously. We visited during their Country Christmas weekend, and can recommend it highly." *(Lynne German, also Michelle & Jonathon Sheppard)*

Another opinion: "Despite the two-night weekend minimum, our Friday night reservation was confirmed. When we arrived at the inn, we were told they had inadvertently overbooked their 18 rooms, and that a reservation had been made for us at another inn, 15 minutes away."

Open All year.
Rooms 7 suites, 11 doubles—all with private bath and/or shower. 15 with air-conditioning, 3 with porch. 7 rooms with whirlpool tub, fireplace in Creekside Lodge.
Facilities Breakfast room, common room with fireplace, TV, games, cards, books, self-serve coffee/tea. Rooftop garden for sunbathing; adult "tree house." 14½ acres with picnic area, barbecue, swing, tandem bicycles, canoe rentals. Dock for fishing, canoeing on St. Joseph River. Golf, tennis, downhill, cross-country skiing nearby.
Location SW Michigan. Halfway between Chicago and Detroit; 22 m S of Kalamazoo. 3 blks. from center of town.
Restrictions Smoking in common rooms only.
Credit cards Amex, Discover, MC, Visa.
Rates B&B, $72–115 suite, $50–72 double. Extra person, $10. Quilting, skiing, craft, holiday packages. Midweek rates. 2-night weekend minimum.

METAMORA

Arizona East Bed & Breakfast ¢ 👫   *Tel:* 313–678–3107
3528 Thornville Road, 48455

To answer the obvious question, the name of this B&B arose when owner Jim Cork said to his wife Melissa: "If I can't find anything in Metamora that I like, we're moving to Arizona." When they found this 8,000-square-foot mansion, built in 1951 as the summer home of a weathy Detroit banker, he named it Arizona East. The Corks have remodeled it as a B&B, furnishing the rooms with traditional period decor. Rates include a breakfast of fruit and juice, eggs cooked to order, toast and rolls, sausage or bacon, and sometimes a daily special like chocolate chip pancakes. "Lovely home, warm hospitality." *(GR)* More comments needed.

An area for improvement: Better lights for reading in bed.

Open All year.
Rooms 6 doubles, 1 single—2 with private bath, 5 with maximum of 4 people sharing bath. All with telephone, desk.
Facilities Dining room with fireplace, living room, TV room with fireplace. 12½ acres. 5 m to cross-country skiing.
Location SE MI. 35 m N of Detroit, 30 m W of Port Huron. Take Rte. 24 N to Dryden Road, turn right and go 5.4 m., turn left onto Thornville, & go 1 m to inn.
Credit cards None accepted.
Rates B&B, $60 double, $45–60 single. Extra person, $10. Children under 3 free. Theme weekends.
Extras Airport pickups. Crib.

PORT HURON

The Victorian Inn ¢ 🍴   *Tel:* 313–984–1437
1229 Seventh Street, 48060

J. H. Davidson, owner of a prominent home furnishings store in Port Huron, built this Queen Anne Victorian in 1896. When Ed and Vicki Peterson and Lew and Lynne Secory purchased the Davidson home in 1983, they were lucky enough to receive the original plans, drawings, and specification sheets, which helped them to make the restoration as accurate as possible. Fortunately, the house had never been divided into apartments, and the original woodwork and leaded glass were still intact. After six months of intensive work, the inn opened, decorated in period with reproduction wallcoverings and window treatments. A dinner at the inn's popular restaurant might include crab and mushroom bisque; quail stuffed with sausage and shallots, served with rice and salad; and chocolate nut pie for dessert. "Beautiful restoration, warm and hospitable staff, enjoyable atmosphere, good food." *(IK)* More comments required.

Open All year. Restaurant closed Sun., Mon.
Rooms 4 doubles—2 with private bath and/or shower, 2 with maximum of 4 people sharing bath. All rooms with radio, air-conditioning. 2 with fireplace.
Facilities Restaurant with fireplace, bar/lounge with TV, fireplace, Fri. entertain-

ment; drawing room, study, wraparound porch. Off-street parking. Lake Huron, St. Clair River nearby for boating. Cross-country nearby.

Location SE MI. 55 m N of Detroit. 4 blocks N of Bus. I-69. On Seventh St., between Union and Court Sts.

Credit cards Amex, CB, DC, Discover, MC, Visa.

Rates B&B, $55–95 double. Alc lunch, $11; alc dinner, $26–37.

Extras Station pickups. Some Spanish, German spoken.

PORT SANILAC

Raymond House Inn
111 South Ridge Street (M-25), 48469

Tel: 313–622–8800

The Raymond House is a red brick Victorian, complete with gingerbread façade, steep, sloping roofs, and white icicle trim dripping from the eaves. Inside, the rooms are furnished with antiques; one bedroom features a "Lincoln" bed, the same kind as the one on display in the White House.

"The moment you walk in the door you feel calm and comfortable. The rooms are large and very clean. In the morning you can help yourself to a continental breakfast of coffee, juice, fresh fruit, and date-nut bread, and the morning paper. If the weather is nice, we take ours outside to the patio. Shirley Denison, the innkeeper, goes out of her way to make everyone's stay pleasant. She is a potter and has quite a collection of local art and antiques that can be purchased or just admired. The inn is located within walking distance of Lake Huron, and during the summer the Arts Council sponsors an arts and crafts fair and a Renaissance fair. We enjoy the fishing, swimming, boating, shopping, and the good restaurants for perch dinners." *(Raymond & Patricia Harkey)* "Friendly hospitable owners. Extra touches included extra pillows, a selection of audiotapes, snacks, ice, and glasses in our room. The delicious sitdown breakfast included fresh fruit and juice, cereal, and breads with homemade jams and jellies." *(Helen Springer)*

Open April through Oct.

Rooms 7 double rooms—all with private bath and/or shower, air-conditioning, fan.

Facilities Parlor with TV/VCR, card games; dining room, library, patio. Pottery studio. 1 1/2 acres with shade trees, patio, bicycles. 1 block from Lake Huron and marina. Beaches, charter boats, golf, horseback riding nearby.

Location "Thumb" area of E MI. 90 m N of Detroit; 30 m N of Port Huron. 2 blocks from center of village.

Restrictions No smoking. No children under 12.

Credit cards CB, DC, MC, Visa.

Rates B&B, $50–65 double or single. Extra person, $15. 10% senior discount.

SAGINAW

The Montague Inn ✕
1581 South Washington Avenue, 48601

Tel: 517–752–3939

"The Montague Inn is a 12,000-square-foot Georgian mansion built in 1929 for a sugar beet baron, and sits well back from the busy road. There is a formal garden on the terraces near the river and an herb garden; the gardens and river at the rear of the grounds foster a secluded feeling. The dining room holds about ten well-spaced tables. The parlor/library contains comfortably elegant furniture and a wide selection of books. The main living room is furnished luxuriously with antique reproductions from the 1930s, and opens onto a sun-room. All the public areas are beautifully decorated and invite relaxation. The original bathrooms still have handmade Pewabic tiles, made by a Detroit woman who took the secret of their manufacture to her grave. "The Bridal Suite, surely the most spacious room in the inn, occupies the entire area above the living room and sun-room. Its private living room comes with TV, coffee table, fold-out couch and upholstered chairs, a TV, and phone. The bedroom is even bigger with a four-poster bed, fireplace, secretary's desk, two wing chairs, and a dining room table with two chairs, plus a window seat and built-in cedar closets and drawers. The huge tile bath has two full-size pedestal sinks, a separate toilet area, a toothbrushing sink (I've never seen one of these before), and a double shower stall with shower nozzles at two heights and on both sides. Other guest rooms in the inn are equally nice, though obviously smaller." *(SHW)*

"The house has many examples of superior, old-fashioned craftsmanship, including the hidden panels in the library. Coffee is served there, among the many volumes of books, all available to guests on a 'return when you visit again' basis." *(Sally Williams)*

"We stayed at the Montague just after Christmas, and the inn was very pretty with its seasonal decorations. One really great feature is the old carriage house, with five guest rooms that are as pretty as those in the main house. Since we were there with two other families, we were able to take over the carriage house, which made for a very homey atmosphere." *(Bob & Sandy Dekema)*

"The cooling color schemes of ice green and forest green and seemingly endless cantilevered circular staircases provided an aura of comforting sophistication. Breakfast was elegantly served on fine china, and the tiny touches (genuine cream in a pitcher and precisely sculptured softened butter) separates the Montague from ordinary inns." *(Zita Knific)* "The dining room offers lunch and dinner to the public, along with a continental breakfast for guests. The food is well prepared and served, and the creative menu is changed regularly. The hospitality of the staff, the elegant decor and furnishings, and the beautiful and spacious grounds all create a delightful atmosphere." *(Donald Gibbons)*

Open Closed Jan. 1, Dec. 25. Restaurant closed Sun., Mon.
Rooms 1 suite, 17 doubles—16 with private shower and/or bath, 2 with maximum of 4 people sharing bath. All with telephone, TV, air-conditioning. 3 with fireplace, some with desk. 5 in Carriage House.
Facilities Dining room, library with fireplace, reception room, lounge. Meeting rooms. 8 acres with river for fishing nearby. Health club nearby.
Location Central MI. Take I-75 100 m NW of Detroit. Exit I-75 at Holland M-46, bear right on Remington, left on S. Washington.
Restrictions Smoking in library, lounge only.
Credit cards Amex, MC, Visa.
Rates B&B, $140 suite, $55–105 double. Extra person, $5. Alc lunch, $15; alc dinner, $35–40.
Extras Wheelchair access; 1 room in Carriage House equipped for disabled. Crib.

SAINT CLAIR

Murphy Inn ¢   *Tel:* 313–329–7118
505 Clinton Street, 48079

The St. Clair River, a historic waterway connecting Lake Huron with Lake St. Clair and Lake Erie, was the scene of busy riverboat traffic through the nineteenth century. What is now the Murphy Inn was built in 1836 as the Farmer's Hotel, a white clapboard structure surrounded by porches; horses were brought here for auction by riverboat from Detroit. The inn was restored in 1985 by Ron and Cindy Sabotka, who have decorated the rooms simply, with queen-sized beds and a few antiques. The dining room serves light meals throughout the day at very reasonable prices.

"Our impeccably clean room was well appointed with a country inn atmosphere. The owners went out of their way to make us feel at home, even delivering the continental breakfast of juice, rolls, and coffee to our door." *(Shelby Fox)* "As you would expect from its name, the Murphy Inn combines an Irish atmosphere with a warm and hospitable staff." *(Vince & Revea Mecallef)* More comments please.

Open All year. Restaurant closed Christmas.
Rooms 1 suite, 6 doubles—all with private bath and/or shower, telephone, radio, TV, desk, ceiling fans, air-conditioning. 1 room with balcony.
Facilities Dining room, bar/lounge. St. Clair river, golf nearby.
Location SE MI, 50 m NE of Detroit, 10 m S of Port Huron, MI and Sarnia, ONT. 2 blocks from center of town.
Credit cards Amex, MC, Visa.
Rates B&B, $55–75 suite, $42–55 double. Extra person, $10. Children stay free. Alc lunch/supper, $4–6.

SAUGATUCK

A well-known art colony on the shores of Lake Michigan, Saugatuck is an attractive resort town. It's most popular in the summer months, for swimming and windsurfing on Lake Michigan, plus hiking in the dunes and canoeing on the Kalamazoo River; cross-country skiing in the winter is becoming very popular as well. Most visitors enjoy browsing through the town's lovely shops and art galleries.

The town is located in southeastern Michigan, 35 miles southwest of Grand Rapids and 10 miles south of Holland. Rates are generally highest on weekends, May through October, and a two-night minimum stay on weekends is usually required for advance reservations.

Information please: The Kirby House (Center Street at Blue Star Hwy., P.O. Box 1174, 49453; 616–857–2904) is a century-old Queen Anne Victorian decorated with period antiques. The hot tub is available for year-round relaxation, and rates include a full breakfast. **The Newnham Inn** (131 Griffith Street, P.O. Box 1106, 49453; 616–857–4249) is a turn-of-the-century home just a block from Saugatuck shopping. Six guest rooms and a cottage are available to guests, and all can enjoy the

MICHIGAN

hot tub and swimming pool. **Twin Gables Country Inn** (900 Lake Street, P.O. Box 881, 49453; 616–857–4346) has 13 guest rooms and three cottages overlooking Kalamazoo Lake. Both the guest rooms and ample common areas are decorated in period antiques and white wicker; also available are a hot tub and heated swimming pool. The **Maplewood Hotel** is a 125-year-old Greek Revival building with 13 remodeled guest rooms, a restaurant serving continental cuisine, and a yellow Rolls Royce to pick you up at the Holland train station (428 Butler Street, P.O. Box 1059, 49453; 616–857–2788).

We'd also like to hear more about **The Park House** (888 Holland Street, 49453; 616–857–4535) listed in earlier editions but dropped for lack of reader feedback. The oldest home in Saugatuck, the Park House has eight guest rooms with wide-plank pine floors, decorated with lots of craftwork; furnishings include Victorian antiques and brass beds. Rates include a continental breakfast of fruit, juices, granola, and muffins.

Kemah Guest House
633 Pleasant Street, 49453

Tel: 616–857–2919

Built at the turn of the century, the Kemah features magnificent stained and leaded glass windows, hand-carved wooden landscapes, and beamed ceilings, all added in 1926. An unusual addition is the airy solarium, built by a contemporary of Frank Lloyd Wright. Rates include a continental breakfast, and in summer, a pre-dinner drink in the Bavarian-style rathskellar.

"Fluffy white towels, eyelet-trimmed sheets, mints at night, and the morning paper were all nice touches. Downstairs, we especially enjoyed the sun porch, a homey, white-wicker oasis." *(Virginia Britton)* "Owners Cindi and Terry Tatsch were more than willing to share the history of the house and its contents with us." *(Mr. & Mrs. Brian Pace)*

"Not a stodgy museum, Kemah House is an active and dynamic place that happens to be a historic home. It has an indoor waterfall, two player pianos, a beer cellar, and a man-made grotto. *Kemah* means "in the teeth of the wind," an appropriate name, given the inn's location on the crest of a hill overlooking this small resort town. I discussed bicycling with Terry, and read a few of his books on sailing. My wife and I enjoyed the Saturday night pre-dinner party, which gave us a chance to meet the other guests." *(David & Carole Marzke)*

"Furnishings are nearly all period antiques, most of them from Michigan. We stayed in the Master Suite, decorated with nine pieces of French Provincial furniture. The room was airy, extremely pretty, and overlooked Kalamazoo Lake. Breakfast is elegantly served on Art Deco-style china in the sunny dining room." *(Roger & Nancy Nelson)* "Our room was spacious, clean, and beautifully decorated with English charm. Breakfast was served immediately upon our arrival in the dining room, and included coffee, juice, fresh fruit, muffins, and pastries. Our hosts were gracious and accommodating , and the location was perfect, within walking distance of restaurants and night life." *(Julie Malcolm)*

An area for improvement: "The lovely grounds could be improved with a bit more attention."

Open All year.
Rooms 6 doubles—all with maximum of 6 people sharing bath. 4 with fan, 2 with air-conditioning.
Facilities Living room with player piano, dining room, study with fireplace, library with TV, stereo, sun porch, solarium with waterfall, rathskellar, game room with pool table. 2 acres with patios, wooded trails. Off-street parking.
Location 40 m SW of Grand Rapids. 3 blocks from downtown, at the corner of Allegan St./ Pleasant St.
Restrictions No smoking. Inn not suitable for young children.
Credit cards MC, Visa.
Rates B&B, $45–95 double or single. Extra person, $20. Senior discount. 2-night weekend minimum May–Oct.
Extras Bus station pickups. Spanish spoken.

Wickwood Inn
Tel: 616–857–1097
510 Butler Street, 49453

Summer is peak season in Saugatuck, when Lake Michigan and the Kalamazoo River attract boaters, bathers, and fishermen in abundance. Although rates are lower in winter, the Wickwood goes in for Christmas in a big way: from mid-November until mid-January, there's a tree in every bedroom, one in the living room, and one in the garden room. Many tree ornaments are handmade and coordinate with each room's decor. Evergreen garlands, tiny white lights, and unusual displays are everywhere.

Stub and Sue Louis have owned the Wickwood since 1982; Dottie Berghuis is the resident manager. The rooms are individually decorated, the baths are modern and comfortable, and the entire inn is air-conditioned. Continental breakfast is served at the guest's convenience, and a special brunch is prepared on Sundays.

"The rooms are extremely comfortable, visually pleasing, with first-class facilities. Hot coffee, fresh juice, fresh-baked goodies, and the morning paper start each wonderful day. The common rooms make Wickwood a wonderful place for relaxing alone, or for having (BYO) cocktails and hot hors d'oeuvres with the other guests." *(Dr. & Mrs. Birmingham)* "You could eat off the hardwood floors; the bathrooms are meticulously clean, with plenty of hot water for bathing." *(Maureen Schell)*

"Saugatuck is small enough to be friendly and intimate, but it offers interesting shops and art galleries, good restaurants, great beaches, and live theater in summer. The Wickwood's location, right on the edge of the main business district, puts all the shops and restaurants within a few blocks' walk, so parking is never a problem." *(Ben & Connie Forcey)*

"The air in the inn is scented by potpourri, just one of the delicate touches. The furniture is exquisite—country English style." *(Steven Braddon & Kathi Best)* "Manager Dottie Berghuis is bright, bubbly, efficient and an instant friend to all guests. We spent two very rainy days at the inn and were not bored for a moment. Every imaginable table game is available along with a well-stocked library." *(Sara Walters)*

"The Carrie Wicks Suite is a romantic Victorian dream. A wonderful four-poster canopy bed with the softest sheets imaginable, a blazing fire, beautiful hardwood floors, and an Oriental rug. Everywhere you look surprises delight the eye; the decor is eclectic but in the best of taste. Personal touches abound—fresh flowers, a refrigerator stocked with juice and soda, morning paper, and elegant breakfast table or the option of breakfast in bed." *(Jenifer Swanson-Meilleur)* "Charming inn, ideal location." *(Deborah Cortopassi)*

Minor niggles: "Our only regret is that we weren't able to meet the owners." And: "We would have appreciated some afternoon snacks and a cold drink, but none were in evidence."

Open All year except Dec. 24, 25.
Rooms 2 suites, 9 double rooms—all with full private bath, desk, air-conditioning. 1 suite with fireplace.
Facilities Living room with fireplace, library with TV, bar; garden room with games, puzzles; screened gazebo; garden with patio. 1 block to lake/river fishing. Cross-country skiing nearby.
Location SW Michigan. 135 m from Chicago. 2 blocks from town center. "1 sand dune from Lake Michigan."
Restrictions Some street noise in first-floor rooms.
Credit cards Amex, MC, Visa.
Rates MAP, $70–120 suites and doubles. 2-night minimum on weekends. Corporate rates.
Extras Ramp; 1 bedroom/bath equipped for disabled. Airport/station pickups.

SOUTH HAVEN

South Haven is located on Lake Michigan, in the southwestern part of the state, about 2 hours northeast of Chicago, and 3½ hours west of Detroit. Area activities include all the water sports Lake Michigan makes possible (including great beaches), plus golf, cross-country skiing, winery tours, and fruit-picking in season. Summer is the area's busiest season, although the many sugar maples make the fall colors glorious. Winter is the quietest time, although many city visitors savor a pre-Christmas weekend in the country, enjoying the courteous service and free gift wrapping offered in local shops, and bringing home a freshly cut, reasonably priced Christmas tree.

Information please: The Ross House (229 Michigan Avenue, 49090; 616–637–2256) is a century-old Queen Anne-style Victorian home on a quiet, tree-lined street, just two blocks from the beach or downtown riverfront shops. Owners Cathy Hormann and Brad Wilcox include a continental breakfast midweek, and a full one on weekends in the $45–55 double rates for their seven shared bath guest rooms. Guests enjoy the inn's collection of memorabilia from the days when steamers traveled the lakes.

A Country Place B&B ¢   *Tel: 616–637–5523*
North Shore Drive, Route 5, Box 43, 49090

The Niffeneggers invite you to share the slow-paced, relaxing atmosphere of their B&B, opened in 1986. "We encourage guests to sleep in—our full breakfast with lots of home-baked goodies is served leisurely on the deck during the summer and by the fireside in winter. Our quiet location and no-smoking policy work well, bringing us well-educated, well-traveled guests, open to new experiences."

"This restored old farmhouse is very comfortably decorated. The owners, Art and Lee Niffenegger, are very friendly, thoughtful, and accommodating. The house is immaculate, and the parking, plumbing, and lighting were all fine. Just one block away is a large Lake Michigan beach—a perfect place to watch the sunset!" *(Susan Jacques)*

"Pleasant surroundings, screened cedar gazebo, friendly resident cat. Our mattress in the Meadow Room provided solid comfort. The aroma of blueberry crumb cake wafting through the air was second only to its delectable taste; each breakfast brought different treat of fresh fruit, delicious breads and muffins, enjoyed on the spacious deck. We were treated like family yet felt like royalty. The house is a solid structure and very soundproof. Our bathroom was spacious and well designed, with ample hot water and good pressure. Adequate night lighting is a big plus." *(Janice & Milton Johnson, also Elizabeth Locallo)*

Open All year.

Rooms 3 cottages, 5 doubles—all with private bath, ceiling fan. Some with air-conditioning.

Facilities Living/dining room with fireplace, TV/VCR, stereo. Enclosed porch with guest refrigerator, games; deck. 6 acres. 1 block to beach. 1½ m to cross-country skiing.

Location 2 m N of town. From I-196, take Exit 22. Go W on N. Shore Dr. 1 m to inn on left.

Restrictions Light sleepers should request room away from street. No smoking.

Credit cards MC, Visa.

Rates B&B, $55–65 double, $40–65 single. Extra person, $10. Weekly cottage rates. Family rates. 2-night holiday weekend minimum.

Extras Limited wheelchair access. Airport/station pickup.

Yelton Manor
140 North Shore Drive, 49090

Tel: 616–637–5220

A rambling Victorian home, Yelton Manor was built in 1873 for Lulu and Dee Delamere of Chicago. They ran it as a rooming house, and in 1947 it was remodeled as a small hotel. It was restored in 1988 as a B&B by Jay and Joyce Yelton, and was purchased in the spring of 1991 by Elaine Herbert and Robert Kripaitis. The recommendation below precedes the change in ownership, so inquire further when booking.

The outside of this painted lady include soft gray clapboards, contrasting with pale pink fishscale shingles, highlighted by white trim and rose detailing. Inside, the inn is decorated in a country Victorian style with antiques, lace curtains, wing chairs and floral carpeting.

"Outstanding! Ample common areas on the first floors, and lovely guest rooms on the second and third floors. Lots of extra touches: fresh popcorn all the time, candy dishes full, fire always agoing. We stayed in Terry's Room for our anniversary, and loved its Jacuzzi tub, king-sized bed with canopy, and sitting area, along with a dish of fudge and cookies." *(Deborah Cortopassi)*

Open All year.
Rooms 1 suite, 10 doubles—all with private shower and/or bath, air-conditioning. Some with TV, balcony, Jacuzzi tub.
Facilities Dining room, 2 parlors—1 with TV/VCR, 1 with fireplace, den with TV, library, porches. Across street from beach.
Location Take Rte. 196 to Phoenix Street (196 Business). Turn right on Broadway. At drawbridge Broadway turns into Dyckman. Take Dyckman to stop sign. Inn is at left corner of Dyckman and N. Shore Dr.
Restrictions No smoking. "Adults only B&B."
Credit cards Amex, MC, Visa.
Rates B&B, $135 suite, $75–135 double.

TRAVERSE CITY

Although originally developed for their lumber, cherry trees were introduced in the 1880s when the timber supply was exhausted, and the area now supplies over a quarter of the world's cherry crop. As a result, the region is especially lovely when the trees bloom in late May. Visitors can make this small city, set at the head of Grand Traverse Bay, their headquarters for drives up the narrow Old Mission Peninsula, which divides the bay into two narrow arms, or west to Lake Michigan and Sleeping Bear Dunes National Lakeshore. Hiking, fishing, and sailing are popular summer activities, while cross-country, sled-dog racing, and snowmobiling occupy snowy winter days.

Traverse City is located in the northwest side of the Lower Peninsula, at the base of the Leelanau peninsula.

Information please: For a real change of pace, book a berth on the **Tall Ship Malabar** (13390 West Bay Shore Drive, 49684; 616–941–2000) a 105-foot two-masted gaff-rigged Maine-built schooner with eight rustic staterooms. The $148 rate include a full breakfast with the crew. "We only had time for an afternoon sail, but would love to come back for an overnight. A beautiful ship, well cared for. Accommodations as advertised. A little cramped maybe, but adequate, with built-in bunks, fresh linens, towels, and warm blankets. We didn't try the food, but the menu looking appetizing." *(Donna Bocks)*

The Stonewall Inn ¢   *Tel:* 616–223–7800
17898 Smokey Hollow Road, 49684

A Victorian farmhouse built in 1865, the Stonewall Inn was remodeled and enlarged in 1910 in the Colonial Revival style. Owners Pat and John Washburn have decorated with a mixture of Victorian antiques and traditional furnishings. Rates include a continental breakfast.

"One of the most elegant B&Bs we've visited. It has genuine Eastlake antiques and other high quality and tasteful furniture and decor, with water views from some rooms. The continental breakfast usually includes delicious, just-baked muffins or breads." *(Edward Bagley)*

Open Closed Dec. 24 to Jan. 1.
Rooms 5 doubles—3 with private bath, 2 with a maximum of 4 people sharing 1 bath.

Facilities Living room with piano, fireplace; dining room, porches. 6 acres on waterfront.
Location Follow M-37 N for 11½ m, bear right and follow Smokey Hollow Rd. for 3½ m to inn.
Restrictions Smoking restricted.
Credit cards None accepted.
Rates B&B, $75 double. 2-night weekend, holiday minimum.

UNION CITY

The Victorian Villa   *Tel:* 517–741–7383
601 North Broadway, 49094

The Villa dates back to 1876, and has kept much of the ambience of that period, with the addition of some modern conveniences. Each room at the Villa is furnished in a style of the 1800s, from Empire to Edwardian; the Tower Suite is a favorite with newlyweds. Rates include an afternoon beverage and a breakfast of home-baked Amish pastries, muffins, and seasonal fruit.

"The unique condition of this restored home, with its antique furniture and finishings, makes it outstanding. The afternoon refreshments are delightful, and the morning breakfast is superb." *(Claude Saum, also Brian Pauley)*

"An inn of immense charm and indescribably excellent Victorian furnishings. Mr. Gibson has an eye for tiny details such as handsome glassware and for great details such as the best pillows and mattresses I have experienced anywhere. Mr. Gibson himself is a most charming and kind host in an understated way." *(M. Landon Spencer)* More comments required.

Open All year.
Rooms 3 suites, 9 doubles—all with full private bath. 6 with air-conditioning, 6 with fan. 2 rooms with fireplace, 1 with Jacuzzi. 4 rooms in annex.
Facilities 2 parlors with fireplaces, piano, games; dining room, breakfast room. 2-acre grounds with Victorian landscaping.
Location S Central Michigan. 2 hrs. W of Detroit; 3½ hrs. E of Chicago; 1½ hrs. N of Fort Wayne, IN. 2 blocks from downtown. From I-94 take I-69 S to Rte. M-60, Exit 25. Take Rte. M-60 W to Union City. Broadway is main street.
Restrictions No smoking.
Credit cards MC, Visa.
Rates B&B, $85–135 doubles & suites, $80–120 single. Extra person, $10. 2-night weekend minimum May–Oct. Set dinner available Friday and Saturday, $45 per couple. Victorian theme, murder mystery, holiday packages.
Extras Free pickup from train/bus. Crib.

UNION PIER

Long a getaway resort for Chicagoans (it's just a 90-minute drive), Union Pier is located on Lake Michigan, in the southwest corner of the state, about five miles north of the Indiana border. Favorite activities include swimming, fishing, golfing, bicycling, and skiing. Roaming the country roads of Harbor County, looking for antique shops, wineries, orchards, and dunes to explore, is no less appealing.

Reader tip: "To the south is the town of New Buffalo, a sailor's port with a large marina and excellent restaurants, Skip's Other Place and the Miller House. Our other favorite pastime is riding our bikes to visit the nearby wineries—it's ten miles to Tabor Hill Winery. The dunes in Warren Dunes State Park make scenic and relaxing hiking terrain; the beaches there are wide and sandy. If you're there on a weekday, drive to the north end of Lakeshore Drive to the Swedish Bakery; people drive the 50 miles from Chicago every weekend to stock up." *(Dave Marzke)*

The Inn at Union Pier   *Tel:* 616–469–4700
9708 Berrien Road, P.O. Box 222, 49129

Chicagoans are thrilled to have found a relaxing retreat less than two hours' drive around the lake—the Inn at Union Pier, opened in 1985 by Madeleine and Bill Reinke. The inn features an open and sunny great room, inviting decks for summer breakfasts or a soak in the hot tub, and elegantly decorated guest rooms. Lake Michigan's beaches are "just two hundred steps from the front door." A typical summer breakfast might include orange juice, popovers with strawberries and Romanoff sauce, omelets to order, sausages, and English muffins; in cold weather, the menu might feature pumpkin muffins, baked apples, baked egg with bacon, and fried tomatoes.

"Madeleine greets you with a special treat of homemade soup in winter, and fresh baked cookies and lemonade in summer. She really cares about her guests and goes out of her way to make you feel at home. Best of all are the rooms, which are lavishly furnished—comfortable without stuffiness." *(Kathryn Havlish)*

"Winter weekends are particularly nice because almost every room has its own Swedish fireplace. If you've forgotten to bring reading matter, each room has an assortment of books and magazines. Plenty of hot water, thick towels, and truly comfy beds make the individually decorated rooms most relaxing. Breakfasts are leisurely affairs; you'll need plenty of time to eat the multiple courses and savor the homemade muffins. The Reinkes manage to make you feel as though you are guests in their home, yet they aren't hovering about. The location is superb as well—beautiful surroundings close to home yet far away from sounds of traffic or jet planes." *(Ann Scher)* Additional comments appreciated.

Open All year.
Rooms 15 doubles—all with full private bath, radio, desk, air-conditioning. Some with balcony, fireplace. 10 rooms in 2 adjoining buildings.
Facilities Dining room, great room with piano, meeting room, library, decks. 1 acre with hot tub, sauna, hammock, croquet, bicycles. Off-street parking. 1/2 block to Lake Michigan for swimming, fishing, windsurfing. 2 m to cross-country skiing.
Location Take Exit 6 off I-94 N onto Townline Rd. Go .7 m to Red Arrow Highway. Go right .6 m, then turn left on Berrien. Go 1 1/2 blocks to inn on left.
Restrictions No children under 12.

Credit cards MC, Visa.
Rates B&B, $98–125 double. Extra person, $10. 2-3 night minimum weekends, holidays. 3-night midweek stays get reduced rate.
Extras Station pickups. Wheelchair access; baths equipped for disabled.

Pine Garth Inn   *Tel: 616–469–1642*
15790 Lake Shore Road, P.O. Box 347, 49129

We are often asked how the B&B business has changed over the years, and the Pine Garth Inn illustrates this change very well. No longer merely an inexpensive place to stay, many B&Bs have become luxurious destination mini-resorts. Russ and Paula Bulin describe their B&B as a place "to feel relaxed and renewed, to celebrate the uninhibited satisfaction of appetite, companionship, and rest, in a place that makes us feel good. It lets us indulge our need for pure unhurried pleasure, and frees us to receive all sensations with delight."

To this end the Bulins, who opened their B&B in 1988, found an old summer estate right on the lake, complete with a 200-foot sugar sand beach. Nearly all rooms have lake views, and they've restored with great flair, decorating eclectically with country florals, brass beds, and some antiques. Guests who enjoy the feeling of sleeping under the trees may want to request the room done in pink and green florals. Its queen-size four-poster bed is made from unpeeled logs—one of which still has several branches intact! In 1991, they purchased four adjacent cottages, refurbishing them to provide additional accommodations.

"This inn has all the elements essential to a perfect weekend—gracious hosts, sunny charming rooms, an ideal location overlooking Lake Michigan, and fresh, delicious full buffet breakfasts. The owners, Paula and Russ Bulin, have done a fantastic job at creating a quaint, quiet B&B. Each guest room has its own soothing color scheme. Exemplary attention to detail: flowers in each room; amenities basket with Caswell-Massey creams and soaps, toothbrushes and sewing kit; wine and cheese, and tea with delicious homemade chocolate chip cookies are served in the afternoon. Each guest room has a VCR and there's an extensive collection of new and old movies." *(Jessica Slosberg)*

One small (but oft-heard) suggestion: "Our exquisitely decorated room would have been made perfect by the addition of a bedside table and lamp on *my* side of the bed."

Open All year.
Rooms 7 doubles, 4 2-bedroom cottages—all with private bath and/or shower, air-conditioning, fan, telephone, TV, VCR. 4 with whirlpool tub, 3 with private deck, some with fireplace. Cottages with kitchen, gas grill.
Facilities Great room with fireplace, TV, games, video library. 2½ acres with decks, 1-acre sand beach on Lake Michigan, beach chairs.
Location 5 min. walk to town. From I-94 take Union Pier Exit and follow Townline Rd. W past flashing light (Red Arrow Hwy.). Continue to stop sign and turn right on Lakeshore Rd. Continue to inn on left.
Restrictions No smoking in guest rooms. Children welcome in cottage units only.
Credit cards MC, Visa.
Rates Room only, $140–225 cottage. B&B, $65–130 double. 5-night discount. Off-season discount. 2-night weekend minimum June–Sept.
Extras Train station pickups.

Minnesota

Pratt Taber Inn, Red Wing

Minnesota is best known for being a nice place to live. The Twin Cities, Minneapolis/St. Paul, have outstanding theaters, museums, and cultural attractions; the countryside has more lakes than you can count, as well as numerous historic river valleys to explore by boat, foot, or bicycle. Travelers driving up Route 61 to Minneapolis would do well to stop and explore the historic Mississippi River bluff towns of Hastings, Red Wing, Frontenac, Lake City, Winona, and Wabasha. Other recommendations: Pipestone National Monument, a sacred Indian stone quarry in the state's southwestern corner; Jeffers Petroglyphs (north of I-90, off Route 71); and, in far northwestern Minnesota, Grand Portage National Monument, dedicated to the voyagers who used this 8½-mile portage during the area's fur trade.

Rates do not include 6% state sales tax, plus additional local taxes, where applicable.

Information please: Located in the lakes region, 50 miles west of Minneapolis/St. Paul, is the **Thayer Inn** (Highway 55, Annandale, 55302; 612–274–3371). Listed on the National Register of Historic Places, this 1895 restored hotel has long been listed in this guide but with little reader feedback. It was sold in 1991 to Al Lovejoy, who has continued the restoration process. The pressed-tin walls and ceilings and much of the woodwork have been retained. Some of the furniture is original to the building; period antiques, including brass and canopied beds, and handmade quilts complete the decor. The restaurant features specially aged meats and fresh vegetables, along with homemade ice cream and baked goods.

BLUE EARTH

Super Eight Motel ₡ 👫   *Tel:* 507–526–7376
1120 North Grove Street, P.O. Box 394, 56013   800–843–1991

If you're driving through Minnesota on I-90 and need a welcoming place
to stay overnight, this motel may be just the thing. Although we're not
particularly eager to add motels to this guide, particularly large economy
chains like Super Eight, this one's a bit different. It's owned by Ernie and
Mickey Wingen, and all the furniture "with the exception of the chairs"
was built by Ernie. The decor includes Mickey's hand-painted murals over
each bed and her hand-sewn drapes, bedspreads, and blankets. "Although
our decor was originally intended to be early American, it has taken an
international flavor, due to friends from near and far who have sent us
gifts." The continental breakfast is served in a cozy area of the lobby,
complete with fireplace, comfortable seating, and country crafts.

"Rooms are warm, cozy, spotlessly clean, and chock full of early American crafts and touches. Throughout the inn you find stenciled pineapples,
the colonial symbol of 'welcome.' Not to mention homemade cinnamon
rolls, juice, and hot coffee in the morning, and iced tea in the afternoon.
The staff is warm and friendly." *(Susan Vass)*

Open All year.
Rooms 1 suite, 39 doubles—all with full private bath, telephone, TV, desk,
air-conditioning, fan.
Facilities Lobby with fireplace, TV, exercise room with hot tub, bicycle. 1 acre
with garden, fountain. Cross-country skiing, snowmobiling, golf, tennis, swimming
nearby.
Location S central MN. 130 m SW of Minneapolis. 1 m from downtown, ¼ m
from I-90. At the jct. of I-90 and US Hwy. 169.
Credit cards Amex, CB, DC, Discover, MC, Visa.
Rates B&B, $40 suite, $36 double, $32 single. Extra person, $4. No charge for
children under 12. 10% senior discount.
Extras Wheelchair access; 2 rooms equipped for the disabled. Crib.

BROOKLYN CENTER

Inn on the Farm ₡   *Tel:* 612–569–6330
6150 Summit Drive North, 55430

Four restored farm buildings are the setting for this B&B on the grounds
of a Victorian horse farm, now the Earle Brown Heritage Center, just
minutes from downtown Minneapolis. Innkeeper Lynn Mottaz finds that
guests enjoy the country-style comfort while being close to big city
attractions; she notes that the inn is owned by the city of Brooklyn Center,
the only city-owned inn in the state. With Minnesota's chilly winters in
mind, the buildings have all been connected by enclosed glass walkways.
Guest rooms, named for Brown family members or farm staff, are individually decorated with period antiques and reproductions. Afternoon tea is

served daily in the parlor, and the midweek continental breakfast expands to a full breakfast of fresh fruit, wild rice quiche, sausage, French toast and muffins on weekends.

"Quiet setting in the midst of a city. The friendly innkeepers offered evening coffee, cool drinks and cookies by the fireside." *(Marilyn Leiseth)* "Each room is different; the hostess gave us a tour of the inn and gave us our choice of room." *(Mike Schultz)* "Couldn't have been cleaner, friendlier, or more hospitable. Rooms are beautifully done, comfortable, with every amenity you could want." *(Bob & Donna Mennenga, and others)* "Make sure you hear the history of the property and its founder extraordinaire, Earle Brown. Charming breakfast in the gazebo overlooking a pond with a gaggle of ducks." *(Frank & Madaline Renshaw)*

Open All year. Closed Dec. 24, Dec. 25.
Rooms 1 suite, 10 doubles—all with full private whirlpool bath, telephone, TV, desk, air-conditioning, fan. Some with balcony. Rooms in 4 connected buildings.
Facilities Dining room, living room with fireplace. Glass gazebo. 7 ½ acres with picnic area.
Location 10 min. NW of downtown Minneapolis. Just off I-94/694.
Restrictions No smoking. Children 13 and older welcome.
Credit cards Amex, Visa, MC.
Rates B&B, $110–120 suite, $70–90 double, $60–80 single. Extra person, $10.
Extras Wheelchair access.

CHASKA

Bluff Creek Inn ¢　　　　　　　　　　　　　　　　*Tel: 612–445–2735*
1161 Bluff Creek Drive, 55318

A Victorian farmhouse, built in 1864, the Bluff Creek Inn was restored as a B&B in 1984, and was bought by Anne Karels in 1988. Rooms are decorated with family antiques, quilts made by the innkeeper, and designer linens. A full breakfast is served on English china with Bavarian crystal, and an evening snack is left at the bedside.

"An Appalachian carved canopy bed waited in our bedroom, which was furnished with antiques, lace linens, handmade quilts, and baskets. The lavish bathroom had baskets of lotions, talcs, and soaps; beautiful cotton linens hung along with the other towels. Drinking glasses from England were on the shelf with other mementos and a grouping of flowers." *(Evelyn Carey)* "A peaceful and relaxing country getaway with fascinating history and lovely authentic decor. The inn was spotlessly clean and well-maintained. Service and breakfast were first-rate. If possible, try the apple puff pancakes." *(Michelle Mueller)* More comments welcome.

Open All year.
Rooms 4 doubles—1 with private bath, 3 with private half-bath share shower. All with air-conditioning, fan. 2 with balcony.
Facilities Dining room with fireplace, parlor with fireplace, porches. 1 acre. Cross-country skiing, bicycling nearby.
Location SE MN. 30 min. SW of Minneapolis. 3 m from town. From I-494, go W on Rte. 169/212; turn right on Bluff Creek Dr.

Restrictions No smoking. No children under 12.
Credit cards MC, Visa.
Rates B&B, $65–95 double, $60–90 single. Extra person, $25. Midweek, corporate rates. Prix fixe dinner, $25.

COOK

Ludlow's Island Lodge 🏃 🏹
Box 1146, Lake Vermilion, 55723

Tel: 218–666–5407
800–537–5308

The Ludlow family has owned and run this rustic family resort for over 50 years. Mark and Sally Ludlow, the second-generation owners, welcome back a fair share of second-generation guests each year. Sally notes that "our staff caters to families with such activities as pontoon rides, hot dog roasts, marshmallow campfires, nature hikes and fishing contests." The cabins are well spaced out over their small private island, with several more on the nearby south and north shore of the lake. To facilitate your travels between your cabin, the main lodge, and the recreation center, rates include both shuttle service and your personal fishing boat for the week (in addition to free use of their many canoes, kayaks, sailboats, and more). Lake Vermilion is 40 miles long, with 365 islands and 1,200 miles of shoreline, and offers fishing for walleye, northern pike, large and small-mouth bass, plus crappies and panfish.

"A great place for a family vacation! Each of the cabins on the island has a rustic, woodsy feeling, yet they come equipped with a popcorn popper, microwave, dishwasher, and grill. The boats and motors are well-maintained, and the dock staff cleans fish and pays attention to your kids. There are no phones in the guest cabins, but a newspaper is delivered each day so you can 'keep in touch.' The island is safe for kids to explore with little paths connecting the cabins, lodge, and beach areas. They can play basketball, football, tennis, racquetball, or watch a movie on a rainy day." *(Al & Joanne Hinderaker, and others)*

"Neither just a fishing camp nor a luxury resort, Ludlow's strikes a balance between the comforts and conveniences we require for a relaxing family vacation, and the solitude, pristine natural beauty, and good fishing we crave. Mark and Sally are hospitable hosts who place a strong emphasis on service. I wish I could bottle whatever they give to their staff to always keep them smiling, enthusiastic, and looking for ways to be helpful." *(Dr. & Mrs. R. DeAngelo)* "Exactly what I wanted—a clean, quiet cabin with a stone hearth, screened-in porch. Luggage is delivered from your car to your cabin. The terry robes are a thoughtful touch." *(Ruth Ronning)*

Open May 5–Oct. 1.
Rooms 19 cabins, with 1–5 bedrooms, full bath, kitchen with microwave and dishwasher, fireplace, decks or screened porches, barbeque grills; whirlpool tub.
Facilities Lodge with fireplace, TV/VCR, library, game room; grocery store, laundry. Recreation center with 2 tennis courts, racquetball. Children's program, playground, water slide, camping island. 4 acres with lake for swimming, fishing, boating; hiking trails. 5 m to golf.

Location NE MN. 8 m from Cook, 80 m N of Duluth, 225 m N of Minneapolis. From Minneapolis, take Rte. 35 W to Cloquet. Then take Rte. 33 to 53 north to Cook. From Cook, take Rte. 1 E, to 78 N to 540 E to lodge.

Restrictions No smoking in lodge.

Credit cards MC, Amex, Visa.

Rates Room only, $160 double, $675–1,500 weekly; includes 16-foot aluminum boat. Extra person, $20 daily, $60 weekly. Weekly maid service $60 additional. 2-night minimum stay. Fishing, honeymoon package. Alc lunch, $8. Alc dinner, $20.

Extras Airport pickup, $20–60; station pickup, free. Crib, babysitting. Spanish spoken.

CRANE LAKE

Nelson's Resort ⊄ 🏃
7632 Nelson Road, 55725

Tel: 218–993–2295

The northeast corner of Minnesota has more than 1,600 lakes, and sitting next to one is Nelson's Resort. Built in 1931 by John and Millie Nelson, the inn is now run by their daughter, Goldie Pohlman, and her family. With seven *million* acres of U.S. and Canadian wilderness around you, you'll find plenty of outdoors adventures here, from canoeing (forty miles without a portage), to fishing for walleye, lake trout and bass, to wildlife camera excursions.

"Check-in was easy; they remembered everything we'd asked about when we called for a reservation. You park in a central area and all your gear is carted along as you are led along a curving shoreline path to your lakeside peeled log cabin. The whole area is beautifully landscaped—never cramped or crowded—with scattered rock outcroppings, impeccably maintained, and a dock for every two or three cabins. Aspen, birch, pine, and spruce trees dot the area and make up the deep forest directly behind the cabins. Each cabin is different, and is far enough from the next for ample privacy. Chairs are set out for relaxing under trees, on rocks, next to the water.

"Our log cabin—the last one available—was called the 'Last New,' although three more were added afterwards. It had a very adequate dining and sitting area, with rag rugs on the floor, and a fully equipped little kitchen. The interior walls are peeled logs, too and everything was shining clean. The bedroom had plenty of storage space, and pretty little curtains with flowers and partridges. The spotless bathroom even had views of the lake and forest (as did the other rooms).

"The attractive main lodge building has a stone foundation, wood above, and a red roof. There's a sitting area on the upper floor with old leather chairs and sofas, and the nautical bar has a funny player piano with a drum set attached to it, and a xylophone on top. Across from the lodge is a log 'trading post'; baskets of bright red impatiens hang from the porch. The dining room is large but cozy, with yellow table cloths, and copper antiques here and there.

"Like the entire staff, our waiter was friendly and efficient. Dinner started with a relish tray of just-picked pea pods, radishes, and more. The salad was equally crisp and fresh, with homemade salad dressings; the bread was obviously homemade and arrived warm. My broiled walleye was lightly seasoned, accompanied by wild rice and baby carrots. Dessert included a chocolate French silk pie; the portions were ample but not gigantic. Breakfast was cheerfully and quickly served, with big hunks of homemade bread and your choice of eggs or omelets of any kind, pancakes, or French toast. Though we found Nelson's purely by chance, we'd recommend it highly, and look forward to a return visit." *(Suzanne Carmichael)*

Open Mid-May to October 1.
Rooms 27 1-3 bedroom cabins—all with private bath and/or shower. 14 with kitchenette, some with fireplace, screened porch.
Facilities Main lodge with sitting room, TV, fireplace; dining room with fireplace; bar with player piano. Trading post with game room with ping pong, pool table, video games, board games, sauna; gift shop; laundry room. Flower, vegetable gardens. 150-foot sand beach, canoes, boats, kayaks, paddle boats, swimming docks, water slide, water skiing, snorkling, fishing. Playground, children's program, shuffleboard, horseshoes; 3 m of nature trails. Fishing guides, seaplanes.
Location NE MN, at Canadian border. 250 m N of Minneapolis/St. Paul, 30 m NE of Orr. Go N on Rte. 53; W on Cty. Rte. 23/24 & watch for signs.
Credit cards MC, Visa.
Rates Room only, $95 double (May & Sept. only). MAP, $148 double. Full board, $184 double. Extra person, $25–90. 12% service. Weekly rate, 10% midweek discount. Children under 3, free; 3–9 half-price; 10–13, ³/₄ price.
Extras Crib, babysitting.

DULUTH

Developed initially as a logging and mining center, Duluth's setting on Lake Superior has made it a major inland port and grain shipping center. Of particular interest is The Depot, a restored railroad terminal converted into a cultural museum, overlooking a square with old-fashioned shops. Duluth is located in east central Minnesota, 165 miles north of Minneapolis, via I-35, on Lake Superior.

Fitger's Inn   *Tel: 218–722–8826*
600 East Superior Street, 55802   800–726–2982

In this creative preservation, a 100-year-old, historic brewery was converted into an inn, restaurant, and group of specialty shops, called Fitger's On The Lake, listed on the National Register of Historic Places. The lobby has many features of the original building, including a leaded glass skylight, an iron cashier's cage, and hand-crafted oak woodwork. The guest rooms have more of a country decor, with some featuring floor-to-ceiling windows overlooking Lake Superior and original stone walls. The restaurant serves classic American cuisine, with walleye pike a particular favorite.

"Cordial staff. Our street-side room was well-appointed and lighted, charmingly decorated with luxurious touches, and quiet. The inn adjoins three stories of specialty shops and restaurants. A walk along the lake offers a spectacular view of the waterfront and the aerial lift bridge. All in all, a fun, different kind of place to stay." *(Betty Ross)* "A fairly expensive place for the area, but rooms have lots of personality, and some have terrific views." *(JH)*

Minor niggle: "Only 29 parking spaces have easy access to the inn; the others are in the lot for the shopping mall."

Open All year. Restaurant closed Christmas, New Year's Day.
Rooms 6 suites, 42 doubles—all with full private bath, telephone, TV, desk, air-conditioning. Suites with Jacuzzi. 22 rooms in annex.
Facilities Restaurant, bar/lounge with dancing, game room. Room service. Off-street parking. 30 specialty shops in complex. Overlooking Lake Superior for fishing, boating. Downhill and cross-country skiing nearby.
Location 3 blocks from center, 6 blocks E of downtown.
Credit cards Amex, DC, MC, Visa.
Rates Room only, $135–270 suite, $85–105 double, $80–100 single. Extra person, $10. No charge for children under 17. Alc breakfast, $3–6; alc lunch, $6; alc dinner, $15–20.
Extras Wheelchair access; 2 guest rooms fully equipped. Crib, babysitting.

Mathew S. Burrows 1890 Inn
1632 East First Street, 55812

Tel: 218–724–4991

Opened in 1989 under the enthusiastic ownership of Pam and Dave Wolff, The Mathew S. Burrows 1890 Inn is furnished with period antiques. The Master Suite has the original bath with oversized footed tub and marble full-body spray shower. Pam reports: "Our guests just love it, and we call it our vertical whirlpool." A full breakfast is served at 9 A.M. by candlelight in the dining room, with a cathedral stained glass window.

"A beautiful Victorian home. Our suite had a sitting room with a partial view of the lake, and everything was clean and inviting. Pam and Dave are warm and friendly people who greeted us with hot cider and home-made bread on a cool, rainy day. Baroque music playing softly in the background added to the atmosphere. Breakfasts were excellent." *(Mark & Mary Kay Vance)*

Open All year.
Rooms 2 suites, 2 doubles—all with private bath and/or shower. 1 suite with fireplace.
Facilities Dining room, library with fireplace, music room with fireplace, player piano; gazebo with hammock, porch, garden.
Location 4 blocks from Lake Superior. From Rte. 35 take Exit 35W. Go East on Superior Street to 17th Avenue. Turn left, go ½ block to inn on left.
Restrictions No smoking. No children.
Credit cards MC, Visa.
Rates B&B, $75–120 suite or double. 2-night weekend minimum for advance reservations.

Stanford Inn ¢
1415 East Superior Street, 55805

Tel: 218–724–3044

The first house on the block when built in 1886, the Stanford Inn had descended from the elegance of a private home to the grim realities of a boarding house, when it was rescued in 1987 by owners Doug Stromley and Kevin Fairbanks. They have removed suspended ceilings, refinished miles of woodwork and floors, and stripped away layers of wallpaper and paint to bring back the house's original charm, garnering an award from the Duluth Preservation Alliance in the process. Now guests can view the hand-gilded tin ceiling and original stained glass windows in appropriate period atmosphere, complete with Bradbury & Bradbury reproduction wallpapers and lace curtains. Doug is now on assignment for AT&T in California, so Ron Garatz is managing the inn is his absence. Breakfast menus vary, but might include fruit cup with orange cream sauce, muffins, peach French toast, and cheese quiche.

"The two parlors are decorated in late Victorian and Mission era furnishings, arranged for both comfort and appearance. The colors and patterns of the paint and wallpaper were striking, adding warmth to the rooms. I especially liked the gilded tin ceiling in the front parlor; although not original to the house, it is a real enhancement. Most guest rooms have a small alcove with a small table, two chairs and an antique tea service— ideal for enjoying an early cup of coffee from the thermos pitcher placed outside our door. We stayed in the Brass Room, with a heavy antique bass bed and lace accents." (Jim & Krisha Pennino)

Room for improvement: "Although the innkeepers may already have seen to it, a light in the alcove, a scatter rug by the bed, and additional storage would have made our lovely room a bit more comfortable."

Open All year.
Rooms 1 suite, 3 doubles—1 with full private bath & TV, 3 rooms sharing 2 baths.
Facilities Dining room with veranda. 2 parlors, 1 with fireplace, TV.
Location From Rte. 35, take Exit 35; go E on East Superior Street 3 blocks to inn.
Restrictions Smoking restricted to parlor.
Credit cards Amex, MC, Visa.
Rates B&B, $90 suite, $65–75 double.

EXCELSIOR

Christopher Inn
201 Mill Street, 55331

Tel: 612–474–6816

You may have been to many Howard Johnson's in your travels, but we can guarantee that you've never stayed at one like this inn, owned by the Howard Johnson family. Built in 1887 and listed on the National Register of Historic Places, the Christopher Inn is a classic Victorian mansion, with lots of gables and porches. Its restoration in 1985 by Joan and Howard Johnson resulted in a handsome decor combining Laura Ashley fabrics with late Victorian furnishings. "We are a Christian family and attempt to promote a Christian atmosphere with peaceful serenity." Breakfast includes fresh fruit and juice, served with such specialities as eggs Benedict on croissants, seafood strata, or Swedish pancakes with apples.

"The house sits on a hill at the edge of town and is surrounded by a huge lawn with many shade trees, and is furnished with Victorian antiques and reproductions. We had a nice lake view from one window in our room. Complimentary mineral water was set on a table for us and ice was available in the kitchen. Our room smelled as fresh as it looked, with a slight scent of potpourri. We had an old-fashioned claw foot tub which my daughter enjoyed using. Later in the evening, dessert and coffee were set out in the upstairs hall. Breakfast was served in the elegant dining room. A fireplace graced one wall and the tables were set with linen cloths, fine china and crystal, and dried flower arrangements. We feasted on peach Melba, juice, and French toast topped with apricot preserves and butter. Though it is just a short drive from Minneapolis, you feel like you are in a small town; within walking distance of the inn are many antique shops." *(Chrys Bolk)*

Open All year.
Rooms 8 doubles—6 with private bath and/or shower, 2 with maximum of 4 people sharing bath. All with radio, desk, air-conditioning; telephone on request. 2 with fireplace.
Facilities Dining room with fireplace, porch. 1½ acres with gardens, croquet, tennis court. Bicycles, cross-country skiing. Across street from Lake Minnetonka for fishing, boating, swimming.
Location 15 m E of Minneapolis. 2 blocks from center. From (I-694, take I-494 to Hwy. 7. Go W on Hwy. 7 to Excelsior.
Restrictions No smoking. No unmarried couples. Children by prior arrangement.
Credit cards Amex, CB, DC, MC, Visa.
Rates B&B, $115–120 suite, $65–100 double. Extra adult, $20. 20–50% midweek discount.
Extras Wheelchair accessible; 1 room specially equipped. Crib.

GOOD THUNDER

Cedar Knoll Farm B&B   *Tel:* 507–524–3813
Route 2, Box 147, 56037

A contemporary Cape Cod-style home is the heart of Cedar Knoll Farm, a working farm bordered by the ravines of the Cobb River. Dormered guest rooms are furnished in an eclectic blend of Minnesota, Pennsylvania, and European antiques and collectibles. Owner Mavis Christensen reports that "guests are welcome to feed watermelon rinds or vegetables to our horse—he's a real salad lover." She starts each day with a tray of juice to each room, and then, in the dining room, serves a breakfast which might include fruit, sweet rolls or bread, a meat dish, pancakes or eggs, home fries and ham, quiche or perhaps apple pie, or on occasion, a breakfast shish-kebab.

"Mavis welcomed our last-minute reservation, and apologized because a 7:30 A.M. meeting would prevent her from providing her usual breakfast. We were glad we decided to come—the entire second floor is turned over to guests, with three comfortable rooms, each with a double bed, ideal for a family or a group traveling together. Antiques, art, and family heirlooms are all cleverly displayed. We felt welcome and at home, and were invited to prepare our own breakfast the next morning. When our hostess returned from her meeting, we accompanied her to the barn to feed the sheep, hens, and horse. Mavis called her farm a peaceable kingdom and indeed it was." *(Betty Ross)*

Open All year.
Rooms 4 doubles—1 with shared family bath, 3 sharing 1 bath.
Facilities Living room, family room, dining room, kitchen, screened porch, patio. 138 acres with working farm.
Location S central MN. 10 m S of Mankato. S Lakes Region. Take Rte. 22 S from Mankato & go 10 m to Beauford. At Beauford, go right (W) on Rte. 10 & go 1.5 m. Watch for sign on right (N) side of Rte. 10. From W, inn is 4.1 m E of Good Thunder.
Restrictions No smoking in guest rooms, barns, woods.
Credit cards None accepted.
Rates B&B, $45 double, $35 single. First child, $10; any additional, $5 each. Family rates.
Extras Wheelchair access. Crib. Pets in barn by prior arrangement.

GRAND MARAIS

Located on Lake Superior in the far northeast corner of Minnesota, Grand Marais is a popular resort for those enjoying water sports in summer, and skiing in winter. It's also the beginning of the Gunflint Trail, leading north into the wilderness of Superior National Forest and Boundary Waters Canoe area.

Also recommended: Although this B&B is too small for a full write-up with only one guest room, contributing editor *Suzanne Carmichael* sent us a rave report on her visit to **Young's Island B&B** (Gunflint Trail, HC 64, Box 590, 55604; 218–388–4487 or 800–322–8327), 32 miles from Grand Marais. Hosts Barbara and Ted Young share their Swedish-style log home and 18-acre private island with guests, and will pick you up in their boat. "There's a screened-in, glassed-in old fashioned porch that's very large, filled with rag rugs and antique wicker rockers. You look out at islands across the way—you can't see any other sign of civilization. Inside are lots of antiques, Oriental rugs, and comfortable furnishings. Up two steps is a warm family kitchen with an enormous antique cook stove. The guest room is quite small but very comfortable, done in blue and white. Breakfasts are wonderful. We had pineapple/banana juice; blueberry muffins; eggs scrambled with mushrooms, onion, bacon, and cheese; sausage patties; and a fresh fruit plate with two kinds of grapes, cantaloupe and bananas. You go off-island for dinner, then return for a scrumptious dessert—raspberry shortcake or homemade sundaes. The B&B is open year-round; in winter the Youngs offer yurt-to-yurt dog-sledding or cross-country skiing trips.

Received too late for a full write-up was an enthusiastic report on the **Rockwood Lodge & Outfitters** (Gunflint Trail, HC 64, Box 625, 55604; 800–942–BWCA). Located 30 miles north of Grand Marais, Rockwood offers a rustic log lodge with a handsome stone fireplace and a well-known restaurant, a lakeside location for fishing and swimming, and private modern cabins set along the lake, equipped with kitchenettes and private baths. There's hiking right from your door, and canoes, motor boats, and other gear can be rented for exploring the Boundary Waters Canoe Area (BWCA). "Two generations of Austins run the lodge, and are about the nicest people you'll ever meet. The restaurant and cabins look just like the pictures in the brochures—not doctored up for the photographer—complete with handmade chairs and a big moose head over the mantle. Delicious meals (no lunch) with homemade bread." *(Yvonne & Arnold Miller)* Also: "We stopped by for dinner, and loved the look of the restaurant; perhaps we hit an off night, because we found the food bland, the service slow."

Information please: In the northeasternmost corner of the state, 2½ hours northeast of Duluth, and about 36 miles from Grand Marais is the **Grand Portage Lodge** (Box 307, Grand Portage, 55605; 218–475–2401 or 800–232–1384), on the Grand Portage Indian Reservation (owned and run by them). Though not a small hotel, the lodge offers 100 well-furnished rooms, a handsome lobby with Native American artifacts, on-site gambling, and a gift shop selling authentic Indian crafts. Nearby is Grand Portage National Monument, worth a visit in itself and the place to get the ferry for Isle Royale.

Cascade Lodge ¢ 🏃 ✕

Tel: 218–387–1112

Highway 61, East Star Route, Box 490, 55604   In MN: 800–322–9543

Cascade Lodge is set in the Cascade River State Park on the shore of Lake Superior. The resort includes guest rooms in the main lodge, log cabins with fireplace, housekeeping cabins and a small motel. As Gene and Laurene Glader, owners since 1981, describe it: the main attractions of the area are provided by God: "Superior National Forest, Lake Superior, the inland lakes, the Boundary Waters Canoe area, the fish and the wildlife. The secondary attractions are the recreational facilities and services that resorts such as Cascade Lodge provide."

"We reached our romantically decorated, rustic cabin by crossing a private bridge over a small brook. The cabin had a fireplace and a modern bath. The lodge has a restaurant offering good food at reasonable prices; it's decorated with numerous wildlife heads and skins. Also available are comfortable common rooms and a game room in the basement. We discovered during our vacation around Lake Superior that it can be difficult to find nice accommodations and were very happy with Cascade Lodge. One note of caution—the facility is, at times, entirely booked by bus tours." *(Jeff & Terri Patwell)* "An excellent place for families, with reasonably priced and delicious food. The area is very pretty, overlooking Lake Superior, with woods surrounding the lodge area." *(KJ)*

Open All year. Restaurant closed Christmas Day.
Rooms 1 suite, 16 doubles, 10 cabins—all with private shower and/or bath, desk. 8 with TV. 2 with whirlpool. Some with telephone. Rooms in Main Lodge, motel, and cabins.
Facilities Restaurant, gift shop, TV lounge, fireplace lounge, game room with pool table, Ping-Pong, games. 14 acres; surrounded by Cascade River State Park. Badminton, horseshoes, hiking, fishing, berry picking, 40 m of cross-country ski trails. Bicycle, canoe, fishing gear rentals. Naturalist conducts evening lectures, slide shows, movies. 9 m to downhill skiing. Golf, tennis, heated swimming pool nearby.
Location NE MN. 100 m NE of Duluth. 9 m S of Grand Marais, on Hwy. 61.

Restrictions Light sleepers should request rooms away from the lodge.
Credit cards Amex, MC, Visa.
Rates Room only, $65–130 suite, $40–110 double, $30–100 single. Extra adult in room, $8–10; extra child age 7–17 $4. 10% senior discount. Alc lunch, $5.50; alc dinner, $11.
Extras Airport pickup. Crib, babysitting. German, Finnish spoken.

Naniboujou Lodge ¢ ♁ ✗

Tel: 218–387–2688

Highway 61, North Shore Drive Star Route 1, Box 505, 55604

Naniboujou was planned in the 1920s as a private club; Babe Ruth, Jack Dempsey, and Ring Lardner were among its charter members. The lodge's most striking feature is its dining room, with the largest native rock fireplace in Minnesota and walls and windows painted brightly with Cree Indian designs. The club couldn't survive the Crash and went bankrupt shortly thereafter. In 1985 Tim and Nancy Ramey bought Naniboujou, now listed on the National Register of Historic Places, and restored it as a comfortable family resort.

"This beautiful lodge is located on the north shore of Lake Superior, where there are many hiking trails and waterfalls, including a spectacular one right across the road. The Brule River, with its great trout fishing, is a few steps from the door. It's in the midst of state and national forests, and one can experience the pleasure of the north woods without the discomforts of primitive camping." *(Marilyn & Arthur Hanson)* " My room faced Lake Superior and I could hear the Brule River nearby. The lodge is very clean and well-kept." *(Pam Little)*

"The Lodge is set back from the highway, halfway between the road and a short bluff overhanging a beach along Lake Superior. The first glimpse one gets is of a very unusual, yet intriguing building—with natural brown shingles and yellow and orange shutters. The overall feeling of the lodge is low key and friendly. The dining room has a 30-foot-high massive stone fireplace with rocks set in a sunburst pattern. The vaulted ceiling is a riot of color without being garish at all. The pointed windows and unusual light fixtures complement the overall geo-metric effect. The solarium stretches the length of the dining room (but is set off completely from it), with comfortable furniture set in conversa-tional groupings.

"The food here is superb. We started off with an hors d'oeuvre of baked brie with raspberry-honey mustard. Homemade ranch dressing with a balsamic vinegar tang complemented crisp lettuce, grated carrots, and red cabbage, topped with toasted wild rice. My entrée of three kinds of pasta with pesto, fresh tomato, artichoke hearts, onion, and toasted pinenuts was hearty without being heavy; the individual flavors blended well but kept their own character. Dessert wasn't up to the same standard. For breakfast, I had eggs with cream cheese, chives, and onions with home-made wheat bread. Nice classical music played in the background.

"We stayed in Room #16, recently refurbished room with a tall ceiling, snugly set under the eaves. It had Craftsman-style oak furniture, a comfortable double bed with a beige handmade coverlet, a nice greyish blue rug, a fireplace, and windows looking over thick lawn towards the lake." *(SC)*

Areas for improvement: "We were told that all the rooms are gradually being redone; we'd strongly recommend requesting one that's been refurbished." And a minor niggle: "The dining room is so gorgeous that I was amazed to see paintings of moose and deer on black velvet in the upstairs hall."

Open Mid-May through mid-Oct.; week between Christmas and New Year's; weekends only Jan. through March.
Rooms 27 doubles—21 with private bath and/or shower, 6 with maximum of 6 people sharing bath. All rooms with fan. Some rooms with fireplace.
Facilities Dining room with fireplace, solarium with games, TV, library; gift shop. 15 acres on Lake Superior and Brule River with hiking, interpretative nature trail, river swimming, fishing, children's play equipment, lawn games. Cross-country skiing nearby.
Location NE MN. 125 m NE of Duluth, 275 m NE of Minneapolis, 65 m SW of Thunder Bay, Ontario. 15 m NE of Grand Marais, on Hwy. 61.
Restrictions No alcohol in public rooms. Minimal soundproofing between rooms.
Credit cards Discover, MC, Visa.
Rates Room only (summer), $40–72 double, $35–48 single. Winter packages, $260 double, $175 single. Alc lunch, $4–5; alc dinner, $10–15. Picnic lunches available.
Extras Limited wheelchair access. Crib, babysitting.

HASTINGS

The Rosewood & Thorwood Inns   *Tel:* 612–437–3297
Rosewood: 620 Ramsey, 55033
Thorwood: 315 Pine, 55033

Hastings is a historic riverfront town, with 62 buildings listed on the National Register of Historic Places. Two of them are The Rosewood and Thorwood Inns, nearby 1880 mansions, rescued from demolition by Dick and Pam Thorsen and restored as B&Bs. The former is built in the Queen Anne style, the latter in French Second Empire. The restoration included the addition of elegant private bathrooms, some in marble, for every room. While the two inns have a number of lovely, reasonably priced double rooms, furnished with period antiques, Victorian country fabrics and wall-coverings, and canopy, sleigh, or brass beds, they are perhaps best known for their extravagant suites. At Rosewood, "Mississippi under the Stars" encompasses 1,200 feet and six skylights to recapture the Victorian vogue for a Turkish hideaway, swathed in paisley fabrics and oozing such sybaritic luxuries as a double whirlpool tub in front of the fireplace, plus a copper soaking tub and round shower in the bath area. In the morning you can choose to have breakfast in the dining room, on the porch, or delivered to your room; guests are also offered an evening snack and local wine. The location is ideal for hiking, swimming, bicycling, golf, and tennis, and of course skiing in winter.

"We stayed in Isabelle's Room at Rosewood, with ruffles, frills, and a very comfortable sleigh bed; warm, delicious brownies and fruit were placed at our bedside. The all-season porch connected to it had a wicker swing and a lovely view. Breakfast was a dream, in a basket delivered to our door. Winery, cross-country skiing, nature paths, and antiques shopping are all nearby. If Thorwood is anything like Rosewood, it is a very special place indeed." *(Liba & Tom Stillman)*

Open All year.
Rooms 3 suites, 11 doubles—all with private bath and/or shower. 6 with fireplace, 8 with double whirlpool tub, 2 with enclosed porch. Rooms in 2 buildings.
Facilities 2 parlors, dining rooms, porches. Hiking, cross-country & downhill skiing, golf, tennis, bicycling, fishing, swimming nearby.
Location SE MN. 25 m SE of Minneapolis/St. Paul. Thorwood: 4th & Pine; Rosewood: 7th & Ramsey.
Restrictions Children not encouraged. No smoking.
Credit cards Amex, MC, Visa.
Rates B&B, $100–225 suite, $75–150 double. Midweek, off-season rates. Dinner packages. 2-night weekend minimum.

LANESBORO

Mrs. B's Historic Lanesboro Inn ¢ ✗   Tel: 507–467–2154
101 Parkway, 55949

Lanesboro is a historic town, most of whose buildings date back to the 19th century. Walled in by wooded bluffs, the village is set on the Middle Fork of the Root River, surrounded by farmland and hardwood forests. By some fortuitous fluke of nature, the area is virtually free of mosquitoes.

The Lanesboro Inn was a furniture shop and undertaker's parlor for about 110 years until previous owners Nancy ("Mrs. B") and Jack Bratrud converted it into an inn and restaurant in 1982. Rooms are furnished with antiques, comfortable chairs, and good lamps. The inn was sold in March, 1991, to Bill Sermeus and Mimi Abell, who plan to continue on the fine path established by the Bratruds. "We hope to keep the same quiet, rural, historic, picturesque, nurturing feeling, with emphasis on comfort, peace, beauty, good plumbing, thick towels, and fresh food. The restaurant style will also remain the same—new American cuisine," reports Bill.

"It has been our good fortune to visit inns throughout much of the western world. Those that we value most have several things in common—an appealing setting (both house and terrain), grand guests, gratifying food and drink, and gracious innkeepers. This combination of virtues makes for a most enjoyable ambience—one so attractive that coming back seems the most natural thing to do. So it is with Mrs. B's." *(Richard and Helga Van Iten)* (This quote precedes the change of ownership; we are eager to hear from guests who have stayed at Mrs. B's since then). More reports required.

Open All year. Restaurant closed Mon., Tues.
Rooms 9 doubles—all with private bath and/or shower, desk, air-conditioning. Telephone, radio, TV on request.
Facilities Lobby with library, piano; bar, dining rooms, decks, porches, garden; bicycles. Cross-country skiing, paved 35-mile bike trail from door. Tennis, canoeing, tubing, hiking, trout fishing, golf, spelunking nearby.
Location SE MN. 120 m SE of Minneapolis, 120 m NW of Cedar Rapids, IA, 300 m NW of Chicago, IL. In center of village.

Restrictions Smoking restricted.
Credit cards None accepted.
Rates B&B, $48—90 double. Extra person, $10. Prix fixe dinner, $20, plus tax, tip, drinks by advance reservation; early theater suppers on Wed., Sun.
Extras Dining room, 1 bedroom has wheelchair access.

MINNEAPOLIS

Minneapolis is a very inviting modern city, as is its slightly more old-fashioned sister city across the Mississippi, St. Paul. Known for its exceptional cultural and educational facilities, it offers outstanding restaurants, theaters, and museums and the largest single college campus in the U.S., the University of Minnesota, with about 65,000 students. Modern art fans should head over to the Walker Art Center and Sculpture Garden, and perhaps stay for an evening performance at the renowned Guthrie Theater. Children of all ages will enjoy the city's fine zoo, as well as its extensive network of lakes and parks for bicycling, jogging, swimming, boating, and cross-country skiing.

Information please: For rooms filled with beautiful Art Deco furnishings and stained glass, **Evelo's B&B** offers a friendly atmosphere, filling and healthy breakfasts and modest prices for shared bath accommodation (2301 Bryant Avenue South 55405; 612—374—9656). Only four blocks from downtown is **Linné B&B** (2645 Fremont Avenue South, 55408; 612—377—4418), an 1896 Queen Anne home constructed by Swedish immigrants and named for 18th century Swedish naturalist Carl von Linné. The three guest rooms, furnished with period antiques and reproductions, share a bath and the reasonable rates include a full breakfast on weekends and a continental breakfast midweek. Reports?

For additional entries, see St. Paul.

Nicollet Island Inn ✕   *Tel:* 612—331—1800
95 Merriam Street, 55401

Built in 1893, this limestone building on Nicollet Island began life as a company making wooden window sashes and doors. After a stint as a Salvation Army headquarters, the inn was virtually gutted and restored. Rooms are decorated with period antiques and reproductions, and rates include morning coffee and the paper, and turndown service.

"Nicollet Island sits in the middle of the Mississippi River in downtown Minneapolis, and is a wonderful place to explore. To the south, is a well-kept park with lots of cottonwood trees and grass; just across the bridge to the west is Riverplace, an attractive amalgamation of chic shops, restaurants, and even a comedy club in refurbished warehouses. You enter the inn through big oak doors with beveled glass windows, into an attractive welcoming area with a grandmother clock, oak flooring, large rug, comfortable wing chairs, and a high tin ceiling painted light aqua. More comfortable chairs, and a sofa facing a small fireplace are found in a second sitting area, along with a miniature old-fashioned carousel horse, and duck decoys. There's a beautiful green marble bar with stools, as well as a section with wing chairs and sofas. The bar is separated from the dining room by modern stained-glass windows. The outside tables and chairs are perfect for a cool drink on a humid summer day.

"The handsome dining room contrasts large windows with dark woodwork; the best tables are by the windows overlooking over the Mississippi and the bridge. The food was good—not great—but a decent value, and highlighted by the wild rice soup—creamy with wild rice, carrots, mushrooms, almonds, and a splash of wine. Our breakfast of freshly squeezed grapefruit juice, perfectly scrambled eggs and sausage was served quickly and efficiently. Even the hallways and elevator are decorated with care and thought, enhancing the old building's charm.

"The best rooms are #209 and 309, on the corner with river views. Numbers 204, 304, 206, 306, 207, and 307 are somewhat smaller, but also look out at the river. The other rooms overlook the parking lot and the uninspiring Minneapolis skyline. We stayed in room #309, a spacious room with black, white and red wallpaper, and black carpeting, and a subdued, pleasant, clubby feel to it. Two windows are set in deep casements that look out towards the river; the third faces the park. The furniture included undistinguished but attractive oak, and two comfortable armchairs. The tiled bathroom was also done in white with black accents, and had particularly thick towels." *(SC)*

Open All year.
Rooms 2 suites, 22 doubles—all with private full bath, telephone, radio, TV, desk, air-conditioning.
Facilities Restaurant, pub with live music, lobby, patio, garden, off-street parking.
Location On island in middle of Mississippi River. Between downtown and Riverplace. Heading NE on Hennepin Ave., cross river at Henn. bridge. Go right on Main St. at light. E. Henn. is at next light; go straight onto Cobblestone Rd. (ignore sign saying rd. is closed). ½ block on right is Merriam St. bridge; go right, then straight through stop sign to inn on right. Heading SW on Hennepin, go left on Main St. before crossing river; then as above.
Restrictions No smoking in guest rooms.
Credit cards Amex, CB, DC, Discover, MC, Visa.
Rates Room only, $100–130 suite or double. Extra person, $10. Alc breakfast, $4–8; alc lunch, $5–11; alc dinner, $12–35. Packages available. Corporate rates.
Extras Wheelchair access; 2 rooms equipped for handicapped. Airport/station pickup. Crib. French, Swedish, Italian, Greek, Spanish spoken.

The Whitney Hotel ✕
150 Portland Avenue, 55401

Tel: 612–339–9300
800–248–1879

For a memorable stay in Minneapolis, readers unanimously recommend the Whitney, a luxury hotel located in a retrofitted 19th-century flour mill, in the historic riverfront mill district. Decorated in rich, dark, slightly masculine tones of deep brown, moss green, peach, and ivory, the hotel claims one staff member for each of its 97 rooms. The traditional decor includes burnished mahogany and cherry woods; brass chandeliers, door handles, and bath fixtures; marble floors and vanities; four-poster beds and wingback chairs. The extensive free amenities list includes the morning paper, in-room hair dryers, bathrobes, toiletries, evening turndown service with chocolates, and free limousine service to the business district and downtown. The Whitney Grille offers classic American cuisine in elegant surroundings (try the pheasant with Minnesotan wild rice, and don't resist anything chocolate for dessert), while the Garden Plaza awaits for casual outdoor meals (weather permitting).

"Very European and top-of-the-line in furnishings, service, and food. Truly exquisite, and the weekend packages are very reasonable." *(Kathleen Novak)* "Our first stay was such a pleasure that we went out of our way to come back. They even put together an English high tea for my wife Doris that put the one at the Empress in Victoria to shame." *(Willard Parker)* "Everything was exactly as you described. Although we arrived in the middle of the night (2 A.M.), we were asked what papers we wanted and they arrived bright and early that morning." *(Susan Roach)*

"One of America's top hotels. From the moment you enter the lobby, you are welcomed with efficient, considerate, and gracious service. The lobby is small, elegant yet friendly. Our duplex suite had a first floor bath, bar area, and living room with comfortable overstuffed off-white contemporary furniture. The wall at the end (with windows overlooking the outside courtyard, the Mississippi and other sights), stretched to the ceiling of the second story. Up a curving wrought-iron stairway is the bedroom—an enormous room with understated but very tasteful contemporary furnishings and a spacious bathroom, and a second TV.

"We went for a drink in the inner courtyard, and took corny photos of each other next to the giant chess board with six-foot pieces, then ordered a light meal from room service. The menu was inventive, the food superb, and the presentation, punctuality, and temperature of the food were just right. What impressed us the most, however, was the service. Anything you wanted came immediately. *Everyone* knew your name, what room you were in, and what you'd asked for last ('just wanted to make sure you got that extra towel you requested'). And all of it done in a cultured, respectful, and friendly way. We've never had better hotel service." *(Suzanne Carmichael)*

A minor note of caution: "Typical of many cities, the commercial district in which The Whitney is located is fairly deserted at night. Although the hotel is an excellent place for a single woman to stay, don't go walking alone after dark."

Open All year.
Rooms 97 suites and doubles—all with full private bath, 2 telephones, radio, TV, air-conditioning. 40 with wet bar, refrigerator.
Facilities Lobby, restaurants with entertainment, bar/lounge, 24-hour room service. Courtyard with fountain, benches, walking paths, gardens. Free parking; valet service. Athletic club privileges.
Location Historic Mill District; 7 blocks to business district. On Portland Ave., between 1st and 2nd sts. From I-94 E take 5th Ave. exit. Follow 5th Ave. 8 blocks to Washington Ave. and go right, then left on Portland Ave. to hotel. From I-94 W take 4th Ave. exit. Turn right on 10th St. S and go 1 block to 5th Ave. From Rte. 35 W, take 5th Ave. exit.
Restrictions No smoking in some guest rooms.
Credit cards Amex, DC, MC, Visa.
Rates Room only, $185–800 suite, $150–160 double. Extra person, $20. Weekend rate: $125 suite, $95 double. Alc lunch, $15; alc dinner, $28.
Extras 4 rooms equipped for disabled. Pets in cages permitted, by prior arrange-

ment. Free limousine service to business district. Crib. Spanish, French, German spoken. Member, Preferred Hotels.

NEW PRAGUE

Information please: Seven miles east of New Prague is the **Archer House** (212 Division Street, Northfield, 55057; 507–645–5661), an imposing French Second Empire hotel with 28 suites and doubles, recently renovated in turn-of-the-century country decor. It's located in Northfield, home to Carleton College, about 30 miles south of Minneapolis. Reports?

Schumacher's New Prague Hotel ✕   *Tel:* 612–758–2133
212 West Main Street, 56071

When John Schumacher bought the New Prague Hotel in 1974, this 1898 Georgian Revival hotel (designed by the architect of Minnesota's Capitol) was a $2.50-a-night rooming house. Since then, Schumacher and his wife Kathleen have invested tremendous amounts of time and money in restoring, remodeling, and upgrading it. New Prague has a large Czech and German population, and John decided the inn should reflect the heritage of those two countries. Accordingly, the guest rooms—named for the months of the year—are decorated with Bavarian decor, hand-painted European folk art, and plump down pillows and eiderdown featherbeds; nearly all have double whirlpools baths and many have fireplaces, and are intended for special-occasion romance. The inn's restaurant is famous, and the Schumachers take no less care with the food than the decor. Everything is made from scratch of the finest ingredients, and the Central European motif is carried through the imported furnishings to the menu, written in English and Czech. Specialities include roast duck; rabbit roasted with caraway, onions, and mushrooms; pheasant with mushrooms and shallots; venison with red currant sauce; veal paprika or schnitzel; homemade Czech and German sausage; and sauerbraten. A variety of dumplings, red cabbage, salads, and homemade sweet and rye rolls accompany the entrées. A roast goose dinner, complete with Czech dumplings and dressing, and cherry strudel for dessert, is served from Thanksgiving through Christmas. *(JH)* More comments welcome.

Open Closed Dec. 24, 25.
Rooms 11 doubles—all with private bath and/or shower, telephone, stereo, air-conditioning, fan, whirlpool tub. 7 with gas fireplace. TV on request.
Facilities 3 dining rooms, bar, lobby with piano, game room with pool table, gift shop. Evening entertainment can be arranged. Swimming, tennis, golf, canoeing, biking nearby. 20 m to cross-country skiing.
Location S MN, LeSueur County. 45 m S of Minneapolis/St. Paul. Center of town. From Minneapolis, take 35W to 19 West.
Restrictions Light sleepers should request quietest rooms. No smoking in guest rooms.
Credit cards Amex, Discover, MC, Visa.

Rates Room only, $100–142 double. Corporate rate; senior packages. Alc dinner $35.
Extras Limited wheelchair access; restaurant bathroom equipped for the disabled

---

ONAMIA

Izatys Golf & Yacht Club 🏃 🎿
Lake Mille Lacs, 56359
In Mnpls: Suite M, 5555 West 78th Street,
Edina 55435

Tel: 612–532–310
800–533–172

In Mnpls: 612–829–089

If your kids can learn to pronounce Izatys (eye-zatees) and Onamia (oh-name-ia), reward them with a trip to this relaxing family resort, set on the shores of the redundantly named Lake Mille Lacs. All will enjoy it well-equipped facilities, and the club restaurant will ensure that you family's chief cook and bottle washer can enjoy a vacation too.

"Our very attractive unit included a first floor with living room, dining area, fully equipped kitchen and bath. The second floor had two bedroom and another bathroom. Everything was decorated in muted colors. Sliding doors led out to a patio and then across a large expanse of lush green grass dotted with trees, to the lake. You had the feeling of privacy even though other units were wall to wall with yours. Dinner is served on the second floor of the clubhouse, with sweeping views of the lake and marina." *(SC*

Open All year.
Rooms 58 2-4 bedroom townhouses—all with full private baths, telephones radio, TV/VCR, air-conditioning, fireplace, patio, kitchen.
Facilities Clubhouse with restaurant, lounge, meeting rooms, 500 acres with indoor/outdoor swimming pools, whirlpool spa, tennis courts, pro shop, 18-hole golf course. Marina with sailing, boating, parasailing, canoeing, fishing. Platform tennis, cross-country skiing, snowmobiling, ice fishing, skating. Children's program.
Location C MN. 90 m N of Minneapolis.
Credit cards Amex, MC, Visa.
Rates Room only, $160–280 3-4 bedroom townhouse (for 6-8 persons), $80–200 2-bedroom townhouse (for 2-4 persons). MAP, $85 per person. Children's rates 10% MAP senior discount. 10% discount for 4-night stay. Midweek, weekend seasonal packages.

RED WING

A historic river town, Red Wing was named for a famous Dakota Indian chief. Although known particularly for its pottery, the town is still home to many prosperous industries as well as several beautiful riverfront parks ideal for hiking and swimming. Climb to the top of Barn Bluff and Sovin's Bluff for dramatic river views and stop by the colorful harbor, Boathouse Village.

Located in southeastern Minnesota, Red Wing is set among the lime stone bluffs lining the Mississippi River Valley, 55 miles southeast of

Minneapolis/St. Paul via Route 61, and about the same distance from Rochester, via Route 58Y.

Pratt Taber Inn ¢
706 West 4th Street, 55066

A. W. Pratt built this 13-room Italianate-style home in 1876 and sold it to his son-in-law, Robert Taber, in 1905, which is why it's listed on the National Register of Historic Places as the Pratt-Taber House. It's been a B&B since 1984, and innkeepers Jane and Darrell Molander have furnished it with a wonderful collection of Renaissance revival and country Victorian pieces. The woodwork is typical of the period, from the gingerbread trim with a star motif (celebrating the 1876 centennial) on the outside of the house to the elaborate walnut and butternut interior carvings.

"The Pratt-Taber provides the essential elements of a wonderful inn—authentic decor, comfortable and inviting common areas and guest rooms, and caring, knowledgeable innkeepers. The guest rooms are beautifully decorated, with ample reading lights and comfortably firm beds. Breakfast was a real treat, with delicious homemade delights that never seemed to stop coming. Jane's knowledge of Red Wing and what it had to offer us was remarkable. Before we even formally checked in, we got a brief history of the area and a room-by-room tour of the inn. What I especially liked was Jane's invitation to play the old player piano, or the Victrola, or to look at the one-of-a-kind stereograph collection which took up an entire shelf in the comfortable library. The pitcher of coffee and morning newspaper that was outside our bedroom door at 7:30 A.M. was an unexpected treat." *(Jim & Krisha Pennino)*

"Our bright and sunny room was the same one chosen by Garrison Keillor when he was in Red Wing. We awoke to the sounds of birds, and enjoyed a breakfast of fresh fruit with a delicious dip, homemade coffee cakes and muffins hot from the oven, juice, and tea or coffee. You can eat in bed, in the dining room, or on the porch. The honey peanut butter served with the muffins was my favorite. During the day we could help ourselves to apple cider, lemonade, coffee and big jar of chocolate chip cookies, from the kitchen. When we showed our room key at the local movie theater, we got in at half price! With the inn's Victorian decor, and hostess in long dress serving breakfast, we felt like we were stepping back in time." *(Chrys Bolk)* "My favorite is Polly's Room, with a slate fireplace—painted to look like marble—crystal chandelier, antique dressers, and a brass bed. The china is lovely Red Wing pottery and the food is delicious." *(Mrs. Marie Hassler)*

An area for improvement: "Although they made it look nice, our room had so many knickknacks on the dressers and tables that it was hard for us to find room to put our toilet articles, books, or eyeglasses."

Open All year.
Rooms 6 doubles—1 with private bath, 1 with private ½ bath, 4 with a maximum of 4 people sharing 1 bath. All with telephone, radio, TV, desk, air-conditioning, fan. 1 with fireplace, 1 with private entrance.
Facilities Dining room, sitting room, parlor, screened and unscreened porches, library, bicycles. 3 blocks from Mississippi River; golf, cross-country, downhill skiing nearby.

Location In historic district, 3 blocks from downtown. 2 blocks off Hwy. 61 on 4th and Dakota sts.
Restrictions No smoking in guest rooms.
Credit cards MC, Visa.
Rates B&B, $69–89 double. Extra person, $10. Midweek, corporate discounts.
Extras Limited wheelchair access. Pets permitted by prior arrangement. Marina/ station pickup. Crib, babysitting.

St. James Hotel 👤 ✕
406 Main Street (Route 61), 55066

Tel: 612–388–2846
800–252–1875

Red Wing's initial prosperity arose from its key role as a port for the shipping of wheat. The St. James built in 1875 as a symbol of this early success. Owned for 72 years by the Lillyblad family, the hotel became famous for fine food. It is said that the trains used to stop in Red Wing "just so the passengers could eat at Clara Lillyblad's restaurant." In 1975 the Red Wing Shoe Company bought the hotel, restoring it completely and combining it with a shopping, parking, and office complex. Each guest room is named for a Mississippi riverboat, and half have views of the river and the bluffs; all the rooms have been individually decorated with period antiques and reproductions and lovely handcrafted quilts. Still known for good food, the hotel is home to two restaurants: the Port of Red Wing Restaurant, serving American food, and the Veranda Café, providing three casual meals daily, overlooking the Mississippi.

"Excellent staff—I arrived by train and they came to the station to greet me at 10:30 P.M. They were also eager to acquaint me with Red Wing and other areas of interest during my stay. The rooms are comfortable, with appealing color schemes." *(Lucia Giliberti)* "Good food, gorgeous decor, great setting. Climb to the top of the nearby bluffs for great river views." *(Jeanne Hanson)* "The hotel is quiet, yet has several nice restaurants and is close to great shopping." *(Thomas Dewey)*

"We liked the gracious high-ceilinged library with dark wood walls and leather chairs and couches, floral patterned rug, and old books including an old set of Encyclopedia Britannica. The hallways are wide and clean, with gingerbread woodwork over the archways to some of the rooms; everything fresh and clean. Hanging on the stairway between the 2nd and 3rd floor is a very well-done antique quilt." *(SC)*

Little quibbles: "Although my born-to-shop teenage daughter didn't agree, I was sorry to see the original lobby cluttered with little shops, and thought it made the check-in area too crowded." Also: "The ersatz marble sink in our bathroom didn't do justice to the decor."

Open All year.
Rooms 60 doubles—all with private bath and/or shower, telephone, radio, TV, desk, air-conditioning. 6 with single or double Jacuzzi. 19 rooms in annex.
Facilities 2 restaurants, pub, lounge with weekend pianist, library. $\frac{1}{2}$ block to YMCA with full athletic facilities. Off-street parking. Heated pool. Tennis, golf nearby. Boating, fishing, swimming nearby. 10 m to downhill and cross-country skiing.
Location Downtown.
Restrictions Light sleepers should request rooms away from street or railway. No smoking in some guest rooms.
Credit cards Amex, CB, DC, Discover, MC, Visa.

Rates Room only, $83–120 double, $65–83 single. Extra person, $10. No charge for children under 18 in parents' room. Theater, "Winterlude" packages. Alc breakfast, $4–7; alc lunch, $5–9; alc dinner, $10–35.
Extras Wheelchair access; 3 rooms equipped for disabled. Station pickup. Crib, babysitting.

ST. PAUL

Just across the river from its flashier twin, Minneapolis, St. Paul offers beautifully restored mansions and historic sights, and a diverse ethnic population. Of particular interest is its impressive turn-of-the-century State Capitol, and the Science Museum of Minnesota, with domed Omni-theater.

The Chatsworth B&B ¢   *Tel: 612–227–4288*
984 Ashland Avenue, 55104

The Chatsworth is a 1902 Victorian home, on a large corner lot shaded by basswood and maple trees, set in a family neighborhood. Guest rooms have been eclectically decorated to reflect the journeys of owner and ardent traveler Donna Gustafson; you can choose Victorian, Oriental, African-Asian, antique Scandinavian, or simple four-poster. After raising eight children and hosting exchange students from three continents, Donna and her husband Earl now enjoy helping out-of-town visitors learn about the Twin Cities. A healthy breakfast of fresh fruit, granola, yogurt, muffins, juice, coffee, tea, and milk is served in the panelled dining room.

"The highlight of our stay was breakfasting in Donna's lovely Victorian dining room, chatting with the bright and interesting people—travelers, visiting professionals, and even an author looking for a peaceful place to write. Donna and Earl are attractive, gracious, and delightful people." *(James Fudge)* "The Gustafsons are a storehouse of knowledge about area activities." *(Jitendra Singh)* "Special touches—candles, tape player, lace bedspreads, thirsty towels and robes—enhanced our visit." *(Kathryn Williams)*

Open All year.
Rooms 5 doubles—3 with private bath and/or shower, 2 with a maximum of 4 people sharing bath. All with radio, fan. 3 with desk, 1 with air-conditioning, 1 with balcony. 2 with whirlpool tub.
Facilities Living room with fireplace, piano; dining room, library, porch, deck.
Location Center of town, 2 blocks from Governor's Mansion. From I-35 E, take Summit Ave. exit and go N on Chatsworth Ave. to inn on left, at corner of Ashland Ave.
Restrictions No smoking.
Credit cards None accepted.
Rates B&B, $60–98 double, $50–88 single. Extra person, $12.
Extras Airport/station pickup, fee varies. Crib.

St. Paul Hotel   ♙ ✕   *Tel: 612–292–9292*
350 Market Street, 55102   Outside MN: 800–292–9292

With an elegant setting overlooking Rice Park in the heart of St. Paul, the St. Paul Hotel is a classic old hotel. Its architects were Reed and Stern, who had just completed New York City's Grand Central Station, and the hotel opened to great fanfare in 1910. As has happened to many center city hotels, it eventually went into a decline and closed in 1979, the furnishings auctioned off. In 1985, the hotel was reconstructed, reducing the room count to provide more comfortable rooms, and moving the main entrance to Market Street, with a graceful circular entrance. A complete remodeling was completed in 1991 under the ownership of the St. Paul Companies, and the management of William Morrissey.

"Although a bit bigger and busier than your usual entries, this old gem merits inclusion for its excellent location and sense of history." *(MW)* More reports required.

Open All year.
Rooms 7 suites, 247 doubles—all with full private bath, telephone, radio, TV, desk, air-conditioning, fan.
Facilities 2 restaurants, bar. On "Skyway" all-weather access system. Parking garage adjacent, fee charged.
Location Downtown. At corner of Market and 5th Sts.
Restrictions Smoking restricted in some areas.
Credit cards All major credit cards accepted.
Rates Room only, $134–525 suite, $120–135 double/single. Extra person, $15. Children free in parents' room. 20% senior discount. Weekend packages. Alc breakfast, $6–10; alc lunch, $7–10; alc dinner, $12–26.
Extras Wheelchair access; some rooms equipped for the disabled. Airport pickup. Crib, babysitting. German, Japanese, Chinese, French spoken.

The University Club of St. Paul ¢ 🛪   *Tel:* 612–222–1751
420 Summit Avenue, 55102

Built in 1890, the University Club was modeled after the Cambridge and Oxford Clubs in London. The club's extensive common rooms have high ceilings and panelled walls, with English antiques and landscape paintings. In the Grill Bar, F. Scott Fitzgerald's initials can be found alongside those of the other members.

"For accommodations in the Twin Cities, the best-kept secret and value is the University Club. An outside terrace overlooks a tennis court, swimming pool, and offers a beautiful night-time view of the city and the river. Owner John Rupp is a knowledgeable art and antique collector and has furnished every room with an eclectic collection of fine art, antique furniture, English brass rubbings, and Persian carpets. For service, cleanliness, location, and overall atmosphere, it can't be beat. Summit Avenue is a tree-lined, divided parkway graced with a number of Victorian homes built by St. Paul's elite railroad and lumber barons of the 19th century." *(R. A. Randall)*

Open All year.
Rooms 1 suite, 7 doubles—all with private bath, air-conditioning. Some with TV, fireplace.
Facilities Dining/breakfast room, bar, lounge with fireplace, library, porch, terrace. On-street parking. Swimming pool, fitness center with whirlpool, tennis court.
Location 1 m from downtown. Exit Hwy. 94 at Dale, take Dale S to Summit Ave. Take Summit E (left) to the University Club.

Restrictions No smoking in guest rooms.
Credit cards Amex, DC, MC, Visa.
Rates Room only, $85 suite, $45–85 double/single. Extra person, $10. Breakfast, $3–6. Alc lunch, $5–9; alc dinner, $8–17.

STILLWATER

Lowell Inn 👫 ✕   *Tel:* 612–439–1100
102 North Second Street, 55082

A Williamsburg-style hotel, the Lowell was built in 1927. Its first managers, Nelle and Arthur Palmer, had traveled through the Midwest—as vaudevillians—and had stayed in so many third-rate hotels that they decided to run a truly superior one. In 1930, they served their first Christmas dinner and also began collecting antiques, fine linens, china, and glassware, and eventually purchased the inn in 1945. Although both senior Palmers have passed away, the inn has continued to prosper under the ownership of their son and daughter-in-law, Arthur Jr. and his wife Maureen.

The inn has several different dining rooms, each with a different character and menu—the elegant George Washington Room, the Garden Room with indoor trout pond, and the Matterhorn Room, filled with antique Swiss wood carvings. Many of the inn's specialties have been served for decades—by guest demand. Rooms are decorated traditionally, highlighted with antiques; some have elaborate draped or gilt beds and marble sinks.

"Very southern atmosphere and delicious dinners. The Palmer family runs this inn with impeccable taste." *(Liba & Tom Stillman)* "The best inn we've ever visited, hence the constant returns. Rooms have many extra touches, the food outstanding, service tops." *(Stephen Shipps)*

"Your current listing does not do this wonderful institution justice. I've been going there for half a century and it not only stays uniform but gets better. Food and service in the George Washington and Matterhorn Rooms is incomparable. In the Garden Room one can net a trout from the spring-fed pond and have it cooked and served right away. The prices are high but worth it. I wish they had an elevator to make an overnight stay easier for older folks (the guest rooms are on the second floor). The rooms have small bottles of wine, special embroidered towels, soaps, and a comfortable, quiet setting. The hall carpets are the thickest I've found anywhere." *(David Fesler)*

Another guest had a slightly different viewpoint: "Stillwater is a delightfully quaint river town, with interesting buildings and neat shops, although the inn is not right in the historic section. I have friends who became engaged at Lowell's 25 years ago, and still love to return on their anniversaries; others visiting recently for the first time found it overrated." More reports needed.

Open All year. Closed Thanksgiving, Christmas.
Rooms 4 suites with Jacuzzi baths, 17 doubles—all with private bath and/or shower, telephone, radio, desk, air-conditioning.

Facilities Restaurant, lounge, lobby with fireplace. Fishing nearby.
Location SE MN, 19 m E of Twin Cities. Take Rte. 35 W north to Rte. 36 E. One block off Main St., on corner of Myrtle and 2nd Sts.
Restrictions Light sleepers might be disturbed by street noise on east side of building.
Credit cards MC, Visa.
Rates Room only, $179 suite, $109–159 double. MAP rates, add $100. 16% service additional. Breakfast platter, $22; alc lunch, $11–19; alc dinner, $20–32. Prix fixe fondue dinner for 2 (Matterhorn Room), $92.
Extras Restaurant wheelchair access. Crib, babysitting. German spoken.

WABASHA

Anderson House ¢ ♪ ✕
333 West Main Street, 55981

Tel: 612–565–4524
In MN: 800–862–9702
In Midwest: 800–325–2270

In Anne Tyler's book *The Accidental Tourist*, the protagonist says that hotel rooms should come with a pet, to keep you company. The Anderson House does just that: You can pick, or even reserve, one of the inn's 10 cats to keep your toes warm for the night.

It's the oldest operating hotel in Minnesota, dating back to 1856, and is owned and managed by the fourth generation of the Anderson family. Grandma Ida Anderson, who started running the inn at the turn of the century, learned how to cook in the Pennsylvania Dutch country, and many of her favorite recipes are still being served—cinnamon rolls, red flannel hash, scrapple, *fastnachts* for breakfast; chicken with dumplings, smoked pork chops with red cabbage for lunch or dinner; plus a dozen different breads and an equal number of desserts ensure that no one goes to bed hungry. Rooms are furnished with period antiques, many of them original to the building.

"Anderson House is a homey inn with over 130 years' worth of character. It's a clean establishment with great food, reasonably priced. The inn is a block from downtown Wabasha, a quaint southern Minnesota town on the Mississippi River; Nelson, Wisconsin, is on the other side." *(Lanie Paymar)* "Many people come here just for the restaurant. Clean, cozy rooms. If time permits, make the drive from here to Red Wing, beautifully scenic along the Mississippi River, with wooded bluffs on both sides." *(Lucia Giliberti)*

Open All year. Restaurant closed Jan. 3–25.
Rooms 4 suites, 27 doubles—18 with private bath and/or shower, 17 with maximum of 6 sharing bath. All with TV, desk, air-conditioning.
Facilities Restaurant, bar/lounge, lobby, ice cream parlor, patio, greenhouse. Mississippi River for swimming, boating, fishing. Cross-country, downhill skiing nearby.
Location SE MN, Mississippi River Valley, off Rte. 61. 1 block from downtown.
Credit cards None accepted.
Rates Room only, $79–109 suite, $40–73 double. Extra person, $5. Midweek family, B&B and MAP rates. Special event, seasonal, weekend packages. Children's menu. Full breakfast, $3–5. Prix fixe lunch, $6–7; dinner, $10–14. Alc dinner, $17–21.
Extras Station pickup. Crib, babysitting.

Missouri

Garth Woodside Mansion, Hannibal

Missouri's two major cities, Kansas City and St. Louis, developed on the state's two major rivers—the Missouri and the Mississippi, which form its eastern and part of its western borders. Children will enjoy Kansas City's Toy & Miniature Museum, while adults will appreciate St. Louis' sophisticated shops and the Cupples House, an enormous pink granite mansion erected in 1890. Northwest Missouri is Mark Twain country, while the central part of the state is more rural, with the Lake of the Ozarks and the Ozark Mountains regions as major tourist attractions. Don't miss the annual Arrow Rock Invitational Craft Festival in October or the National Ragtime Festival in June.

Information please: In the central part of the state is the enormous man-made Lake of the Ozarks. Although most accommodations here consist of huge resorts, condos and camps, one small family-owned place is **Bay Ridge Resort** (HCR 77, Box 6, Sunrise Beach 65079; 314–374–5320) offering rustic but clean waterfront cottages on a quiet cove ideal for fishing, swimming, and waterskiing. Children are welcome, and families return year after year to the shady setting.

In the southwest corner of the state (7 miles north of I-44 via Route 71), is Carthage, site of the first battle of the Civil War. Several turn-of-the-century marble mansions built by prosperous mine owners are now B&Bs including: **The Leggett House** (1106 Grand Avenue, 64836; 417–358–

0683); the **Grand Avenue Inn** (1615 Grand Avenue, 64835; 417–358–7265); and the **Maple Lane Farm** (RR1, 64836; 417–358–6312). It's worth leaving the interstate just to see Carthage's imposing, castle-like courthouse, quarried from local gray marble; inside is a mural of the town's history by Lowell Davis. Reports?

Rates do not include 7½% state sales tax and room tax.

ARROW ROCK

Information please: About 30 minutes southeast of from Arrow Rock is the town of Boonville with over 400 buildings and locations listed on the National Register of Historic Places, and the site of two Civil War battles. The **River City Inn** (311 East Spring Street, Boonville 65233; 816–882–5465) is an 1843 home decorated in period, both private and shared baths; in the process of renovating the former slave quarters a room sealed since 1904 was uncovered. Rates include a full breakfast.

Borgman's Bed & Breakfast ¢   *Tel: 816–837–335C*
706 Van Buren, 65320

Founded in 1829, Arrow Rock is a Historic Landmark town, the home of artist George Calib Bingham, and located near the beginning point of the Santa Fe Trail. Its most prosperous period was when it served as a Missouri River steamboat port; its decline started with the Civil War, and by the turn of the century the town was largely forgotten. In the 1920s local groups began restoring its historic buildings, and today people come to visit those buildings as well as the local antique shops and Arrow Rock's well-regarded summer repertory theater, the Lyceum.

"Kathy and Helen Borgman have personally restored and decorated this two-story white frame house. The food is home-cooked, and the smell of homemade cinnamon rolls makes you aware that Helen is preparing breakfast especially for you. Parking is ample and the house is within walking distance of the historical area and the Lyceum Theater." *(Darleen Mueller)* "Warm and friendly innkeepers. Very quiet location. Cathy is a wealth of information about the town and area." *(Jacque & Steve Dougherty)* "My immaculate room was furnished with antiques, including a cradle with dolls sleeping peacefully. A visit to Arrow Rock and Borgman's is like stepping back in time to a more peaceful, friendly era." *(Jo Kieselback)*

Open All year.
Rooms 4 doubles sharing 3 baths. All with air-conditioning.
Facilities Kitchen/breakfast room, 2 sitting/TV rooms with games, porches. Missouri River nearby for fishing.
Location Central MO. 2 hrs. E of Kansas City, 3 hrs. W of St. Louis. 50 min. W of Columbia. From I-70 W, take exit 98 to Hwy. 41 to Arrow Rock. From I-70 E take exit 89 to Hwy. K to Hwy. 41. B&B is 1 block E of Hwy. 41.
Restrictions No smoking.
Credit cards None accepted.
Rates B&B, $40–45 double, $35 single, including tax. Extra person, $5. 10% discount on 3-night stays.
Extras Crib.

ONNE TERRE

ansion Hill Inn ✕   *Tel:* 314–731–5003
ansion Hill Drive, 63628
ail: 11215 Natural Bridge, Bridgeton, MO 63044

ention scuba-diving and most people envision the sunlit waters of the
aribbean or another exotic locale. But not Catherine and Douglas Goer-
·ns, who operate Bonne Terre Mine with its ten-square-mile *underground*
ystal-clear lake as a Midwestern scuba-diving center. (Non-divers can
ke a 17-mile underground boat ride.) With the defunct St. Joe Lead Mine
·w attracting thousands of visitors each year, the Goergens purchased
e dilapidated estate that was once the home of the mine's president.
ith the same energy that led them to create a successful business out of
 eyesore, they renovated and reconstructed the 32-room building to
come the Mansion Hill Inn. Decorated in turn-of-the-century style with
utical accents, the inn has an old English steamer chest in the library and
sleigh bed in one of the guest rooms. The restaurant and pub, of the
me name, offer an eclectic menu: appetizers of toasted ravioli, shrimp
cktail, and Louisiana-style chicken wings; and such entrées as fried
hole catfish, broiled beef short ribs, Italian meatloaf, and plantation-style
ed chicken.
 Catherine and Douglas also purchased the old train station and con-
·rted it to an small inn and restaurant, the **1909 Depot**, adding a dining
·r and caboose to all the railroading memorabilia that serves as its decor.
he 1909 Depot has seven guest rooms, with private bath, and is open
uesday through Sunday. Reports on both properties needed.

pen All year. Fri., Sat. only. (1909 Depot open Tues.–Sat.)
ooms 5 doubles—2 with private bath, 3 with maximum of 4 sharing bath. All
th radio, air-conditioning, fan, balcony/deck.
cilities Dining room, living room, library—all with fireplace, library with TV/
CR, stereo, books. Piano bar Sat. nights. 133 acres, golf, picnic area. 3 blocks from
·nne Terre Mine for scuba diving, boating.
·cation SE MO, 60 m S of St. Louis.
·strictions No smoking in guest rooms.
·edit cards Discover, MC, Visa.
·tes Room only, $80 double. Extra adult, $40; child, $30. Alc lunch, $6; alc
nner, $24. 10% AAA discount.

RANSON

he Branson House ¢   *Tel:* 417–334–0959
·0 Fourth Street, 65616

'he Ozarks are a wonderful place for a vacation, even for Missourians.
·oms in this area are expensive and often full. To our delight we found
ace in this quiet turn-of-the-century home. Guests are also offered
ternoon sherry and evening milk and cookies. We had a chance to visit

with owner Opal Kelly and the other guests, but also had lots of p
vacy—a perfect combination." *(Kathy & Helen Borgman)*

"One of the few historic homes left in Branson, and a welcome resp
from the amalgam of motels, fast food joints, and country music shov
that line the Highway 76. Set in a quiet, shady, residential area, Bransc
House is within walking distance of downtown with its small tov
ambiance. Opal Kelly has done a marvelous job restoring this two-sto
bungalow—painting, carpeting, refinishing the walnut woodwork, ar
modernizing the plumbing and kitchen facilities. The guest rooms a
simply but comfortably decorated. Everything works—parking is ad
quate, the food is tasty and ample, and our room had been tidied up befo
we returned from breakfast.

"But the biggest plus is Opal and her personable family. When she isr
busy in the kitchen, she joins her guests on the front porch for entertainir
conversation. Opal is a native, a rarity among B&B owners in the Ozark
she remembers when there was no strip and when tourists came main
to float fish (before the dam was built)." *(Kristen Morrow)*

Open March through Dec.
Rooms 1 suite, 6 doubles—all with private bath and/or shower, air-conditionin
Facilities Parlor with books, games; dining room, porch. Shaded lawn. Walkir
distance to Lake Taneycomo, shops, restaurants.
Location SW MO. Center of town. 45 m S of Springfield, 250 m SW of St. Lou
100 m NE of Fayetteville, AR.
Credit cards None accepted.
Rates B&B, $50–65 double.

HANNIBAL

Mark Twain (born Samuel Clemens) lived in Hannibal as a boy and as
young man, when the prosperity of the river and of steamboating we
at their height. Scenes from both *Tom Sawyer* and *Huckleberry Finn* we
inspired by his days here. Twain remains Hannibal's main claim to fan
to this day, and there are many worthwhile historic and entertainir
sights to see, including Mark Twain's Boyhood Home; a summer outdoc
drama based on his life and characters; narrated riverboat rides; and tt
Mark Twain Cave, in which Tom Sawyer and Becky Thatcher were los
Also of interest is the Autumn Folk Life Festival, where traditional craf
are demonstrated, and the high bluffs overlooking the river, the souther
migration point for many bald eagles.

Fifth Street Mansion ¢ 👫   *Tel:* 314–221–044
213 South Fifth Street, 63401

Situated on a block known as "Millionaire's Row" for its imposing, 19t
century homes, the Italianate-style Fifth Street Mansion was the in-tow
home of the same John Garth who built the Garth Woodside Mansio
(listed below). In this house in 1902, Mark Twain saw his childhoc
sweetheart, Laura Hawkins, for the last time (he lived the remainder of h
life in the East); she was the real-life model for Tom Sawyer's girlfrien

ecky Thatcher. Much of the home's original architectural detail remains,
om the large Tiffany stained glass window that graces the stairway to
ie imported, hand-molded tiles around the parlor fireplace (one of eight
 the home), hand-grained walnut panelling, and original chandeliers and
rass gasoliers. Innkeepers Mike and Donalene Andreotti have decorated
ie rooms with period furniture and floral wallpapers, highlighted with
mple lace curtains. A welcoming beverage is served each afternoon,
ther in the parlor or on the broad front porch. A typical breakfast might
iclude fresh fruit and orange juice, Mike's French toast, sausage, blue-
erry muffins, assorted breads, coffee and tea.

"I felt like a princess in our room decorated with antiques, lace, and fine
nens. Our bathroom had a claw-foot tub and large bath sheets. We
alked to all the attractions and restaurants." *(T.D. Haiser)* "Delicious
ood, immaculate housekeeping." *(Jane Jensen)* "Homey and relaxed atmo-
phere." *(Yuki Komaki)* "We had the top floor room, in the cupola, with
 wonderful view of the Mississippi River." *(Judy & Randy Bouwens)*
Welcoming atmosphere, interesting history, convenient location." *(Ward
atz)*

Open All year.

ooms 1 suite, 6 doubles—all with private bath and/or shower, air-conditioning.
Most with desk, fireplace; 1 with fan. Telephone on request.

acilities All public rooms with fireplace: Dining room, parlor, music room with
rgan, library with TV/VCR, games; wrap-around porch. Near Mississippi River
or boating, fishing.

ocation 100 m NW of St. Louis. In town near Historic District.

estrictions No smoking.

redit cards Amex, Discover, MC, Visa.

ates B&B, $60–85 suite, $50–75 double, $40–60 single. Extra person, $15.
amily rate.

xtras Free local airport/station pickup. Crib, babysitting by prior arrangement.

Garth Woodside Mansion ¢   *Tel: 314–221–2789*
New London Gravel Road, R.R.#1, 63401

n 1871 John W. Garth built Woodside, an imposing Victorian mansion
n the Second Empire style, complete with mansard roof and cupola, as a
ummer retreat. A longtime friend of Mr. Garth's, Mark Twain is believed
o have stayed in the mansion in 1882 and again in 1902.

"Prior to its present ownership, the mansion was open only as a
nuseum, and it is listed on the National Register of Historic Places. It has
lmost all the original furniture in each of the rooms, with 12-foot-high
ieadboards, tables, and even knickknacks. Our room had a claw-foot tub
nd a European hand-carved armoire with mirror. Even 19th-century-style
iightshirts are provided for guests to wear! The fresh homemade break-
asts are served on a different china pattern every day." *(Cristina Goodman)*
"The outstanding features include a magnificent flying staircase that floats
o the third floor with no visible means of support and seven hand-crafted
talian marble mantels." *(Duane & Clare Baylor)*

"This B&B is located on a park-like hillside shaded by stately oak and
naple trees. While we enjoyed tea on the veranda, a young doe grazed

in the nearby meadow. Our third-floor room had a lovely view, th hospitality was friendly and relaxed, and the delicious breakfast w elegantly served by owner Dianne Feinberg and her daughter Carrie *(Doris & R.B. Thomas)*

"Irv took time to answer our questions and fill us in on the history the Garth family. The Garths had a tradition of hospitality which th Feinbergs are clearly upholding." *(Dianne Lutz)* "Our delicious breakfa included fresh pineapple and watermelon with yogurt sauce, still-war lemon sponge cake, and outstanding peach French toast." *(Pat DeLane also Kimberly Holzerland)*

"The busy innkeepers gladly answered our frequent questions abo the fascinating history of the mansion, gave complete information abo local points of interest, teased our children, and in every way develope a homey atmosphere during our stay." *(J. Regis O'Connor)* "We felt total at home yet transported back to the Victorian era. The Garth famil history, illustrated by many photographs, was especially interesting *(Marilen Pitler, and others)* "We stayed in the Clemens Room. It was a thr to sleep in the same bed as Mark Twain." *(Robert Slotta)*

Open All year.
Rooms 8 doubles—all with private bath and/or shower, air-conditioning; som with desk; telephone on request.
Facilities Dining room, living room, parlor, library, verandas, porches. Parking c site. 39 acres with gardens, fish pond, croquet. Swimming, boating nearby.
Location NE MO. 2 m S of town. From town go S on Hwy. 61, go E on Warre Barrett Dr. (1st rd. S of Holiday Inn); at 2nd bridge follow signs S to inn.
Restrictions No smoking. No children under 12.
Credit cards MC, Visa.
Rates B&B, $59–79 double. Extra person, $15. Tipping encouraged. 2-nigl holiday minimum. Midweek specials. "An Evening with Mark Twain" speci event by prior arrangement.

HERMANN

A Missouri river town founded by German immigrants over 150 year ago, Hermann has maintained a strong sense of its heritage, celebrate vigorously in May, August, and of course in the fall, with Octoberfes Hermann boasts over 100 buildings and two districts listed on the Na tional Register of Historic Places. The community's winemaking root reach back to its founding, and two local wineries welcome visitors.

Information please: The Seven Sisters B&B (108 Schiller Stree 65041; 314–486–3717) has guest rooms decorated with handmade quilt its reasonable rates include a breakfast of home-baked cinnamon rolls, an a horse-drawn carriage tour of the historic district. **Das Brownhaus** (12 East Second Street, 65041; 314–486–3372), is a 1896 Queen-Anne styl home with original woodwork and stained glass, and a decor combinin Victorian and contemporary elements; rates include an imaginative fu breakfast. A local miller built what is now the **William Klinger Inn** (10 East Second Street; 314–486–5930), a sturdy red brick house, in 1878. I was converted into an inn a little more than a century later, with a great deal of its hand-crafted woodwork, stained glass, and ceiling medallions still intact. Rates include a full breakfast.

Birk's Goethe Street Gasthaus ¢
700 Goethe Street, P.O. Box 255, 65041

Tel: 314–486–3143
800–748–7883

Birk's Gasthaus was built in 1886 by William Herzog, who owned Stone Hill Winery during the period when it was the third largest in the world. The mansion was used both as a private home as well as a gasthaus where the Herzogs entertained friends and customers. Elmer and Gloria Birk acquired the mansion in 1977, opening it as a B&B in 1984. A full breakfast is served promptly at 8:30 A.M. in the dining room; a typical menu includes fresh fruit and juice; mushroom, sausage and egg casserole; and sweet rolls, coffee and tea. Furnished in period, the guest rooms are spacious (the smallest is 10 by 15 feet), with country Victorian decor. Many have reproduction brass beds, enormous antique armoires and dressers, and bathrooms with oversize claw-foot tubs.

Although murder mystery weekends are now available at many inns, the Gasthaus was one of the first to offer them. Presented the first two full weekends of every month, these elaborate productions are extremely popular, usually booked well in advance; the many nooks and crannies of this 12,000-square-foot house lend themselves well to the creation of a mysterious atmosphere.

"Elmer and Gloria have ancestors that helped settle the area and brought the art of winemaking with them. The inn is located away from the main district so evenings are peaceful, particularly on the wrap-around porch in the back of the house. Breakfast is served in an extension off the kitchen. The cooking aromas wafted upstairs so we came downstairs early for a cup of coffee." *(Trish Smith)* "The dinners were very special—smoked turkey, sauerbraten, and homemade soups were some of the memorable entrées made by Gloria. The mystery weekend is like a live Clue game with a real who-done-it atmosphere. The local actors who played out the mystery were very talented and drew us into the scenario. We received a kit to solve the crime and were encouraged to dress in period costumes." *(Mary Thouvenot & David Lipsey)* More comments welcome.

Open Feb. 1 through Dec. 23.
Rooms 9 doubles—7 with private bath, 2 with a maximum of 4 people sharing bath. All with air-conditioning.
Facilities 2 dining rooms, 2 lounges with TV, library—all with fireplace. Swimming, golf, tennis nearby.
Location E central MO. 90 m W of St. Louis. Take I-70 W to Hwy. 19 (Hermann-Montgomery City exit) and go 14 m to Hermann. Go 6 blocks (road name becomes Market St.) and turn right on W. 6th St. Go 3 blocks and turn left on Goethe St. to inn at corner of Goethe and 7th Sts.
Restrictions Smoking permitted in 1st floor lounge only. No children under 16.
Credit cards Amex, MC, Visa.
Rates B&B, $58–68 double, $48–58 single. Extra person, $13. No tipping. Mini-

mum stay required during Maifest, Octoberfest activities. "Mansion Mystery" weekend packages.

Extras Local airport/station pickup.

INDEPENDENCE

Woodstock Inn ¢ 🛉🛉   *Tel:* 816–833–2233
1212 West Lexington, 64050

One of Missouri's most historic cities, Independence was the starting point of the Santa Fe Trail, and is best known as the hometown of President Harry Truman. Sites of interest include the Truman Library, the Truman Home and other places connected with his career, as well as several restored buildings and mansions now open as museums.

Built in 1916, the inn has been modernized and expanded many times over the years, and is conveniently located to all historic sites. Rooms are decorated simply, with period antiques and reproductions, comfortable traditional furnishings, and handmade quilts. Rates include full breakfast; a sample menu might include a choice of fresh fruit and juice, a variety of breads, bagels, and English muffins, thick French toast and sausage or Swedish pancakes with fruit, syrup, and whipped cream, and banana chocolate chip muffins.

"Friendly, comfortable, relaxed atmosphere, with many homey touches. The inn is very clean, quiet, with delicious food graciously served." *(Mr. & Mrs. Ralph Ryan)* "Hospitable owners, helpful with restaurant ideas." *(Margaret Rothchild)*

Open All year.
Rooms 2 suites, 9 doubles—all with private bath and/or shower, telephone, air-conditioning, fan. 2 with desk, suites with TV.
Facilities Living/dining room with piano, TV, games, library. 10 min. to sports stadiums, theme parks.
Location Historic district. 10 m E of Kansas City. 8 blocks from center of town. Inn at corner of Short and Lexington Sts.
Restrictions Traffic noise in front rooms. No smoking.
Credit cards MC, Visa.
Rates B&B, $59 suite, $45–49 double, $40 single. Extra person, $5. Children under 2 free in parents' room. 10% senior discount, Oct.–March. 10% discount for 3-night stay. 2-night summer weekend minimum preferred.
Extras Wheelchair access; suites equipped for the disabled. Airport/station pickup, $15. Crib, babysitting. German spoken.

KANSAS CITY

Located close to the geographic center of the continental U.S., Kansas City has long been a favorite of convention planners. Lesser known is the fact that it is a pleasant city, with lots of parks and open spaces, several museums of note, including the Nelson Gallery of Art, with world-class collections, and the Liberty Memorial, with museums dedicated to World War I artifacts. Although KC has several major shopping and restaurant plazas of note, serious shoppers will want to pay homage (and probably more) at the many fine shops of Country Club Plaza, with its Spanish towers and Moorish tiled fountains—probably the country's first suburban-style shopping mall, built in the 1920s.

Also recommended: Received too late for a full write-up was an enthusiastic report from *Annette Anderson* on the **Apple Creek Inn** (908 Washington Street, Weston 64098; 816–386–5724). This B&B has four guest rooms with private and shared baths, and is located in Weston, 30 minutes northwest of Kansas City on the Missouri River. "Comfortable beds. Susan Keith, the innkeeper, graciously bent over backwards to cater to our every need. Breakfast was superb, with fresh fruit and juice, banana bread, pumpkin muffins, sausage, and wonderful quiche."

Kansas City is located in western Missouri, straddling the Kansas border.

Doanleigh Wallagh Inn
217 East 37th Street, 64111

Tel: 816–753–2667

Ed and Carolyn Litchfield were so sure that they wanted to run an inn that they spent their honeymoon looking at properties in Key West, Florida. They didn't find their dream house there but have done considerably better here in Kansas City. Doanleigh Wallagh consists of two architecturally interesting houses, built in 1907. Both are handsomely restored and decorated with American and European antiques and quality reproductions. Rates include a full breakfast with an entrée such as French toast with honey and orange glaze, eggs Benedict, Russian pancakes with sour cream and fresh fruit, popover pancakes with cinnamon apples, or Scotch eggs with hollandaise, plus a breakfast meat, fruit, juice, coffee, and tea. Lighter breakfasts are available and special dietary restrictions can be met with advance notice.

"A lovely inn in a quiet section, walking distance to the art museum and Country Club Plaza. Our room was beautifully restored with modern amenities; breakfasts are varied and tasty, and the innkeepers most accommodating." *(Adam Platt)* More comments welcome.

Open All year.
Rooms 10 rooms in 2 adjacent homes—all with private bath or shower, telephone, radio, TV, desk, air-conditioning. 2 rooms with fireplace. Fully equipped kitchen for guest use in 1 home.
Facilities 3 Dining rooms, 2 living rooms with grand piano, pump organ, fireplace, library; solarium with TV/VCR, video library; porch. Off-street parking. Park with tennis across street.
Location 5 min. to Crown Center, Country Club Plaza, and Westport; 10 min. to downtown. 3 blocks E of Main.
Restrictions Smoking on first floor only.
Credit cards Amex, MC, Visa.
Rates B&B, $60–110 double. Extra person, $10. 2-night holiday/weekend minimum. Extended stay discount.

The Raphael ✗ ♦♦
325 Ward Parkway

Tel: 816–756–3800
800–821–5343

Originally built as an apartment house, the Raphael was converted to a hotel about a dozen years ago. The lobby is paneled in beautiful woods, with traditional furnishings; guest rooms are warm and comfortable, and most have been updated with classic reproduction decor. The suites are an excellent value in comparison to the newer hotels in the area; ask about their "Suite Deal" package for $98. Rates include the morning paper and breakfast of juice, roll, and hot beverage, delivered to your door each morning." *(Virginia Slimmer)* "Superb service in every aspect; elegant dining in the restaurant. If you are visiting Kansas City during the holiday season, book a room at the Raphael facing the Country Club Plaza with all of its holiday lights. It is spectacular!" *(Jim & Tina Kirkpatrick)*

Open All year. Restaurant closed Sunday.

Rooms 90 suites, 33 doubles—all with full private bath, telephone, radio, TV, desk, air-conditioning, refrigerator, mini-bar.

Facilities Restaurant, lounge with nightly piano bar. Swimming pool across street. Free valet parking. 24-hour room service. Tennis courts, jogging course nearby.

Location Country Club Plaza, 10 min. from downtown.

Credit cards Amex, DC, MC, Visa.

Rates B&B, $98–121 suites, $98–111 double. Extra adult, $15; no charge for children under 12. Weekend package, $98.

Extras Crib, babysitting. Spanish, German, French spoken.

Southmoreland Inn
116 East 46th Street, 64112   *Tel: 816–531–7979*

Kansas City was ahead of most of the country when it launched its first planned community in 1922, complete with high-rise apartments, private homes, and shopping enclave. Now the cultural, shopping, and entertainment heart of the city, this well-manicured district, known as Country Club Plaza, is home to an urban inn, the Southmoreland. Missouri natives Susan Moehl and Penni Johnson left corporate careers to follow the long-nurtured dream of becoming innkeepers, and found the best opportunity in their own backyard. "We learned the importance of being flexible. When we started out we wanted a country location, but we got urban. We wanted East Coast, we got Midwest. We wanted Victorian, we got 1913 Colonial." The outcome of months of renovation, which combined the city's stringent commercial building code with vintage construction and decor, is a Colonial Revival home with a cheery solarium furnished in white wicker with an Amish rag rug, and a convivial living room decorated with antiques and reproductions, accented with brass sconces and collectibles. New white-tiled bathrooms were added to complement the existing ones, and guest rooms are supplied with sherry, fresh fruit and flowers, down comforters and pillows (hypo-allergenic ones available on request), and Caswell-Massey toiletries. Wine and cheese is served every afternoon, and in the morning, breakfast is served at the long harvest table in the dining room. On recent mornings, breakfast included apricot-banana frappes, Virginia ham with apple pie and Edam cheese, and cheddar cheese muffins with peach preserves; or broiled grapefruit, French toast stuffed with Swiss cheese and ham, and apricot sour cream bread. "Warm, comfortable inn. Each room is named and decorated for a well-known Kansas City celebrity. Breakfasts were excellent and varied."*(John Jurco)* "The innkeepers made every effort to accommodate each guest's needs at check-in, check-out, and breakfast." *(Mary Cole)* "No detail of renovation or decorating was omitted, from the plumbing and lighting fixtures to the wreaths on the doors." *(Nancy Kurten)*

Open All year.
Rooms 12 doubles—all with full private bath, telephone, desk, air-conditioning, ceiling fan. Some with fireplace, deck; 1 with TV, Jacuzzi.
Facilities Dining room with fireplace, living room with fireplace, wet bar, TV/VCR, VCR library; solarium, porches. Courtyard, croquet lawn. Business hook-ups (fax, modem). Swimming, tennis privileges at nearby club. Off-street parking.
Location 1 1/2 blocks E of Country Club Plaza.
Restrictions Smoking restricted to living room. No children under 13.
Credit cards Amex, MC, Visa.
Rates B&B, $110–135 double, $90–115 single. Corporate discount.
Extras Wheelchair access; 1 room equipped for disabled.

ROCHEPORT

School House B&B ¢   *Tel:* 314–698–2022
Third and Clark Streets, 65279

The School House B&B was built in 1914 as a three-story brick school house and served the local area into the 1960s. In 1987 John and Vicki Ott purchased the building and restored it as a B&B. Student desks and wheezing radiators have been replaced with antique beds and dressers and old-fashioned bathtubs, but the big blackboard in the reception room reminds guests of their grade school days. Guest rooms are spacious with 13-foot ceilings, large windows, lace curtains, and bright wallpaper. Rates include a full breakfast. *(MW)* More reports required.

Open All year. Closed Christmas.
Rooms 8 doubles—all with private shower and/or bath, telephone, air-conditioning. 2 rooms in annex.
Facilities Common room with blackboard, TV. 1 acre with patios, fountains, gardens, hot tub. Off-street parking. 2 blocks to walking, biking trail.
Location Central MO. 12 m W of Columbia on I-70. In town.
Restrictions No smoking. No children under 5.
Credit cards MC, Visa.
Rates B&B, $55–95 double. Extra person, $20.
Extras One guest room and bath has wheelchair access.

ST. CHARLES

Founded by French Canadians in the 1770s, St. Charles was Missouri's first capital when statehood was achieved in 1821. Another historic moment came when Lewis & Clark made the town the starting point for their explorations of the Louisiana Purchase. Many German settlers arrived throughout the 19th century, and the town prospered as a shipping center because of its location on the Missouri River. Today, many historic homes and buildings have been restored in the South Main Street Historic District, and in the Frenchtown Antiques District; a riverboat cruise will give you another perspective on the town. And yet it's just a 30-minute drive from the St. Louis Arch.

Boone's Lick Trail Inn ¢   *Tel:* 314–947–7000
1000 South Main Street, 63301   8 A.M.–5 A.M. CST: 800–366–2427

Built as an inn in 1840, the Boone's Lick Trail Inn—also known as the Carter-Rice building—is one of the oldest buildings in town. Early adventurers and settlers stayed at this last outpost before moving westward, while the little rooms off the back gallery were once used for a brothel. Begun in 1853, Boone's Lick Road led from the inn up to Arrow Rock, where it joined the Santa Fe Trail. The inn is owned by V'Anne Mydler and her family, and rooms are furnished with fresh flowers, old quilts, lace curtains, late 19th-century beds, and yellow pine floors. A breakfast of fresh fruit, homemade rolls and breads, homemade jams and jellies, and a main dish, such as an egg casserole or French toast, is served in the dining room on Haviland china and fine silver.

"The beds were comfortable, and the furnishings a nice compromise between 19th-century atmosphere and 20th-century comfort. Even the small, claw-foot tub in the bath was set up nicely for showers. Mrs. Mydler was always scurrying around trying her best to make all her guests feel at home. Everything was neat as a pin. Breakfast the first morning included coffee, orange juice, cantaloupe with strawberries, muffins and terrific buckwheat pancakes. The second morning we had cinnamon rolls, hot cross buns, cheese omelet and a fruit compote with apples, grapes, and yogurt sauce." *(Walter & Paula Briggs)* "Service was downright homey—friendly, courteous, and helpful, with care for my special dietary needs. The corner location is not especially quiet, but the scene from the porch was active and interesting, right in the middle of the historic district and close to the river." *(Lois Warburton)* "Perfect location in a quaint part of town. V'Anne was concerned with all the little touches that make a stay enjoyable. We were surprised that a town so close to a big city could have so much charm." *(Debbie Mishkin & Michael Swiatek)*

Open All year. Closed Christmas.
Rooms 1 suite, 4 doubles—all with private shower, telephone, radio, TV, air-conditioning, fan. Suite with balcony.
Facilities Dining room, family room with TV, game table; porch, patio.
Location E MO. Approx. 20 m N of St. Louis. From St. Louis, take I-70 W & exit at First Capitol Dr. Continue to Main St. & turn right to inn at Main & Boone's Lick Rd.
Restrictions Light traffic noise in early evening. No smoking.
Credit cards Amex, Discover, MC, Visa with $3 surcharge.
Rates B&B, $95–115 suite, $65–69 double, $53–69 single. Extra adult, $20; child, $15. Discount for 2-night stay on holiday/festival weekends.

STE. GENEVIEVE

Ste. Genevieve is the oldest town west of the Mississippi; it sits on the Mississippi River, about 60 miles south of St. Louis. Settled in the 1750s by French Canadians when this area was still part of French-owned Upper Louisiana, the town has preserved a rich collection of 18th and 19th-century French Creole buildings. Later immigrants included Yankees from Kentucky, and Germans in the 1850s. Be sure to follow the town's walking tour, visiting the many restored dwellings now open as museums.

Information please: The Steiger House is a B&B offering reasonably priced suites and cottages and use of the inn's indoor swimming pool (1021 Market Street 63670; 314–883–5881).

Listed in previous editions is the **Inn St. Gemme Beauvais** (78 North Main Street, 63670; 314–883–5744), a sturdy red-brick home built in the 1850s. Owned by Paul Swenson and Marcia Willson since 1988, it offers a stone-walled common room in the basement, a charming restaurant with marble fireplace on the first floor, and comfortable guest rooms, simply decorated with some Victorian antiques on the second. A well-traveled reader reported with delight on the friendly helpful innkeeper and delicious food, but with less enthusiasm on the peeling paint and mildew in his bathroom. We hope this problem has long been remedied, and appreciate your comments.

The Southern Hotel ¢   *Tel:* 314–883–3493
146 South Third Street, 63670   800–275–1412

If you were traveling the Mississippi back in the mid-1800s, you might well have spent a comfortable night at The Southern Hotel. A Federal-style building constructed in 1820, it was known as the finest accommodations between Natchez and St. Louis; additional attractions included the gambling rooms and the first pool hall west of the Mississippi. Although the gambling is gone, this historic inn is still welcoming travelers, thanks to the restoration and reconstruction job completed in 1988 by owners Barbara and Mike Hankins. The interior was entirely gutted and rebuilt, with ample common rooms, and guest rooms individually decorated with period antiques.

"A painstakingly restored building now listed on the National Register of Historic Places. Each room is individually decorated, one with folk art, another with a Japanese accent, a third with country Victorian charm. The inn has a relaxed but romantic atmosphere, and the owners have clearly given much attention to detail. Each guest room is comfortable, spacious yet cozy, and most have working fireplaces. The Hankins are warm, generous, caring people who obviously love sharing the charms of their old building. The full French country breakfast was wonderful, the coffee superb." *(Deborah Bianco)* "Our hosts worked hard to create a private, comfortable and beautifully decorated inn. The parlor and dining room offered countless items of interest for antique lovers, and our room had fascinating books." *(Roger & Janis McCurley)* "Private, immaculate, homey and full of antiques. We arrived, were shown to our room, and left alone—just what we wanted. The splendid breakfast included champagne and orange juice, artichoke strata, croissants, and excellent coffee." *(Rebecca Haidt)*

A word of advice: Although all the rooms have wonderful claw foot tubs, in a number of them, the bathroom is a part of the guest room, separated only by a screen.

Open All year.
Rooms 1 suite, 9 doubles—all with private bath and/or shower, air-conditioning, fan. 3 rooms in annex.
Facilities Dining room, 2 parlors, game room with pool table. ½ acre with gardens.
Location E MO, Mississippi River. Historic district, across the street from town square. At the corner of Market and Third Sts.
Restrictions No smoking in guest rooms. Children discouraged.
Credit cards MC, Visa.
Rates B&B, $140 suite, $55 double, $45 single. 2-night minimum 2nd weekend in August.

ST. LOUIS

Long known as the Gateway to the West, St. Louis is located in eastern Missouri, at the Illinois border. Although the Gateway Arch remains its premier tourist attraction, there's lots else to keep you busy. The once-decaying downtown area has been transformed in recent years by several major restoration projects. The once-proud Union Station has been restored to its original glory and now functions as a shopping, entertainment, and hotel complex. The *U.S.S. Admiral* is now permanently moored on the Mississippi as an entertainment complex, and Laclede's Landing has been transformed from an abandoned warehouse district into a 19th-century river town. The St. Louis Science Center offers lots of hands-on exhibits, while the free tours (and samples) available at the Anheuser-Busch plant provide hands-on experiences of a totally different kind.

Also recommended: Although this hotel is too big at 301 guest rooms to be included in this guide, once again a reader has reported in with the highest of accolades for a member of the Ritz-Carlton hotel chain. The St. Louis **Ritz-Carlton** (One Ritz-Carlton Drive, 63105; 314–863–6300 or 800–241–3333) is located in Clayton's Carondelet Plaza, halfway between downtown St. Louis and Lambert Airport, and constructed of brick and limestone accented with arched windows and wrought iron balconies. The decor is highlighted by 18th century art and antiques, marble floors, and wood paneling. An exceptional value is the $129 weekend rate, including welcoming drinks and continental breakfast. "Everything was exceptional. Our room had a luxuriously comfortable king-sized bed, down pillows, pile carpeting, a TV hidden in a beautiful cabinet, a small seating area and French doors which opened out to a balcony overlooking the rooftops of the city. The bathroom was sparkling marble with a large well-lit mirror and all the amenities, including a hair dryer and monogrammed bathrobes. The color scheme was a soothing cream and moss green. At night we were enveloped in total silence. Truly a bargain when you consider the same hotel in a larger city would be twice as expensive." (*Kathleen & James Conley*)

Information please: Once part of France's Louisiana Territory, the 1790 **Geandaugh House** (3835-37 South Broadway, 63118; 314–771–5447) is one of the few buildings surviving in St. Louis to have been constructed by French settlers. Located in the downtown area known as Dutchtown South, the inn and its 19th century, Federal-style addition have been authentically restored to provide four guest rooms with shared baths. Rates include breakfast of freshly baked breads and muffins, cereal, coffee and tea.

In neighboring Illinois, the **Westerfield House** (RR 2, P.O. Box 34, Freeburg, 62243; 618–539–5643) is shielded by evergreen trees planted from seed; adjacent is an herb garden home to 120 varieties, including 30 species of mint. The inn is a three-level log cabin, furnished with antiques, some dating back to Colonial times. Promptly at seven, guests are seated on antique Windsor chairs, at candlelit tables, and are served a leisurely seven-course meal by their hosts, clad in colonial garb.

For additional entries in neighboring Illinois, see entry for **Elsah**, about 40 miles upriver from St. Louis, for pleasant B&Bs in a 19th-century village.

Lafayette House ¢ 👫   *Tel: 314–772–4429*
2156 Lafayette Avenue, 63104

Overlooking Lafayette Park, this 1876 brick Queen Anne house has been owned by Sarah and Jack Milligan since 1984 and is decorated with many Victorian antiques. Sarah serves a full breakfast of casseroles, quiches, waffles, pancakes, or eggs, with bacon or sausage, and fruits, juices, and homemade breads. She says, "I love to cook, so there is something different every day."

"Excellent service with very gracious and helpful hosts. Wine, cheese, and crackers always available. This Victorian mansion has been elegantly restored and is very comfortable." *(Dr. William Mania)*

"The Lafayette Square area has been extensively and attractively restored and is very convenient to many attractions in St. Louis. We stayed in the third-floor suite with our kids and had room to spare. The Milligans were gracious and helpful hosts who were eager to provide whatever advice or assistance we needed. The full breakfast was very good and included Sarah's excellent home-baked speciality breads. The Milligans have several resident cats so allergic persons should take note." *(James & Janice Utt)* More comments welcome.

Open All year.
Rooms 1 suite, 3 doubles—2 with full private bath, 2 with maximum of 4 people sharing bath. All rooms with air-conditioning. Suite with kitchen.
Facilities Dining room, living room, lounge, library. Park across street.
Location 2 m from center. Exit I-44 at Jefferson; go N 1 block and turn right on Lafayette; or exit Rte. 40 at Jefferson and go S 7 blocks to Lafayette and turn left.
Restrictions Smoking in lounge area only.
Credit cards None accepted.
Rates B&B, $75 suite, $50–60 double, $45–50 single. Extra adult, $15; extra child, $10. 2-night minimum stay in suite.
Extras Airport/station pickup, fee charged. Crib, high chair.

Seven Gables Inn 🍴   *Tel: 314–863–8400*
26 North Meramec, Clayton, 63105   Outside MO: 800–433–6590

Inspired by Nathaniel Hawthorne's *House of the Seven Gables* and its illustrations, a St. Louis architect designed the Seven Gables as an apart-

MISSOURI

ment building in the early 1900s. In 1985 it was completely renovated and converted to a hotel and restaurant. Rooms are traditionally furnished, and its two French restaurants have excellent reputations: Chez Louis, the fancier one, was named as one of the country's top hotel restaurants by *The New York Times*.

"The Seven Gables is just 10 minutes from the St. Louis airport and is very much like one of the Relais de Campagne in France. The service was faultless and the food exquisite." *(Ethel Aaron Hauser)* "This lovely little European-style hotel provides quiet and tasteful accommodation in a historic building in the middle of a bustling office and shopping area. The furnishings and service are impeccable, worthy of a large, luxury establishment. The crowning glory of the Seven Gables is its food. Chez Louis is a marvelous French restaurant, and Bernard's is a bistro with a lighter menu. Both are very popular with St. Louisans as well as with the inn's guests. The restaurants share an outstanding wine cellar." *(Irving Litvag)*

"This is a classy place, with huge, beautifully decorated rooms and all the amenities a business traveler could want. Vacation travelers will have to decide if they want the extras that come with an urban hotel—valet parking, people opening doors, newspapers at your door, etc—and if they are willing to pay for them." *(Barry Gardner)*

One well-traveled writer noted that light sleepers should request the third-floor rooms to eliminate overhead noise, and felt that rooms in this price range should come with a proper closet, not just an open rod. Comments?

Open All year.
Rooms 4 suites, 28 doubles—all with full private bath, TV, telephone, radio, desk, air-conditioning.
Facilities Restaurant, bistro, bar, garden courtyard. Shaw Park nearby for jogging, swimming, tennis, ice skating. Valet parking. Room service.
Location E central MO. Clayton is at the intersection of Hwys. 40 and I-70. 7 m from downtown. ½ block from St. Louis County Government Center.
Credit cards Amex, DC, Discover, MC, Visa.
Rates Room only, $146–370 suite, $115–140 double, $100–126 single. Extra person, $30–45. Weekend B&B rate, $85 double. Honeymoon packages. Alc breakfast, $6–11; alc lunch, $15–20; alc dinner, $20–50 (lower prices in bistro, higher in restaurant).
Extras Wheelchair access; some guest rooms equipped for disabled. French, Italian, Spanish, German spoken. Member, Relais et Chateaux.

SPRINGFIELD

Walnut Street Inn ¢   *Tel:* 417–864–6346
900 East Walnut, 65806

Some of the most interesting B&Bs began life as a designer showcases, and the Walnut Street Inn is no exception. A Queen Anne Victorian home built in 1894, the inn was bought by Nancy and Gary Brown in 1988, and is managed by their daughter Karol Brown. To benefit the local symphony orchestra, the house was featured as a designer showcase with all of the rooms done by area artists and decorators. Although each room has a very different look, all pay tribute to the inn's Victorian heritage, complementing its beveled leaded glass windows and hardwood floors. One handsome guest room is done in hunter green and burgundy, with exuberant reproduction paisley wallcoverings and draperies, while another is light and cheery with four windows and a decor of white wicker, white floral comforters and window swags, and yellow striped wallpaper. The Browns have been inveterate antiques collectors for years, and often sell the furnishings of some of the rooms, replacing them with other pieces from their acquisitions. Rates include a breakfast of such Ozark specialties as persimmon muffins, walnut bread, or feather cakes, with smoked ham or bacon, seasonal fruit, freshly squeezed orange juice, and coffee. Wine and cheese is also offered from 5 to 6 P.M. each afternoon.

"The location is ideal, and the inn's decor is distinctive. Food and atmosphere were tops, and Karol's warmth and helpfulness will bring us back many times." *(Amy Cole)* More reports appreciated.

One area for improvement: "More bedside lights for night-time reading would be helpful."

Open All year.
Rooms 1 suite, 6 doubles—all with private bath, telephone, radio, TV, desk, air-conditioning, fan. 2 with balcony.
Facilities Living room, gathering room with fireplace, TV, stereo, guest refrigerator; porch, deck. Garden. Tennis, golf, children's play equipment nearby. Off-street parking. Boating, fishing, skiing nearby.
Location Ozark Mt., SW MO. 3 m S of I-44. Center of town. From I-44 take Exit 82A and go S on Hwy. B65. Turn right on Rte. 13, then turn left on Sherman Pkwy.-John. O. Hammons Pkwy. Go 1 block to Walnut St. and turn right to inn.
Restrictions No smoking. No children under 8.
Credit cards Amex, Discover, MC, Visa.
Rates B&B, $95 suite, $65–95 double or single. Extra person, $10. Tipping "not encouraged." Midweek rate, weekend packages.
Extras German spoken.

WASHINGTON

Information please: Washington House (3 Lafayette Street, 63090; 314–239–2417) offers antique-filled rooms in the 150-year-old home of Mr. and Mrs. Charles Davis. Most rooms have river views, and all have private baths and queen-size canopy beds. The reasonable rates include wine and cheese on arrival, and breakfast. Reports, please.

The Schwegmann House ¢   *Tel:* 314–239–5025
438 West Front Street, 63090

With a population of 10,000, Washington is the largest town of the Missouri Rhineland, so named by the many Germans who settled here in the early 1800s. Schwegmann House was built over a century ago by a prosperous miller who needed a house large enough to provide overnight accommodation for his customers. Owned by George Bocklage, it has been run as a B&B since 1983 and is furnished with antiques and hand-made quilts. Innkeeper Mary Ann Page serves a continental breakfast of juice and fruit, croissants, jam, and cheese.

"The house is very clean and attractive inside and out, and the breakfast is plentiful and healthy. The atmosphere is homey and friendly." *(Glen Steele)* "The rooms were decorated with wonderful antiques. Innkeeper Mary Ann Page was gracious and served a delightful breakfast that included locally made grape juice, sausage, and cheese." *(Nancy Lamb)*

Open All year.

Rooms 9 doubles—7 with private bath and/or shower, 2 with maximum of 4 people sharing bath. All rooms with air-conditioning, fan; some with desk.

Facilities Living/dining room, parlor with fireplace. Grape arbor, patio, gardens. River for fishing across street.

Location E central MO. Wine country, 1 hr. W of St. Louis. 1 block to center. From Hwy. 44, drive W 10 m to Hwy. 100. Turn right on Jefferson, left on Front St. to inn.

Restrictions Train noise might disturb light sleepers. No smoking.

Credit cards MC, Visa.

Rates B&B, $65 double, $55 single. Extra person, $10. Reduced family rates.

Extras Limited wheelchair access.

We Want to Hear from You!

As you know, this book is only effective with your help. We really need to know about your experiences and discoveries. If you stayed at an inn or hotel listed here, we want to know how it was. Did it live up to our description? Exceed it? Was it what you expected? Did you like it? Were you disappointed? Delighted? Have you discovered new establishments that we should add to the next edition?

Tear out one of the report forms at the back of this book (or use your own stationery if you prefer) and write today. *Even if you write only "Fully endorse existing entry" you will have been most helpful.*

Thank You!

Nebraska

The Offutt House, Omaha

Although Nebraska is the fifteenth-largest state, this chapter was once the shortest one in our guide. Fortunately, this has changed. Although Nebraska is discovering B&Bs late in the game, they're substantially on the upswing, and we are pleased to list many of them in our guides. Some are a bit primitive yet when it comes to the question of private baths, but the modest prices and genuine hospitality should more than compensate guests for any inconvenience. We would love to hear more about these or any other bed & breakfasts, country inns, guest ranches, or city hotels of character and distinction. So, if you're doing business in Omaha, visiting the university in Lincoln, or stopping in North Platte while traveling on Interstate 80, please do join our corps of inn-vestigators!

Also recommended: Although it is too large for a full listing, *Betty Ross* wrote to tell us about an agreeable hotel in South Sioux City in the northeastern corner of the state. "Right on the Missouri Riverbank, the **Marina Inn** (4th & B Street, South Sioux City 68776; 402–494–4000 or 800–798–7980), having undergone a refurbishing and a three story new addition, is sparkling fresh. Our room was tastefully decorated, well-ventilated to catch the fresh breezes, equipped with all necessary amenities, with easy access to parking. It was pleasant to walk in the nearby park and along the river. The desk clerks were courteous and helpful, the restaurant had pleasant views of the river, a bounteous salad bar, and good staff. A good night's stay in an area with rather mundane motels."

BROWNVILLE

Thompson House ¢   *Tel:* 402–825–6551
Fifth and College Streets, 68321

Homesteaded in 1854 by Richard Brown, Brownville was one of Nebraska's first settlements, and was a prosperous river town at the middle
of the century. Guests enjoy touring the town's restored 19th-century
buildings, poking into local antique shops, and taking a cruise down the
Missouri River. A three-level, brick house constructed in 1869, Thompson
House has been authentically restored and furnished with period antiques,
stained-glass windows, and handmade area rugs. Rates include breakfast,
but guests are also welcome to fix an evening meal in the kitchen.
    "Lovely B&B, small but comfortable, with great antiques." *(JS)*

Open All year.
Rooms 5 doubles—3 with private shower and/or bath, 2 rooms sharing 1 bath.
All with air-conditioning.
Facilities Living room, kitchen with wood-burning stove. Yard with creek,
bridge.
Location SE NE. In town. Call for directions.
Restrictions No smoking. No children under 12.
Credit cards MC, Visa.
Rates B&B, $45–70 double. Discount for extended stay.

GRAND ISLAND

Kirschke House ¢   *Tel:* 308–381–6851
1124 West Third Street, 68801

Located nearly halfway between Omaha and North Platte in the Platte
River Valley, Grand Isle was settled in 1857 by German immigrants
moving west from Iowa. Later, the railroad helped to bring prosperity to
the region, and with it came fine, solid homes. One such home was the
two-story brick home built in 1902 by successful contractor Otto
Kirschke, with such embellishments as a windowed cupola, turret, stained
glass windows, and oak woodwork. Rooms have been cheerfully decorated with country Victorian antiques and reproductions by owner Lois
Hank, who discovered the pleasures of B&Bs on several trips to Europe,
and decided to introduce the concept to Grand Isle in 1989. In a creative
combination of new and old, guests will enjoy relaxing in the wooden hot
tub, found in the lantern-lit brick wash house. Rates include a full breakfast
of fresh fruit or hot fruit compote, a egg and cheese dish, sausage or
Canadian bacon, homemade oatmeal or whole grain bread, blueberry or
other muffins, juice, and fresh ground coffee.
    "The Kirschke House is a delightful place full of old-world charm and
modern conveniences. The entire house is bright, clean, and pleasant to
be in. Each room has been meticulously restored in a comfortable, work-
able manner. Lois is a superb cook whose breakfasts and dinners were real

feasts." *(Phyllis & Robert Kimbrough)* "Very friendly innkeeper, excellent service, delicious food, spotless accommodations, and beautifully decorated, romantic rooms." *(Marilyn Chadwell)* "Fresh popcorn and cold beer were the perfect midnight snack when I arrived late at night, after a seven-hour drive. Coffee was hot, gourmet, and waiting outside my room the next morning." *(Kelly Taylor)* More comments welcome.

Open All year.
Rooms 4 doubles—3 with sink in room, all sharing 1 bath. All with desk, air-conditioning, fan. TV on request.
Facilities Dining room, parlor with fireplace, TV/VCR, courtyard with patio, hot tub, croquet, picnic area.
Location Central NE. 9 m N of I-80. From I-80, take Exit 312 and go N 9 m on Hwy. 281. Turn E at Hwy. 30 exit. Continue E into town and go 4 blocks past Broadwell St. traffic light. Turn N on Washington St. and go 1 block to inn.
Restrictions No smoking.
Credit cards Amex, MC, Visa.
Rates B&B, $45 double, $40 single. Extra adult, $15; extra child, $10. Prix fixe lunch, $7; prix fixe dinner, $15.
Extras Station pickup. Babysitting.

LINCOLN

State capital and home of the University of Nebraska, Lincoln is home to beautiful parks and interesting museums, ranging from the sunken gardens of Antelope Park to the history of Nebraska on display at the New State Museum, and the fossilized elephants at the university museum. Of course, if you're heading for cultural overdose, you can always take in a free visit to the National Museum of Roller Skating!

The Rogers House ¢   *Tel:* 402–476–6961
2145 B Street, 68502

A brick Jacobean Revival house built in 1914, The Rogers House features windows of leaded and beveled glass, French doors, and polished hardwood floors. It's furnished in period antiques; beds have down comforters. Nora Houtsma, who converted Rogers House into a B&B in 1984, enjoys guests with business in town or at the university, as well as folks just passing through. Rates include a hot entrée, fresh fruit, pastry, and fresh-squeezed orange juice. "Lovely, comfortable house; very gracious hostess." *(Jeannie Swoboda)* More comments appreciated.

Open All year.
Rooms 8 doubles—all with private bath.
Facilities Dining room, living room with fireplace, library, 3 sun-rooms. Walking distance to park with gardens.
Location E central NE. 35 m SW of Omaha. Historic Near South neighborhood. 5 min. from downtown and university.
Credit Cards Amex, MC, Visa.
Rates B&B, $45–55 double. $40–50 single.

OMAHA

The Offutt House ¢   *Tel:* 402–553–0951
140 North 39th Street, 68131

Even if you're not familiar with "Chateauesque-style" architecture, you'll still recognize it immediately when you see the Offutt House. An imposing yellow brick 14-room mansion, with a red-tile roof, it sports the massive chimneys and gables that you would expect. Built in 1894 in a section developed by Omaha's wealthiest residents, the area is known today as Omaha's Historic Gold Coast. The house was one of the only ones to survive the Easter Sunday Tornado of 1913; according to a local source, "an open decanter of sherry was carried 35 feet from the dining-room sideboard to the living room without spilling a drop." Jeanne Swoboda has owned the inn since 1978.

"The house, simply but elegantly furnished with many antiques, is clean and exceptionally comfortable. Jeanne Swoboda is a gracious and charming hostess." *(Dr. William Mania)* "Great atmosphere; furniture and linens delightfully in tune with the building; friendly and helpful owner; peaceful setting in a cul-de-sac; ample and easy parking, with quick access to all points of interest and downtown. Three minutes' walk to public transport." *(Barbara Edna Kaye)* "A historic house in a wonderful neighborhood, serene living rooms, beautifully appointed dining room and bar, promptly served breakfast with ample homebaked breads and fresh fruit. My bedroom had a Dutch tile fireplace, beautifully decorated porch, mahogany sleigh bed, generous closets, and was clean and well maintained. Sharing a bath did not prove inconvenient and the claw foot tub was like a small swimming pool, a great relief from the 95° heat. Parking was on the street, but close to the house." *(Polly Noe)*

Open All year.
Rooms 1 suite, 6 doubles—3 with private bath, 4 with maximum of 4 people sharing bath. All with telephone, radio, TV, desk, air-conditioning, fan. 2 with fireplace, 1 with deck.
Facilities Dining room with fireplace, living room with fireplace, books, stereo, piano; library, lounge, guest laundry, porch, picnic area. Golf nearby.
Location 2 miles from center; Historic Gold Coast. 1 block N of main thoroughfare.
Restrictions Children by prior arrangement.
Credit cards Amex, MC, Visa.
Rates B&B, $75 suite, $45–65 double, $45–55 single. Extra person, $15. Weekly rates.
Extras Airport/station pickup, $5. Pets "possibly" allowed. Crib.

PAWNEE CITY

My Blue Heaven ¢   *Tel:* 402–852–3131
1041 Fifth Street, 68420   402–852–9114

Yvonne Dalluge has recently opened her comfortable country home to B&B guests. Rooms are furnished with some antiques, handsewn quilts, tatting, and many handcrafted items; as you might expect, blue is a favored color in the simple decor. The Dalluges welcome guests who would like a taste of quiet small-town hospitality; you can spend the day exploring the area lakes and other attractions—even a museum displaying 800 varieties of barbed wire—and return to sit on the porch swing and listen to the birds. Rates include a full breakfast—perhaps blueberry pancakes, quiche, or "whatever else guests enjoy," with home-baked muffins and fresh fruit.

"Mr. and Mrs. Dalluge were kindness personified. The rooms are spotlessly clean; the beds are comfortable, and the guest rooms well equipped with ample storage space. The only sounds were those of birds nesting. The breakfast was a generous well-cooked farm breakfast pleasingly presented. The Dalluges are knowledgeable about the community and local restaurants, and helpful with directions and suggestions. Pawnee City is a quiet farming town located in an area of diversified activity. The area is spotted with a number of lakes, hunting areas, and historic buildings." *(Stanley Hess, also Mrs. Willadean Merrill)*

Open All year.
Rooms 2 doubles sharing 1 bath. Both with air-conditioning, fan.
Facilities Dining room, living room with TV, kitchen, porch with swing. Swimming, tennis, golf nearby. Lakes nearby for fishing, boating.
Location SE NE, 5 m N of Kansas border. 70 m S of Lincoln. From intersection of Rte. 50 and 8, go S 2 blocks and turn E. Go 3 blocks to inn.
Restrictions No smoking. No children under 10.
Credit cards MC, Visa.
Rates B&B, $30–35 double.
Extras Local airport pickup.

RED CLOUD

The Meadowlark Manor ¢   *Tel:* 402–746–3550
241 West 9th Avenue, 68970

Named for the famous Sioux chieftain, Red Cloud is today a farming and ranching community, best known as the childhood home of Willa Cather. The Meadowlark is within walking distance of the Cather Historical Center, and is part of a historic district listed on the National Register. Frankie Warner, along with her husband Mark and children Tammy and Mark Jr., has owned this B&B since 1987, opening it to B&B guests after nearly a year of renovations.

Built in 1915, the inn is highlighted by beveled and leaded windows, period decor, and original stenciling, along with flowered wallpapers, freshly painted trim, gleaming oak floors, and Oriental carpets. The living and dining room combine period and contemporary decor, while the inviting front porch is supplied with chairs and tables for relaxing.

"Meadowlark Manor jumps right out of the pages of Cather's writings. One can see 'Lucy Gayheart' strolling down 'Quality Street' which fronts this lovely home. The food is delicious, creative, and beautifully served; the hospitality always felt but never intrusive." *(Beverly Cooper)* "The whole house is devoted to the guests; the owners' quarters and entrance are entirely separate. The splendid dining room has a huge table, making it pleasant to visit with other guests at breakfast. The food is excellent, especially the quiche and the giant German pancakes with lemon butter. The guest rooms are lovely. Everything, from sheets to pillows to comforters to the terry-cloth robes are of the highest quality. The bathroom has a deep soaking tub with a separate shower, a huge dressing table and mirror. The towers are large and thick, the soap and shampoo soft and fragrant. Everything is spotless. Frankie is a most gracious smiling hostess, always ready with a glass of ice tea, beds turned down at night, and mints on the table." *(Sylvia Wolff)* "I reread Cather's story 'Old Mrs. Harris' while lying on the Victorian oak bed, with the late afternoon sun filtering through the lace curtain. Frankie's breakfasts are terrific, especially her French toast." *(Susan Parry)*

Open All year.
Rooms 1 suite, 2 doubles, 1 single—sharing 1 full bath and 1 half bath. All with desk, air-conditioning, fan.
Facilities Dining room, parlor with fireplace, library, piano, games. Children's play equipment. Swimming, tennis, golf nearby.
Location S central NE, approx. 5 m N of Kansas border. In historic district. From Hwy. 281 turn left on 9th Ave. and go 2 blocks to inn.
Restrictions No smoking.
Credit cards None accepted.
Rates B&B, $40 suite, $36–40 double, $27 single. Extra person, $7. By prior arrangement, "High Tea" $6; prix fixe lunch, $8; prix fixe dinner, $20.
Extras Airport pickup. Crib, babysitting.

SPALDING

Esch House ¢
Highway 92, Rte. 1, Box 140, 68665

Tel: 308–497–2628

"This lovely hilltop home overlooks the beautiful Nebraska Sandhills. Nearly all of the second floor of this relatively new home is just for the guests. Mrs. Esch is a writer and a very delightful and interesting hostess. She's also a fabulous cook; her excellent breakfast of fresh baked cinnamon rolls, and an egg and meat casseroles proved that Nebraskans do know good food. The southern exposure is all glass, upstairs and down. The bedrooms are beautifully but comfortably furnished. A large skylight in my bedroom was lovely; one can actually count the stars in Nebraska, and here you have a chance to do that while going to sleep. The upstairs loft living room has a fireplace and TV for guests' use.

"The small town of Spalding is on the other side of the highway, and has a steak restaurant, several shops, and a huge Catholic cathedral. Best of all are the Sandhills. It is a shame that people travel across our lovely state and never see their desolate beauty. Highway 91 is only a short distance north of Interstate 80, and one can travel across most of the state and be thrilled by the wildflowers, the varied grasses, and the magnificent sunsets and sunrises." *(Sylvia Wolff)*

Open All year.
Rooms 5 doubles—1 with private bath, 3 with maximum of 6 people sharing bath, 1 sharing bath with family. All with telephone, air-conditioning.
Facilities Dining room, breakfast room, living room with fireplace, TV on each level; guest laundry, deck. 19 acres with fields. Swimming, tennis, golf within 1 m. Canoeing on river nearby.
Location Central NE. 70 m N of Grand Island; ½ m from town on Hwy 91.
Restrictions No smoking.
Credit cards None accepted.
Rates B&B, $35 double. Rollaway bed, $5. Discount for 2-night stay.
Extras Station pickup. Crib, babysitting.

Key to Abbreviations and Symbols

For complete information and explanations, please see the Introduction.

¢ Especially good value for overnight accommodation.

👪 Families welcome. Most (but not all) have cribs, baby-sitting, games, play equipment, and reduced rates for children.

✗ Meals served to public; reservations recommended or required.

🎾 Tennis court and swimming pool or lake on the grounds. Golf usually on grounds or nearby.

Rates: Range from least expensive room in low season to most expensive room in peak season.

Room only: No meals included; European Plan (EP).

B&B: Bed and breakfast; includes breakfast, sometimes afternoon/ evening refreshment.

MAP: Modified American Plan; includes breakfast and dinner.

Full board: Three meals daily.

Alc lunch: À la carte lunch; average price of entrée plus nonalcoholic drink, tax, tip.

Alc dinner: Average price of three-course dinner, including half bottle of house wine, tax, tip.

Prix fixe dinner: Three- to five-course set dinner, excluding wine, tax, tip unless otherwise noted.

Extras: Noted if available. Always confirm in advance. Pets are not permitted unless specified; if you are allergic, ask for details; *most innkeepers have pets.*

North Dakota

We've been waiting *for years* to find some hotels, inns, B&Bs, or even ranches to recommend in North Dakota, but nothing has ever worked out. So, in desperation, we're noting some possibilities below, in the hope that some of our intrepid scouts will report back on their findings.

Information please: After extensive research, we've been able to find one historic hotel, the **Rough Rider** (Box 198, Medora 58645; 701—623-4444 or 701—223—4800) in Theodore Roosevelt National Park in the Badlands of southwestern North Dakota. A non-profit organization administers most of the museums, restaurants, and hotels of Medora, including the Rough Rider, rebuilt with materials from the original hotel where Roosevelt stayed. The nine rooms are simply furnished, but are said to evoke the days when Medora was a booming cattle town, and rates are modest. Medora is the state's most popular tourist attraction, with travelers coming to explore the land once described as "hell with the fires out," to visit the museums and shops of Medora, and to see the well-known Medora Musical, playing all summer.

North Dakota has a number of B&Bs, and you can even get a brochure listing them from the state tourist office (see Appendix). Most are home-stay B&Bs, where a family rents a few spare bedrooms to travelers. In general, the hospitality is genuine, the prices low, the baths typically shared, and the furnishings basic. One promising possibility is **Kirkland** (R.R. 2, Box 18, Carrington 58421; 701—652—2775), about 47 miles north of I-94 at Jamestown. Listed on the National Register of Historic Places, this working wheat farm offers three guest rooms in its Colonial-plantation farmhouse, built in 1910, and is owned and run by the great-grandson of the founders. Stained and leaded glass windows highlight the decor, and the $45 rates include a breakfast of blueberry pancakes, deer sausage, fresh-squeezed orange juice, and homemade muffins and jam. In Jamestown is the **Country Charm B&B** (R.R. 3, Box 71, Jamestown 58401; 701–251–1372), a 1920s home decorated with antiques and collectibles; the $35 double rates include a full breakfast and afternoon tea, and the location is a convenient 1½ miles from I-94.

Of interest on the Minnesota border is **Lord Byron's B&B** (521 South Fifth Street, Grand Forks 58201; 701–775–0194), a century-old home, complete with stained glass and oak woodwork, and furnished with Scandinavian antiques and Mission Oak pieces. The $60 double rate includes a creative breakfast—possibly cold blueberry soup, phyllo dough filled with ham, cheese, and mushrooms, and waffles with plum sauce.

We Want to Hear from You!

As you know, this book is only effective with your help. We really need to know about your experiences and discoveries. If you stayed at an inn or hotel listed here, we want to know how it was. Did it live up to our description? Exceed it? Was it what you expected? Did you like it? Were you disappointed? Delighted? Have you discovered new establishments that we should add to the next edition?

Tear out one of the report forms at the back of this book (or use your own stationery if you prefer) and write today. *Even if you write only "Fully endorse existing entry" you will have been most helpful.*
Thank You!

Ohio

The Buxton Inn, Granville

Ohio, with an economy based on manufacturing and agriculture, has both major industrial cities and rich farmland.

Although once plagued by bad press, Ohio's urban centers actually offer visitors a wealth of options: Cleveland is ringed by a necklace of lovely parks and has a lively theater and art scene, Cincinnati's zoo is a favorite with children of all ages, and Columbus' German Village is a great place to explore antique shops and sip beer. Other surprises include 46 wineries (6th largest wine-producing state in the country), 2,000-year-old Indian burial mounds near Chillicothe, and a group of scenic Lake Erie islands located offshore from Port Clinton.

Architecturally, parts of northeastern Ohio will look very familiar to aficionados of New England's colonial heritage. Known as "Connecticut's Western Reserve" when it was deeded by Charles II of England to residents of Connecticut, the area was settled by immigrants from that eastern colony, who proceeded to construct homes and towns reminiscent of those they'd left behind. From these origins, Cleveland derives its "Western Reserve" style; one of the most notable towns in this genre is the small community of Hudson, about 20 miles southeast of Cleveland. Another appealing area is Holmes County, in the north central part of the state, home to a large Amish community. (See entries for Danville, Loudonville, and Millersburg.)

Information please: There are some interesting possibilities in the Toledo area we'd like to hear more about. The **Mansion View Inn** (2035 Collingwood Boulevard, Toledo 43620; 419–244–5676) is just 3 blocks north of I-75, in the Victorian Old West End. Listed on the National Register of Historic Places, this century-old Queen Anne mansion combines such period details as corbelled red brick, feathered slate, beveled and stained glass, and period antiques with such 20th century amenities as private baths, kitchenettes, and in-room telephones. About 50 miles east of Toledo is Sandusky, home to **Wagners 1844 Inn** (230 East

Washington Street, Sandusky, 44870; 419–626–1726) an Italianate Victorian home. Period decor in the three guest rooms is paired with private baths and air-conditioning; rates include a continental breakfast, served in the dining room or on the screened veranda. About 50 miles southeast of Toledo is the historic college town of Tiffin. The **Zelkova Inn** (2348 South CR 19, Tiffin 44883; 419–447–4043) is named for the zelkova trees that line the driveway of this 30-acre estate just outside of town. Rooms are furnished with antiques and reproductions, complemented by cherry woodwork and a muted 18th century color scheme. Outdoors, the inn offers a swimming pool, ornamental gardens, and nature trails. Reports would be most welcome.

Rates do not include 5.75% sales tax, and local hotel occupancy taxes where applicable.

AURORA

The town of Aurora, located midway between Cleveland and Akron, and 6 miles north of I-80, is best known as the home of Sea World of Ohio. The center of Midwestern cheese production in the mid-1800s, Aurora developed into an area of elegant farms and Western Reserve homes during the 1920s real estate boom; the crash of 1929 ended those plans, but lovely homes and estate farms dot the community.

During the summer, local highways become clogged with traffic as families arrive to enjoy Sea World and its neighboring amusement park, Geauga Lake. The town of Aurora itself is little more than a crossroads, with a scattering of quaint shops among century-old homes. To take advantage of the visitors generated by Sea World, various discount outlets have sprung up. To add to the confusion, Aurora Farms has an old-time flea market on Wednesday and Sunday, where you can rent a 4-by-8 plot of land and sell whatever legal wares you choose.

The Aurora Inn 🏃 ✖ 🎋   *Tel:* 216–562–6121
State Routes 306 & 82, 44202   800–444–6121

If you come to the Aurora Inn expecting a quaint country inn, you'll be disappointed. Built in 1927 by the Van Swearingens, famous Ohio real estate developers, the original structure was destroyed by fire in 1963 and was completely rebuilt. Designed to replicate the outward appearance of the old inn, the reconstruction provides both the amenities and the atmosphere of a modern business travelers' hotel. "The rooms are very comfortable, with reproduction antiques that lend a homey feeling. But the crowning touch is the food. From excellent pastries in the morning to superb steaks for dinner, everything is Midwestern mouthwatering." *(Mark Rechner)* Also: "Too motel-like for our tastes."

Open All year.
Rooms 10 suites, 36 doubles, 23 singles—all with private bath and/or shower, telephone, radio, TV, desk, air-conditioning.

Facilities Restaurant, tavern with fireplace, music on weekend evenings; lobby with fireplace. 3 acres with patios, heated indoor and outdoor swimming pools, Jacuzzi, saunas, tennis courts.
Location NE OH. 30 m SE of Cleveland, 20 m NE of Akron. At intersection of Rtes. 82 & 306 (crossroads of road to Sea World and Geauga Lake Park).
Restrictions No smoking in some guest rooms.
Credit cards Amex, MC, Visa.
Rates Room only, $96–143 suite, $85–133 double, $72–123 single. Extra person, $15. Children's, senior discounts. Full breakfast, $3–8. Alc dinner, $20–35. 15% service additional for meals. Weekly rates.
Extras Pets permitted by prior arrangement. Crib.

CHAGRIN FALLS

The Inn of Chagrin Falls ✗   *Tel:* 216–247–1200
West Street, 44022

Neat white clapboard homes primly set along tree-lined streets, and sedate Colonial storefronts on Main Street give Chagrin Falls the look of a New England village. The eponymous waterfall is right in the center of town; local legend says that early settler Moses Cleaveland found it while travelling down the river, much to his "chagrin."

The Inn of Chagrin Falls occupies a building long known as Crane's Canary Cottage, built in 1927 as the country home of Ohio-born poet Hart Crane. A group of local investors spent a year gutting and rebuilding this traditional Colonial-style cottage, with steeply pitched roofs and multi-paned windows, while maintaining its rich canary yellow color. The inn's restaurant, the Gamekeeper's Taverne, has occupied one wing of the building for decades and remains as popular as ever, with its dark wood panelling, intimate booth seating, and hunting trophies on the walls. Rates include a continental breakfast and afternoon sherry.

"The building looks deceptively small from the outside, but the interior has high ceilings and generously-sized rooms. The living room has dark green-striped wallpaper, antique and reproduction furniture, and feels like an English club, complete with shelves of books and deep wing chairs. The reproduction furnishings in the guest rooms vary from wicker, to Victorian oak, to Colonial cherry four-poster beds. Coordinating wallpapers and borders highlight the walls, and lush bouquets of silk flowers accent each room. The luxurious bathrooms have brass fittings and sconces, and large tiled showers; some have a Jacuzzi tub with a view of the bedroom fireplace. Every room has a good reading lamp next to a comfortable chair or sofa, and interesting prints hang on the walls." *(NB)* More reports welcome.

Open All year.
Rooms 4 suites, 11 doubles—all with full private bath, telephone, TV, desk. 11 with fireplace, 3 with double Jacuzzi tub.
Facilities Restaurant, library, patio.
Location NE OH. 20 m E of Cleveland. 1 block from falls, 2 blocks from the center.
Restrictions No smoking in guest rooms. No children under 8.

Credit cards Amex, MC, Visa.
Rates B&B, $165–180 suite, $95–155 double. Corporate rates.

CINCINNATI

A cosmopolitan city with a slight touch of the South due to its proximity to Kentucky, Cincinnati abounds in sports fever (the Reds and the Bengals) and fine restaurants. After the city's initial importance as a port for cargo-bearing riverboats, pigs later became the basis of its economy when river traffic declined; a wave of German immigration in the mid-1800s resulted in the city becoming a major center for the slaughtering and butchering of hogs. Both economic and ethnic heritages are reflected in the city's festivals (steamboating, Oktoberfest) and culinary style.

Also recommended: Just across the Roebling Suspension Bridge from Riverfront Stadium in Covington, Kentucky, is another area possibility, the **Amos Shinkle House** (215 Garrard Street, Covington, KY 41011; 606–431–2118). An 1850s brick riverboat house with many original plaster cornices and ceiling medallions, the Amos Shinkle House was restored by owners Bernie Moorman and Don Nash, who uncovered some of the original wall murals in the process. Much of the decorating was completed when it was a designer showcase for a local fund-raiser. A full breakfast is provided, often with crisp-fried German sausage, a local specialty.

The Cincinnatian ✕
6th & Vine Streets, 45202

Tel: 513–381–3000
513–381–3000
In OH: 800–332–2020
In US: 800–942–9000

The Cincinnatian was built in 1882, and was renovated in 1986 as a contemporary hotel surrounding an eight-story atrium. The decor is sleek and modern; bathrooms are equipped with Roman tubs, bathroom phones, terry robes, dressing areas, and hair dryers.

"We had afternoon tea in Crickets, the lobby bar/lounge, which included one's choice of tea, sandwiches, tea breads and scones, and dessert. The food was good, the setting comfortable, and service unhurried. Our third-floor non-smoking room was large, with desk, several tables, couch, chairs, king-sized bed, and ten-foot ceilings in most of the room. The bathroom had contemporary decor in black, light blue, and tan. Both the turndown service and room-service breakfast were on time and good. The front desk staff were competent and friendly, as was the valet parking attendant." *(LG)*

Open All year.
Rooms 149 suites & doubles—all with full private, telephones, TV, radio, air-conditioning, hair dryers. Some with atrium balcony.
Facilities Atrium lobby, restaurant, piano bar/lounge, valet parking.
Location Downtown. 1 block to Fountain Sq.; 3 blocks to Riverfront Stadium. 20 min. to airport.
Restrictions Non-smoking guest rooms. Traffic/construction noise in some rooms.

Credit cards Amex, MC, Visa.
Rates Room only, $450–750 suite, $190–240 double, $165–215 single. Corporate rate, $1435–160. Weekend rate, $99–125. Packages.
Extras Member, Preferred Hotels.

Prospect Hill B&B ¢   *Tel:* 513–421–4408
408 Boal Street, 45210

A restored 1867 Italianate townhouse located in a National Historic district with a hillside view of Cincinnati, the Prospect Hill was opened as a B&B in 1989. Owner Gary Hackney notes that he hosts many business travelers because of the inn's proximity to downtown, but that vacationers would also find the location convenient. Rates include a full breakfast buffet.

"Rooms are authentically decorated to the era, and the combination of woodburning fireplaces, spectacular views, and relaxed atmosphere made for a very romantic weekend. Breakfast was tasty and plentiful, and Gary made us feel right at home." *(Jill Kartisek)* Additional reports welcome.

Note: As we went to press, this inn was for sale; inquire further when booking.

Open All year.
Rooms 2 suites, 2 doubles—2 with private bath and/or shower, 2 with a maximum of 4 people sharing bath. All with radio, TV, air-conditioning, fireplace. 1 with private entrance.
Facilities Dining room, porch. 1 m to river for boating.
Location Prospect Hill National Historic District; N edge of downtown. ½ m from center. From I-71 S, take Reading Rd. exit. Turn right on Liberty, then at Sycamore St. turn right and go 2 blocks to Boal St. Turn right on Boal to inn. From I-71 N, take Reading Rd./Florence, Dorchester exit. Continue on Dorchester and turn left at 2nd light onto Highland. Go 1 block to Boal St. and turn right on Boal to inn.
Restrictions No smoking. No children under 13.
Credit cards MC, Visa.
Rates B&B, $79 suite, $69 double. Extra person, $15. 10% weekly discount.

CLEVELAND

Cleveland has long been known as an industrial zone of factories and less-than-inspiring housing developments and office buildings. For a more appealing view, head for the University Circle area, where the city also provides outstanding cultural activities, such as its world-renowned symphony orchestra and the Cleveland Museum of Art, considered one of the top five art museums in the country. For those whose interests run in other directions, there is the Crawford Auto-Aviation Museum, Case Western Reserve University and the Rock 'n' Roll Hall of Fame. The newest area of interest, with up-and-coming restaurants, nightclubs, and shops in restored factory buildings, is known by locals as the "Flats" because of its low-level terrain in the Cuyahoga River basin.

Just 30 miles south of the city, in Cuyahoga Falls, is the Blossom Music Center, which hosts a music festival every summer similar to the Tanglewood Festival in Massachusetts; The Football Hall of Fame, in Canton, is just 60 miles south of Cleveland.

Information please: Newly opened in 1992 are the restored **Pelton and Franklin House B&Bs** (2830 Franklin Boulevard, Cleveland 44113; 216–861–1646) two adjacent Queen Anne-style Victorian homes located in the downtown district called Ohio City. Just 10 minutes west of downtown Cleveland is **The Captain's House** (16807 Hilliard Road, Lakewood 44107; 216–521–7070). Dating from the 1850s, it was owned for many years by a Great Lakes ship captain, and is listed on the National Register of Historic Places. The house has Italianate and carpenter Gothic detailing, and rates include a home-baked continental breakfast.

In the country village of Chardon—maple syrup capital of Ohio—45 minutes east of Cleveland, and 7 miles from I-90, is the **Bass Lake Inn** (400 South Street, Route 44, Chardon 44024; 216–285–3100). Well-known for its restaurant, the Bass Lake Tavern, the newly built inn overlooks a man-made lake; the 12 spacious guest rooms each have a gas fireplace, Jacuzzi, microwave, refrigerator, and patio or deck. Rates include a breakfast basket of juice, muffins, cereal, milk, and coffee brought to your door.

If you're looking for a weekend getaway, or are traveling through on I-90, two lakeside communities convenient to both will be of interest. Painesville, 30 miles northeast of Cleveland, is home to **Rider's Inn** (792 Mentor Avenue, Painesville 44077; 216–942–2742), an inn since 1812. A large restaurant and tavern occupy the ground floor, while eight upstairs guest rooms, each with private bath, are appealingly decorated with antiques and collectibles, reflecting different periods of the inn's history. Rates include a continental breakfast served in your room, and a guest sitting room offers a private place to read.

In the opposite direction (35 miles to the southwest), is the college town of Oberlin, home to the 75-room **Oberlin College Inn** (State Route 58, On Tappan Square, Oberlin 44074; 216–775–1111). Recently redecorated with period furnishings; its restaurant has an excellent reputation for imaginative cuisine.

Also recommended: Sixty miles northeast of Cleveland and 40 miles from the Pennsylvania border is Ashtabula. The harbor area is currently undergoing a revitalization as a historic district, with antique stores, gift shops, and museums. The 1887 Stick-style **Michael Cahill B&B** (1106 Walnut Boulevard, 44004; 216–964–8449) has been restored as a B&B, and is listed on the National Register of Historic Places. Painted in authentic Victorian colors of dark green and burgundy, it sits high on the hill overlooking the harbor, and offers four air-conditioned guest rooms with private and shared baths. "Like staying at grandma's house, with vintage collectibles and Victorian antiques. A tasty breakfast is served family style, and included fruit-filled corn muffins and frittata." *(NB)*

The Baricelli Inn ✕

2203 Cornell Road, 44106

Tel: 216–791–6500

The Baricelli Inn, with an imposing, hand-carved stone exterior that dominates its street corner, was built in 1896. Owned by the Minnillo family, who have also created three other restaurants widely regarded for their sophisticated cuisine (the Bella Luna, the Greenhouse, and the Ninth Street Grill), the inn opened in 1986. Rates include a continental breakfast of coffee, juice, fresh fruit, muffins and pastry. The Baricelli is famed for its restaurant, serving creative cuisine with an Italian accent. Menus change seasonally, and entrée possibilities include lobster ravioli in a Dijon mustard and dill sauce or roasted lamb in a spinach mousseline with a Cabernet Sauvignon wine sauce.

"The Baricelli is located near University Circle, an elegant neighborhood close to the huge Cleveland Clinic complex, adjacent to the University Hospitals and Case Western Reserve, and just up the street from Severance Hall, winter home of the Cleveland Orchestra. The Minnillos redid this large old house, saving the beautiful woodwork and stair rails, and obviously took great pains to make the new blend with the old. The front entrance is porticoed and faces the brightly lit parking lot. There are four dining rooms, with about five tables in each." *(Pete Blake)* "The food is superb and presented as a culinary and visual feast. Within walking distance of the Symphony Hall, Art Museum, Garden Center, Natural History Museum, Western Reserve Historical Society, and the Auto Museum." *(Mrs. S. Busch)*

"Guest rooms are simply furnished with matching floral comforters and draperies accenting pastel walls. The original fireplaces, with carved mantels reaching almost to the ceiling and inset with mirrors, are the prominent features of two rooms, accented by antique armoires (holding the TV) and traditionally-styled, comfortable chairs complete with reading lamp. The modern baths have theatrical-style lighting strips and built-in hair dryers. The dining room in the original part of the house has beautiful oak woodwork. Comfortable upholstered chairs circle the tables, and wall-to-wall carpeting in subtle shades of moss green cover the floors." *(NB)*

Area for improvement: Except for the atrium lobby, which is often filled with waiting dinner patrons, there is no common area for guests.

Open All year, except major holidays. Restaurant closed Sun.
Rooms 7 doubles—all with full private bath, telephone, radio, TV, air-conditioning, fan, fireplaces. 5 with desk.
Facilities Restaurant, lobby, patio, garden. Near Lake Erie for fishing, boating.
Location 5 m from downtown, in "Little Italy," on the East Side. At corner of Cornell & Murray Hill. 2 blocks from Severance Hall.
Restrictions No cigar or pipe smoking in guest rooms. "Not recommended for children."
Credit cards Amex, MC, Visa.
Rates B&B, $90–125 double. Continental breakfast for non-resident guest (with 24 hr. notice), $6.50. Prix fixe dinner, $60; alc dinner, $50.
Extras Airport/station pickups by prior arrangement. Spanish, French spoken.

Glidden House   Tel: 216–231–8900
1901 Ford Avenue, 44106

This French Gothic-style mansion was built in 1909 and is listed on the National Register of Historic Places; a modern addition houses all the guest rooms except the suites. A continental buffet breakfast is served in what was originally the library, with stone fireplace, dark carved paneling and ceiling beams; dishes are stored where dusty tomes once rested. The guest rooms have a country Victorian decor, with teal-colored carpeting, lace curtains, and cream-colored chenille spreads. Wallcoverings are either plain or floral, with rose, dark green, blue, and cream among the key colors. Some of the more interesting pictures include old framed ads for Glidden Paint, and black-and-white pictures from the Western Reserve Historical Society.

"The lobby and entry are posh; staff is courteous and accommodating. The hotel is lovely, within walking distance of Severance Hall, major museums, and Little Italy." *(Zita Knific)* "A striking stone and brick Tudor home that gives you a glimpse of the grandeur of the era, especially the first floor common rooms. Upstairs, the only remnants of the past are the ornately carved fireplaces in some of the suites. But the rooms are spacious, with crystal bedside lamps and ornate brocade- or floral-patterned wallpapers, comfortably upholstered Queen Anne-style wing chairs with good reading lamps, and modern bathrooms. The rooms in the addition, while of generic hotel design, are large, with the same quality furnishings and floral wallpaper." *(NB)*

Minor niggle: "Some of the rooms have scrubbed pine furniture—attractive, but it seemed a bit out of sync with the building's era and architecture."

Open All year.
Rooms 8 suites, 52 doubles—all with telephone, radio, TV, air-conditioning.
Facilities Lobby, breakfast room with fireplace, enclosed porch, meeting rooms, courtyard. Limited off-street parking.
Location University Circle, 5 m from downtown.
Credit cards Amex, DC, Discover, MC, Visa.
Rates B&B, $105–120 suite, $94 double, $84 single. Extra person, $10.

COLUMBUS

The third of the "C" cities of Ohio, and also its capital city, Columbus seems to be known best as the home of a Big Ten college football team, the Ohio State University Buckeyes. While in football season this does dominate the local atmosphere, Columbus has other attractions for the traveler: its zoo is the only one in the world with three generations of gorillas; and the restored Ohio Theatre and the Palace are lavishly designed 1920s buildings providing entertainment extending from ballet to an annual "Three Stooges Film Festival." Every August, the 17-day Ohio State Fair dominates the local calendar, with 56,000 animals, ranging in size from tiny gerbils and rabbits to draft horses and championship beef cattle. In 1992, numerous special events will also be focused on the 500th anniversary of Christopher Columbus's "discovery" of America.

Information please: Less than 30 minutes southeast of Columbus is Pickerington, a bustling suburb with an "old town" little changed since the 19th century. Built in 1860, the **Central House** (27 West Columbus Street, Old Village Area, Pickerington 43147; 614–837–0932) is a totally restored country hotel.

OHIO

Note: Rates do not include the whopping 15.75% sales tax.

Also recommended: See also entry for **The Worthington Inn** in Worthington.

50 Lincoln, A Very Small Hotel   Tel: 614–291–5056
50 East Lincoln Street, 43215

Owned by Jack and Zoe Johnstone, 50 Lincoln is a 19th-century brick manor house, situated between downtown Columbus and Ohio State University, in a transitional neighborhood of restored homes, art galleries, unique shops, and restaurants known as Short North. Originally a large two-family home, the building was converted to a rooming house in the 1950's. The Johnstones renovated it in 1986, decorating eclectically to create a European-style business hotel. Rates include a full breakfast.

"Simply but tastefully decorated, 50 Lincoln is a well designed inn; the subdued color scheme effectively produces a calming atmosphere. Creative use of space and interesting 'foot' windows make all the bedrooms feel spacious and well-lit; even those under the eaves don't make you feel closed in. Each guest room is thoughtfully furnished with Parsons tables which serve as generous night stands as well as desks, equipped with a good reading lamps and a business telephone system. Jack and Zoe are knowledgeable, interesting, and gracious hosts who were more than happy to make dinner reservations for us at an outstanding nouvelle Italian restaurant nearby, Nonni's. The next morning our breakfast was simply yet elegantly presented; Jack's homemade bread was a real treat. The location is very quiet, and the small backyard with parking area has been intensively landscaped into an inviting garden oasis. This neighborhood is still developing so both restored and unrestored homes sit side by side, with creative new construction tucked here and there." *(NB)*

"Highly recommended, particularly for the business traveler working in downtown Columbus or at Ohio State University. Jack & Zoe are superb innkeepers." *(Jim King, also D. Koyama)* "We stayed here last here when our convention hotel was full, and liked it so much we came back again this year." *(Wilbur Graham)*

Open All year.
Rooms 3 suites, 6 doubles—all with private bath, telephone, radio, TV, desk, air-conditioning.
Facilities Dining room, parlor with piano, garden, off-street parking.
Location Central Ohio. 1 m from downtown, 1 m S of Ohio State Univ., in Short North gallery district.
Credit cards Amex, MC, Visa.
Rates B&B, $119–129 suite, $109 double, $99 single. Extra person, $25.
Extras German, Swedish spoken.

The Great Southern Hotel ✕   Tel: 614–228–3800
310 South High Street, 43215   Outside OH: 800–328–2073
                                        In OH: 800–228–3789

Built in 1896 as one of the first fireproof buildings in the country, the Great Southern Hotel was placed on the National Register of Historic Places when it was totally restored and reopened in 1985. Guest rooms feature Victorian cherry wood reproduction furnishings, and public areas reflect their original elegance, with a marble lobby and stained glass ceiling. The hotel's restaurant, Chutney's, offers California cuisine with such entrées as pork with cranberry chutney and salsa verde; sole stuffed with prosciutto, spinach, and grapefruit in red pepper coulis; and duck breast with shiitake mushrooms, glazed with mulled cider." *(Susie Preston)* "Accommodating, comfortable hotel, perfect for the business traveler in need of a downtown location. Found both the restaurant and the lobby bar very enjoyable." *(Jim King)*

Open All year.
Rooms 30 suites, 166 doubles—all with private bath and/or shower, telephone, radio, TV, desk, air-conditioning.
Facilities Restaurants, bar, lobby. On-site parking.
Location Downtown. Adjacent to City Center Mall; 2 blocks from Capitol. Take High St. exit off I-70/71 to hotel at corner of S. High and Main Sts.
Credit cards Amex, DC, MC, Visa.
Rates Room only, $120 suite, $100 double, $90 single. Weekend rate, $67. 10% senior discount. Alc breakfast, $5–9; alc lunch, $8; alc dinner, $22.
Extras Wheelchair access; some rooms equipped for the disabled. Airport/station pickups. Crib.

Harrison House B&B ¢   *Tel:* 614–421–2202
313 West 5th Avenue, 43201

Not far from the university crowds, fast food restaurants, and tee-shirt shops of High Street is the sedate neighborhood known as Victorian Village with its vintage homes, surrounded by antique wrought iron fences and flowering trees. One such residence is Harrison House, a Queen Anne-style Victorian built in 1890, freshly painted in shades of beige and brown, and listed in the National Register of Historic Places. Innkeepers Maryanne and Dick Olson, who opened the inn in 1990, invite you to "relax and enjoy the original cut glass windows, magnificent woodwork, elegant lace curtains, and picturesque landscaping." The generous breakfast includes juice, fresh fruit, eggs, freshly baked breads, coffee and tea.

"A welcome addition to the Columbus scene. Gorgeous decor, surrounded by other Victorian homes. Near the university, Columbus City Center, new mall, Battelle Institute, and 'Short North' art district. You feel as if you're in your own home (but what a home); service is warm, helpful, accommodating, and Maryanne is a delight. Good breakfast with fresh squeezed juice and homemade muffins and breads." *(Carol Juniewicz)* "We found the Olsons to be comfortable hosts. The rooms are well decorated and very comfortable." *(Mr. & Mrs. John Langdon, also Susan Bush)*

Open All year.
Rooms 2 suites, 2 doubles—all with private bath and/or shower, radio, TV, desk, air-conditioning.
Facilities Dining & living room with fireplace, guest refrigerator.
Location Victorian Village. 5 min to downtown.
Restrictions No smoking in guest rooms.
Credit cards Amex, MC, Visa.

Rates B&B, $85 suite or double, $75 single.
Extras Airport pickups. Crib.

COSHOCTON

Also recommended: The 1890 B&B (663 North Whitewoman Street, 43812; 614–622–1890) is a century-old Victorian home set high above historic Roscoe. Rates for its three guest rooms range from $50–65, and include a breakfast of home-baked pastries. It's just a short walk to Coshocton's museums and restaurants, and guests are welcome to relax in the gazebo, or before the parlor fireplace. "Though imposing and formal on the outside, the inn is warm, comfortable, and friendly inside." *(Doris Blackmun)*

Roscoe Village Inn ✕ ¢   *Tel:* 614–622–2222
200 North Whitewoman Street, 43812   800–237–7397

In the 1830s the 308-mile Ohio & Erie Canal connected Lake Erie with the Ohio River, bringing instant prosperity to a then-depressed agricultural region. The last of the canal boats passed through just after the turn of the century. The area slumbered for generations, until 1968, when Edward and Frances Montgomery established a non-profit foundation to restore the village to its glory days. In all, the restoration consists of 28 buildings lining Whitewoman Street, given its name by the Delaware Indians— Walhonding in their language. Most are restored, although a few are reconstructed; two buildings are new. One of the new buildings is the inn itself, built in 1985 in a Greek Revival style of red brick with white trim similar to the surrounding homes. Although the entire complex can easily be explored on foot, guests enjoy taking a ride on the horse-drawn trolley or the replica canal boat on a restored section of the canal.

The inn itself combines modern amenities with historic charm. Polished wood beams, huge wrought-iron chandeliers, high-backed wing chairs, antiques, and a fireplace invite guests to relax in the lobby; guest rooms are furnished with simple hand-crafted pieces—four poster beds and Windsor-style rockers—fashioned by the Amish workers of neighboring Holmes County. The inn's tavern, King Charley's, was named for the town's first white settler, who allegedly gave the boot to the heir-apparent to the French throne. The restaurant menu is surprisingly ambitious; a recent meal included mushrooms stuffed with walnuts and cheese, spinach salad with bacon dressing, and scallops and lobster au gratin, with an almondine torte for dessert.

"We visited during the spring dulcimer festival, and found that the old-fashioned music fit perfectly with this 19th-century restoration. Our room was quite modern and comfortable, yet blended well with the general historic atmosphere. Although expensive, the quality of the food and service in the hotel restaurant were a pleasant surprise." *(MW)* "Handmade pottery and ironwork, from the village's craftspeople, nicely accented the simple country decor." *(NB)*

Open All year. Restaurant has limited hours Jan. 1, Thanksgiving, Dec. 25.
Rooms 1 suite, 50 doubles—all with full private bath, telephone, radio, TV, desk, air-conditioning.
Facilities Restaurant, tavern with entertainment, lobby with fireplace. Golf, swimming, hiking nearby. On-site parking.
Location E central OH. Approx. 70 m NE of Columbus, 98 m S of Cleveland. On Rte. 16/83 near junction of Rte. 36.
Credit cards Amex, DC, Discover, MC, Visa.
Rates Room only, $72 double. Extra person, $10. Theme, weekend getaway, golf, senior packages. Alc breakfast, $5–10; alc dinner, $25–30. AAA, AARP discount.
Extras 2 rooms equipped for the disabled. Local airport pickups. Crib.

DANVILLE

The White Oak Inn ¢   *Tel:* 614–599–6107
29683 Walhonding Road (Route 715), 43014

Set deep in the countryside of the Walhonding Valley, The White Oak is decorated with nineteenth-century antiques and handmade quilts. Rates include breakfast and afternoon tea and cookies; the inn's "signature" breakfast is French toast made with homemade bread.

"A beautifully restored old farmhouse, with all new plumbing and wiring. One outstanding feature of The White Oak is its quiet country setting on a little-used back road." *(Philip Eramo)* "Wide, welcoming porches; gleaming woodwork; comfortable bed with crisp, sweet-scented linens; spacious, light, airy rooms; peaceful, quiet, rolling countryside. The Actons are warm hospitable people who make you feel like you're going home for the weekend." *(Lee Siegrist, also William MacGowan)*

"No question but that the inn and its keepers are of the highest quality. Most rooms are named after the dominant wood in which it is furnished—oak, cherry, birch, balsam, 'ply,' and 'Natalie'(!). Our room, the Cherry, was the last one available at this popular inn, and was clean, crisp, with a high double bed with an excellent mattress, and a beautiful view of the majestic oaks and hemlocks, providing a romantic milieu. Breakfast was wonderful, with a puffy pancake filled with fresh fruit and blueberry sauce, sausage, homemade pastry, and freshly squeezed orange juice. A prix fixe dinner is served family-style on weekends; in this instance roast beef and Yorkshire pudding was topped off with an almond cake with chocolate sauce. If you'd prefer a more romantic or private meal, plan ahead and ask Jim and Joyce if you can be served a private dinner in one of the fireplace bedrooms." *(Zita Knific)*

Open All year.
Rooms 10 doubles—all with private bath, radio, air-conditioning, ceiling fan. 3 with fireplace. 3 rooms in annex.
Facilities Dining room, common room with fireplace, stereo; porch, screenhouse. Conference room with business equipment. 14 acres. ½ m to river. Hiking, fishing, biking, golfing, canoeing nearby.
Location N central OH. 50 m NE of Columbus. 4 m E of junction of Rtes. 36 & 62 at Millwood. On SR 715.

Restrictions No smoking. No children under 12.
Credit cards MC, Visa.
Rates B&B, $90–100 suite, $70–80 double, $60–80 single. Extra person, $25. 2-night weekend minimum, April–May, Aug–Nov. Weekend packages. Prix fixe dinner (by prior arrangement only), $15–22; 15–20% service additional.

DAYTON

Home of aeronautical pioneers Wilbur and Orville Wright, Dayton is also the site of the U.S. Air Force Museum, art and natural history museums, and several historic districts. The Carillon Historical Park traces the progress of transportation, from a restored Wright Brothers' airplane to trolley cars and vintage automobiles.

Prices' Steamboat House B&B ¢   *Tel:* 513–223–2444
6 Josie Street, 45403

Ruth and Ron Prices' Steamboat House is located in the city's second oldest historic district, St. Anne's Hill, a quaint neighborhood of Federal and Romanesque architectural styles, originally laid out in 1815. The Steamboat House was built in 1852 and then "Victorianized" in 1889; its unusual attributes include rounded porches on both the first and second floors (presumably the source of its name), as well as a rooftop widow's walk. Ruth and Ron bought the 22-room home in 1987 and have furnished it with Victorian antiques and Oriental rugs, which complement the handsome woodwork. Breakfast is served in the dramatic scarlet-colored dining room beneath a 19th-century crystal chandelier; a typical menu includes fresh fruit, juice, eggs, homemade breads, coffee and tea.

"An imposing home, set on the crest of a hill. The interior is a jewel furnished with the Prices' family heirlooms and many more antiques collected over the years. Ruth's breakfast was a highlight of our visit, enhanced by the pleasant company of the other guests. Thoughtful touches include the second floor guest refrigerator and a coffee/tea caddy, with a selection of homemade cookies for late evening or early morning snacks. All the practical aspects—lighting, plumbing, housekeeping, and parking—are right up to snuff. The location is convenient to the Convention Center and Memorial Hall, and close to the freeways for activities beyond." *(Polly & Jack Hornickel)*

Open All year.
Rooms 3 doubles—all with private bath, radio, TV, air-conditioning. 1 with desk, deck.
Facilities Dining/breakfast room, living room, family room, laundry facility, unscreened porch, guest refrigerator. ½ acre. Off-street parking. Tennis nearby.
Location SW OH. 56 miles N of Cincinnati, 72 m W of Columbus. St. Anne's Hill district. Edge of downtown; 1 m from center.
Restrictions No smoking. Children over 12 welcome.
Credit cards None accepted.
Rates B&B, $69 double, $59 single. Extra person, $10.
Extras Airport/station pickups.

DELLROY

Dellroy is a convenient base from which to tour the historic settlements of northeastern Ohio. Within a thirty-mile radius you will find Zoar, the first commune in the New World, and Schoenbraunn, the first settlement west of the Allegheny Mountains, plus contemporary attractions like the Football Hall of Fame in Canton. Boating, fishing, and swimming in Atwood Lake is just one mile away. Dellroy is located 90 miles south of Cleveland.

Information please: Located right on the lake with its own pontoon boat for rental is **Whispering Pines B&B** (P.O. Box 340, 1268 Magnolia, 44620; 216–735–2824), with three guest rooms, each with private bath. Built in 1880 and decorated with period antiques, rates include a breakfast of fresh fruit cup with cream, juice, homemade bread or muffins, and a hot entrée—eggs Benedict, baked French toast with strawberries, or spinach-sausage casserole.

Pleasant Journey Inn ¢   *Tel:* 216–735–2987
4247 Roswell Road S.W., 44620

Innkeepers Jim and Marie Etterman are so eager for visitors to see all the local attractions that they have created a five-day itinerary for their guests. Their 1870s Italianate Victorian home has seven marble fireplaces, twelve-foot ceilings, a curved walnut staircase lit by an antique oil chandelier, and elegant porches on three sides. Breakfast includes a fresh fruit platter, an entrée (maybe eggs Florentine or eggs Benedict), and homemade bread, juice, and coffee.

"Beautifully decorated in a lovely, quiet rural setting. Our room was cozy with a four-poster bed with extra blankets and antique quilt. There were lots of towels in the commodious shared bath. Marie is an excellent cook and prides herself on serving a different breakfast on each day of a guest's stay. The baked pancake was a special treat, and lots of fresh fruit accompanied each meal." *(Mary Davis)* "The friendly innkeepers are very knowledgeable about places of interest and the fascinating history of the inn. Furnished with comfortable antique furniture." *(Wayne & Judith Peskura)* "Nice and clean with a homey atmosphere and excellent, imaginative breakfast." *(Mr. & Mrs. Don Harper, and others)* More comments welcome.

Open All year.
Rooms 4 doubles—1 with full private bath, 3 with maximum of 6 sharing bath. All with clock/radio, fan.
Facilities Dining room, living room with TV/VCR, stereo, books; porch. 12 acres with antique/gift shop, gardens, Christmas tree farm. Off-street parking.
Location Atwood Lake Region. 18 m S of Canton, OH. ½ m from downtown.
Restrictions Smoking only allowed in living room. No children under 10.
Credit cards MC, Visa.
Rates B&B, $60 suite, $46 double, $36 single. Extra person, $10. Golden Buckeye discount. Golf packages.

GRANVILLE

Reader tip: *Christine Adkins* heartily recommends dining at the **Bryn Mawr Restaurant** (614–587–4000) when you are in Granville: "A beautifully restored home and restaurant with food and service of the highest quality, where local residents go for special occasions. The atmosphere is elegant, with classical guitar played in the lounge. Each dining room is very different and can be closed for off for private parties or romantic dinners for two." Also: "Although we didn't see the guest rooms, we had a delicious lunch at the **Granville Inn** (614–587–3333), a hotel built in 1924 in the style of an English Tudor manor house."

The Buxton Inn ¢ 🛏 ✕   *Tel: 614–587–0001*
313 East Broadway, 43023

Granville was settled by New Englanders from Granville, MA, and Granby, CT, at the beginning of the nineteenth century. The town was laid out to look like a New England village; it is still a small town today, and the home of Denison University.

The Buxton Inn was one of the town's first buildings, constructed in 1812, and now listed on the National Register of Historic Places. It changed hands a number of times before 1865, when it was purchased by Major and Mrs. Buxton, who ran it for 43 years. During that time, the inn was expanded often; additions included a two-story wing with a Victorian dining room and guest rooms. Orville and Audrey Orr bought and restored the inn in 1972; according to local sources, inhabitants at the inn include not only the paying guests, but two (friendly) ghosts, both innkeepers here at different stages of the inn's history.

"This is truly a restored, not reconstructed, inn; the floors are uneven and sagging, the rooms are furnished with genuine antiques and quilts. The food is continental and some of the best anywhere, with excellent wine choices. We ate in a lush courtyard." *(EJS)* "Lovely rooms; we especially recommend room #5. The food is prepared by an excellent chef and the town of Granville has a real New England feel to it. Much of the inn's charm is owed to the manager, Cecil Snow, who juggles the making of desserts along with an excellent staff. Cleanliness, attention to detail, and historical importance are all superb; the decor is eclectic." *(Kit Weilage)*

"While staying at the Buxton Inn, be sure to try the Bryn Mawr restaurant for dinner. It's a beautifully restored, white-columned mansion with wonderful dinners and brunches, located a couple miles south of Granville on Route 37." *(Susie Preston)*

"Despite its size, the inn really has the atmosphere one expects but so rarely gets from a country inn. The owners, Orville and Audrey Orr, are great people. They do not formally manage the inn but are very actively involved in its operation. Everything about this inn is first class—the rooms, the antique furnishings, the decor, and the food. The Orrs have bought most of the block that comprised the original owner's holdings, and are expanding their lodging options a house or so at a time." *(Barry Gardner)*

Less favorably: "Our annex room, in a house dating from the early 1800s, smelled musty and was poorly lit. We were not impressed by the staff—seemed like they had too many part-timers." Your opinions welcome.

Open All year. Restaurant closed Jan. 1, Dec. 25.
Rooms 5 suites, 10 doubles—all with private bath and/or shower, telephone, radio, TV, desk, air-conditioning. 11 rooms in annex.
Facilities Restaurant, tavern, wine cellar, courtyard with gazebo, fountains.
Location Central OH. Approx. 30 m E of Columbus, 8 m N of I-70. In center of town.
Credit cards Amex, CB, DC, MC, Visa.
Rates B&B, $65–80 double, $55–70 single. Extra person, $10; children under 5 free. Full breakfast, $2–6; alc lunch, $5–7; alc dinner, $24. Children's menu.
Extras Limited wheelchair access. Crib, babysitting.

LEBANON

The Golden Lamb Inn ✕ ¢
27 South Broadway, 45036

Tel: 513–932–5065

Lebanon was founded in 1796, and The Golden Lamb just seven years later, making it Ohio's oldest hotel. A two-story brick Federal-style building replaced the original log structure in 1815; this building now houses the lobby, but it has been added to many times over the years. The Golden Lamb had many famous visitors in the 19th century, including ten U.S. presidents (most recently Ronald Reagan), Charles Dickens, and Mark Twain. The inn's guest rooms are individually furnished with antiques and reproduction furniture. Rates include a continental breakfast and the daily paper.

"We visited just before Christmas and thoroughly enjoyed two meals at the inn, including their traditional 'Mount Vernon' dinner, featuring smoked ham and turkey. Carollers dressed in 19th-century costumes visited each of the dining rooms. The eggnog, served from a large polished pewter punch bowl during our brief wait in the lobby, was an extra treat. Christmas is an excellent time to visit here; the inn is decorated with hand-stitched Christmas samplers from all over Ohio, and the tree beside the fireplace is hung with handmade ornaments." *(Kathy Still)*

"Since our last visit, we noticed that bathrooms have been improved throughout, with new tubs and showers, and vanity sinks. Bedroom furniture is mostly antique, with pine and maple the most prevalent woods. The most elegant rooms are the Charles Dickens and the Ulysses S. Grant, with massive carved beds; on the third floor is the light and airy Samuel Clemens room with its two four-poster beds. Second floor rooms have central air-conditioning, while those on the third have window units. We had lunch in the restaurant, and found it jammed, though service was prompt and our iced tea was replenished often. We were served generous portions of salad, and enjoyed a Shaker sugar pie and strawberry-filled angel food cake, for dessert; all were reasonably priced." *(SHW)* "Excellent food; we would return to the restaurant anytime." *(Ruth McBride)*

Areas for improvement: Although the management is working to remedy these problems, one reader reported a erratic hot water supply during her visit, and another noted a balky window air-conditioner.

Open All year. Restaurant closed Christmas Day.
Rooms 1 suite, 17 doubles—all with private bath and/or shower, telephone, TV, air-conditioning.
Facilities Restaurant, tavern, lobby/parlors, gift shop, Shaker museum. Hiking, canoeing, boating, tennis, golf nearby. Off-street parking.
Location SW OH. 35 m N of Cincinnati, 15 m S of Dayton. Just off I-75 and I-71, on Rte. 42.
Restrictions Restaurant noise in some rooms: light sleepers should note that inn (including upstairs Shaker Rooms) is open to visitors until 10:30 P.M. Inn is not appropriate for children.
Credit cards Amex, CB, DC, MC, Visa.
Rates B&B, $94 suite, $68 double, $54 single. Extra person, $6. Alc lunch, $8; alc dinner, $23.

LEXINGTON

White Fence Inn ¢   *Tel:* 419–884–2356
8842 Denman Road, 44904

Situated almost halfway between Columbus and Cleveland, the White Fence Inn is a 98-year-old farmhouse owned by Bill and Ellen Hiser. This B&B offers a country retreat among apple trees, grape vines, gardens, and fields. Rates include a full country breakfast with homemade jams, juices, and cider.

"This immaculately clean farmhouse has owners who went out of their way to make us comfortable. Each guest room has a different decorating theme, from Amish to Victorian to Southwestern. Breakfast was delicious, and our young son loved the farm animals and the tire swing." *(RMN)* "Freshly decorated with just the amount of detail to make it inviting, but not fussy." *(NB)*

"The Hisers have completely renovated this old farmhouse—ask to see the before and after pictures. It's surrounded by farmland, woods, and with its own fishing pond. When traveling under the stress of business, it's incredibly relaxing to see a full moon in a night sky and hear only the sound of crickets. When sitting on the front porch or back deck, be sure to have some of Ellen's iced tea—there's always a pitcher in the fridge. You literally wake up to birds singing and if it's a nice morning you can have breakfast on the deck. Don't miss Ellen's blueberry muffins." *(Bob Fletcher)*

"What makes the White Fence Inn a great place to stay is the hosts, Bill and Ellen—they made us feel like family. Their attention to detail covers everything from the decor of the rooms to the outstanding breakfasts and desserts. The fresh strawberry pie was so irresistible that I ate three pieces." *(Scott Daley)* "An unexpected breakfast treat was homemade grape juice." *(Walter Wittich)*

Open All year.
Rooms 6 doubles—4 with private bath, 2 with a maximum of 4 people sharing a bath. All with fan. 1 room with fireplace, deck.

Facilities Dining room, parlor with fireplace, piano, games; TV room with stereo; library, porch. 73 acres with orchard, chicken yard, pond and brooks for fishing, hay and sleigh rides, tennis, walking and cross-country skiing trails, children's play equipment.

Location N central OH. 2.5 m from town. From I-71 take exit 165 to Rte 97. Go through Lexington and follow signs to Mid-Ohio Racetrack. Go left on Lex-Steam Corners Rd. Go 2 m then turn left onto Denman Rd. Inn is 1st farm on right.

Restrictions No smoking.

Credit cards None accepted.

Rates B&B, $58–95 double, $48–58 single. Extra person, $12. Children under 5 free. 2-night minimum on race weekends. Discount for 5-night stay.

Extras 1 room has wheelchair access. Station pickups. Crib, babysitting.

LOUDONVILLE

The Blackfork Inn ¢   *Tel:* 419–994–3252
303 North Water Street, P.O. Box 149, 44842

Built in 1865, The Blackfork is listed on the National Register of Historic Places. Albin and Suzanne Gorisek have owned the inn since 1983, and have furnished it with a collection of antiques ranging from the colonial to the Victorian.

"The Blackfork Inn is a lovely, graceful Victorian mansion in a quiet town in the heart of Amish country. Every room is beautifully done with Victorian antiques and memorabilia. Sue and Al Gorisek strike that rare balance that allows one to feel like a privileged guest in their home, with the freedom to enjoy as much privacy or interaction as desired. Morning begins with leisurely breakfasts around the dining room table, chatting with other guests or simply concentrating on the delicious Amish pastry and apple butter, fresh croissants, cheese, fruit, and more. Guests are given keys to come and go as they please, in order to enjoy the area attractions—canoeing, antiquing, visiting craft and specialty shops, or simply exploring the winding back country roads. Sue and Al are full of ideas and have maps for newcomers. The inn has several cozy nooks for conversation or reading, in addition to the spacious bedrooms. Each is decorated differently, and all have updated baths." *(Marion Carroll & Bill Brink)*

"Midway between Cleveland and Columbus, we found a finely tuned mixture of pampering, privacy, graciousness, wit and elegance. Amenities are well rooted in this century—long, hot showers, electric blankets, and fresh flowers year-round." *(Marcy Hawley)* "The original interior woodwork is outstanding—window frames, doors, and archways—all with lovely curved lines. The rooms are furnished in decorator Victorian, with floral wallpapers in rooms and matching or coordinated papers in the baths, and lace curtains at the windows. Good reading lights were next to the bed; and bright lights in the bathroom. Everything was immaculately clean, and positively lovely to look at. Breakfast was superb, with fresh squeezed orange juice, cinnamon tea, fruit compote of citrus, kiwis, and cantaloupe, topped with frozen yogurt. This was followed by quiche, and then 'dessert,' frozen strawberries and raspberries topped with Swiss cream (a delicious Amish invention). Sue loves to make suggestions for

activities; as a writer for *Ohio* magazine she certainly knows her territory."
(SHW)

Some areas for improvement: "There was no place to set our suitcases,
nor were luggage racks provided. Bathrooms were beautifully done, but
there were no hooks to hang robes or nightclothes. The staircase is steep,
yet the handrail stops two feet short of the top." Another reader com-
mented that just a few doors away is the railroad crossing, with train noise
lasting long into the evening, though "people who love trains will enjoy
this inn—there's a railroad museum in town, too."

Open All year.
Rooms 6 doubles—all with full private bath, air-conditioning. 1 with TV, 2 with
desk.
Facilities Dining room, 2 parlors with pump organ, Victorian puzzles, games,
stereo, CD player, books, library. ¾ acre. Hiking, swimming, fishing, canoeing,
cross-country skiing nearby.
Location N central Ohio, halfway between Columbus and Cleveland. Holmes
County, 20 m NW of Millersburg. In village, 2 blocks from Main St.
Restrictions Train noise/whistle on nearby tracks can disturb sleepers. No smok-
ing. Children permitted only by special arrangement.
Credit cards MC, Visa.
Rates B&B, $65–75 double, $43 single. Midweek corporate packages.
Extras Pets allowed by prior arrangement. Airport/station pickups.

Cannon House B&B ¢   *Tel:* 419–994–5546
109 South Market Street, 44842

While small as entries go for this book, the Cannon House offers comfortable accommodations in a circa-1823 stagecoach inn. Having survived
many uses since its inception, this B&B, owned by Betty and Donn Kieft,
returned to its origins in 1989 when it once more began hosting overnight
guests. Situated right on Fountain Square, in the center of busy street
traffic, this 170-year-old house has walls that are 2 to 3 bricks thick,
creating a very effective sound barrier. Betty has furnished the house with
antiques and reproductions, and a wonderful collection of Majolica pottery—the inspiration for the dramatic accent colors used throughout.
Rates include morning tea or coffee in your room, and a buffet breakfast
of juice, fresh fruits, rolls, cereal and coffee, served in the dining room or
porch.

"The original woodwork and hardwood floors in the house are refinished and accented with Oriental or rag rugs. Both the library and living
room are reserved for guests; the Kiefts have their own quarters at the
rear. But this is truly a home, and Betty is pleasant, warm and welcoming
without being intrusive.

"A good choice for elderly guests, who want to minimize stair-climb-
ing, is the suite on the first floor; the bedroom has twin beds and its sitting
room has a daybed and wicker chairs, boldly painted to complement the
dramatic, large-scale floral wallpaper. The two rooms upstairs are nicely
finished and equally comfortable, though their ceilings are lower than
those on the first floor. While there's a busy road nearby (and the railroad
tracks not too far away), the thick brick walls blocked out traffic noise."
(SHW)

Open All year.
Rooms 1 suite, 2 doubles—all with private bath and/or shower.
Facilities Dining room, living room with TV, library, sun porch, porch.
Location Center of town. On Fountain Square (Rte. 3), just S of intersection of Rtes. 3 & 39.
Restrictions No smoking in guest rooms. No children under 11.
Credit cards None accepted.
Rates B&B, $65 suite, $55 double.

MILLERSBURG

Yellow highway signs bearing a silhouette of a horse and buggy give you the first inkling of the ways of the Amish and Mennonite—the "plain people," the skilled farmers and craftspeople of Holmes County. Amidst rolling fields, unadorned frame houses, and immaculately maintained farm buildings, you can see children playing, outfitted just like their parents in black trousers and jackets or long dresses and bonnets. Millersburg is the county seat, so often you'll find a simple black buggy, horse hitched to a rail, "parked" outside the imposing stone Italianate county courthouse.

Millersburg is located in north central Ohio, 85 miles south of Cleveland, 85 miles northeast of Columbus.

Reader tips: "For an Amish sampler, visit the Guggisburg Cheese Company—considered the best of its kind by local residents. Then go to Miller's Dry Goods (in the village of Charm), the oldest quilt shop in the county, with striking Amish quilts and an extensive selection of fabrics. The Wooden Toy Shop (north of Winesburg on Route 62) has a marvelous array of trains, rocking horses, blocks, and toddler-sized furniture; nearby is the Holmes Chair Company for contemporary wooden furnishings. The Rastettler Mill (between Berlin and Millersburg on Route 39), one of three remaining woolen mills in the U.S., sells woven rag rugs—one hangs in the Smithsonian's Museum of American Folk Art." *(NB)* "During the summer, I recommend the 20-mile drive to Wooster to see the Gilbert & Sullivan productions." *(Susie Preston)*

Information please: About 10 miles southeast of Millersburg is the Amish village of Charm, home to the **Charm Countryview Inn** (State Route 557, P.O. Box 100, Charm 44617; 216–893–3003) offering 15 guest rooms with private bath. The $65–95 rates includes a hearty full breakfast and an evening snack; no smoking, alcohol, or Sunday check-ins allowed. A couple miles east of town, this newly built inn offers an old-fashioned rocking porch, and spotless rooms simply furnished with solid oak furnishings and handmade quilts.

Hotel Millersburg ¢ ♀ ✕   *Tel:* 216–674–1457
35 West Jackson Street, 44654

The oldest and largest building in town, the Hotel Millersburg was built in 1847 and renovated in the 1980s. While the exterior was maintained in conformity with the Ohio Historic Preservation Society, very little of the original interior detailing was salvageable above the first floor. Although ornate cherry doors with etched glass panels grace the entrance and the lobby has its original pressed-tin ceiling and oak trim, guest rooms are somewhat motel-like in appearance. Amish quilts warm the atmosphere of the non-smoking rooms, which are furnished with locally made pine and oak furniture. Owners Robert and Cheryl Bird, and daughter Robyn, the manager, are lifelong residents of the county, and bring a wealth of experience as restaurateurs to the hotel. They have moved one of their popular restaurants, Emperor's Cove, from another location to occupy half of the hotel's ground floor; recent entrées included salmon with Dijon mustard sauce, pork chops with mushroom gravy, and chicken with a champagne glaze.

"Gives one the opportunity to experience the warmth and flavor of Amish country in a pleasantly modern atmosphere. Food and friendliness were great." *(Edwin Lewis, also SHW)* "The guest rooms are large, simply furnished, and clean. The restaurant is well designed with oak and brass trim and cozy lamps that give you plenty of light to see your food, without making you feel like you're in a cafeteria." *(NB)*

Open All year.
Rooms 1 suite, 21 doubles, 2 singles. All with private bath and/or shower, telephone, TV, desk, air-conditioning.
Facilities Dining room, bar/lounge with weekend entertainment, family room with games, TV. Swimming pool, tennis, golf nearby.
Location Holmes County. Center of town.
Restrictions Traffic noise possible in front rooms. No smoking in some guest rooms.
Credit cards Amex, MC, Visa.
Rates Room only, $70–80 suite, $39–54 double, $30 single. Extra person, $5. Children under 12 free in parents' room. Alc lunch, $5–5.50; dinner, $15–18. Special packages.
Extras Dining room with wheelchair access. Local airport pickups. Crib, babysitting by prior arrangement.

The Inn at Honey Run ✕   *Tel:* 216–674–0011
6920 County Road 203, 44654   In OH: 800–468–6639

Built in 1982, the Inn at Honey Run is a handsome contemporary structure of glass, wood, and stone, surrounded by trees. Rates include continental breakfast, and the cuisine at lunch and dinner is straightforward American cooking—beef, pork, turkey, chicken, locally caught rainbow trout, fresh vegetables, and homemade breads and desserts—all prepared "from scratch." The inn attracts many executive seminars during the week; weekends bring professional couples looking for rest and relaxation. Added in 1988 were the earth-sheltered Honeycomb rooms, set on a hillside above the inn, overlooking a pasture of wildflowers and grazing sheep.

"The decor is a lovely blend of Amish pieces, e.g., rockers, quilts, handmade furniture (much of it made in Holmes County), and contemporary work. In our room, a floor-to-ceiling window looked out onto a bank of ivy and a bird feeder. The inn has a small library for its guests; you can take home unfinished books and return them by mail. Meals are served in a dining room whose only decoration is baby-size Amish quilts hung between the large windows. The food was delicious, very generous in

)ortion, and well presented. The grounds are wooded and hiking trails are narked, the longest being a mile and a quarter." *(Shirley & Perry Noe)*

"Our second-floor corner room overlooked a heavily wooded area. No :urtains were needed, and we felt as though we were in the forest, with ıll the comforts of a first-class hotel. The inn is immaculate. Sunday night upper is called 'Raid the Kitchen,' and included fresh roast turkey, ham, :alads, soups, and rolls, all set up in the kitchen. Six or seven desserts were)n a table in the dining room." *(KLH, also Mary Wabeke)*

"Very relaxed and quiet atmosphere, with extremely friendly, courte-)us, and eager-to-please staff." *(Mr. & Mrs. James Grigsby)* "Each guest :oom has a helpful notebook, filled with information about everything we ıeeded to know." *(Marjie Berens)* "Simplicity and elegance, combined with ınusual attention to detail." *(Mary Starr)* "I relaxed in my room in a cozy :hair, feet propped up, reading and watching the birds feasting at the :eeder outside my window. A bird book is in each room, and is a great ıid in identifying many species I'd never seen before. Truly down-home :ooking." *(Susie Preston, and others)*

"My favorite rooms are in the Honeycomb, an earth-sheltered structure)uilt into the side of the hill. Forget every pre-conceived notion you've ·ver had about this type of construction—here hallways are light and ıiry, and the luxurious guest rooms have an uninterrupted view of wood- ands and farms—even from the bed. A sandstone quilt, quarried within ₿0 miles of the inn, 'hangs' in the building entrance; its 'Trip around the Vorld' pattern is composed of six-inch squares of stone in shades of pink, ·ed, yellow, brown/purple, and white." *(NB)*

Open All year. Closed Jan. 1–18. Restaurant closed to public Sun.

Rooms 1 suite, 35 doubles—all with private bath and/or shower, telephone, :assette/radio, TV, desk, air-conditioning. 12 Honeycomb rooms with fireplace, vhirlpool tub, patio.

Facilities Restaurant with occasional Sat. evening entertainment, lobby with ʿireplace, family/game room with fireplace, games, bumper pool; meeting rooms, ²ing-Pong, movies. 60 acres with hiking trails, farm animals.

Location N central Ohio, Holmes County. 85 m S of Cleveland, 85 m NE of Columbus. 3 1/2 m from Millersburg. Take E Jackson St. in town to Rte. 241 and :urn left. Go 2 3/4 m to County Rd. 203 and turn right. Go 1 1/2 m to INN sign ınd turn right.

Restrictions No alcohol in public rooms; no smoking in dining room, some guest ·ooms. Children discouraged.

Credit cards Amex, MC, Visa.

Rates B&B, $95–125 suite, $69–150 double. Extra person, $15. 2-night weekend ninimum. Alc lunch, $7; alc dinner, $14.

Extras Limited wheelchair access—elevators, ramps, no stairs. Local airport ›ickup. Crib, $15 per night. German spoken.

MOUNT VERNON

The Russell-Cooper House ¢   *Tel: 614–397–8638*
115 East Gambier Street, 43050

ῑn 1987, Tim and Maureen Tyler moved from New York City to one of Ohio's historic towns, home to Kenyon College and to the oldest surviving opera house in America. They had been searching for a home to restore as a B&B, and were particularly attracted to the Russell-Cooper House because it had remained in the same family over the decades. Although many alterations had been made (the Tylers removed 8 layers of linoleum) over the years, many of its original furnishings and historical memorabilia were intact. They've returned the house to its original elegance by using such authentic restoration products as Lincrusta, Anaglypta, NMC Crown Mouldings, Bradbury & Bradbury wallpapers, and Victorian reproduction lighting fixtures to complement their home's original embossed ceilings, rich cherry, maple and walnut woodwork, etched and stained glass windows, and numerous fireplaces. History buffs will especially enjoy the array of Civil War items, antique medical devices, and rare books. Most recently restored is a ceiling fresco of the four seasons in the mansion's ballroom, long covered by strips of canvas, an elaborate effort involving gold-leaf underlay and floral appliqués.

No less striking is the mansion's exterior. A high Victorian fantasy, the house has been painted a soft gray-green, contrasting with the cream and carmine used on the elaborate trim—columns, pilasters, balustrades, and unusual mini-turrets. The Russell-Cooper Mansion was built in 1830, and was long the home of Dr. John Russell, a prominent surgeon, and later his son-in-law, Colonel William Cooper, a U.S. congressman and Ohio Adjutant General.

Rates include a full breakfast and evening cordials. A typical breakfast might include coffee or tea and juice, fresh-baked rolls, muffins or biscuits, melon and strawberries, egg and cheese soufflé, sausage, and cinnamon/cheese blintzes.

"Tim and Maureen personify hospitality. Tim is an expert on local history and willingly fills the evening with interesting stories in front of a crackling fire in the library. Maureen's delicious breakfasts and friendly conversation with the other guests makes leaving this delightful B&B even harder." *(David & Heather Samuels)* "The house has been painstakingly restored to its original glory and then some. It's spotlessly clean—not a speck of dust was to be found from the private bath to the window sills. Our breakfast was served at a table set with crystal, fine china, and linen." *(Priscilla Wilde)* "A guest refrigerator held soda and wine, and there were lots of common areas for relaxing. The French toast was especially good." *(Elisabeth McLaughlin)*

"Situated on a lovely, tree-lined street, the Russell-Cooper House is a magnificent 'Painted Lady,' with just the right contrasting colors to emphasize its elaborate turrets and brackets. The interior is no less impressive, with shining woodwork, period antiques and lamps. All is not stiff-backed formality; the Tylers have furnished the sun porch with white wicker, flowered chintz pillows, and a TV for those who can't do without." *(NB)*

Open All year.
Rooms 6 doubles—all with private bath and/or shower, radio, desk, air-conditioning, fan. 4 with fireplace.
Facilities Dining room with fireplace, piano, library, sun porch with TV. ½ acre with patio, garden. State park nearby.
Location Central OH. 45 m NE of Columbus. 1½ blocks from center.

Restrictions No smoking in guest rooms. No children under 13.
Credit cards MC, Visa.
Rates B&B, $75 double; $50 single. Extra person, $15. Midweek rates.

PENINSULA

Peninsula, once an important stop on the Ohio Canal, is now a quaint little
village of antique stores, old factory sites, and vintage houses, surrounded
by the Cuyahoga Valley National Recreation Area. Within this 32,000-
acre region, you'll find Hale Farm, an authentic 19th century midwestern
farm and village complete with a steam-powered train which passes
through Peninsula once daily.

Tolle House B&B   *Tel:* 216–657–2900
1856 Main Street, 44264

Named for its friendly owners Ina and Jerry Tolle (not the cookie), the
Tolle House B&B is a restored turn-of-the-century home, located just a
few blocks from the river. Beautiful oak moldings and stairways are
accented with antiques and collectibles, the latter thoughtfully labelled
with their name and original purpose; if you still can't figure out what a
gadget is, Jerry is delighted to tell you. The guest parlor has what the
Tolles' call a "comfortable English pub" feeling with easy chairs, games
such as cribbage, British Monopoly, and checkers. The cozy guest rooms
have fluffy comforters with matching pillows, brass or early American-
style beds, and simple country accents on the walls. Breakfast is served at
a large round table in the parlor and includes fruit, bacon, ham or sausage,
potatoes, juice, and coffee, with eggs, pancakes or Belgian waffles. On
weekends the Tolles offer guests a choice of special dishes such as a Creole
Scramble; Jerry has yet to have anyone choose "Hangtown Fry" (an
oyster omelette).

"While guest rooms are small (one verges on 'tiny' and is almost
wall-to-wall bed), they boast excellent reading lights and firm mattresses.
The bathrooms, down a short hall, are immaculate; fluffy robes are available in your room, along with bubble bath for a leisurely soak. Little fact
sheets explain everything about the inn: when tea is served, the breakfast
menu, the guest refrigerator—all those questions which you forget to ask
until you're already in bed." *(NB)*

"We arrived at 5 P.M. to find tea and muffins awaiting us. Ina and Jerry
were most hospitable but never intrusive. Breakfast was delicious and the
Tolles were very accommodating. We had told them that we are vegetarians and they served us a generous portion of sautéed mushrooms to
substitute for the sausage the other guests were having." *(Karen & Larry
Fournier)*

Open All year.
Rooms 3 doubles share 2 baths. All with air-conditioning.
Facilities Parlor with TV, radio, games, library; porch with swing. Park for hiking,
bicycling, fishing, swimming, golf. 2 m to downhill skiing, 1 m to cross-country
skiing.

OHIO

Location N Ohio. 25 m SE of Cleveland, 10 m N of Akron. In center of village. From I-271, take Rte. 303 E to town.
Restrictions No smoking in guest rooms. No children under 10.
Credit cards None accepted.
Rates B&B, $45–55 double, $40–45 single. Extra person, $5. No tipping.

SAGAMORE HILLS

The Inn at Brandywine Falls   *Tel:* 216–467–1812
8230 Brandywine Road, 44067

Brandywine Falls is located in the heart of the Cuyahoga Valley National Recreation Area (see description under "Peninsula"). Leased from the National Park Service, this farmhouse has been restored by George and Katie Hoy, who warn guests that "our gift certificates expire on April 15, 2037, so that gives you only 45 years to plan a stay with us." Ohio antiques and paintings are showcased in rooms decorated in the spare style appropriate to the 1850s Greek Revival design of the house. Over the parlor fireplace hangs a watercolor by one of Ohio's first Impressionist artists, and floors are covered with the patterned carpets popular during that period. Guest rooms have antique beds fitted with firm mattresses, pure cotton bedding, and handmade coverlets or quilts. The once-condemned hen house has been imaginatively transformed into two suites, each with a greenhouse window overlooking the woods, a loft bedroom, and exposed barn board walls. Rates include a welcoming glass of Ohio wine or tea and biscuits, and a hearty home-made breakfast, served in the dining room, with fruited oatmeal soup a popular item; a continental breakfast is delivered to the door of guests in the hen house suites.

"Charming, authentic rural setting with animals, fields, split-rail fences, and personable and interesting hosts." *(George Ubogy)* "George and Katie have done a magnificent job restoring both the inn and the Granary, the circa 1848 hen house where we stayed. The Hoys couldn't have been more hospitable, as were their cats, dogs, and horses. Even the roosters spared us. Expensive and reasonable restaurants abound locally, and we enjoyed both types. We hiked to the magnificent falls just 300 feet away, and bicycled for miles in the surrounding area." *(William Bennett)*

"Unprepossessing from the exterior, this simple white frame farmhouse hides a treasure trove of Ohio history and craftsmanship. George and Katie Hoy are personable and witty hosts who can explain the ancestry of each item. The first floor guest room has a signed, handwoven coverlet dating from 1844 on queen-sized antique sleigh bed, and window shades painted (a popular decorating technique in that time) to depict the view you would have seen in the 1850s. In the dining room, the large round table is handpainted in the 'toleware' style of the era, and each guest has a different fruit or berry design in front of them. Everything is authentic to the period, so guests accustomed to the lavish style of the later Victorian period will be surprised by the simple pleasures found within. The Hoys want their antiques to be seen and appreciated: two of the upstairs bedrooms even have antique quilts as shower curtains (used with plastic liner, of course), and they assured me that the quilts are better out of the sunlight, with a more constant humidity, than if they were folded away or arranged on a bed. For a feeling of the delightful atmosphere of this inn, ask the Hoys to send you a copy of their most recent newsletter, filled with 'inn' puns and news of the inn's menagerie." *(NB)*

Open All year.
Rooms 3 suites, 3 doubles—all with full private bath, desk, air-conditioning. Telephone, radio, TV on request. 2 suites in Hen House with microwave oven, refrigerator; 1 with woodstove, double Jacuzzi tub.
Facilities Kitchen with fireplace, living room with piano, dining room, study with books, unscreened porch. 3 acres. Tennis, golf nearby. National Park for hiking, biking, canoeing, fishing, cross-country nearby.
Location NE OH. Approx. 20 m S of Cleveland. 12 m N of Akron.
Restrictions No smoking. Children under 6 in Loft Suite only.
Credit cards MC, Visa.
Rates B&B, $95–165 suite, $80–85 double, $70–75 single. Extra person, $20–25. Reduced rates for families, children.
Extras Wheelchair access. Airport/station pickups, $25. Crib, babysitting.

TROY

Information please: Listed in earlier editions is the **Willowtree Inn** (1900 West Route 571, Tipp City 45371; 513–667–2957) on Route 571 about three miles south of Troy. A gracious Georgian mansion, with a Victorian-style patterned roof and widow's walk, The Willowtree was built in 1830, and was purchased in 1989 by Tom and Peggy Nordquist. Guest rooms are simply furnished, and rates include a full breakfast.

H.W. Allen Villa B&B ¢   *Tel:* 513–335–1181
434 South Market Street, 45373

A prosperous banker, H.W. Allen built an elegant villa to house his growing family in 1874. It remained in the Allen family until 1945, when the local Hobart Corporation bought it for use as a corporate guest house. In 1985, the corporation put it up for sale, and June and Robert Smith decided that it would be the perfect home for their 20-year collection of Victorian furnishings and LaBelle Flow Blue china. The Smiths worked for months replacing fluorescent fixtures with period lighting, and restoring the original stenciling, crown moldings, and white and black walnut floors and trim. The decor is formal high Victorian throughout, balanced by plain white walls and simple window treatments in most rooms. The outside has been newly repainted, transforming a white elephant into a beautiful painted lady of three shades of greenish gray, from pale to dark, with accent touches of burgundy and rose, highlighting the fine construction work of the house.

"Each room is beautifully furnished with a personality of its own, carried out with an individualized color scheme. Water pressure was very good, which surprised us as the fixtures were antique; we learned later that they had taken lots of time to install authentic fixtures when they redid the plumbing. Just a short walk from downtown, the area is very quiet, as is the villa. Bob and June Smith are friendly and helpful hosts, but not intrusive; the morning paper was ready when we came downstairs for breakfast and June had available books on antiques and antique shops when she found out that we were interested." *(Lynn & Steve Kocher)*

"This is genuine Victorian, not decorator Victorian. June has done fantastic research on the history of the house and can even tell you when and where the bathroom fixtures were manufactured. A patch of 1884 stencil work remaining in the parlor illustrates the meticulous restoration. While the house sits on the main street of town, it is high, up two terraced levels, and the interior is cool and quiet. The original maids' quarters form a suite accessible by its own staircase; hand-crocheted spreads on brass beds set the tone of these simpler, smaller rooms. June is a warm and hospitable innkeeper; there is no doubt that June loves this house, and she goes the extra mile to see that her guests—both business and vacation travelers—are happy." *(SHW, and others)*

"On a return visit, we stayed in the largest room, the Allen Suite, with a set of antique natural wicker furniture, and two enormous matching lamps with pierced brass shades, and an antique king-size four poster bed with an authentic period quilt roll. The bathroom was equipped with all conceivable amenities for travelers who may have forgotten some toiletry, and the original 1915 full-body soaker tub. The inn is comfortable, quiet, immaculate, and livable, with luggage racks and shelves for possessions. Breakfast was fantastic. It was served in the formal dining room and it consisted of a fresh fruit cup, orange juice, and a croissant with bacon and tomato; French toast, omelets, and eggs were gladly prepared to order as well." *(Susan W. Schwemm)*

Open All year.
Rooms 1 suite, 3 doubles—all with private bath and/or shower, telephone, TV, desk, air-conditioning, fireplace.
Facilities Dining room, living room with fireplace, TV, player piano; parlor with fireplace, piano; guest refreshment center, porch. ¾ acre with lawns. Off-street parking.
Location 4 blocks from center. From I-75 take Exit 73 and go E 1 m on Rte. 55 to S. Market St. Turn left to inn at corner of S. Market and Simpson Sts.
Restrictions No smoking in public rooms. No children under 12.
Credit cards Amex, MC, Visa.
Rates B&B, $60 double, $40 single. Extra person, $10. Family rates for extended stay. 10% senior discount. Weekly, monthly rates.
Extras Airport/station pickups, $2–10.

WEST MILTON

Locust Lane Farm ¢   *Tel:* 513–698–4743
5590 Kessler Cowlesville Road, 45383

While a little on the small side, the Locust Lane Farm received such an enthusiastic report from a contributing editor that we couldn't resist.

"When you see the sign on the quiet country road for Locust Lane, you are happy to turn onto the gravel driveway bordered by locust trees that goes straight as a die to the farmhouse, surrounded by fields. What a find for lovers of peace and quiet! Owners Ruth and Don Shoup are members of a German Baptist sect who call themselves 'plain people.' Their religion is not advertised or mentioned to guests, but they do not have radios or TV in their home (there are telephones). Unlike other sects which shun more modern ways, Don and his son make their living in the plumbing business; and the farm and B&B are hobbies for the family. The Shoups are warm, interesting, thoughtful, and receptive hosts.

"The family and dining rooms are furnished with reproduction Queen Anne furniture, accented with lace and brass. Guest rooms are furnished simply, but all possible comforts are supplied, including night-lights and window air-conditioners. There are lots of towels and everything in the entire house is immaculate. Abundant breakfasts are served on the sun porch or in the dining room; fresh fruit compote of melon, strawberries, pineapple, bananas and grapes followed by homemade granola topped with vanilla yogurt, cream fruit scones, orange muffins, cranberry juice and golden pecan coffee, eggs and bacon, and sautéed mushrooms." (SHW)

Open All year.
Rooms 3 doubles—1 with private bath, 2 with maximum of 4 sharing bath. All with air-conditioning.
Facilities Dining room, living room, screened porch, deck. 58 acres with patio, herb garden, gazebo.
Location W central OH. Approx. 5 m N of I-70 via Rte. 40, 5 m W of I-75 via Rte. 571. Take Exit 69 off I-75. Go 5 1/2 m on Kessler Cowlesville Rd. to in on left.
Restrictions No smoking. No alcohol.
Credit cards None accepted.
Rates B&B, $45–50 double. Extra adult, $10; extra child, $5.

WOOSTER

The Wooster Inn ¢ 🛏 ✕   *Tel:* 216–264–2341
801 East Wayne Avenue, 44691

"With a lovely location adjoining the College of Wooster's golf course, the classic, immaculately maintained brick structure of the college-owned Wooster Inn (built in 1959) immediately gives the impression of quiet comfort. The dining room is sunny and spacious, overlooking a flower-filled patio. While the hallways are indistinguishable from those of a good chain hotel, the spacious guest rooms, individually decorated with Colonial print wallpapers and coordinating draperies, at least one comfortable reading chair, and maple "early American" furniture, are most appealing. The institutional-style bathrooms have sparkling white grout and shiny tile surfaces and are accented with print wallpapers. The inn's restaurant has an excellent reputation, serving tried and true favorites, expertly prepared, at very reasonable prices: chicken breast with artichokes, fettuccine primavera, rainbow trout, veal Marsala, and lamb chops are among the entrées. The homemade soups are inventive, salads are fresh, and the desserts are all baked on the premises, with mocha mousse and apple pie among the favorites." *(NB)*

"Great home-cooked food. Guest rooms are very clean and nice, but lack the individual character of a true country inn. If you visit in the summer be sure to go to the Light Opera series—they do a different Gilbert & Sullivan production every evening." *(SP)*

Open All year. Closed Christmas.
Rooms 2 suites, 12 doubles, 3 singles—all with private bath and/or shower, telephone, TV, desk, air-conditioning, fan.
Facilities Restaurant, terrace. 10 acres with college golf course, cross-country skiing adjacent, tennis courts and swimming nearby.
Location NE OH. 50 m S of Cleveland, 90 m NE of Columbus. 2 m from center of town. From US Rte. 250, exit to Rte. 585. Go N onto Wayne Ave. Follow Wayne Ave. to inn on the left.
Credit cards Amex, CB, DC, MC, Visa.
Rates B&B, $140 suite, $68–77 double, $53–62 single. Extra adult, $15; child under 12, $5. Alc lunch, $6–10; alc dinner, $15.
Extras Limited wheelchair access. Pets permitted by prior arrangement. Crib, babysitting. German, Spanish spoken.

WORTHINGTON

The Worthington Inn � ✕   *Tel:* 614–885–2600
649 High Street (Route 23), 43085

The Worthington Inn was built in 1831 as a stagecoach stop. It was expanded many times over the years, most notably in 1901, when the mansard roof, front porches, and exterior spiral staircase were added. After many changes of ownership, the inn was a decaying white elephant when it was bought and totally renovated in 1983 by Hugh Showe. Some guest rooms have hand-stenciled walls and are furnished with early American reproductions, while others have a Victorian decor. Rates include a breakfast of fresh fruit and juice, coffee, and pastry—and the inn's restaurant serves an ambitious menu of French and continental specialties.

"We watched the renovation in progress—one of the most well done I've seen. They've restored the old-time flavor with elaborate attention to detail. Meals are elegantly served, with rich desserts, in a very charming atmosphere. The inn is on a street with lots of quaint shops with crafts and quilts." *(ES)* "Dinner was excellent and we enjoyed the New England flavor of the shops on the old town square. We especially enjoyed the fortuitous combination of 19th century charm and 20th century comfort." *(Lisa Craig)* "Be sure to ask to see the Van Loon ballroom, with its elegant Czechoslovakian chandelier." *(Nancy Brightman)*

"Even the new rooms at the Worthington Inn are something special. While motel-like in design, the rooms have high ceilings, reproduction furniture, carpeting and lighting fixtures, and Caswell-Massey amenities. The rooms in the original inn and the adjacent Snow House are even more attractive. Suite 28 has a crocheted canopy bed and many other antiques; the large bathroom has a separate shower with enormous antique brass shower head, a six-foot tub, and an oak dressing table. The four suites in the Snow House have a Laura Ashley-style decor which accentuates the antique oak and walnut beds (fitted with queen-size mattresses); the headboards to these beds are almost eight feet tall." *(NB)*

Open All year. Restaurant closed Christmas, New Year, Memorial Day.
Rooms 7 suites, 19 doubles—all with full private bath, telephone, radio, TV, desk, air-conditioning, fan. 4 rooms in annex.
Facilities Restaurant, pub and wine bar, meeting rooms. Evening entertainment throughout the week. Golf, swimming, boating, fishing nearby.
Location Central OH. 15 m N of downtown Columbus, 5 m N of Ohio State University. 1 block S of Rte. 161. 2 m S of I-270 N.
Credit cards All major cards.
Rates B&B, $110–150 suite, $95–105 double, $85–95 single. Extra person, $10. Children under 12 free in parents' room. Alc lunch, $9; alc dinner, $35. Holiday, weekend rates.
Extras Airport pickup, $25. Crib.

YELLOW SPRINGS

Morgan House ¢   *Tel: 513–767–7509*
120 West Limestone Street, 45387

Built in 1921 as the home of Antioch College president Arthur Morgan, Morgan House became a dormitory, then a food co-op and office, before Marianne Britten renovated it as a B&B, opening in November 1986. Rates include a continental breakfast of homemade breads and muffins, fresh fruit, juice, and coffee or tea.

"Marianne Britten, an enterprising woman from California, cooks the wonderful breakfast herself, and has found lovely antiques at local auctions to decorate the rooms. Yellow Springs is a town of about 4,500 people transplanted from East and West. John Bryan State Park is a mile away, and Glen Helen, a 1,000-acre nature preserve, is adjacent to the town. Small but diverse shops and restaurants abound." *(Sue Parker)*

"Yellow Springs is one of our favorite places, an old, progressive, cultured town in rural Ohio. The Morgan House fits right in. Rooms are small but comfortable. The parlor and screened-in porch are great places to sit with a good book. Plenty of nice walks, interesting shops, and fine places to eat. Marianne is a terrific innkeeper." *(Jack Johnstone)* More comments please.

Open All year.
Rooms 4 doubles with maximum of 4 people sharing bath. All rooms with air-conditioning.
Facilities Living room with fireplace, TV/sitting room, dining room, screened porch. ½ acre with flower garden. Swimming, hiking, cross-country skiing nearby.
Location SW OH. 15 min. NE of Dayton, 45 min. NE of Cincinnati, 1 hr. W of Columbus. 9 m S of I-70. In historic district, ½ block from downtown.
Restrictions No smoking.
Credit cards MC, Visa.
Rates B&B, $50–60 double, $40 single. Extra person, $10. Weekly rates. Saturday afternoon tea every other Sat.
Extras Crib. Chinese spoken.

ZOAR

Information please: The Cowger House (4th & Parks Streets, Zoar 44697; 216–874–4672), is a 150-year-old home offering antique-filled rooms, full breakfasts, and reasonable rates.

Cider Mill Bed & Breakfast ¢   *Tel: 216–874–313?*
Second Street, P.O. Box 441, 44697

During the 1860s, Zoar was the nation's most successful communal religious village; later, because of its charm and serenity, President McKinley picked it for his summer retreat. Today, the entire village is listed on the National Register of Historic Places. The cider mill was built in 1863, and was used as a cabinetmaker's shop in the off-season. In 1972 Judy and Ralph Kraus renovated the mill and have opened it up to B&B guests.

"The mill is located on a side street of the tiny artist colony and Separatist community of Zoar. It is very quiet and secluded, though only about a 5-mile drive from the interstate. The ground floor of the inn is an antique shop, the main floor has lots of space and high ceilings and is decorated with antiques, featuring the owners' favorite motifs of violets and geese (but not together). Up a spiral staircase, the two guest rooms are relatively small, but beautifully decorated with antiques. We asked for an extra lamp for reading, which Judy gladly provided. Judy Kraus loves animals and has several different kinds. She was very friendly, and we had interesting conversations while she was preparing our breakfast in the lovely country kitchen. We had sliced cantaloupe, sausage and omelet, homemade pear jam, and grapes." *(SHW)* "Our room was quiet, cool, and comfortable, and the excellent breakfast included German pancakes with fresh peaches. Ralph and Judy are excellent hosts." *(Pat & Jim Carr)*

Open All year.
Rooms 2 doubles with air-conditioning, sharing 1 bath.
Facilities Living/family room with TV, fireplace; antique shop. Fishing, canoeing, swimming, sailing, golf, bicycling, hiking nearby.
Location NE OH. 75 m S of Cleveland; 15 m S of Canton. On Rte. 212, 3 m SE of I-77. In town center.
Restrictions Smoking in family room only. No children under 6.
Credit cards MC, Visa.
Rates B&B, $55 double, $50 single. Extra person, $15.
Extras Pets allowed. Airport/station pickups.

South Dakota

Hotel Alex Johnson, Rapid City

Visitors come to South Dakota to enjoy its outdoor pleasures—hiking, fishing, swimming, cross-country and downhill skiing—and to see the natural and man-made wonders found in the southwestern part of the state. Must-see sights in the Black Hills include Mt. Rushmore, Custer State Park, Jewel and Wind caves, and the gold rush towns of Deadwood and Lead; many are fascinated by the Mammoth Site in Hot Springs. Just to the east of the Black Hills is Badlands National Park, an extraordinary landscape of sharply eroded spires, ridges, and buttes.

Information please: More reader feedback on existing entries, and suggestions for new listings are—to be honest—desperately needed.

Reader tip: *Mark L. Goodman* suggests that although "most people see Mt. Rushmore at night, it was made to be seen by natural light. A drive along the scenic Needles Highway and Iron Mountain road is a must."

Rates listed do not include 4 to 7% state and local sales taxes.

CUSTER

State Game Lodge & Resort ¢ 👫 ✕   *Tel:* 605–255–4541
US Hwy 16A, Custer State Park   800–658–3530
HCR 83, Box 74, 57730

Located near the center of Custer State Park, the State Game Lodge complex is composed of the original lodge, listed on the National Register of Historic Places; forty modern motel units; and a variety of cabins of different sizes. The lodge rooms, decorated with period furnishings, once hosted Presidents Coolidge and Eisenhower. The motel rooms were recently remodeled, so be sure to specify your preference.

The lodge restaurant specializes in buffalo, pheasant, pike, and trout. If you've never had buffalo, here's your chance—you can try the steaks, burgers, or stew." *(Ralph Miller)* Comments needed!

Open May through mid-Oct.
Rooms 20 cabins, 47 doubles (in lodge and motel)—all with private bath and/or shower. Most with telephone, TV, desk, air-conditioning, fan. 2 with fireplace, some with deck. 7 cabins with kitchenette.
Facilities Dining room, cafeteria, bar/lounge with fireplace, piano; lobby with fireplace, grocery store, gift shop. 80 acres with children's play equipment, picnic area, creek for fishing. Hiking, jeep rides to buffalo herds, horseback riding, ranger programs nearby.
Location SW SD, in Black Hills. 30 m SW of Rapid City, 14 m E of Custer. Lodge is on Alt. 16, approx. 7 m E of Rte. 87 (Needles Hwy.) and 13 m W of Rte. 79.
Credit cards Amex, Discover, MC, Visa.
Rates Room only, $65–75 double, $55 single. 15% service suggested. State park entrance fee additional. Alc breakfast, $4–6; alc lunch, $7; alc dinner, $20. Children's menu.
Extras Dining room, some guest rooms have wheelchair access. Pets permitted in cabins only. Crib, babysitting. Airport/station pickups, $25.

DEADWOOD

In the Black Hills of southwestern South Dakota, Deadwood retains much of its flavor as a wild-west mining town. Built along the bottom of Deadwood Gulch and climbing the steep hillsides, the town features such attractions as reenactments of the Wild Bill Hickok murder trial, steam train rides, and underground gold mine tours. Also worthwhile is a visit to the Homestake Gold Mine, in nearby Lead (pronounced Leed); this working mine has been in continuous production since 1876. Lead also has an interesting mining museum and beautiful views from the top of Terry Peak.

In an effort to increase the amount of gold mined from tourists, gambling has been legal in Deadwood since 1989; slot machines, poker, and blackjack are permitted, and over 80 gaming licenses have been issued locally.

Reader tip: "Take time to tour the Chinese Museums and tunnels, and to poke through the Public Library (right behind Franklin Hotel), with a fascinating collection of books and papers covering western history; visit the Chamber of Commerce on Main Street for more suggestions." *(MA)*

Information please: Another possibility in Deadwood is the **Adams House** (22 Van Buren, 57732; 605–578–3877), a century-old Queen Anne B&B decorated in period with wallcoverings, linens, and china original to the house. Reports most welcome.

Franklin Hotel ¢ ✗   *Tel:* 605–578–2241
700 Main Street, 57732   800–688–1876

"Deadwood is a picturesque mining town filled with the spirit of the gold rush days and wild-west history as well as a fair share of tourist traps.

Entering the Franklin Hotel, a big brick building in the center of town, is like stepping back to the turn of the century in an honest, comfortable, non-glitzy way. Built in 1903, the Franklin was a premier hotel of its day.

"The friendliness of the owners and staff and its great location for exploring Deadwood's famous saloons, graveyard, shops, and museums make this a delightful place to stay. Deadwood is within easy driving distance of Mt. Rushmore, downhill skiing, the Passion Play in Spearfish, the Homestake Opera House and Gold Mine in Lead, buffalo herds, the Badlands, and the Black Hills.

"Many famous people have stayed at the Franklin, including Pearl Buck, Teddy Roosevelt, and John Wayne. Their presence can still be felt in the spacious lobby, with its dark wood, Doric columns, molded ceilings, huge fireplace, and grand staircase. In the early days the hotel's large dining room was the scene of some fine meals, and that tradition is being revived. The menu is impressive and imaginative, but not overpriced.

"The owners are putting a lot of effort into restoring the hotel. Drab carpeting and heavy drapes in the dining room have been removed to expose a lovely wood floor and huge beveled glass windows. Early American-style chairs and wagon-wheel lighting fixtures have been replaced with bentwood chairs and chandeliers. The effect is open, airy, and elegant.

"Our room was large, clean, and comfortable, with iron beds, rocking chairs, and a dresser that probably dated back to when the hotel was new. Our bath had a big claw-foot tub but no shower, although one was available down the hall." *(Linda Meyer)*

Open All year.
Rooms 1 cabin, 13 suites, 60 doubles—all with private bath and/or shower, telephone, TV. Most with desk, air-conditioning. Some suites with refrigerator. 14 rooms in motel annex.
Facilities Dining room, pub with band on weekends, gambling hall with slot machines, poker, blackjack; dances in lobby for special occasions, gift shop, veranda. Swimming pool, tennis nearby. 3 lakes within 20 m; 15 m to snowmobiling, cross-country/downhill skiing.
Location SW SD, Black Hills. 50 m NW of Rapid City. Take I-90 NW from Rapid City, E 12 on Alt. 14 to Deadwood. In center of town, at the end of Main St.
Restrictions Light sleepers should request rooms away from street.
Credit cards Amex, CB, DC, Discover, MC, Visa.
Rates Room only, $75–150 suite, $40–68 double. Extra person, $5. 10% senior, AAA discount. Alc breakfast, $3–5; alc lunch, $5; alc dinner, $12–15.
Extras Limited wheelchair access. Crib.

HILL CITY

Sylvan Lake Resort ¢ ♚ ✕   *Tel:* 605–574–2562 (May–Sept.)
Needles Highway, Custer State Park   800–658–3530
P.O. Box 752, Custer, 57730

This resort is located at the northwest tip of Custer State Park, a 72,000-acre home to elk, mountain goats, deer, buffalo, bighorn sheep, antelope, and eagles. The lodge was built in 1936 as a WPA project and has undergone a complete face-lifting in recent years.

"Probably the nicest place to stay in the Mt. Rushmore area. Our room #210, was very large and looked out over the lake. The buffalo steak at dinner was gamy but very good, and there was a fire in the lodge fireplace even in June! All in all, a comfortable, quiet, relaxing place." *(Mark L. Goodman)* Reports needed!

Open All year.
Rooms 24 lodge rooms—5 suites, 19 doubles; 43 cabins. All rooms with private bath and/or shower, telephone, TV, desk. Some cabins with fireplace, kitchenette (no utensils provided).
Facilities Dining room, lounge, lobby/living room, terrace, game room, café, gift/food shops, coin-operated laundry, meeting rooms. 50 acres with sandy beach on lake, canoeing, paddle boating, trout fishing, children's play equipment, cross-country skiing, snowmobiling. Rock climbing, hiking nearby.
Location SW SD, Black Hills. 28 m SW of Rapid City. From Rapid City, take Hwy. 16 (Rushmore Rd.); left onto Rte. 385 S; left on Rte. 87 S (Needles Hwy.) to lodge. 7 m N of Custer.
Credit cards CB, DC, Discover, MC, Visa.
Rates B&B, $90–99 suite, $72–95 double, $84–180 cabin. Extra person, $5. Crib rollaway, $5 per night. State park entrance fee additional. Alc breakfast, $2–5; alc lunch, $3–7; alc dinner, $17. 3-night minimum for cabins.
Extras Some guest rooms and baths have wheelchair access. Crib, babysitting.

RAPID CITY

Hotel Alex Johnson ¢ 🍴 ✗ *Tel:* 605–342–1210
523 Sixth Street, P.O. Box 20, 57709 800–888–2539

Construction on the Alex Johnson began in 1927, about the same year as Gutzon Borglum started work on Mt. Rushmore. Intended to be "the Showplace of the West," the hotel's lobby is highlighted by a massive fieldstone fireplace, hand-carved Sioux Indian busts, and a chandelier of warrior lances; in 1991 more Sioux Indian artifacts were incorporated into the decor. The rooms were fully remodeled in the early 1980s and are decorated with contemporary furnishings. The hotel restaurant, the Landmark, serves South Dakota specialty items such as buffalo, pheasant, walleye pike, and beef.

"The atmosphere is wonderful throughout. Paddy O'Neill's Pub is designed for fun and the lounge for quiet discussion. The rooms are tastefully decorated, and the staff is friendly and willing to accommodate." *(Pat Kurtenbach)*

An area for improvement: We understand that the guest rooms are gradually being redone with furnishings more in keeping with the western feel of the common areas. Many are still decorated in standard hotel/motel furnishings, with little regional flavor, so specify your preferences when booking. Your comments most welcome.

Open All year.
Rooms 35 suites, 85 doubles—all with full private bath, telephone, radio, TV, desk. air-conditioning. Suites with Jacuzzis and/or wet bars.
Facilities Lobby, restaurant, pub with weekend entertainment, lounge with paramutual betting (horse and dog racing, Thurs.-Sun.), sauna, health club.

Location SE SD. 35 m NE of Custer, 42 m S of Deadwood. On Sixth St., between Main and St. Joseph Sts.
Restrictions No smoking in 9th floor guest rooms.
Credit cards Amex, DC, Discover, MC, Visa.
Rates Room only, $65–95 suite, $50–90 double. Extra person, $8. No charge for children under 18 in parents' room. Weekend packages. 10% senior, AAA discount. Alc breakfast, $3–6; alc lunch, $5–10; alc dinner, $20.
Extras Wheelchair access.

Key to Abbreviations and Symbols

For complete information and explanations, please see the Introduction.

¢ Especially good value for overnight accommodation.
ᴴ Families welcome. Most (but not all) have cribs, baby-sitting, games, play equipment, and reduced rates for children.
✗ Meals served to public; reservations recommended or required.
ᴛ Tennis court and swimming pool or lake on the grounds. Golf usually on grounds or nearby.
Rates: Range from least expensive room in low season to most expensive room in peak season.
Room only: No meals included; European Plan (EP).
B&B: Bed and breakfast; includes breakfast, sometimes afternoon/evening refreshment.
MAP: Modified American Plan; includes breakfast and dinner.
Full board: Three meals daily.
Alc lunch: À la carte lunch; average price of entrée plus nonalcoholic drink, tax, tip.
Alc dinner: Average price of three-course dinner, including half bottle of house wine, tax, tip.
Prix fixe dinner: Three- to five-course set dinner, excluding wine, tax, tip unless otherwise noted.
Extras: Noted if available. Always confirm in advance. Pets are not permitted unless specified; if you are allergic, ask for details; *most innkeepers have pets.*

Wisconsin

The Thorp House Inn & Cottages, Fish Creek

Wisconsin is a big state, with abundant agricultural and natural resources; it is also vacationland for many Midwesterners. Called "America's great freshwater playground," Wisconsin offers summer visitors everything from deepwater sport fishing on the Great Lakes to boating, waterskiing, fishing and foot-dangling in 15,000 inland glacial lakes. In winter, take advantage of the state's downhill and cross-country ski areas or pursue less rigorous activities—tour breweries and cheese factories, visit Mineral Point's Shake Rag Alley crafts community (southwest of Madison), or tour Old World Wisconsin, west of Milwaukee, for an introduction to the state's Scandinavian heritage.

From Milwaukee in the southeast corner of the state to our northern-most listing in Bayfield, on Lake Superior, it's 380 miles. Most of our listings are found in Door County (noted under "Location" heading), an attractive and accessible resort area, with several more in the Madison area. We know of a number of interesting B&Bs and lodges around the state, but need more feedback before proceeding.

Information please: Recommendations for hotels in **Milwaukee** would be greatly appreciated. The **Astor Hotel** (924 East Juneau Avenue, 53202; 414–271–4220 or 800–558–0200), listed on the National Register of Historic Places, is a 94-room hotel, restored with antiques and period reproductions; rates are reasonable and many rooms have kitchenettes. The **Pfister Hotel** (424 East Wisconsin Avenue, 53202; in WI, 800–472–4403, outside WI, 800–558–8222) is a beautifully maintained century-old hotel, with many works of fine art on display. Although the hotel is a bit big for the guide at 333 rooms, their tradition of quality makes it a worthy contender. Let us know what you think.

About 20 miles south of Milwaukee is an intriguing possibility in Racine. Just a short walk from downtown and the marina is **Lochnaiar** (1121 Lake Avenue, Racine 53043; 414–633–3300). Built in 1915, this English Tudor mansion sits on a bluff overlooking Lake Michigan and was recently restored as a B&B. Rooms vary widely in size and price, but all are equipped with private bath, and in-room telephone and TV. Farther south, just at the Illinois border, is the **Manor House** (6538 Third Avenue, Kenosha 53140; 414–658–0014) a stately brick Georgian mansion built by a vice-president (who married the president's daughter) of the Nash Motor Company. It overlooks the lake, and offers four guest rooms elegantly furnished with Chippendale, Queen Anne, and other English antiques; the spacious common rooms are equally posh. Across the street is the Kemper Center, bordering Lake Michigan, with tennis courts and a fishing pier. The $85–115 rates include a continental breakfast.

A different experience awaits at the other end of the state in southwestern Wisconsin. **Just-N-Trails** (Route 1 Box 274, Sparta 54656; 608–269–4522) is a 175-acre working dairy farm and B&B, owned by the Justin family since the 1900s. Accommodations are available in four guest rooms in the farmhouse, plus three additional buildings—two are converted farm buildings, and the third is a Scandinavian log house. Rooms are highlighted by antiques and Laura Ashley fabrics, and the $60–125 rates include a full breakfast. Guests are welcome to accompany the Justins during their farm chores, or cross-country ski or bike the 15 miles of trails. The farm is just 5½ miles from I-90. Comments?

Door County Located in northeastern Wisconsin, 150 miles north of Milwaukee, Door County is a peninsula that extends like a pinkie finger from the town of Green Bay 80 miles out into Lake Michigan. Its extensive shoreline provides plenty of opportunities for fishing, boating, and swimming; its many trails and country roads are perfect for walking and bicycling. There are wildflowers in spring and summer, foliage in autumn, and cross-country skiing in winter; the county is home to five state parks. Door County is also well supplied with attractive shops, art and craft galleries, summer theaters, and 400 apple and cherry orchards, as well as a major Great Lakes shipbuilding center in Sturgeon Bay. Don't expect to be the first to have discovered Door County; from mid-June through Labor Day, "summer tourists descend with a vengeance," reports one reader.

The area is famous for its fish boils, started 100 years ago by the Scandinavian settlers of the peninsula. Here's how the White Gull Inn describes it: "Fresh Lake Michigan whitefish is cut in chunks and cooked (in boiling water with small red potatoes) in a cauldron over an open fire. Salt is the only spice used. Fish oils rise to the surface of the boiling water, and when the fish is perfectly done, the 'master boiler' tosses a small amount of kerosene on the flames underneath the pot. The great burst of flames causes a boilover, spilling the fish oils over the sides of the pot and leaving the fish steaming hot and ready to serve." The fish and potatoes are then served indoors with homemade breads and coleslaw.

Rates quoted do not include Wisconsin sales tax of 5%.

ASHLAND

Hotel Chequamegon ¢ 🏃 ✕   *Tel:* 715–682–9095
101 Lakeshore Drive West, 54806

Founded in 1854, Ashland became a thriving port city soon after the railroad was completed in 1877, enhancing Ashland's natural harbor on Lake Superior. The original Hotel Chequamegon (pronounced sha-WA'-me-gun) was built in 1877 by the Wisconsin Central Railroad (now the Soo Line), not far from the location of the current hotel. Destroyed by fire in the 1950s, the hotel was rebuilt in 1986. Though not a reproduction of the original building, this symmetrical four-story white clapboard building, anchored by turrets at each end, attempts to evoke its grandeur, style, and service. Inside, it also gives the feeling of an older hotel because of its traditional styling and period decor; the extensive oak and mahogany paneling used in the reception area was salvaged from nearby docks once used for shipping ore.

The hotel offers lake views from many guest rooms and from its public spaces, including Fifield's for formal dining, and Molly Cooper's pub for drinks and for casual meals. Guest rooms are decorated with period reproductions and a color scheme of burgundy, soft mauve and blue. The old-fashioned mood is enhanced by the absence of plastic, chrome, or fiberglass in the furnishings." *(Keith Jurgens)* More reports appreciated.

Open All year.
Rooms 18 suites, 44 doubles—all with full private bath, telephone, TV, desk, air-conditioning. Suites with refrigerator, sunken tub or whirlpool.
Facilities Restaurant, bar/lounge with TV, lobby, parlor with fireplace, porches. Off-street parking. Indoor heated swimming pool, hot tub, sauna, gazebo, picnic area. On lake for swimming, boating, fishing. Snowmobiling, cross-country skiing nearby.
Location N WI, on Lake Superior. In town.
Restrictions No smoking on 2nd floor.
Credit cards Amex, MC, Visa.
Rates B&B, $90–140 suite, $70–80 double. Extra adult, $10; children free. Rollaway/crib, $5. Corporate, senior discount.
Extras Crib.

BARABOO

The Barrister's House   *Tel:* 608–356–3344
226 9th Avenue, 53913

Mary and Glen Schulz invite guests to share their colonial-style home built in the 1930s. Baraboo is home to the Circus World Museum, and is close to Devil's Lake State Park and the Wisconsin Dells.

"Beautifully decorated, very clean, quiet neighborhood. We were served wine, cheese, and crackers on the screened porch before dinner; later we returned to sit and visit with Mary Schulz on the patio. Breakfast, served formally in the dining room, consisted of fresh fruit compote and two kinds of freshly baked muffins, accompanied by more good conversaion." *(Geri & Jim Becknell)* "A peaceful, relaxing home with warm, friendly ospitality. We especially enjoyed the evening wine and cheese and the ibrary reading room." *(ML)* "Beautiful furnishings; excellent cinnamon ·uns and rolls at breakfast." *(GR)* Additional comments welcome.

Open All year.
Rooms 4 doubles—all with private bath and/or shower, air-conditioning.
Facilities Dining room with fireplace; living room with piano, game table, fireplace; library with fireplace; screened porch; veranda; terrace. Downhill, cross-country skiing nearby.
Location S central WI. 40 m N of Madison, 12 m S of Wisconsin Dells. 5 blocks rom center. From I-90, take Hwy. 33 (Ringling Blvd.) to Baraboo. Go 1 block past :nd blinking light and go right onto Birch St. Go 1 block to inn at corner of 9th Ave. From Hwy. 12, turn E onto Hwy. 33; go left onto Birch St. 1 block to inn.
Restrictions No smoking. No children under 6.
Credit cards None accepted.
Rates B&B, $50–60 double, $45–55 single. Extra person, $5.
Extras Station pickups.

BAYFIELD

Also recommended: Although perhaps not right for a full entry, island ·uffs will enjoy ferrying over from Bayfield to Madeline Island, for a stay at the **Inn on Madeleine Island** (P.O. Box 93, La Pointe 54850; 715–747–6315 or 800–822–6315). This resort complex offers dining in the Pub restaurant, a full range of watersports, a marina, tennis courts, bicycles, and an 18-hole Robert Trent Jones golf course. Accommodations are provided in lakeside condominiums and cottages in the woods. *(KJ)*

Old Rittenhouse Inn **♦♦** ✗   *Tel:* 715–779–5111
301 Rittenhouse Avenue, P.O. Box 584, 54814

The Old Rittenhouse Inn is a beautiful Victorian mansion built in 1890. It has 26 antique-filled rooms and twelve working fireplaces, and is located in Bayfield's historic district, only a few blocks from the shores of Lake Superior. Jerry and Mary Phillips renovated the inn in 1976, and have also acquired two other nearby historic homes, **Le Chateau Boutin**, a handsome yellow Queen Anne Victorian, and the **Grey Oak Guest House**, a less elaborate turn-of-the-century home, which also offer B&B accommodation to guests. Guests at these two houses take a four-block walk (or drive) to the Rittenhouse in the morning for a continental breakfast of homemade preserves, fresh-baked rolls, fresh fruit, and juice. A full breakfast is available at a extra charge, and includes such entrées as creamed eggs, omelets, French toast, fresh lake trout, hash browns, bacon, sausage, and a tempting variety of pancakes: wild blueberry, wild rice, apple, oat, and raspberry. The dinner menu changes daily, but always features fresh fish, fruits and vegetables, homemade breads, and tempting desserts; favorite entrées include trout in champagne, roast lamb, and scallops Provençale.

Mary and Jerry are actively involved in the operation of the inn. "If we're open," she notes, "Jerry is always on the floor and I am always in the kitchen. It's been that way for 15 years." If there are ever any problems, she hopes that guests will let them know, so the situation can be remedied.

"Bayfield is a New England-type town, its economy once based on commercial fishing and logging. Today it is a vacation village, located at the northernmost tip of Wisconsin, at the gateway to the Apostle Islands National Lakeshore. Mary's cooking is presented by Jerry and the staff in a mouth-watering oral menu style that make you want to holler 'Uncle.' Our favorite room is Number 7, with a view of the lake, a wonderful king-size bed, private bath and fireplace with wood just waiting to be lit." *(Carol Thacher & Steve Rossa)* "A truly beautiful inn." *(Yvonne & Arnold Miller, also KJ)* "Rooms in the main building are, for the most part spectacular—large and beautifully furnished. The 'Chateau' rooms are a shade below the main building in opulence but have the advantage of a quiet and secluded location. A marvelous wide veranda overlooks the harbor and lake, and is perfect for after-dinner visits with other guests. At breakfast we were served delicious berries with whipped cream, juice, and average biscuits." *(John Blewer)*

Areas for improvement: "Everything was pleasant, but at approximately $100 a night—not in peak season—I expected more." Similarly "Perhaps the day was unusually hot, but our warm room was un-air-conditioned—at $110 a night. Also: "Though dinner for two with wine totaled $100, it seemed only average in quality to us; other guests were delighted with every aspect of the meal. *De gustibus non disputandum est!*"

Open Mid-May–early Jan. Weekends only, early Jan.–May.
Rooms 4 suites, 17 doubles—all with shower and/or bath, desk, fan. 7 other rooms in Le Chateau Boutin, 4 in Grey Oak Guest House 4 blocks away. Suite with whirlpool bath, library. All but 1 with fireplace.
Facilities Guest lounge with books, games, fireplace, TV, piano. Indoor community pool, whirlpool, racquetball, tennis, cross-country skiing, sailing, fishing, boating nearby. Off-street parking.
Location In historic district. 80 m E of Duluth, MN; 370 m N of Milwaukee. Short walk to shops, galleries.
Restrictions No smoking in public rooms.
Credit cards MC, Visa.
Rates B&B, $69–169. 16% service. Extra person, $15. Crib in parents' room, $10. 2-night weekend minimum at Rittenhouse. Continental breakfast included; $5 extra for full. Prix fixe lunch, $12.50; prix fixe dinner, $32 plus 16% service. Off-season "Mystery Weekend" packages, holiday dinner concerts. 10% AAA discount.
Extras One guest room wheelchair accessible. Children's portions, crib, babysitting. Vegetarian entrées with advance notice. French spoken.

BRANTWOOD

Palmquist's "The Farm" ¢ 🏂   *Tel: 715–564–2558*
River Road, Route 1, Box 134, 54513

"The Farm" is a logging, dairy, and beef cattle operation sprawling over 800 acres that has been in the Palmquist family for nearly 100 years. Rustic, family-style accommodation has been available for the last thirty. The atmosphere is friendly, relaxed, and unpretentious: Helen Palmquist notes that "breakfast is not served in bed unless someone is ill."

"The day we arrived, one of the Holsteins presented the herd with its newest heifer, and our children watched and clucked encouragement as the baby struggled to his feet for the first time. Later, the kids commandeered some bales of hay at the front of the barn and played hide and seek with the tiny kittens. They picked green apples to feed to the horses; watched a swallow sitting on her eggs in the horse barn; trekked off to round up 'Houdini,' a spirited heifer who managed to escape any confinement; supervised the four o'clock milking; and explored fields and buildings until they finally collapsed in the swing before dinner.

"And what a dinner! Roast chicken, Finnish meat loaf, wild rice with wheat berries, fresh vegetables from the garden, homemade bread, and peach shortcake. Helen serves guests and family together around a big table in the country kitchen. The conversation is as good as the food!

"After dinner, Jim and Art harnessed the Belgian horses to a flatbed wagon and we set off on a hayride through fields, pine woods trails, and groves of sugar maples. On our final turn through a clover field, a doe emerged from the woods and leapt across the field into the sunset. That night, we heard coyotes howl.

"During the winter, cross-country skiing and sleigh rides are the main activities. The farm is open during the holidays, and traditional Finnish dishes are served. The Palmquists maintain over 20 miles of groomed trails and a ski shop where you can rent equipment. Summertime activities include hiking, swimming, wandering country roads, and picnicking.

"The rustic charm of the farmhouse and guest cottages (simple, but comfortable—no TV) and incomparable hospitality of the Palmquist family make this a marvelous place to really get away." *(Maria & Carl Schmidt)* "All the Palmquists are wonderful. Despite a dilly of a rainstorm, our stay was all one could ask for." *(Yvonne & Arnold Miller)*

Open All year.
Rooms 4 cabins sleep 4 to 12—all with bath and/or shower, woodstove.
Facilities Country kitchen; living room; lodge with large fireplace, games; sauna. 800 acres with farm buildings. Hiking, biking, children's play equipment, hay rides, pond, 20 m cross-country ski trails, sleigh rides. 20 min. to lake for swimming, fishing, boating.
Location N central WI. 20 m W of Tomahawk, 12 m E of Prentice. "Farm" is ¾ m N of U.S. Hwy. 8, 2½ m E of Brantwood.
Restrictions No smoking.
Credit cards MC, Visa.
Rates MAP, $46–50 per person; $23–25 for children under 12. Ski trail fee, $3 per day, per person.
Extras Airport/station pickups. Pets permitted by prior arrangement. Crib, babysitting. Finnish spoken. Ski rentals.

BURLINGTON

Hillcrest Inn ¢   *Tel: 414–763–4706*
540 Storle Avenue, 53105

Hillcrest was built in 1908 by a prominent New York radiologist; originally three gardeners were employed full-time to look after the grounds.

Eighty years later, Dick and Karen Granholm spent a full year restoring Hillcrest to its original splendor, though today's gardens are a bit more modest in scope. When you drive through the gates, past the original stone pillars, up the curving drive to the house, you may feel that you're traveling back in time as well. Rooms are highlighted by antiques—one is done in country French decor; another has a king-size white iron bed with fabrics in shades of melon and aqua; and the third combines antique oak furnishings with a handmade quilt, lace curtains, and braided rug. Rates include a breakfast of a hot entrée, fresh fruit, muffins or croissants.

"Located high above several lakes and a rivers this B&B offers exceptional views; the building itself is equally handsome. Karen is a lovely caring hostess and a wonderful cook. Breakfast was served on fine china on the porch, overlooking the water. Outstanding!" *(Yvonne & Arnold Miller)*

Open All year.

Rooms 3 doubles—1 with private bath, 2 with maximum of 4 sharing bath. Central air-conditioning.

Facilities Dining room, living room, kitchen, balcony, porches. 4 acres with gardens, gazebo, fountain. Lakes for water sports, golf, bicycling nearby.

Location SE WI. 25 m W of Racine, 75 m SE of Madison, 75 m NW of Chicago. From downtown, take Hwy 11 W approx. 7 blocks to Pleasant Ave. Go S on 2 blocks on Pleasant, & turn right onto Storle Ave.

Restrictions No smoking. No children under 12.

Credit cards MC, Visa.

Rates B&B, $60–75 double.

CEDARBURG

Less than half an hour away from Milwaukee, Cedarburg offers a relaxing escape back to a slower time. With its many restored 19th-century buildings, the little town offers plenty of attractions—a visit to the Cedar Creek Settlement, a collection of antique and specialty shops, restaurants, and a winery, housed in an old woolen mill; the Ozaukee Art Center; and Pioneer Village. Other more vigorous pastimes include swimming, hiking, golf, tennis, horseback riding, and canoeing. In winter, there's cross-country skiing and ice-skating on Cedar Creek. Wisconsin's last original covered bridge is just a few miles outside of town.

Cedarburg is located in southeast Wisconsin, in Ozaukee County, 20 miles north of Milwaukee. From Milwaukee, take I-43 or Route 57 north to Cedarburg, where it becomes Washington Avenue.

Stagecoach Inn ¢   *Tel:* 414–375–0208
W61 N520 Washington Avenue, 53012

The Stagecoach Inn, which dates back to 1853, was built to accommodate both passengers (upstairs) and drivers (in the basement) traveling by stagecoach. Brook and Liz Brown, who have owned the inn since 1985, describe the Stagecoach as "a cozy and comfortable place. We have authentically restored the inn, using period furniture and fixtures. We used pictures from the late 1800s to help us." In addition to the guest rooms, the inn houses a candy shop, a bookstore, and the Stagecoach Pub, where guests can enjoy evening games of Trivial Pursuit and cards. The pub functioned as a bar for over 100 years, and the Browns spent many long hours scrubbing off decades of tobacco smoke to expose the original stamped tin ceiling.

"Liz and Brook Brown are the most congenial of hosts. The rooms are always well kept and project a feeling of early American warmth, due in part to the antique decor. The Stagecoach Pub is an ideal setting for a pleasant breakfast of cereal, hot croissants, coffee, and juice. A wide selection of beers, wine, and special summer and winter drinks are also available. Pretzels with mustard-honey dip complement the drinks. There are activities in the town of Cedarburg 28 out of 52 weekends a year, along with appealing shops and restaurants." *(Jack & Sharyl Dobson)* "Our room was lovely, and the continental breakfast of hot chocolate (or coffee or tea), juice, and warm croissants was delicious." *(Laura & William Hitt)*

"Our room had pretty stenciled walls and antiques. We were greeted with hot drinks to welcome us in from the cold. This cozy, romantic inn has a warm, old-fashioned atmosphere." *(Eileen Kalasa)* "Our suite was beautifully decorated, and the innkeeper took care of my special requests for champagne glasses and a flower vase." *(Tobi Steinberg)* "Existing entry is accurate; double rooms are attractive, clean, and small." *(John Blewer)*

Areas for improvement: "From our room, we could clearly hear the sounds of showers running (at a reasonable hour), or toilets being flushed (at an unreasonable hour). Its windows had ¾ shutters, which permitted the sun to flood the room with light at 5 A.M.. Regrettably, the one common room is locked until 8 A.M., which meant that I had nowhere to go for some early morning reading time."

Open All year.
Rooms 5 suites, 7 doubles—all with private bath, air-conditioning, TV. Suites with whirlpool tubs. Some with clock, tape deck.
Facilities Tavern with games; gift and chocolate shops. Boating, canoeing, bicycling, hiking, ice-skating, cross-country skiing nearby.
Location SE WI; 25 m N of Milwaukee. In center of town historic district.
Restrictions No smoking. Traffic noise in front rooms.
Credit cards Amex, MC, Visa.
Rates B&B, $95 suite, $55 double, $45 single. Extra person, $10.

The Washington House Inn
W62 N573 Washington Avenue, 53012

Tel: 414–375–3550
800–369–4088

The Washington House Inn, a Victorian cream-city brick building, was built as a hotel a century ago. Rooms are decorated either with a Victorian look, including period antiques, lace, Laura Ashley prints and papers; or in a country decor, with pencil-post canopy beds, planked floors, patchwork quilts, and exposed beamed ceilings. The inn was restored in 1983 by Jim and Sandy Pape, developers of the Cedar Creek Settlement; Wendy Porterfield is the innkeeper. A new wing opened in 1988 with nine country-style suites with fireplace and large whirlpool tub. Rates include a continental breakfast of muffins, breads, cereals, fresh fruit, and juices, plus an afternoon social hour with local wines and Wisconsin cheeses.

"Friendly helpful staff, enjoyable atmosphere in both gathering room and in guest rooms." *(Marsha Jones)* "The country-style rooms are more rustic, while the Victorian ones are classic in style; all are very clean and attractive. The afternoon social hour was great—fantastic cheeses, crackers and fruit, with local wines—it was the highlight of our stay here. Cedarburg is a fun place to go for a weekend away from Chicago." *(Kimberly Hawthorne)*

Some areas for improvement: "More fruit at breakfast; when we visited, the staff didn't seem knowledgeable about antique shops and local attractions." Additional reports needed.

Open All year.
Rooms 10 suites, 19 doubles—all with full private bath, telephone, radio, TV, desk, air-conditioning, fan. 26 rooms with whirlpool baths, oversize tubs. 9 rooms with fireplace.
Facilities Gathering room with fireplace, lobby with fireplace, harp entertainment on holiday weekends; sauna. Off-street parking. Golf nearby.
Location SE WI. Historic district.
Restrictions Traffic noise in front rooms may disturb light sleepers.
Credit cards Amex, DC, Discover, Enroute, MC, Visa.
Rates B&B, $95–139 suite, $59–119 double. Extra person, $10. 10% senior, AAA discount. Midweek packages.
Extras Wheelchair access; 2 rooms equipped for disabled. Crib, babysitting. Airport pickups, $16.

EGG HARBOR

Information please: If you are looking for a reasonably priced B&B with a comfortable family atmosphere, the **Country Gardens B&B** (6421 Highway 42, 544209; 414–743–7434) offers a turn-of-the-century farmhouse with four guest rooms sharing two baths. A full breakfast is served, and children will love to explore the farm's 160 acres. Reports?

The Alpine Resort ¢ 👪 ✗ 🦅
7715 Alpine Road, P.O. Box 200, 54209

Tel: 414–868–3000
414–868–3236

The Alpine is a comfortable family resort, founded by the Bertschinger family 70 years ago and staffed by college students. Activities are offered for all ages, and many families return year after year at the same time. Food is hearty, and rooms are simply furnished with motel-style furniture. The Alpine's 27-hole golf course has the most scenic hole in Wisconsin: the 9th hole is set high on a bluff with the green 130 feet lower than the tee.

"The Alpine Resort is run by lovely people. Every year they make improvements, adding new attractions. Home-cooked meals, beautiful, clear water, golf courses, music for dancing, and much more bring us back every year. The area offers over 8 miles of lovely parks, with Green Bay on one side and Lake Michigan on the other. There are islands to visit, charming little towns, lighthouses, nice shops, and boat rides." *(Mrs. Merrit Gates)*

"Marvelous lake views from the lodge and grounds; quiet setting off the beaten path; excellent building maintenance and housekeeping; friendly accommodating staff; good wheelchair access." *(Mr. & Mrs. Chester Virtue)* "The food is excellent, especially the home-baked pastries. The grounds are well cared for, including the golf course." *(Edward Decancq)*

Minor niggle: "Better lights for reading in bed." More reports welcome.

Open Memorial Day to mid–Oct. Dinner served mid–June through mid–Sept.
Rooms 40 doubles, 21 cottages—all with private bath and/or shower, TV, desk, ceiling fan.
Facilities Dining room, game room, sitting rooms; evening activities in July, Aug. 300 acres with ½ mile lake frontage, 27-hole golf course, heated swimming pool, 3 tennis courts, game room, swing set, picnic area, bicycle rentals, hiking. Swimming, fishing, boating, dockage in Green Bay.
Location Door County. 60 m NE of Green Bay. ¾ m SW of village, on Hwy. G.
Credit cards Amex, MC, Visa.
Rates Room only, $68–80 suite, 47–72 double. MAP, $101–120 suite, $80–103 double. Extra person, $9–26. Tipping encouraged. Full breakfast, $6.50. Prix fixe dinner, $15. Inquire for cottage, housekeeping home rates; accommodates 4–9 people.
Extras German spoken. Station pickups. Cribs, babysitting. Wheelchair access. Station pickups.

ELLISON BAY

The Griffin Inn ¢
11976 Mink River Road, 54210

Tel: 414–854–4306

Antique beds and hand-pieced quilts will soon put you in the mood for a relaxing stay at the Griffin Inn. Built in 1910 with a New England look, a gambrel roof and ample porches, the inn has been owned by Jim and Laurie Roberts since 1986. A recent breakfast included juice and fresh fruit, an egg-apple-bacon-cheese bake, scones and muffins; cottage guests receive a continental breakfast basket. Laurie cooks a five-course dinner on Saturday nights.

"The inn is restored and decorated beautifully. Breakfast is homemade everything—even the syrup. You won't be hungry for five hours if you eat it all. We had no problems with the shared baths. Lively conversation fueled by popcorn in front of the living room fireplace in the evening. Excellent restaurants within two blocks." *(M. Voigt)* "The Roberts' friendliness made our stay special; I give Laurie's breakfasts top marks. Our room was cozy and comfortable." *(Pat Borysiewicz)* "Jim and Laurie are the warmest innkeepers we've ever met. Looking forward to a return visit." *(Debbie Mishkin and Michael Swiatek)*

Open All year. Cottages open May through Oct.
Rooms 4 cottages with private bath, 10 doubles sharing 2½ baths. Inn rooms with air-conditioning, fireplace.
Facilities Living room with fireplace, dining room with wood stove, library, veranda with swings, guest refrigerator, unscreened porch. 5 acres with sports court, gazebo, cross-country skiing. Tennis, golf, watersports nearby.

Location Door County. 10 m N of Fish Creek via Rte. 42 N. After descending the Ellison Bay hill, turn right onto Mink River Road, at Trinity Church. Continue about 2 blocks to inn on left.
Restrictions No smoking. No children under 6 in main house.
Credit cards None accepted.
Rates B&B, $71–75 cottage or double, $67–70 single. Extra person, $6–10. 2-3 night weekend/holiday minimum. Winter midweek, weekend packages.

EPHRAIM

Eagle Harbor Inn & Cottages
9914 Water Street, P.O. Box 72, 54211

Tel: 414–854–2121

Regardless of whether you're traveling with kids and want a relaxed family vacation, or whether you're looking for an elegant adult atmosphere, Eagle Harbor may be the right place for you. The white clapboard inn is furnished with antiques, hand-pegged wooden floors, period wall coverings, and coordinated fabrics. Rates include a full breakfast of juice and fresh fruit, coffee cake, muffins, French toast, ham and eggs. The nearby cottages with casual furnishings, TVs, play equipment, and barbecue grills are ideal for families. Both the inn and cottages have been owned by Ronald and Barbara Schultz since 1986.

"Each room is different, clean, and classy, decorated with antiques and many comforts of home. The common areas are cozy and relatively private. The breakfast porch is refreshing; the food is elegant, ample and just plain 'good eating.' I love the quiet, the charm and Door County." *(Mary Karegeannes)* More reports welcome.

Open All year. Cottages open May through Oct.
Rooms 9 doubles, 12 cabins—all with private bath and/or shower, fan. Cottages with 1 bath each, TV, fan, barbecue grill.
Facilities Dining room, living room with fireplace, TV; library. 5 acres with children's swing set. Across the street from lake for swimming, fishing, boating. Golf, cross-country skiing nearby.
Location WI peninsula. 65 m NE of Green Bay. Center of town.
Restrictions No children under 15 in main house.
Credit cards MC, Visa.
Rates B&B, $68–135 cottage, $70–100 double. Extra person in cottage, $12. 2-3 night weekend/holiday minimum. Children under 3 free in cottages.
Extras Airport pickups. Crib.

FISH CREEK

Fish Creek is a pleasant resort village with many specialty shops. It offers swimming at a clear, sand-bottomed beach, a full range of water sports and tennis, and a summer theater company and music festival. The village is adjacent to Peninsula State Park, with thousands of acres of forest, miles of beaches, and bicycling, hiking, and cross-country ski trails. Three golf courses are within an easy drive.

Information please: About six miles from Fish Creek, on the east side of the peninsula, is the well-known **Baileys Harbor Yacht Club &**

Resort (Ridges Road, Baileys Harbor, 54202; 414–839–2336). A weather-beaten replica of the U.S. Coast Guard watchtower that once stood on this site dominates the club's architecture. Originally a restaurant with a few summer cottages, Baileys now offers accommodations in rustic cottages and more luxurious lodge rooms and villas. The restaurant serves American cuisine, specializing in fresh fish and vegetables, along with home-baked breads and desserts. Full resort facilities are available—marina, swimming pool, tennis, golf, and more. Reports needed.

Thorp House Inn & Cottages
Tel: 414–868–2444
4135 Bluff Road, P.O. Box 490, 54212

Thorp House is named for Asa Thorp, founder of Fish Creek. In 1902, Asa's nephew, Freeman Thorp, began building this Victorian home for his wife, Jessie. Freeman perished in a shipwreck, but Jessie saw to the house's completion, and opened it as a guest house. Christine and Sverre Falck-Pedersen acquired the house in 1986; after much restoration work they now welcome B&B guests into a home they're tried to make "warm, relaxed, and friendly."

The rooms, named in honor of the Thorp family women, are decorated with period antiques, including lace-canopied and brass beds. Although the house is perched on a hill overlooking the harbor and town center, it's just a block from Fish Creek's main street with its shops, restaurants, bike and ski rentals, and more. Rates include a breakfast of homemade scones and muffins, fresh fruit and juice, served in the old-fashioned kitchen or on the front porch in summer. Chris notes that "our English scones, made with sour cream and butter, are the house speciality, baked fresh each morning, along with either a coffee cake or muffins—perhaps lemon ginger muffins or apple streusel coffee cake. Romance novel fans will enjoy knowing that LaVyrle Spencer's best-selling novel *Bittersweet* was inspired by the author's visits to Thorp House.

"This place is positively elegant, with marvelous hosts. We also attended a fish boil while we were in town—lots of fun." *(Pat Borysiewicz)* "Just as wonderful on a return visit." *(PB)*

Open All year.
Rooms 7 2-bedroom cottages, 4 doubles. Some with desk. Cottages with private bath, living area with TV, fireplace; refrigerator, deck, charcoal grill. Rooms in inn with 2 shared baths, air-conditioning.
Facilities Living room with fireplace, library, porch. Beach, boating, fishing, cross-country skiing, Peninsula State Park nearby.
Location Door County. 1 block above Main St. on Bluff Rd.
Restrictions No smoking in inn. Children in cottages only.
Credit cards None accepted.
Rates Room only, $71–101 cottage, $70–105 double, $65–100 single. Extra adult in cottage, $10; child, $5. 'No tipping.' Weekly cottage rates June–Aug. 2-3 night weekend/holiday minimum.
Extras Local airport pickup. Crib. Norwegian spoken.

The Whistling Swan
Tel: 414–868–3442
4192 Main Street, P.O. Box 193, 54212

Although built in 1887, The Whistling Swan has been at its present location since the winter of 1896, when Dr. Herman Welcker suddenly decided to get into the resort business. To save construction time, he bought a number of whole buildings in Marinette, and used teams of horses and giant sleds to move them across the frozen waters of Green Bay. What is now The Whistling Swan was called Dr. Welcker's Casino; it had gaming tables for gentlemen guests and fourteen small bedrooms. Jan and Andy Coulson, longtime owners of the White Gull (see above), renovated it in 1985, rebuilding the interior to provides the comforts expected by modern tastes. Rooms are furnished with original and newly acquired antiques and period pieces, and summer and fall rates include a continental breakfast served on the porch.

"A Gatsby kind of house, with large rooms and a wide side veranda. We've been there twice since it opened in the summer of 1986 and we love it. On the ground floor is a sitting room with sofa and books and a baby grand piano. There is also a lovely shop that carries children's clothes, quality linens, Crabtree & Evelyn products, and thick sweaters. Our favorite suite is done in bright yellow and blue; the sitting and sleeping areas are separated by curtained French doors. The bathroom is old, with new, convenient fixtures, special soaps, and a view of the street below. No welcoming detail is forgotten, and the staff is friendly. Jan Coulson is part of nearly every day, and is a wonderful person, truly a professional innkeeper." *(Kathleen Novak)* "Our room (#7) was large, bright, and well appointed. There was ample and comfortable seating for reading and relaxing. The lighting was good, an often overlooked detail. A queen-sized four poster bed provided comfortable sleeping." *(John Blewer)*

Open May through Oct. Weekends Nov.–April.
Rooms 2 suites, 5 doubles—all with full private bath, TV, air-conditioning. Suites with desk.
Facilities Dining room, lobby with fireplace. 1 acre with flower gardens. 2 blocks from lake.
Location Door County. Take Hwy. 42 to Fish Creek. Turn left at stop sign and watch for inn.
Restrictions No smoking. Street noise in some rooms.
Credit cards Amex, MC, Visa.
Rates B&B, $135 suite, $95–115 double. Extra person, $10. 2-night weekend minimum.
Extras Local airport pickups. Crib.

White Gull Inn ♦ ✕   *Tel: 414–868–3517*
4225 Main Street, P.O. Box 160, 54212

What is now the White Gull was originally part of Dr. Welcker's resort (see The Whistling Swan, above). Guests would arrive from Chicago and Milwaukee by steamship for long relaxing visits. Many of the original furnishings—iron and brass beds, wicker chairs, and walnut and oak dressers—are still in use at the inn today. The White Gull has been owned and operated by Andy and Jan Coulson since 1972.

The White Gull's restaurant is open to the public, serving three home-made meals a day. The fish boil steals the spotlight several nights a week (see chapter introduction), although other entrées are also available.

"Although the lodging is pleasant, what we recommend most are the ish boils. We have savored a few of Door County's fish boils and feel that he White Gull does the best job. The food is wonderful, especially the ut breads, and the 'show' is great. The fish boilmaster is Russ, who has een there over 20 years; he entertains the guests with an old-fashioned concertina while he cooks." *(Terri & Jeff Patwell)* "With fear and trepidation ve booked reservations for the fish boil. The fish was served with melted utter, lemon, small red potatoes, and cole slaw. An extraordinary flavor, well worth experiencing." *(John Blewer)*

"We stayed at the inn just before the summer rush, so we could peek nto all the lovely rooms. Our room led onto a balcony filled with comfortable wicker furniture. Thick terry robes were provided for the walk to our shared bath." *(Ethel Peterson)* "It is clear that customer service s a top priority here." *(Pam & Mike Wilson)*

Open All year.

Rooms 14 doubles, 1 single—9 with private bath and/or shower, 5 with maximum of 5 sharing bath. All with air-conditioning, 5 rooms with fireplace, 4 with TV. 4 cottages with 1 to 4 bedrooms, fireplace, TV; 1 fully equipped 2-bedroom home with kitchen, laundry.

Facilities Lobby with fireplace, TV; dining room, porch. 2 acres with patio. 3 blocks to beach. 1/2 m to cross-country skiing. Golf, tennis nearby.

Location Door County. 73 m N of Green Bay. Take Hwy. 42 to Fish Creek. Turn left at bottom of hill to inn. 3 blocks from only stop sign in town.

Restrictions No smoking in lobby or dining room.

Credit cards MC, Visa.

Rates Room only, $120–185 cottage (sleeps 2-8 people), $58–106 double, $36 single. Extra person, $10. No charge for infants in cribs. 2-3 night weekend, holiday minimum; 3-night minimum in cottages July, Aug. 10% discount on weekly stays. Midweek packages Nov.1–Dec. 23, Jan. 2–May 11. Alc breakfast, $4–6, lunch, $6; alc dinner, $16–20.

Extras Crib, babysitting.

GREEN LAKE

Oakwood Lodge ¢   *Tel: 414–294–6580*
365 Lake Street, 54941

The first resort built west of Niagara, the Oakwood Lodge overlooks the entire seven-mile length of Green Lake. The inn's large lakefront provides guests with a full range of water sports; its old-fashioned rooms are furnished with antiques, white wicker, and flowered wallpapers. Owned by Marcy and Wayne Klepinger since 1985, the inn is a popular place for breakfast for guests and visitors alike. Buttermilk pancakes, omelets, and homemade coffee cake and sweet rolls are even more delicious when eaten on the deck overlooking the lake.

"A pleasant and comfortable inn, with a considerate and efficient staff. The lodge makes an ideal base from which to explore this beautiful region. The lake itself is one of the deepest in the state, and is famous for its lake trout fishing. The area was originally home to the Decorahs, a tribe of the Winnebago Indian Nation, and reminded me of Carl Sandburg's *Land of Liver and Onions.*" *(Willard Parker)*

Open April through Oct., Dec. through Feb.
Rooms 11 doubles—7 with private bath and/or shower, 4 with a maximum of 6 people sharing bath. All with fan, 4 with desk.
Facilities Dining room with fireplace, family room with TV, piano; screened porch, deck. On lake with pier, raft for fishing, swimming. ¼ m to marina for boating. Cross-country skiing nearby.
Location 60 m NE of Madison. ½ m from center.
Restrictions Smoking restricted in dining room. "Well-behaved children welcome."
Credit cards MC, Visa.
Rates B&B, $52–120 double, $42–66 single. Extra adult, $10; extra child under 10, $5; crib, $5. 2-3 night weekend, holiday minimum. Golf packages.
Extras Crib, babysitting available by prior arrangement.

HAYWARD

Edgewater Inn ¢ 👤   *Tel:* 715–462–9412
Turner's Road, Rte. 1, Box 1293, 54843

Purchased by Mel and Chris Christensen in 1990, the Edgewater Inn sits (as you might expect) on the shores of Clear Lake. The rooms are clean and neat with simple furnishings, but guests return to the Edgewater for the fresh air and warm hospitality, not the decor. Breakfasts vary daily, but start with fresh fruit and juice and might include homemade waffles, scrambled eggs and bacon; or ham and cheese strata with toast and hash browns.

"We especially enjoyed the living room with many windows overlooking the lake. We spent our days exploring the area, and returned in the evening to visit with the other guests and our hosts, in a warm family atmosphere. A delicious breakfast was served in the dining room, overlooking the lake. We soaked up the rays on the wrap-around deck, then took a leisurely canoe trip around the lake, and saw several deer and beautiful birds. We returned in the fall on a fishing trip; Mel proved to be an excellent guide when we fished for the elusive Musky. We also played a round at the beautiful golf course, tucked away in the woods." *(Daniel Murphy)*

Open All year.
Rooms 1 suite, 4 doubles, 2 quads—all with private bath and/or shower, air-conditioning. 1 with radio, TV, fireplace. 2 with deck.
Facilities Dining room, living room with fireplace, TV/VCR; deck. 3.6 acres on Clear Lake, with dock, fishing, water skiing (limited hours), sailing, cross-country skiing. Adjacent to 9-hole golf course. Guide service. Ice fishing, hunting. Boat rental/launch 1 m. 3 m to Birkebeiner ski trail for cross-country skiing, snowmobiling. Hiking, bicycling nearby.
Location NW WI. 15 m E of Hayward. From Hwy. 77 E, take Murphy Blvd. N to Turner's Rd. Turn E on Turner's; deadends at inn.
Restrictions Smoking in living room only. Children over 6 preferred.
Credit cards MC, Visa.
Rates B&B, $75 suite, $55 double, $50 single. Extra person, $10. Children under 3 free. Mid-week senior discount. Golf, bicycling packages.
Extras Airport/station pickup, $5. Babysitting.

HAZEL GREEN

Mustard Seed ₵   *Tel: 715–634–2908*
205 California Avenue, Box 262, 54843

"Our region attracts young and old to outdoor fun year-round: fishing, hunting, hiking, biking, sailing, golfing, canoeing, skiing, and snowmobiling. Our home offers country comfort and Scandinavian hospitality; our guests arrive as strangers but depart as friends." That, in a nutshell, is the Mustard Seed, according to innkeepers James & Betty Teske. Having purchased the 100-year-old lumberman's home in 1990, the couple now offers guests a taste of Scandinavia—in more ways than one. Included in their three-course breakfast of 'Texas-sized' lumberjack muffins and stuffed French toast with bacon or sausage and maple or apricot syrup is a Scandinavian sweet soup served with melted ice cream.

"Warm, welcoming hospitality; clean, comfortable, and attractively decorated rooms with traditional furnishings. In the evening, a hot beverage and delicious homemade Danish pastry are served by the fireside; breakfasts are different each day but always delicious. Jim and Betty are good sources of area information, but they also make it easy to relax, providing quiet areas to read or chat." *(Judith & Kenneth Schure)*

Open All year.
Rooms 1 suite, 4 doubles; 2 with private bath/whirlpool and/or shower, 3 with maximum of 3 people sharing bath. All with radio, air-conditioning; suite with TV, fireplace.
Facilities Dining room, living room with fireplace, stereo, books. Tennis, golf nearby. Children's play equipment. Near lake for swimming, boating, fishing. 2 m to cross-country skiing.
Location 70 m S of Duluth, MN; 130 m E of Minneapolis, MN. 1½ blocks from town center. From US 63, take California Ave.
Restrictions No smoking. School-aged children preferred.
Credit cards MC, Visa.
Rates B&B, $65 suite, $45 double, $40 single. Extra person, $10. Senior discount.
Extras Airport/station pickup. Danish spoken.

HAZEL GREEN

Wisconsin House Inn ₵ ✕   *Tel: 608–854–2233*
2105 East Main Street, 53811

Wisconsin House is an 1846 stagecoach inn, sturdily built of native white oak in post-and-beam construction. From 1853 to 1958 the house was owned by the Crawford family of Crawford & Mills Mining Company; Ulysses S. Grant was a close friend of Jefferson Crawford and a frequent visitor. When John and Betha Mueller bought the inn in 1985, it had been converted into apartments; the Muellers did a total renovation, installing new wiring, heating, and plumbing, and decorating the inn with their exceptional collection of country antiques and collectibles, including a beautiful display of cast-iron toys in the breakfast room. John's creative wall stenciling is found throughout the house. Rates include a full breakfast, served family-style at a 16-foot southern pine table. A set menu dinner is served on weekends and includes wine, dessert, and ethnic

235

entertainment (John's family is from Switzerland, Betha's from Norway). Guests enjoy antiquing in Galena's shops and visiting its historic buildings; nearby Platteville is home to the Chicago Bears' Training Camp in summer.

"Each room of the inn is furnished in early American antiques and fine collectibles. What catches one's eye upon entering each room are the hand-painted stencil borders, which differ from room to room. All the guest rooms are ample in size and are named after notable people from Hazel Green's past. This inn is quiet and comfortable at all hours. Betha's breakfasts are scrumptious; a typical one might be French toast with fresh strawberry sauce or applesauce/pecan pancakes with fresh country sausage. A special blend of coffee complements the food. Most notable are the innkeepers, who have a very special way of making one feel at home. They delight in giving their guests a complete tour of their home upon arrival. In the morning Betha moves from room to room, knocking on guests' doors to give them personal wakeups, eliminating traffic jams in the shared baths." *(Susan Laugal)* "We've stayed in three different rooms, and all have been delightful." *(Tom & Diane Kandziora, also Frank & Marilyn Van Nuffelen)*

"John is an adept tinsmith. His lanterns throughout the house are handsome indeed. Betha's applesauce pancakes or her chili sauce with scrambled eggs are delicious. Weekend dinners (for up to 24 people) are equally superb. John and Betha do all the preparation themselves; Yankee pot roast and stuffed pork loin with chestnut dressing are favorites. The lovely gazebo in the side yard is a pleasure in good weather." *(Dorothy Timm)*

"We enjoy John's wry humor, his yodeling and Betha's accordion playing after dinner. Relaxing in the kitchen, drinking coffee and visiting with Betha and John while they're baking sweet-smelling pies is a favorite memory." *(Frank & Bonnie Malone)* "We changed our plans in order to stay here—it was worth it; John & Betha are great hosts. They are well known in Wisconsin for their music and story-telling and we are glad that they have continued with this for the entertainment of their guests." *(Glen Lush, also Frank & Marilyn Van Nuffelen)*

Open All year.
Rooms 1 suite, 8 doubles—6 with private bath and/or shower, 3 with maximum of 4 people sharing bath. All with air-conditioning.
Facilities Dining room, living/TV room with bar, porch, balconies. Flower garden, gazebo. Cross-country skiing; Mississippi River nearby for fishing, boating, swimming, riverboat gambling. Tennis, golf nearby.
Location SW WI. 9 m N of Galena IL, 13 m E of Dubuque IA, 14 m S of Platteville, WI. In center of village, 1 block E of intersection of Hwys. 11 & 80 on County Trunk W.
Restrictions Traffic noise possible in two rooms. No smoking in guest rooms. Children over 12 welcome.
Credit cards MC, Visa.
Rates B&B, $75–100 suite, $35–65 double, $30–60 single. Extra person, $15. Prix fixe lunch $6–8; prix fixe dinner $16.95. Winter specials Jan.–Mar.
Extras Swiss spoken. Airport/station pickups. Babysitting.

HUDSON

Information please: Built in 1857, the **Jefferson-Day House** (1109 Third Street, 54016; 715–386–7111) is an Italianate home, built with doorways wide enough to the accommodate the hoop skirts then in vogue. Now restored as a B&B, its three guest rooms are furnished with antiques; rates include a full breakfast and afternoon refreshments.

The **St. Croix River Inn** (305 River Street, Osceola, 54020; 715–294–4248) is located approximately 25 miles north of Hudson. Rates range from $100–200, making it one of the most expensive inns in Wisconsin. The inn offers canoeing and hiking in summer and cross-country or downhill skiing in winter. All rooms have Jacuzzi tubs and stereos, and all but one have beautiful river views. We've listed this inn in past editions, but need more feedback from you as to whether the experience is worth the price.

The Phipps Inn   *Tel: 715–386–0800*
1005 Third Street, 54016

An imposing Queen Anne mansion built in 1884, the Phipps Inn was restored as a B&B by Cyndi and John Berglund in 1990.

"The rooms are a perfect blend of historical appointments with modern conveniences. The dining room and living room are gorgeous, and the delightful music from a player baby grand piano added just the right touch. John and Cindi were never without a smile and were ever ready to do whatever they could to make our stay enjoyable." *(Rhoda & Ron Doty, and others)* "The atmosphere was warm and friendly; the rooms clean, spacious and well lighted." *(NN)* "As a Christmas gift to each other we spent the night in the incredibly romantic bridal suite. It had a cozy queen-size bed with a half canopy, tiled wood-burning fireplace, and Jacuzzi. Our gracious hosts baked us cookies and left us bedtime sweets, and were sensitive to our need for a private, romantic weekend together. The delicious breakfast included homemade rolls and pastries, sorbet and fresh-squeezed juice." *(Sarah & Robert Johnson)* "The lovely Garden Suite made me feel as though I were in my childhood bedroom of long ago." *(Mary Schnell)* "Our cozy, clean attic room had a whirlpool and a fireplace. The delicious four-course breakfast was served on beautiful china. The innkeepers were quiet, friendly and helpful: we had car trouble and they offered us the use of their own for the day!" *(Mary Kay & Mark Vance)*

Open All year.
Rooms 2 suites, 2 doubles—all with full private bath, radio, desk, air-conditioning, fan. 3 with fireplace, double whirlpool tub; 2 with deck.
Facilities Dining room with fireplace, 2 parlors with fireplace, music room with piano, porch. Guest refrigerator, bicycles. 2 blocks from St. Croix River for beach, boating. Cross-country and downhill skiing nearby.
Location W central WI. 20 m E of Minneapolis/St. Paul MN. 4 blocks to downtown. From 94 W, take N. Hudson exit. Go through town, turn right onto Myrtle St. Inn at corner of Myrle & 3rd.
Restrictions No smoking. No children under 8.

Credit cards MC, Visa.
Rates B&B, $139–159 suite, $109–129 double, $79–95 single. Extra person, $10.
Extras Marina/bus station pickup. Babysitting.

KOHLER

The American Club   🛏️ ✕ 🍴   *Tel:* 414–457–8000
Highland Drive, 53044   800–344–2838

Now a magnificent resort and conference center, the American Club began modestly in 1918 as a temporary home for Kohler Company's European immigrant workers, and served as their classroom and meeting place. The building was enlarged in 1924, and remodeled in 1941. In 1978 it was listed on the National Register of Historic Places, and in the early 1980s it was completely renovated and redecorated as a luxury resort and conference center. The club has received the AAA's five diamond award annually since 1986. The rooms combine elegance and comfort in a traditional mood, with hand-crafted oak paneling, stained glass, crystal chandeliers, Oriental rugs, and some antiques. Since Kohler is a famous manufacturer of just about everything you find in a bathroom, it's not surprising that the bathrooms here are both modern and luxurious. A variety of dining experiences are offered, ranging from the elegant atmosphere of The Immigrant restaurant (reflecting Wisconsin's varied cultural heritage) to the wine-cellar atmosphere of the Winery to the Greenhouse, built entirely of stained glass.

"Rooms are heavenly, with skylights to let in the morning sun, bathrooms fit for a king, down comforters, and more. Even when the hotel is booked to capacity, it is still very quiet. As for housekeeping: The day I witnessed one of the cleaning people on his hands and knees with a toothbrush, cleaning the corners of a corridor, is one I'll never forget." *(Therese Lukaszewski)*

"Our luxurious suite had a long narrow sitting room, a rather small bedroom dominated by a brass four-poster bed, and a state-of-the-art bathroom with mirrors everywhere. There were a half-dozen bed pillows (down at our request), ceiling fans in both rooms, and touch-activated reading lights. Everything I saw—our room, the public areas, even the exterior—was spotless.

"There's lots to do in Kohler Village. We took a tour of the factory, visited the Design Center with its extensive designer displays, and had lunch at the River Wildlife Lodge. It was one of the best meals we've ever had—trout chowder, lamb hash, and venison shepherd's pie. After this meal we hiked the trails nearby the club. We rented bicycles to explore the countryside and enjoyed ourselves; the local residents are very friendly, perhaps because the area is not heavily touristed. "Dinner at The Immigrant restaurant was outstanding; the highlight was a trio of soups—pheasant consommé, lobster bisque, and cream of asparagus. The chef agreeably prepared my Dover sole to my request, and the menu listed several appealing 'light' selections." *(Linda Bamber)*

"Expensive by Wisconsin standards, but an outstanding facility. The

taff is particularly accommodating." *(Charles Krause)* "Food is excellent.
The only problem with this place is that it's hard to get a reservation."
(Jim Wilkes)

Open All year.
Rooms 88 doubles, 72 singles—all with private whirlpool bath, telephone, radio,
TV, desk, air-conditioning. Some with refrigerator, wet bar, or double whirlpool.
2 rooms in annex, some with hot tub on enclosed terrace or special "Kohler
Masterbath."
Facilities Sitting rooms, library; 9 restaurants, some with entertainment; patio,
room service, separate conference center, underground parking. Health & fitness
center on private lake, with beach, 12 tennis courts, heated swimming pool, hot
tub, fitness classes, massage, jogging trail, Nautilus, racquetball. 27 holes of golf;
formal gardens; 500-acre wilderness preserve with hunting, fishing, hiking, canoe-
ing, skeet shooting, dining lodge; 20 m of marked cross-country ski trails.
Location SE WI. Near Lake Michigan, 5 m W of Sheboygan, WI. 55 m N of
Milwaukee. From Milwaukee, take I-43 N to Exit 53B to Hwy. 23B, go 1 m W to
County Trunk Y—Kohler and go S on County Trunk Y to inn.
Restrictions No smoking in some areas.
Credit cards Amex, CB, DC, Discover, MC, Visa.
Rates Room only, $112–338 double, $88–292 single. Extra person, $15. Children
under 10 free in parents' room. 2 night weekend minimum July–Sept. Breakfast
buffet, $9. Alc lunch, $6.50; alc dinner, $12–42. Holiday, sport, getaway, spa,
winter packages.
Extras Wheelchair access; some rooms specially equipped for disabled. Airport/
station pickups, $18. Crib, babysitting. Spanish, French, German, Japanese, Italian
spoken.

LAKE MILLS

Fargo Mansion Inn ¢   *Tel:* 414–648–3654
406 Mulberry Street, 53551   Bayberry: 414–648–3654

Not quite halfway between Milwaukee and Madison is the little town of
Lake Mills, named for Rock Lake and the sawmills which were the town's
most distinguishing features at its founding around 1840. It's hardly the
sort of place you'd expect to find an imposing stone and yellow brick
Queen Anne mansion listed on the National Register of Historic Places.
Much less would you expect to find an antique-filled inn, its winding
staircase leading to suites complete with fireplaces and Jacuzzi baths. But
that's just what Tom Boycks and Barry Luce have created since they
bought the Fargo Mansion in 1985. Built at the turn of the century by
Enoch Fargo, a descendant of the Wells Fargo family, the inn has guest
rooms named for persons who had a unique relationship with the town's
most famous and somewhat eccentric family—ask the innkeepers for
details. A favorite room is the E.J. Fargo Suite, with a bath that's more
private than most: it's hidden behind a bookcase that swings out when a
certain volume is moved. These enterprising innkeepers have recently
renovated a second inn, the **Bayberry**, a turn-of-the-century hotel with a
two-story porch filled with plants and white wicker.

"The inn is set on a quiet street, and the people of Lake Mills are warm and friendly; you feel like you've gone back in time. Tom Boycks and Barry Luce are delightful and so accommodating. Classical music fills the house and the house's architecture and decor is fascinating—we loved the sunken tubs and marble treatments. Breakfast is served at a huge old-fashioned dining table, and the freshly baked fruit muffins with an egg and vegetable casserole were delicious. Guests visit and compare notes on their explorations, and Barry's young children help to serve the breakfast. Afterwards, we saw a tape of the mansion as it looked before the restoration—the transformation is unbelievable." *(Kathy & Rod Kadet)*

"We were in this area because we planned to stay at the Wisconsin Dells. We hated it, but came upon the lovely town of Lake Mills—right out of a Norman Rockwell painting, with peonies blooming everywhere, flags waving, and delicious painted Victorian "wedding cake" houses. Barry and Tom have worked hard on both the Fargo Mansion and the Bayberry, and both are charming. We stayed at the less expensive Bayberry, but breakfasted at the Fargo; the raspberry muffins were out of this world." *(Yvonne & Arnold Miller)*

Open All year.

Rooms Fargo Mansion: 5 suites—all with full private bath and/or shower, radio, air-conditioning, fan. 2 with whirlpool tub; 1 with fireplace. Bayberry: 8 doubles—all with private bath.

Facilities Dining room, music room, library, entertainment lounge, foyer, wrap-around porch. 1½ acres with picnic area, tandem bicycle. Lobby area available in Bayberry. Bike trails nearby.

Location 30 m E of Madison. 50 m W of Milwaukee. 2 blocks from town square.

Restrictions No smoking.

Credit cards MC, Visa.

Rates B&B, $65–130 suite, $45–55 double. Extra person, $10.

Extras Airport/station pickups. Babysitting by prior arrangement.

LEWIS

Seven Pines Lodge ¢
Route 35, Box 104, 54851

Tel: 715–653–2323

These days, the environment is on everyone's list of priorities, but in the early 1900s only a few realized that our supply of natural resources was finite. Charles Lewis, a prominent grain broker from Minneapolis, decided that one of the area's last natural stands of white pine, along with a wonderful natural trout stream, were worth saving from the lumber mills. He bought 1,500 acres in the late 1800s and built a trout hatchery (still in operation) to ensure a goodly supply of fish. In 1903, he built Seven Pines to provide comfortable wilderness accommodation for himself and his cronies, including President Calvin Coolidge. Now listed on the National Register of Historic Places, Seven Pines was bought in 1975 by Joan and David Simpson, who restored many of the lodge's original furnishings, adding a minimum of modern amenities—there are no phones or TVs. The lodge is still a favorite with trout fishermen, offering year-round trout fishing for the purist, with a private stream teeming with wild brookies. Not surprisingly, trout is the house dinner specialty. Joan notes that "we feature a warm, rustic atmosphere. Love, laughter, and friends are always welcome."

"Unbelievable atmosphere—the peace and quiet of the north woods combined with great accommodations and outstanding service. Cleanliness, lighting, and plumbing were all in good order. Their blue ribbon, privately managed trout stream is a research area for the University of Wisconsin, with large hatchery adjacent. Of course, the trout dinner was superb." *(Bruce Miles)* More reports needed.

Open All year.
Rooms 2 cabins with private bath, 7 doubles—1 with private bath, 6 with a maximum of 6 people sharing bath (1 with private half-bath). 1 cottage with fireplace.
Facilities Dining room, living room, screened porch. 57 acres with trout fishing, hiking. Fly fishing schools. Canoeing, bicycling, horseback riding, cross-country/downhill skiing, sleigh rides nearby.
Location NW WI. 1½ hrs. NW of Minneapolis. From Minneapolis, take I-35 N to Exit 132, Forest Lake. Go E on Rte. 8, then N on Rte. 35 to Lewis. Turn right at "76" gas station, go to end and turn right on 115 St. Go 1 m to 340 Ave. and turn left. Go 1 m to 1st road on right and turn right to lodge.
Restrictions No smoking.
Credit cards Visa.
Rates B&B, $85–150 cabin (for 2 people), $74–94 double. Extra person, $15. 15–20% service additional. Children under 10, ½-price meals. 2-3 night weekend, holiday minimum. Alc dinner, $21. Holiday, special event, ski packages.
Extras Airport pickups.

MADISON

Set between two lakes, Madison, the capital of Wisconsin, is best known as the home of the main campus of the University of Wisconsin. Take in the view from the top of the domed State Capitol, attend one of the many concerts, plays, and sport competitions on campus (but park elsewhere), and take a self-guided tour of Frank Lloyd Wright's architecture.

Madison is in south-central Wisconsin, 77 miles west of Milwaukee, and 150 miles northwest of Chicago.

Information please: We delighted to note that the **Poynette House** (407 North Franklin Avenue, Poynette 53955; 608–635–4100 or 2277), a reader favorite in past years, has re-opened last year with Heidi Hutchison as owner, and Carl Povlick as innkeeper. Closed since 1987, this Victorian inn and restaurant comprises three buildings, with guest rooms decorated with period antiques, including carved headboards, and marble-topped dressers. Rates are reasonable, and include full breakfast; some rooms have sunken baths or whirlpool tubs. Poynette is 25 miles north of Madison via I-90/94.

The Collins House ¢   *Tel: 608–255–4230*
704 East Gorham Street, 53703

In the early 1900s, Frank Lloyd Wright started the Prairie School of Architecture, then considered a fresh and innovative architectural form typifying the spirit of the Midwest. In 1911, lumber executive William

Collins commissioned local architects to build his home in the Prairie style It's now listed on the National Register of Historic Places.

Barb and Mike Pratzel opened The Collins House for B&B in 1986, and have carefully and thoughtfully decorated it with Arts and Crafts and Mission furnishings that complement the architecture perfectly. The living room highlights the original mahogany-beamed ceiling, leaded-glass windows, and wall stencils; while not contemporary in style, it has a distinctive post-Victorian appeal. The spacious guest rooms are furnished with antiques and homemade quilts, and rates include such breakfast specialties as Swedish oatmeal pancakes or soufflés. Homemade chocolate truffles, a house specialty, always greet guests on arrival. "Unusual decor, great hospitality." *(AR)* Comments most appreciated.

Open All year.
Rooms 3 suites, 2 doubles—all with full private bath, telephone, radio, desk, air-conditioning.
Facilities Breakfast room, sitting room, library with TV/VCR, living room. On lake, beach nearby. Off-street parking.
Location On Lake Mendota, 6 blocks from Capitol, at corner of E. Gorham & N. Blount Sts.
Restrictions No smoking in guest rooms. Street noise in some rooms in summer.
Credit cards MC, Visa.
Rates B&B, $90–99 suite, $65–80 double. Extra person, $10; extra child age 2–9, $5. 2-night minimum some weekends. University, government rates by prior arrangement. Frequent traveler discounts.

Mansion Hill Inn
424 North Pinckney Street, 53703

Tel: 608–255–3999

The Mansion Hill Inn, listed on the National Register of Historic Places, is a luxurious B&B which opened in 1985.

"The Mansion Hill Inn is an intimate facility that includes every amenity a guest could desire. The mansion was constructed in 1858 by the architect who built the second state capitol in Wisconsin, using many of the same materials—thick limestone for the exterior, and Carrara marble, Venetian glass on the inside. Built as a private residence, the mansion was last used as student apartments. A $1 million renovation began in the summer of 1985, and the inn has evolved into an exceptional lodging experience. Each room is decorated in a different theme, but all are appropriate to the Victorian era. Bathrooms are spacious and lavish, with marble walls and whirlpool baths. The rooms have floor-to-ceiling windows, complete stereo systems, and sophisticated telephone systems.

"The inn serves a continental breakfast and an elegant afternoon tea; they will even shine shoes left outside the door at night. There's a marvelous view from the fourth-floor cupola up on top of the inn—Lake Mendota, with spectacular sunsets, to the west, and the white-domed capitol to the east." *(Mrs. Ward Remington)*

"The staff was happy to give us a tour of the unoccupied rooms, but I liked ours—the McDonnell Room—the best. It had a fireplace, whirlpool tub, and a romantic ten-foot-tall draped tester bed. Double French doors lead outside to a veranda overlooking a garden, where we enjoyed breakfast the next morning." *(Kathleen Mahoney)* "The elegantly furnished rooms are equalled by the courteous, friendly, and helpful staff. We were greeted at the door and shown immediately to an antique-filled room; an armoire contained such luxurious modern comforts as a stereo, TV, VCR, and stocked mini-bar. The bathroom, hidden behind a movable bookcase, had tall shuttered windows, a pedestal sink, beautiful antique mirror, and a sunken double whirlpool tub. All was immaculate. Service was outstanding, from fresh towels to bedside mints to a second pot of coffee immediately upon request in the morning." *(Benée Hoxie)*

Open All year.
Rooms 2 suites, 9 doubles—all with private bath and/or shower, telephone, radio, TV/VCR, desk, air-conditioning, stereo, mini-bar. 8 with whirlpool tub, 4 with fireplace, 1 with balcony.
Facilities Parlor, wine cellar, conference room. Victorian garden with fountain, lawn furniture. Health spa privileges. 1 block to Lake Mendota, swimming beach. Valet parking.
Location Downtown, 4 blocks to State Capitol, 1 block to U. of Wisc. At the corner of E. Gilman and N. Pinckney Sts.
Restrictions No children under 12.
Credit cards Amex, MC, Visa.
Rates B&B, $180–250 suite, $100–230 double, $80–140 single. Extra person, $20. Tipping appreciated. Frequent traveler discounts.

OCOWOMOWOC

Inn at Pine Terrace ¢   *Tel:* 414–567–7463
351 East Lisbon Road, 53066   800–421–INNS

Built in 1884 as a summer home for the Anheuser and Schuttler families (of brewing and wheelmaking fame), this inn occupies a magnificent site overlooking Fowler Lake. A later owner of the house attempted to modernize it during the 1950s, removing much of the original exterior detailing—including its distinctive turrets and porch woodwork. It was rescued in 1986 by present owner Cary James O'Dwanny, who had architects work from old photographs to restore the home to its early elegance. Equal attention was paid to the furnishings, with custom-made antique reproduction furnishings and fabrics. While new, the bathrooms also have an old-fashioned feel due to the Victorian-style baths, vanities, and tank toilets. In the Henry Schuttler suite, the clawfoot bathtub occupies a regal position in an elevated bay window alcove; in a third-floor room, a double whirlpool tub sits on a marble platform, underneath the pointed turret ceiling. Innkeepers Tim and Sandy Glynn offer a breakfast of fresh fruit, baked goods, cereal, juice, and hot beverage, served in your own room. *(MW)* More comments needed.

O'Dwanny is also the president of "Classic Inns of Wisconsin," a group of five inns in restored historic buildings in the southeastern part of the state. Information on all is available from the toll-free number above; reports are most welcome.

Open All year.
Rooms 1 suite, 10 doubles, 2 singles—all with private bath and/or shower, telephone, TV, desk, air-conditioning. 6 with whirlpool tub.

Facilities Living room with books, fireplace; sun room. 1 acre with heated swimming pool. 20 to cross-country skiing. Lakes nearby for boating.

Location SE WI. Approx. halfway between Milwaukee & Madison. 35 m W of Milwaukee. 1 min. from downtown. From I-94 take Exit 282 to Hwy. 67. Turn right at top of ramp, & go N to 3rd intersection. At stop sign, turn right. After bridge between Lac LaBelle and Fowler Lake, take Lisbon Rd on right.

Restrictions Smoking permitted only in 4 guest rooms, sun room. "No facilities for very small children."

Credit cards Amex, Discover, DC, MC, Visa.

Rates B&B, $140 suite, $80–130 double, $70 single. Extra person, $15. No tipping.

PORT WASHINGTON

Grand Inn   *Tel:* 414–284–6719
832 West Grand Avenue, 53074

Though small, the Grand Inn is run with the kind of professionalism that makes it appropriate for inclusion here. Owned by Richard and Joyce Merg since 1989, this turn-of-the-century Victorian home elegantly furnished with period and antique decor. Each oversize guest room has a sitting area, a queen-size bed, and a private bath with oversize whirlpool tub. Extra touches include early morning tea or coffee brought to your room with the morning paper, fresh flowers, candy, slippers and robes. Breakfast is served at guests' requested time, and rates include a continental breakfast weekdays, full on weekends, served on fine china, crystal, and silver. Fresh fruit, juice, granola, and muffins are served weekdays. On weekends a hot entrée is added; perhaps apple fritters with maple syrup, huevos rancheros, or Belgian waffles with whipped cream and strawberries.

"Our room was quiet, comfortable, and large. The inn is well-located on a main street, within easy access to Cedar Point and a short drive to Milwaukee. For us, it was a great getaway from Chicago—yet so close! Port Washington is a nice town on Lake Michigan, near beaches along the lake. Dick and Joyce really made us feel at home. At breakfast they were always ready with coffee refills and second helpings but were never obtrusive. The upstairs guest parlor is comfy and relaxing, decorated with antiques and big old leather wingback chairs. We felt neither rushed nor unwelcomed when it came to check out—something we've encountered at other B&Bs." *(Eileen & Robert Kolasa)*

Open All year.

Rooms 2 doubles—both with private full bath, oversize whirlpool tub, telephone, radio, TV, fan. 1 with deck.

Facilities Dining room, family room with Franklin stove, games; porch, deck. Marina, fishing, cross-country skiing nearby.

Location SE WI. 25 m N of Milwaukee. 1 m from town. From I-43, exit at Hwy. 33 (Grand Ave.) Go E to inn on left.

Restrictions No smoking. No children under 12.

Credit cards Amex, MC, Visa.

Rates B&B, $60–95 double. Fri./Sat 2-night rate, $150. Extra person, $10. Senior discount.

Extras Airport/station pickups, $25. German spoken.

ST. GERMAIN

Information please: About 10 miles northeast of St. Germain in an even more remote Northwoods setting is the **Whip-Poor-Will Inn** (County Trunk K, P.O. Box 64, Star Lake 54561; 715–542–3333 or 3600), a dramatic log lodge. Built of local Norway pine logs 18″ thick, it has a great room with a 2½ story vaulted ceiling and a 30′ native stone chimney, a 28′ indoor pool and hot tub, and a loft library with views of Star Lake. The four guest rooms each have private baths, and rates include a full breakfast featuring local maple syrup and smoked meats, often served on the screened porch overlooking the lake. Hiking and water sports keep summer visitors busy; in winter, cross-country skiing starts at the front door. Reports?

St. Germain B&B ¢ 🏃   *Tel: 715–479–8007*
6255 Highway 70 East, 54558

Ron Rhodes and Joyce Zeimetz invite guests to base their explorations of the Northwoods in their four-level modern home—not that you'll have to go far afield, with a swimming pool and tennis court on the premises, and miles of trails leading into the forest. Joyce notes that three of the area's best restaurants are conveniently located within walking distance of the inn. Rooms are furnished with antiques and crafts, with homey touches—one room has a pile of stuffed bears on the bed; another has lots of lace-trimmed pillows and a grapevine wreath. Ron's handmade wooden toys are also found throughout the room. Rates include breakfast of fruit and juice, muffins and a hot dish; cookies, hot chocolate, and tea are available anytime.

"Comfortable accommodations, gracious hospitality, excellent breakfast." *(Ruth Hay)*

An area for improvement: "Better lights for reading in bed." More comments welcome.

Open All year.
Rooms 4 doubles share 2 baths. 1 with ceiling fan. All with clock/radio.
Facilities Great room with Franklin stove, stereo, TV/VCR, games; heated indoor swimming pool, hot tub. 3 acres with tennis court, patio, sun deck with wading pool, lawn games. Adjacent to 19,000-acre natl. forest; hiking, cross-country skiing, snowmobiling from back door. Bicycling, fishing, canoeing, tubing, golf nearby.
Location N central WI, "Northwoods." On Hwy. 70, 10 m W of Eagle River, 15 m E of Minocqua.
Credit cards Not accepted.
Rates B&B, $45–70.

STURGEON BAY

Sturgeon Bay, in mid–Door County (see chapter introduction for more on Door County), marks a historic portage point between Sturgeon Bay and Lake Michigan, now connected by a canal. Potawatomi State Park, along the bay, is nearby for waterskiing, fishing, boating, and canoeing, with trails for hiking in summer and cross-country skiing in winter; several other state parks are close as well, as are golf courses and tennis courts.

Gray Goose B&B ¢   *Tel:* 414–743–9100
4258 Bay Shore Drive, 54235

Jack and Jessie Burkhardt, long-time owners of Egg Harbor Antiques, turned their attentions to a new challenge in 1987, when they opened the Gray Goose, combining their love of antiques with their enjoyment of entertaining. The exterior of this 1850s red clapboard farmhouse is highlighted by a second-story porch which runs the full length of the house. Inside, the inn is beautifully decorated with antiques and collectibles; although there's a goose or two in every room, as you might expect from the inn's name, the overall effect is spare and elegant, devoid of the country clutter that litters many other inns. Most of the rooms have white iron beds, and two have five-foot dormer windows facing the bay and sunset.

Jack and Jessie describe the Gray Goose as a "truly intimate B&B, close to all famous Door County attractions, yet in a quiet area. We offer honest, friendly hospitality without being intrusive. We suggest restaurants, allow free use of our telephone, make dinner reservations, and provide detailed, knowledgeable answers to what to see, where to go, and what to do. Our guests sleep well on firm mattresses with quality linens, enjoying fresh towels daily."

The Burkhardt's "skip-lunch" breakfast is an extended multi-course affair, with never a repeat even on a five-day stay. A possible meal might include endless orange juice, coffee, and tea; baked Granny Smith apples, scrambled eggs with cheddar cheese and sausage; hash browns with red and green peppers; and cinnamon croissants, apple nut coffee cake, and cranberry bread—all homemade from scratch. Snacks, cookies, popcorn, cider, or lemonade are available any time.

"We felt right at home munching popcorn and sipping cider, to say nothing of the very comfortable beds and delicious breakfast." *(LC)* "Whitefish Dunes State Park was a perfect place to ski off all the yummy bread and coffee cake we had for breakfast." *(JS)* More comments welcome.

Open All year.
Rooms 4 doubles share 2 baths. All with ceiling fan, desk.
Facilities Dining room; sitting room with TV, library, games, piano; porch with swing. 1 acre with picnic area, apple orchard. Tennis, golf nearby. Beach, fishing, boating nearby.
Location 50 m NE of Green Bay. 3 m to town. Travel N on Hwy 42/57 around Sturgeon Bay over the "new" bridge. About 2 m after bridge, turn left (W) on County BB (Gordon Rd.). Go 2 m to end of Cty. BB and turn right (N) on Cty. B (Bay Shore Dr.). Go 1.1 m to inn on right.
Restrictions Smoking in guest sitting room only. No children under 14.
Credit cards Amex, MC, Visa.
Rates B&B, $60–75 double, $50–60 single. 2-night holiday weekend minimum. Non-holiday winter weekend packages.

Inn at Cedar Crossing ✗

Tel: 414–743–4200

336 Louisiana Street, 54235

Built in 1884, this brick vernacular-style building has seen many changes, originating as a series of small shops, an apothecary, and a doctor's office; after extensive renovation in 1986 by owner Terry Wulf, it opened as an inn. Now listed on the National Register of Historic Places, the inn features pressed-tin ceilings, period antiques, and hand-stenciling; guest rooms are individually styled, some with American country antiques or reproductions, others with French or Norwegian antiques accented with appropriate wallpapers and window treatments.

In the spring of 1989 Terry realized a long-term dream by expanding her restaurant; the original dining space has become the Gathering Room where her B&B guests can play a board game, relax in front of the fireplace, or linger over their breakfast coffee. Entrées in the restaurant, seating 95, are described by Terry as "elegant country cuisine." A recent menu listed smoked turkey layered with avocado, poppyseed cream cheese, and pineapple for lunch; and lamb roasted with mustard and red potatoes for dinner. An in-house bakery prepares all the breads and pastries; a carry-out service is available. Rates include a breakfast of homemade muffins, coffee cake, granola, fruit and juice. *(KJ)* More comments needed.

Open All year.
Rooms 9 doubles—all with full private bath, air-conditioning. 4 with whirlpool tub, 2 with private porch.
Facilities Restaurant, living/dining room with games, fireplace. Beaches, parks nearby.
Location 45 m NE of Green Bay. Historic district. At corner of 3rd & Louisiana Sts.
Restrictions Smoking restricted in some areas. Children over 5 welcome. Street noise in two rooms.
Credit cards Discover, MC, Visa.
Rates B&B, $69–116 double. Extra person, $12. 2-night weekend minimum.
Extras Airport pickups. Babysitting by prior arrangement.

Scofield House

Tel: 414–743–7727

908 Michigan Street, P.O. Box 761, 54235

Hidden for decades under layers of gray paint, Scofield House has been returned to its original glory—both inside and out—by Bill and Fran Cecil, owners since 1987. This beautifully restored Queen Anne mansion, built in 1901, boasts a five-color paint job, authentic to the period; the interior combines Victorian furnishings with floral fabrics and wallcoverings, and white lace. Especially fine is the original woodwork with oak paneling and inlaid borders on the hardwood floors. Rates include breakfast, afternoon tea and home-baked cookies.

"The atmosphere is warm, comfortable and charming—the antiques are usable, the furnishings comfortable, and the rooms spotless. The inn is located in a safe, quiet residential area, conducive to long walks in the early morning or late evening. The front porch is a wonderful gathering spot with a swing and chairs for guests to sip coffee early in the morning or relax later in the day with homemade cookies and hot cider. Breakfas is served on fine china, with sterling and crystal—perhaps hot appl cinnamon crisp, homemade mini-muffins; then, either an omelet, a bacon egg-cheese casserole, apple-walnut pancakes or eggs Benedict. Fran an Bill's genuine hospitality is exceptional." *(Kathy & Michael Quast)*

"As chef, Bill claims his goal is to get you past the first McDonald's He far surpasses his objective by filling you with more food than th average person needs for a whole day. If you feel the need to leave you lovely room, Bill and Fran are happy to offer suggestions on things to se and do that off the beaten track." *(Nora & Colin Frykman, also Joan & Scot Styles)* "Bill and Fran are warm, gracious, entertaining, and fun. Bill' breakfasts are superb and Fran bakes the best cookies and brownies ir town." *(Darlene Roberts)*

Open All year.
Rooms 2 suites, 3 doubles—all with private bath and/or shower, radio, air conditioning, ceiling fan. 2 with fireplace, double whirlpool bath. 3 with TV/VCR stereo.
Facilities Parlor with piano, board games; sitting room with fireplace, TV/VCR stereo. VCR library. Gazebo. Golf, beaches, boating, fishing, skiing nearby.
Location WI peninsula. 40 m NE of Green Bay. 5 blocks from center.
Restrictions No smoking. No children under 14.
Credit cards None accepted.
Rates B&B, $80 suite, $60–120 double, $55–115 single. 2-3 night weekend holiday minimum. Thanksgiving, Christmas packages.
Extras Airport/station pickups.

White Lace Inn

16 North 5th Avenue, 54235

Tel: 414–743–1105

After serving as a meeting hall for 40 years, this Victorian home was returned to its original beauty by Bonnie and Dennis Statz. The golden oak-panelled walls, the maple floors and antique-filled rooms were opened to guests in 1982; with a successful year behind them, Bonnie and Dennis realized more guest rooms were needed. Two blocks away, an 1880s home about to be razed fit the bill. Bonnie and Dennis bought it, moved it to a site behind their main house, gutted it, and rebuilt it from the inside out. Opened to guests in 1984, it is now the Garden House. Their most recent addition is the Washburn House, across the backyard from the inn, with four luxurious guest rooms.

"This renovated Victorian inn is beautifully decorated with period antiques, lace curtains, decorator towels, crocheted bedspreads, and live plants. Breakfast includes muffins, juice, coffee, and tea. The bran muffins alone are worth a return trip, and over twenty kinds of tea are available. A downstairs closet is loaded with games for guests to play in the parlor or in their rooms. The grounds are beautifully landscaped, with lovely rock gardens. We have been there several times, and Bonnie and Dennis go out of their way to make us feel remembered." *(Terri & Jeff Patwell)*

"Bonnie and Dennis Statz are two of the most personable people we have ever met. They spent much time visiting with us and sharing favorite sights and restaurants." *(Celeste Ruebe)* "Top notch! Beautifully done, fine food, lovely Victorian home." *(Pat Borysiewicz, also Glen Lush)*

Open All year.
Rooms 1 suite, 14 doubles—all with private bath and/or shower, radio, air-conditioning. 5 rooms in Main House, 4 rooms in Washburn House with fireplace, double whirlpool tub, stereo, TV; 6 rooms in Garden House with fireplace. Some rooms with desk.
Facilities Dining room, parlor with fireplace, sitting room with game tables, TV, stereo. 1 acre with gardens. Beaches, hiking, cross-country skiing nearby.
Location 2 blocks to downtown; 5 blocks to bay. Take Business Rte. 42/57 into Sturgeon Bay; cross the bridge into downtown and follow road to 5th Ave. Turn left (N) onto 5th Ave. The inn is on the right.
Restrictions 7 non-smoking guest rooms. Rooms accommodate 2 persons only.
Credit cards MC, Visa.
Rates B&B, $120–145 suite, $80–100 double. 2-3 night weekend, holiday minimum. 3-5 night winter, spring packages.
Extras 1 guest room equipped with ramp. Airport/station pickups.

WAUSAU

Right in the middle of the state, in a busy cheese-producing area, the town of Wausau is a good place to overnight. There's hiking in the unusual rock formations at nearby Eau Claire Dells, and skiing at Rib Mountain. Also of interest is the Woodson Art Museum, with an exceptional collection of porcelain birds and art glass.

Information please: About 11 miles north of Wausau is the town of Merrill, with two B&Bs of interest. **The Brick House** (108 South Cleveland Street, Merrill 54452; 715–536–3230) is a Prairie-style house built in 1915, with oak woodwork and beveled glass French doors, and two guest rooms. The $45 double rate includes a full breakfast. Somewhat larger, with five guest rooms, is the **Candlewick Inn** (700 West Main Street, Merrill 54452; 715–536–7744) an 1880s home furnished in period. A full breakfast is included in the $60 double rate.

Rosenberry Inn ¢   *Tel:* 715–842–5733
511 Franklin Street, 54401

Listed in the National Register of Historic Places, the Rosenberry Inn was constructed of stucco and brick in the Prairie School style, in 1908, for Marvin Rosenberry, a Justice of the Supreme Court. Gerald, Patricia, and Doug Artz purchased it in 1985 to rescue it from the perils of apartment conversion and opened it as a B&B after extensive restoration. Rooms have been decorated with a country flavor, using Victorian antiques in some areas and country primitives in others. Rates include a continental breakfast served in the third floor "gathering" room.

"This inn deserves three stars—the light breakfast was very good, the rooms are clean and decorated with antiques and interesting dolls, and the public rooms are pleasant. Downtown Wausau with its many antique shops is within easy walking distance." *(Sheila & Joe Schmidt)*

Open All year.
Rooms 10 doubles—all with private bath and/or shower, radio, desk, ceiling fan, fireplace, coffee maker. 2 cottages with housekeeping facilities also available.

Facilities Breakfast room, game room with TV, porch. Swimming, boating nearby. 5 m to downhill, cross-country skiing.
Location Central WI. 150 m N of Milwaukee. 5 blocks from center.
Restrictions No smoking on first floor or in guest rooms. No children under 6.
Credit cards MC, Visa.
Rates B&B, $50–90 double, $40–80 single. Extra person, $10.

Key to Abbreviations and Symbols

For complete information and explanations, please see the Introduction.

¢ Especially good value for overnight accommodation.

Ṁ Families welcome. Most (but not all) have cribs, baby-sitting, games, play equipment, and reduced rates for children.

✕ Meals served to public; reservations recommended or required.

ᚥ Tennis court and swimming pool or lake on the grounds. Golf usually on grounds or nearby.

Rates: Range from least expensive room in low season to most expensive room in peak season.

Room only: No meals included; European Plan (EP).

B&B: Bed and breakfast; includes breakfast, sometimes afternoon/evening refreshment.

MAP: Modified American Plan; includes breakfast and dinner.

Full board: Three meals daily.

Alc lunch: À la carte lunch; average price of entrée plus nonalcoholic drink, tax, tip.

Alc dinner: Average price of three-course dinner, including half bottle of house wine, tax, tip.

Prix fixe dinner: Three- to five-course set dinner, excluding wine, tax, tip unless otherwise noted.

Extras: Noted if available. Always confirm in advance. Pets are not permitted unless specified; if you are allergic, ask for details; *most innkeepers have pets.*

Canada

McGee's Inn, Ottawa, Ontario

Canada is a huge and beautiful country with a number of wonderful places to visit, from the exciting, cosmopolitan cities to the peaceful countryside and rugged interior. Far from a carbon copy of the United States, Canada offers visitors subtle "foreign" experiences from French Quebec in the east to the very British city of Victoria, in British Columbia, to the west.

A few notes for first-time visitors to Canada: Radar detectors are illegal and seat belts are mandatory. When consulting maps and speed limits remember that Canada is metric. Ask your auto insurance company for a free "Canadian Non-Resident Inter-Provincial Motor Vehicle Insurance Card"—it will speed up immeasurably any procedures if you are involved in an accident. Finally, it is often advantageous to purchase Canadian currency in the U.S.—make some comparison calls first (the rate varies from bank to bank).

Rates quoted in this section are noted in Canadian, not U.S. dollars. *US $1 = Canadian $.88;* exchange rates are subject to constant fluctuations.

And a final note from the "bite-the-hand-that-feeds-you department." In January, 1991, a federal Goods and Services Tax of 7% (GST) went into effect, which also applies to accommodation and restaurant meals, *in addition* to existing sales taxes. Non-residents are eligible for refunds on most goods and accommodations but not meals, alcohol, or fuel; inquire to obtain appropriate forms or call 800–66VISIT (in Canada) or 613–991–3346. Original (not photocopied) bills must accompany your claim for a refund. Refunds can be obtained by mail, or on the spot at Canadian Land Border Duty Free Shops. Charges made on your credit card to a non-Canadian address may circumvent this unpleasantness, or facilitate a refund.

251

Northwest Territories

Some folks like to get away from it all, and others *really* like to get away from it all. A visit to the Northwest Territories will suit the latter group. Imagine an area equivalent in size to India, with a population of only 50,000! Over half the area of the Northwest Territories is above the Arctic Circle, so it's not surprising that the region enjoys over 20 hours of sunlight daily during June. The Northwest Territories are home to the Dene, Inuit, and Metis peoples as well as more recent arrivals from the south.

All rates are quoted in Canadian dollars.

RESOLUTE BAY

High Arctic International Tourist Home   *Tel:* 819–252–3875
Box 200, X0A 0V0

Owners Terry and Bezal Jesudason welcome those visiting Resolute but are primarily involved in organizing a variety of snowmobile/sledge expeditions in the High Arctic. They write: "We can show visitors some of the interesting cultural and historical sites of this Eskimo village. It's a scenic snow-covered area for almost 10 months of the year, but during the short Arctic summer, flowers bloom and birds come back to breed. It is possible to experience some of the old Eskimo culture and live in the modern world too. The best months to visit are in May, when there are 24 hours of sunshine and beautiful ice and snow formations, or in July, when the snow is gone and the Arctic summer is at its height. If guests want to try northern specialties, we can prepare local foods such as caribou, musk-ox, Arctic char, or seal. We get salad makings and fruit from Yellowknife so we offer a pretty balanced diet."

"Try to imagine comfort and convenience in the bleak, awesome, and austere setting of the Canadian High Arctic, where summer as we know it never comes and where there are only a few miles of roads in a tiny Inuit (Eskimo) village. There are two flights from Montreal and two from Edmonton every week. The nearest highway system is 1,000 miles away.

"This place is the best there is between here and the North Pole. The home is spotlessly clean, and there is the ultimate Arctic luxury of flush toilets and hot showers. It is comfortably furnished and even has satellite TV and a VCR for those interested. There is a fine library of Arctic lore and a paperback collection for escape reading. The living and dining area are spacious and light, and the bedrooms, while simply furnished, are very comfortable and afford privacy and coziness.

"The bottom line in this austere and trying environment, aside from companionship, is good food. Both are here in abundance. Considering that all food is flown in by jet from Yellowknife, 1,000 miles away, the quantities of fresh fruits and vegetables, homemade baked goodies, fresh meats, and fresh milk are remarkable. Breakfasts are as small or as hearty as requested, lunches are simple but plentiful, and dinners are often gourmet if not haute cuisine. All food is prepared with care and imagination.

"Terry and Bezal Jesudason make people feel welcome and at home, and have a knowledge and love of the environment that they successfully impart to those who stay with them. Everyone has the run of the house, but somehow everyone's privacy is respected." *(Arthur & Victoria Spang)* More reports required.

Open Feb. 15–Dec. 15.
Rooms 5 doubles share 2 baths. All with desk.
Facilities Living room with TV/VCR, library of Arctic books and videos; dining room; common room with desk.
Location 1000 m N of Yellowknife and Frobisher Bay, NWT. 4 m from Resolute Bay airport. 1/4 m from Northwest Passage.
Restrictions No smoking in guest rooms.
Credit cards None accepted.
Rates Full board, $105 per person. 5- to 11-day Arctic expeditions to Resolute Bay, Northern Ellesmere Island, Beechey Island, and the Magnetic North Pole; inquire for rates.
Extras Free airport pickups. Eskimo, German, minimal French spoken.

Ontario

Ontario offers much to travelers—the cosmopolitan city of Toronto; the country's capital in Ottawa; and, of course, Niagara Falls (which some visitors claim is more dramatic on the Canadian side). But beyond these population hubs is a quieter province, with pleasant farmland, huge tracts of forest and miles of shoreline along over 250,000 lakes. Most accessible, of course, are areas along Lakes Superior, Huron, Erie and Ontario.

The popular Georgian Bay area offers spiffy resorts and water-related recreation of all types, as well as sleepy towns such as Wiarton. It's easy to see how this area inspired Canada's famous Group of Seven landscape painters. For a longer trip, follow Route 17 along the northern shore of Lake Superior, then take Route 11 to the idyllic Lake of the Woods area in far southwestern Ontario, where there are numerous lodges and rustic resorts.

Major festivals include the Shakespeare Festival in Stratford, and the Shaw Festival at Niagara-on-the-Lake. Several provincial parks offer outstanding facilities for outdoor recreation.

Rates do not include 5% provincial sales tax on room, 7% on meals.
All rates quoted in Canadian dollars.

ALGONQUIN PARK

Algonquin is Ontario's oldest and largest provincial park. Founded in 1893, it has nearly 3,000 square miles of wilderness and more than 1,000 lakes; families of moose roam the territory and bear sightings are common. Although the park is a government-designated wilderness area and primarily accessible by canoe, Highway 60 traverses the southern portion. Naturalist services and museum, a pioneer logging exhibit, conducted trips, and canoe rentals are available by checking with the main information center (705–633–5572) at the east gate, on Highway 60 near Whitney. The park is open all year; admission is obtained by buying a $5 daily vehicle permit.

Information please: 160 miles north of Toronto and 75 miles west of Whitney is a luxurious wilderness resort, where 64 lucky guests are pampered with outstanding French cuisine, a brand-new fitness center, and superlative tennis courts and instruction. Called **The Inn at Manitou** (summer—McKellar Center Road, McKellar P0G 1C0; 705–389–2171; winter—251 Davenport Road, Toronto M5R 1J9; 416–967–3466 or 6137), the inn is a complex of contemporary cedar townhouse-style buildings, many with balconies overlooking Lake Manitowabing, vaulted cedar ceilings, fireplaces, or marble whirlpool baths. The decor is elegant country French, the food imaginative and creative (with both regular and spa menus), the service excellent, and the rates surprisingly reasonable considering that they include almost everything. Owners Sheila and Ben Wise also run a decidedly upscale children's camp next door, where youngsters have their own radio station, photography studio and summer theater. Comments?

Arowhon Pines 👭 ✕   *Tel:* 705–633–5661
Algonquin Park, P0A 1B0
Winter: 297 Balliol Street, Toronto, M4S 1C7   Winter: 416–483–4393

Arowhon Pines was established in the 1930s as a resort for parents visiting their children at nearby Camp Arowhon. Today the resort provides a full complement of water sports and miles of hiking trails in a private lake setting. Accommodations are in rustic but comfortable cabins and lodges, built of peeled logs and accented with Canadian pine antiques and modern furnishings. Rates include all meals and most all resort activities.

A well-known feature of Arowhon Pines is its food, served in the hexagonal shorefront dining room; both lunch and dinner feature salad and dessert buffets in addition to daily menu selections. Some recent luncheon entrées were a mini-club sandwich, marinated salmon, mushroom quiche, or calf's liver with onions. A typical dinner might include smoked trout, minestrone soup, veal medallions with Basmati rice, or whitefish Parisienne.

"Arowhon Pines is very private and peaceful, reached by driving down a beautiful dirt road through the woods. Sitting on a lake are several small lodges with adequate, but not remarkable, guest facilities. The high points are the delicious food and the very courteous staff. The pier and diving platform on the lake are lots of fun." *(Lisa Taylor Crouse)* "Fully endorse existing entry. Try to book a private cabin for complete tranquility." *(LI)*

Open May 12–Oct. 12.
Rooms 3 suites, 47 doubles—all with full private bath, heating, desk. Rooms in 14 cabins, each with 1–12 guest rooms, common lounge with fireplace.
Facilities Dining room with fireplace, family room with fireplace, piano, TV/VCR.

Cabin lounges with fireplace. Movies nightly in family room. 10 acres on lake with swimming, boating, fishing, tennis, hiking. Sauna, children's play equipment, shuffleboard.
Location Central Ontario. 175 m N of Toronto, 35 m NE of Huntsville. From Huntsville, go E on Hwy. 60 to W Algonquin gate. Continue 10 m past gate to private road, turn in and go 5 m to lodge.
Restrictions No smoking in some cabins.
Credit cards None accepted. BYOB.
Rates Full board, $340–482 suite (for 2 people), $220–332 double, $140–200 single. Extra person, $80–110; children under 13 in parents' room, $\frac{1}{2}$ adult rate. 15% service; absolutely no tipping. 3-night minimum during peak season.
Extras Limited wheelchair access. Crib, babysitting. French spoken. Member, Relais et Chateaux.

Killarney Lodge ✕ ♣

Algonquin Park, P0A 1K0

Tel: 705–633–5551
Winter: 416–482–5254

Killarney Lodge, built in 1935, allows one to combine modern comfort with wilderness exploration. Outside, the piercing cry of the loon echoes over the lake while beavers paddle through quiet waters; a morning walk might result in a peek at a moose or a white-tailed deer. Inside the inn itself, guests relax and become acquainted by the natural stone fireplace in the guest lounge.

"Beautifully situated on a peninsula jutting into the Lake of Two Rivers. The lodge is located on the only road through the southern section of Algonquin Provincial Park, a wildlife sanctuary with beautiful rugged scenery and a real sense of wilderness. It is best explored by canoe and on foot, and includes picnic grounds and nature trails.

"The main building contains the reception and dining room. Accommodation is in well-built, comfortable log cabins dispersed under trees along the lakeside. The food was among the best we have found anywhere— fresh vegetables and homemade dishes, with great care and attention to detail. Breakfast included delicious pancakes and maple syrup, jams and marmalade, and homemade rolls. At dinner we were delighted with the local specialties and a variety of fruit pies." *(Harry Robinson)*

"Each cabin is built of Algonquin's native white pine, decorated in rustic chic decor. Each has a view of the lake and its own canoe. The central lodge has a classic Canadian atmosphere including the requisite stone fireplace. The food is robust and satisfying. The owners, Linda and Eric Miglin, circulate throughout the dining area chatting with each table in their friendly and hospitable manner. Housekeeping is prompt, efficient, and friendly. One of the lodge's best features is the landscaping, with hundreds of annuals planted around the brightly painted cabins. Killarney provides civilized accommodations in a Canadian wilderness with full access to the park's activities and scenery." *(Barry Crouse & Kelli Carroll)*
"Immaculate accommodation, firm beds, good food. But best of all is the magnificent scenery." *(Frank Laslow, also Murray Corlett)* "The dining facilities are excellent, with fish, fowl, or roasts of beef, lamb, or pork on the menu. Baking is done on the premises, and desserts are invariably tempting. The staff is congenial, pleasant, and caring about every detail of a guest's visit." *(G.A. Fraser)*

255

ONTARIO

"Immaculate housekeeping, modern plumbing, and more than adequate lighting. The lodge is located on a spit of land jutting into the Lake of Two Rivers. Each cabin comes with plenty of comfortable seating and its own canoe. There's a nice sandy beach with deck chairs and tables. There are nature trails everywhere and we spotted moose, loons, herons, beavers, and otters." *(Ann & Terry Brunstrom)* Reports welcome.

Open May–Oct.
Rooms 27 1- and 2-bedroom cabins—all with private bath and/or shower, electric heat, deck, private canoe. Some with desk.
Facilities Restaurant with fireplace, reception area, guest lounge. 12 acres on lake with sandy swimming beach. Hiking, canoeing, fishing, shuffleboard, play equipment, nature talks, rental boats.
Location SE ONT, on Rte. 60. 48 m East of Huntsville, 188 m N of Toronto. Lodge at 22-mile post, about midway between east and west gates of park.
Restrictions Smoking permitted in cabins only. No alcohol in lodge or restaurant.
Credit cards MC, Visa.
Rates Full board, $166–338 double. Extra adult in cottage, $60–80. Children's rates, $12–59. Tipping appreciated. 2-night weekend minimum. Picnic lunches by prior arrangement. Prix fixe lunch, $9–14; dinner, $35–40.
Extras Crib.

ALTON

The Millcroft Inn ✕
John Street, P.O. Box 89, L0N 1AO

Tel: 519–941–8111
416–791–4422
800–268–8415

The Millcroft is set in an 1881 knitting mill, built of hand-cut stones. Its guest rooms combine both antique and contemporary decor, and an additional 20 condo-style units are located in the Crofts, just across the bridge. Just opened in 1990 is the Manor House, the former mill owner's residence, converted into nine luxury rooms with fireplace and hot tub. The Millcroft is known for its fine food; you can eat in the timbered dining room or in the glass "pod" overlooking the old mill falls. *(WVE)* More comments, please.

Open All year.
Rooms 51 doubles—all with full private bath, telephone, radio, desk, air-conditioning. Some with fireplace, hot tub, refrigerator, patio.
Facilities Restaurant, bar/lounge, lobby, atrium, sitting room with fireplace, game room with billiards, Ping-Pong; patio. 100 acres with conference center, heated swimming pool, 2 hot tubs, sauna, 4 tennis courts, hot air ballooning, hiking. Golf, downhill, cross-country skiing nearby.
Location 50 m NW of Toronto. Take Hwy. 10 N to Caledon 24 km. Turn left on Hwy. 24 and go 5 km to Rte. 136. Turn right and go N 5 km to Alton. Go left at stop sign. Go 1 km. to 2nd stop sign. Bear right on John St. to inn.
Credit cards Amex, DC, Enroute, MC, Visa.
Rates Room only, $155–170 double. 15% service. 2-night weekend/holiday minimum. Alc breakfast, $5–10; alc lunch, $25; alc dinner, $50. Weekend, midweek packages.
Extras Member, Relais et Chateaux.

BAYFIELD

Also recommended: The Benmiller Inn (Huron Road #1, RR #4, Goderich N7A 3Y1; 519–524–2191) is a complex of restored woolen mills and houses, spread over 70 acres; the inn's contemporary furnishings complement the original hand-hewn beams and masonry. Elements of the mill's machinery have been used as lamps, sconces, and decorative elements. Rooms are quite luxurious, with prices to match. "Beautiful facility in a secluded setting. We stopped in for lunch, and enjoyed the creative menu and home-baked breads. An unusual entrée was the salmon cheesecake. Well-stocked gift shop." *(John Blewer)*

The Little Inn of Bayfield 👫 ✕
Main Street, P.O. Box 100, N0M 1G0

Tel: 519–565–2611

An old coaching inn dating back to the 1830s, this once little inn is now actually a small hotel, where antique furnishings and decor are combined with some very modern amenities and a reputation for excellent food.

"Bayfield lies on the shore of Lake Huron, less than an hour, along good country roads, from Stratford. The village was built in the expectation of the railway, which went to Goderich instead, leaving a Victorian ghost town of large houses set on spacious, shady lots, beside a small estuary. This is a comfortable adaptation of an earlier tavern where good food is served and a cheerful and welcoming atmosphere prevails." *(Dugal Campbell)* "We had a lovely lunch here, and would definitely return for an overnight stay. Bayfield has some interesting shops with unusual items." *(Karen Hughes)*

"Delightful inn in every respect, on a quiet street filled with quaint shops. The food and service at dinner were good, and breakfast was excellent. Our room had an extremely comfortable bed and pillows, and the appointments were most attractive. We would definitely return." *(John Blewer)*

Open All year.
Rooms 11 suites, 20 doubles—all with full private bath, radio, desk, air-conditioning. Some suites with whirlpool, fireplace. 10 rooms in adjacent cottage.
Facilities Restaurant, living room with fireplace, bar with TV, parlor with fireplace, games, library; porches. Spa with sauna, whirlpool. Beach swimming, bicycling, golf, tennis, fishing, boating, hiking, horseback riding, cross-country skiing, snowshoeing nearby.
Location SW Ontario on Lake Huron. 55 m N of London, 135 NE of Detroit, 13 m S of Goderich. From Goderich, take Rte. 21 S to Bayfield.
Restrictions Smoking restricted in dining room.
Credit cards Amex, DC, Enroute, MC, Visa.
Rates Room only, $150–185 suite, $95–125 double, $65–110 single. Extra person, $15. Senior discount midweek. 1-2 night packages, $170–250 double. MAP packages, June 1–Labor Day. Breakfast, $4–7. Alc lunch, $8–14; alc dinner, $20–30.
Extras Limited wheelchair access. Crib, babysitting by prior arrangement. French, German spoken.

BRIGHTON

Main Street B&B ¢
96 Main Street, Box 431, K0K 1H0

Tel: 613—475—0351

"Our B&B is a gracious old home (circa 1843) where we treat guests as family," report owners Robert Dodds and Tom Cunningham. The broad porch is welcoming, with white wicker chairs and sofas fitted with plump cushions. Both the common areas and guest rooms are furnished with period antiques and reproductions, accented with the owners' collection of fans and paintings. Robert serves a hearty breakfast of bacon and eggs, juice, fruit, cereal, muffins, coffee and tea at the antique dining table, beneath an elaborate crystal chandelier. Guest can enjoy Presqu'ile Provincial Park, internationally known for bird watching, visit the many area antique stores, or take a dip in the above-ground pool.

"This is a relaxing spot in rural Ontario and a good stopover point when travelling leisurely between Toronto and Ottawa. Hospitality is excellent as is the food. Our room was comfortable and clean. It is a quiet town and parking is ample." *(Steve Bond)*

Open All year.
Rooms 3 doubles—all with shared bath, radio, fan. Some with TV, desk.
Facilities Dining room, living room with fireplace, library with TV, lounge. Swimming pool, bicycles. Beach, fishing, cross-country skiing, provincial park nearby.
Location Northumberland County. In center of village. 100 m E of Toronto. From Toronto or Montreal, turn S on Hwy. 30 and go to Hwy. 2 and turn right to town.
Restrictions Smoking in lounge only. Children welcome by prior arrangement.
Credit cards Visa.
Rates B&B, $45 double, $35 single. Extra child on cot, $10.
Extras Station/harbor pickup. Pets by prior arrangement. Some French spoken.

FERGUS

Breadalbane Inn ¢ 🛉 ✖
487 St. Andrew Street West, N1M 1P2

Tel: 519—843—4770

One of the finest examples of Scottish limestone architecture in this area, the Breadalbane Inn was built in 1860 by the co-founder of Fergus, and stayed in the Ferguson family for over sixty years. A picturesque little town on the Grand River, Fergus is home to 200 similarly built stone structures, including the Farmer's Market, where local produce and arts and crafts are sold each weekend.

"Phil Cardinal and his wife escaped Toronto in 1975, bought this lovely old Victorian home on the main street of Fergus, and made a B&B and restaurant out of it. He is a jovial host and excellent cook (steaks, scallops, ribs, and rack of lamb are specialties) and she does wonderful things with breakfast. The rooms are large and clean, and if you share one of the many baths (some with saunas), cozy bathrobes are provided. The dinner was exceptional, and if weather permits you can eat or drink on the attached patio in the delightful garden. Fergus and nearby Flora make for a great day of exploring, with lots of shops and antiquing." *(Wendi Van Exan)*

"A pleasant inn located in an unexceptional small town. Our room was small but comfortable, the dinner excellent, the service friendly. The seafood dishes were very good, and their wine list offers a first-rate selection at reasonable prices." *(John Blewer)*

Open All year. Restaurant closed Mon.
Rooms 1 suite, 7 doubles—2 with private bath, 6 with a maximum of 4 people sharing a bath. All with telephone, radio, air-conditioning; 5 with TV. 1 room in annex with private bath, kitchenette, patio.
Facilities Restaurant, TV room, patio, children's play equipment. Tennis, canoeing, fishing, sailing, hiking nearby.
Location S ONT. Approx. 65 m W of Toronto. 12 m N of Guelph on Hwy. 6. Turn left at traffic light on St. Andrew St. to inn in center of town.
Credit cards MC, Visa.
Rates B&B, $90 suite, $70–90 double. Extra person, $5. Tipping appreciated. Full breakfast, $3 extra. Alc lunch, $8–10; alc dinner, $25–30. Children's portions.
Extras Limited wheelchair access. Crib, babysitting. French spoken.

GANANOQUE

Trinity House Inn ✕
90 Stone Street South

Tel: 613–382–8383

If you want to have a prolonged stay at Trinity House, you can check into jail—the 1840s constabulary, that is, renovated by partners Jacques O'Shea and Brad Garside. For a more traditional visit, guests can choose the main building at Trinity House, a Victorian home refurbished to provide up-to-date amenities, and named after the district in Scotland where its bricks were made. The rooms are painted in rich shades of burgundy and green, with the extensive woodwork highlighted in ivory tones, and furnished with antiques, Oriental rugs, and bronze sculptures. Brad describes the guest room decor as "eclectic Chinois," and several have magnificent gold and black lacquer screens. The art gallery on the first floor features local works in watercolor and oil, wood carving, and also antique collectibles. An expanded continental breakfast is served in the cafe, which specializes in lunch and dinner of natural, home-cooked cuisine with emphasis on garnishes and presentation.

Gananoque is located at the western end of the St. Lawrence River, in the region known as the Thousand Islands, considered to be one of the finest sailing areas in the Northeast. Fulfilling the dream of many a sailor, Jacques and Brad left Toronto to live among their favorite islands, and offer sailing charters on their 30-foot sailboat as a way of combining the best of all worlds. *(BAB)* Reports needed.

Open April–Jan. Restaurant closed Jan.–April.
Rooms 1 suite, 6 doubles—all with private bath and/or shower, radio, air-conditioning, fan. Some with TV, desk, deck.
Facilities Guest lounge with TV, books, stereo; dining rooms with fireplace; deck.

Victorian gardens. Tennis, golf, children's play equipment nearby. Boat rentals, fishing, beaches on St. Lawrence River nearby.

Location E Ontario. 180 m E of Toronto, 60 m S of Ottawa, 20 m E of Kingston. Center of town. From Hwy. 401 turn S on Stone Rd. and continue to intersection with Hwy. 2. Go through intersection 100 yds. to inn at NW corner of Pine & Stone Sts.

Restrictions No smoking in guest rooms.

Credit cards MC, Visa.

Rates Room only, $75–125 suite, $65–105 double. 2-night holiday weekend minimum. Alc lunch, $7; alc dinner, $28.

Extras Airport/station pickup by prior arrangement.

JACKSON'S POINT

Briars Inn 🏃 ✕ 🏕   Tel: 416–722–3271
Hedge Road, Box 100, L0E 1L0   In Toronto: 416–364–5937

This resort dates back to 1839, and has been owned by the Sibald family for nearly a century. It's been taking summer visitors since the 1900s, and became a full-scale year-round facility in 1977. A full program of activities for both children and adults is offered and included in the rates, with the exception of greens fees for golf.

"This family-run inn and resort is elegant, yet relaxed and informal. The rooms are clean and the public rooms attractive. It's especially appealing to families and older couples. The kitchen produces excellent meals using local produce. Accommodations include modern motel units, summer cottages, and antique-furnished rooms in the main house. The owners take an active interest in the needs and desires of their guests. The golf course is excellent and is used for cross-country skiing in winter." *(Mr. & Mrs. V. Raymond)* Additional reports most appreciated.

Open All year.

Rooms 4 suites, 75 doubles, 11 cottages—all with full private bath, telephone, TV, air-conditioning. Some with radio, desk, fireplace, balcony. Cottages with kitchenette. Rooms in 3 8–10 bedroom lodges, main house and annex, cottages.

Facilities Dining room, bar/lounge, living rooms with fireplaces, library, game room with billiards, exercise room, sauna, hot tub. 200 acres with children's program, indoor and outdoor swimming pools, lakeside beaches, canoeing, boating, windsurfing, sailing, tennis, shuffleboard, walking trails, fishing, 18-hole golf course, cross-country skiing, skating, tobogganing, snowshoeing.

Location Central ONT, 45 m N of Toronto. On Lake Simcoe, ½ m E of Jackson's Point. From Toronto, take Hwy. 48 and bear left into Sutton; go right on Dalton Rd. to Lake Dr. E at light. Go right on Lake, right again on Hedge to resort.

Restrictions No pipe or cigar smoking in dining room. Jackets, dresses required in dining room for dinner.

Credit cards MC, Visa.

Rates Rates per person. Full board, $150–225 suite, $110–165 double, $155–210 single. Extra person over age 12, ¾ adult rate; extra child age 2–12, ½ rate; extra child under 2, $25; infant, $15. 15% service additional. Weekend, weekly rates. Tennis, golf, holiday, getaway packages.

Extras Wheelchair access. Station pickup. Crib, babysitting. French, German spoken.

KENORA

Dogtooth Lake Resort 🏃   *Tel:* 807–548–5101
P.O. Box 437, P9N 3X4

There are three good reasons people come to Dogtooth Lake on vacation: fishing, fishing, and fishing, although there's plenty of hiking in the area, and great blueberry picking in July and August, if you want a day away from the water. There's a wide variety of species to be caught in the lake's 6,200 acres of clear, unpolluted waters, depending on the season: lake trout, walleye, smallmouth bass, crappies, and northern pike all await your baited hook. Even the most avid of fishermen have to eat and sleep now and again, and owners Wayne and Patty Jones provide clean, well-equipped modern cabins, many right on the lake. It's very much a family place, and kids spend lots of time on the beach and in the cool waters. You'll want to bring your camera and binoculars along to keep an eye on the marvelous variety of local wildlife: bald eagles, loons, beaver, otters, deer, moose, and black bears. *(CF)* Reports appreciated.

Open All year.
Rooms 14 2- to 4-bedroom cabins—all with full private bath, radio, TV, fully equipped kitchen, barbecue grill. 5 with desk, 4 with air-conditioning, 3 with fan. Some with chest freezer.
Facilities Lounge with snack/grocery shop. 6 acres on lake with beach, fishing, boating, swimming, boat rentals, guided fishing trips. Adjoins cross-country trails. 15 min. to downhill skiing.
Location NW ONT. 125 E of Winnipeg, Manitoba. 15 m E of town on Hwy. 71.
Credit cards Visa.
Rates Room only, $60–110 double. Extra adult, $14–35. No charge for children under 7; negotiable rate for children 7–16. 7-night minimum during high season. Daily housekeeping service available.
Extras Airport/station pickup. Pets by prior arrangement, must be kept on leash; $5 daily. Crib, babysitting (in summer).

KINGSTON

Information please: About 30 miles northeast of Kingston (about 60 miles south of Ottawa) is the historic town of Portland-on-the-Rideau, home to the **Gallagher House** (West Water Street, Portland-on-the-Rideau K0G 1V0; 613–272–2895). A complex of four historic buildings on the lake, Portland was a favorite docking place for steamers in the 1860s. Rates for the 13 guest rooms are reasonable, and the inn's restaurant is open for three meals every day but Wednesday.

Readers who find physical exertion relaxing should check out the **Blueroof Farm** (Rural Route 1, Verona K0H 2W0; 613–374–2147) with its 15 kilometers of wilderness trails for cross-country skiing and jogging, and small lake system for canoeing. Innkeeper Kim Ondaatje has renovated an old farmhouse to provide luxury accommodations, with some friendly Dalmations serving as a welcoming committee. Verona is 27 miles north of Kingston. Rates include an elaborate breakfast. Reports?

The Hochelaga Inn 🏃🏃
24 Sydenham Street South, K7L 3G9

Tel: 613–549–5534

The Hochelaga Inn was constructed as a private house in the 1880s by John McIntyre. After his death the Bank of Montreal used it as a residence for the bank's managers. It was eventually divided up into small apartments, until its 1984 restoration by "Someplace(s) Different," a company focusing on the renovation and restoration of historic properties. An Italianate Victorian folly, complete with tower, Hochelaga has a brick facade highlighted by ornate pillars and brackets, accented in shades of green and cream. Rooms are decorated with period antiques and reproduction furnishings. Rates include a continental breakfast of fruit and juice, cereal, croissants, muffins, coffee, and tea. The manager is Jo-anne Munro-Cape. "Comfortable accommodation in a handsome mansion. Inviting porch and gardens." *(Mary Beth O'Reilly)*

Someplace(s) Different Ltd. also owns four other recently restored Ontario properties: The Glenerin Inn, Mississauga; the Idlewyld Inn, London; the Isaiah Tubbs Inn—a brick farmhouse built in 1820— and The Merrill Inn—an 1870s gothic villa—in Picton.

Open All year.
Rooms 8 suites, 15 doubles—all with private bath and/or shower, telephone, radio, TV, fan, air-conditioning. Most with queen-size beds. 1 with whirlpool tub.
Facilities Living room with TV, breakfast room, guest kitchen, patio, meeting room. Tennis, golf, swimming, sailing, boating, fishing nearby.
Location SW ONT, SE end of Lake Ontario. 200 m E of Toronto, 250 m S of Ottawa. Downtown, historic area.
Credit cards Amex, DC, Enroute, MC, Visa.
Rates B&B, $100–140 suite, $80–130 double or single. Extra person, $10. No charge for children under 3. Senior, AAA discounts. Special rates off-season.
Extras Crib. Some French spoken.

Hotel Belvedere 🏃🏃
141 King Street East, K7L 2Z9

Tel: 613–548–1565

Originally a family home of a building contractor who lavished so much money on its construction that he went bankrupt, the Belvedere first became a hotel at the turn of the century; in the 1960s, it was converted into an apartment building. Owners Donna Mallory and Ian Walsh spent two years restoring brass fixtures, cleaning original hardwood floors and tiles, and scouring antiques markets for furniture before the hotel re-opened in 1986 to the applause and commendations of the community. Guest rooms are furnished in an eclectic mix of Art Deco chairs, Victorian settees, cabinets of cherry and bird's eye maple, and oversized brass beds. Rates include a breakfast of juice, pastry, and coffee or tea, brought to your door or served in the lounge or outside.

"From the outside, the hotel is unassuming except its unusual sign—a bell, a 'V', and a deer, but the entrance and lounge hint at the delights beyond. Each room has its own theme or style, but all are spotlessly clean, attractive, and well appointed. Our suite was in the basement and was light, airy, and spacious enough so that our children could move around. Soundproofing was good. It seems each guest has their favorite room—my husband took a fancy to the one with its own hot tub while I like the room with the captain's bed. Perhaps the most spacious is the room occupied by Queen Beatrix of the Netherlands on a recent visit, a rose pink suite with balcony.

"Our hosts were very helpful and cots, blankets, and plenty of towels were on hand for our family when we arrived, including a rocking horse for our children to play on. It is very easy to feel looked after here." *(Margaret Henderson)*

Open All year.
Rooms 6 suites, 14 doubles—all with private bath and/or shower, telephone, TV, desk, fan. 14 with air-conditioning. Some with kitchenette. 1 with whirlpool tub.
Facilities Lounge with fireplace, lobby, atrium, terrace with gardens. 1 block from beach for sailing, fishing, swimming, children's play equipment.
Location Downtown area. From Hwy. 401, go S on Division St. to Johnson St. and turn left. Turn right on King St. to hotel.
Credit cards Amex, DC, Enroute, MC, Visa.
Rates B&B, $119–179 suite, $89–149 double. Extra person, $10. Children under 12 free in parents' room. 10% discount for 2 adjoining rooms.
Extras Crib, babysitting. French, Dutch spoken.

LONDON

Idlewyld Inn   *Tel: 519–433–2891*
36 Grand Avenue, N6C 1K8

A Victorian mansion built in 1878 as a home for Charles Hyman, a member of Parliament, the Idlewyld was restored by Someplace(s) Different Ltd. in 1985, and is managed by Dave and Nancy Jarrett. The exterior of this Queen Anne-style inn is light-colored brick, with intricate "gingerbread" details on the porch and balcony railings, highlighted in shades of cream and slate blue. Inside you'll find intricately carved woodwork, impressive stained glass and a massive staircase, with lavishly patterned period wallpapers and carpets to complete the decor. The bedrooms combine modern comfort with period accents, some finished in tones bright and airy, while others have rich, dark colors to create an intimate feeling. Juice, croissants, muffins, and pastries, cereals, toast, and coffee is available in the breakfast room on a help-yourself basis; the kitchen is open to guests throughout the day and evening.

"Charming inn, decorated through an interior designer showcase, when different designers did each room according to their particular vision." *(Helen Nisbet)* "The best place to stay in London. Request a larger room with a whirlpool bath. Excellent theater company, the Grand." *(LI)*

Open All year.
Rooms 10 suites, 17 doubles—all with full private bath, telephone, radio, TV, desk, air-conditioning, fan. Some with whirlpool, fireplace.
Facilities Lobby with fireplace, breakfast room; living room with fireplace; 2

meeting rooms. Patio, garden. Off-street parking. Downhill, cross country skiing nearby.

Location SW ONT. 6 blocks from center. Take Exit 186 from Hwy. 401. Go N on Wellington 3 blocks; turn left at Grand to inn between Carfrae and Ridout Sts.
Credit cards All major.
Rates B&B, $110–135 suite or double, $110 single. Extra person, $10. Senior, AAA discounts.
Extras Wheelchair access; some rooms equipped for the disabled. Crib. Member, Someplace(s) Different Ltd.

NEW HAMBURG

New Hamburg is a small town, set halfway between Kitchener and Stratford (12 miles each way) in southeastern Ontario. Many travelers combine a stay in New Hamburg with visits to the Shakespeare Festival in nearby Stratford.

The Waterlot Inn ¢ ✗   *Tel: 519–662–2020*
17 Huron Street, N0B 2G0

Since The Waterlot opened in the fall of 1974, travelers have been detouring to enjoy an outstanding meal at this historic inn, built in 1846 and now owned by W. Gordon Elkeer. The restaurant specializes in French cuisine. Whenever possible, only fresh local produce is used, along with skim milk, yogurt, and whole-grain flours, to produce dishes that are both healthy and rich in taste. A recent dinner included an appetizer of tomatoes stuffed with mussels, followed by tenderloin of lamb baked in phyllo with fresh local goat cheese in Madeira wine sauce, and concluded with fresh fruit and champagne. The guest rooms, far less well known than the restaurant, are tucked upstairs under the eaves, allowing guests to sample The Waterlot's excellent list of Canadian wines untroubled by worries about driving home. *(Dugal Campbell)* More comments required.

Open All year. Closed Christmas, Good Friday. Restaurant closed Mon.
Rooms 1 air-conditioned suite with private bath, 2 doubles sharing 1 bath. Both doubles with fan.
Facilities Restaurant, gift shop. 1 acre on river for boating, fishing. Tennis, golf, downhill skiing nearby.
Location In center. From Hwy. 7/8, turn onto Peel St., then go left at Huron.
Restrictions No smoking in guest rooms. No children.
Credit cards Amex, Enroute, MC, Visa.
Rates B&B, $85 suite, $65 double. Alc lunch, $12–15; alc dinner, $25–35; half-price meals for children under 10.
Extras Wheelchair access in restaurant. German spoken.

NIAGARA FALLS

In spite of an abundance of fast food restaurants and T-shirt shops, the town of Niagara Falls can still claim one of the most beautiful and breathtaking natural wonders in the world, Niagara Falls—technically

:alled the Canadian (also known as Horseshoe) Falls and the American ¹alls. A popular tourist attraction almost since its discovery in 1678, the ush of over 3 million liters of water *per second* down a 54-meter cliff still hrills the 12 million visitors that come each year to the Canadian side of he Falls.

"What hasn't changed in the 30 years since I was last here is the ¡ll-pervasive roar of rushing water, which you hear over the highway and ourist noise, and the heavy mist that engulfs the beauty of Queen ⅃ictoria Park at dusk. You can really appreciate the vision of the Canadi-¡ns, who, in 1885, created a parks commission to preserve the landscape ⁮or the public's non-commercial enjoyment." *(NB)*

Information please: While typical hotel chains abound in the area near he Falls, there are two small B&Bs within walking distance that we'd like ⁮o hear more about. The **Rainbow View** (4407 John Street, L2E 1A4; ₄16–374–1845), right across from the Rainbow Bridge and 2 blocks from he Falls, provides 4 doubles with private and shared baths. Rates range ⁮rom $45–75 and include afternoon snacks and a continental breakfast. ⁺ust a 5-minute walk away from Horseshoe Falls is the **Glen Mhor ⃒uesthouse** (5381 River Road, L2E 3H1; 416–354–2600), a turn-of-the-⁚entury home overlooking the Niagara River gorge; its guest rooms have ⁾rivate and shared baths, air-conditioning, and a private entrance. Ample ⁾arking is available and nondrivers can make arrangements to be picked ⁴p at the bus or train station. Guests have a choice of continental or full ⁾reakfast with home-baked muffins and breads. Comments?

NIAGARA-ON-THE-LAKE

---

⁵et on Lake Ontario, at the mouth of the Niagara River, Niagara-on-the-Lake, with its many restored nineteenth-century homes, is one of On-⁞ario's prettiest towns. From May to September, its main attraction is the ⁵haw Festival, with plays presented at three local theaters. For a break ⁞rom all that culture, the town is amply supplied with tennis courts, golf ⁚ourses, and bicycle trails, plus cross-country skiing in winter.

Also recommended: We were unable to obtain enough information to ⁚omplete a full write-up on the **Moffatt Inn** (60 Picton Street, L0S 1J0; ⁴16–468–4116), built as an inn in 1834 and renovated in 1983 after years ⁾f use as offices and apartments. The 22 rooms have private baths, and there's also a tea room and bar. "Everything was absolutely spotless. The ⁾wners are British and charming. The breakfast, not included in the rate, ⃶as delicious, with fresh biscuits and scones, and homemade jams and ⁅ellies to die for." *(James Johnson)*

Information please: We'd like to hear more about the **Old Bank House** (10 Front Street, P.O. Box 1708, L0S 1J0; 416–468–7136), built in 1817 as a financial institution and now dispensing hearty English country breakfasts and warm hospitality instead of debit slips. Owned by Don and Marjorie Ironmonger, the rates for its 8 suites and doubles are reasonable, and the inn is a short walk from the theater, shops, and restaurants. Another possibility is the **Queen's Landing** (Byron Street, P.O. Box

1180, L0S 1J0; 416–468–2195), a newly constructed hotel in the Georgian brick style, which offers 137 guest rooms furnished with period reproductions and antiques (many have a fireplace, canopied bed, and whirlpool tub). Summer rates range from $135–$200, and include use of the hotel's indoor swimming pool, hot tub, and exercise room. The hotel restaurant is expensive, but offers an imaginative selection of dishes. Reports please.

The Kiely House Heritage Inn ¢
209 Queen Street, P.O. Box 1642, L0S 1J0

Tel: 416–468–4588

A gracious inn originally built as a private home in 1832, The Kiely House Heritage Inn offers period decor, antique furnishings—some original to the house—handsome moldings, and floral wallpapers. Rates include a buffet breakfast of fresh fruit and juice, scones, muffins, and cold cereal. Meals are served in the dining room, its dark blue Victorian reproduction wallpaper contrasting with the pastel tablecloths and wood floors. The elegant parlor is equally inviting for an afternoon cup of tea. Many of the guest rooms are reached via the second-story porch which wraps around much of the inn; it offers views of the inn's flower gardens and the golf course beyond. The four suites are extremely spacious with antique furnishings, while the double rooms, in the original servants wing, are much smaller and more basically furnished. *(DLG)* Reports most welcome.

Open All year.
Rooms 4 suites with fireplace, 9 doubles—all with private bath and/or shower, telephone, fan. Radio on request. Some with desk, private porch, fireplace.
Facilities Dining room with fireplace, parlor with fireplace, veranda, screen porches. 1 acre with flower gardens, bicycles. Lake nearby for fishing, boating. Golf course adjacent.
Location S ONT. 5 min. walk from downtown. At the corner of Queen & Simcoe Sts.
Restrictions No smoking in dining room. No children under 13.
Credit cards Amex, MC, Visa.
Rates B&B, $140–150 suite, $75–95 double. Extra person, $20. Midweek, weekend packages off-season.

Oban Inn ✗
160 Front Street, Box 94, L0S 1J0

Tel: 416–468–2165
416–468–7811

Built in 1824 by Duncan Milloy, a lake captain from Oban, Scotland, the Oban Inn has been owned by the Burroughs family since 1963. The grounds have a lovely English feeling, with lots of flowers everywhere and the rooms are decorated with traditional furnishings and flowered wallpapers. The menu is also an Anglophile's delight, with such traditional favorites as steak and kidney pie for lunch, or prime rib with Yorkshire pudding for dinner.

"Our first choice of accommodation here. Just off the hustle and bustle of the main street, towards the lake where it is peaceful and lovely. Most of the rooms are not large, but all are decorated beautifully. The hotel has a great piano bar. The dining room has the best food in town and overlooks the lake and golf course. They have a great front porch where you can have light lunches or drinks." *(Wendi Van Exan)*

"We stayed in the Garden Room of the Oban House (just next door), and were delighted with our accommodation and in every aspect of the inn. The food was outstanding, especially the poached salmon." *(Carol & Nick Mumford)*

Open All year.
Rooms 1 suite, 22 doubles and singles—all with private bath and/or shower, radio, TV, desk, air-conditioning. 3 rooms in cottage.
Facilities Dining room with fireplace; lounge/bar with fireplace, weekend piano music; meeting room. 2 acres with gardens. Lake Ontario for fishing, boating; theater, golf, orchards, wineries nearby.
Location S ONT, on Lake Ontario. Center of town. 12 m N of Niagara Falls, Ontario, 75 m S of Toronto, 60 m N of Buffalo, NY. Take Niagara Pkwy. (Rte. 55) and exit at Gate St. in Niagara-on-the-Lake. Turn N on Gate and go N 2 blocks to inn on corner of Gate and Front Sts.
Restrictions Smoking in public rooms only.
Credit cards Amex, MC, Visa.
Rates Room only, $95–155 suite, $95–140 double, $70 single. Extra person, $10. Off-season packages. Alc lunch, $12; alc dinner, $35–45.
Extras Airport/station pickup. French, Portuguese, Italian spoken.

The Pillar and Post Inn ♦ ✕
King and John Streets
P.O. Box 1011, L0S 1J0

Tel: 416–468–2123
In Toronto: 416–361–1931

Built in the 1890s as a fruit canning factory, and converted into a basket factory in 1957, the building started a new life in 1970 as a restaurant and craft center. Shortly thereafter, The Pillar and Post expanded to add rooms for overnight visitors. Guest rooms are furnished in Colonial-style hand-crafted pine with patchwork quilts; there is a gift shop featuring the work of over 200 Canadian artists and craftspeople. The continental menu offers such specialties as beef medallions with wild mushrooms, shallots, and tomatoes; or rack of lamb with grainy mustard and mint Provençale. During the Shaw Festival, the prix fixe dinner is a very good value. *(NA)* Comments essential.

Open All year.
Rooms 91 doubles—all with private bath, telephone, radio, TV, desk, air-conditioning. Most with fireplace.
Facilities Dining room; living room; lounge/bar with fireplace, piano; meeting rooms; craft shop. Heated swimming pool, saunas, whirlpool, tandem bicycle rental. Golf, tennis, theater nearby.
Location S Ontario, on Lake Ontario. 4 blocks from town center. 75 m S of Toronto, 60 m N of Buffalo, NY. From Niagara Parkway (Rte. 55), exit at King St. and go S to inn at corner of King and John Sts.
Credit cards Amex, DC, JCB, MC, Visa.
Rates Room only, $132–195 double. Extra person over age 12, $15. Off-season packages. Breakfast buffet, $8.95. Prix fixe dinner, $29.50. Alc lunch, $10; alc dinner, $32.
Extras One room equipped for disabled. Crib, babysitting. French spoken.

Prince of Wales Hotel ♦ ✕
6 Picton Street, L0S 1J0

Tel: 416–468–3246
800–263–2452

A restored Victorian hotel dating back to 1865, the Prince of Wales presents a very stately face to the public with its three-story brick and stone, mansard-roofed façade. Owned and managed by Henry and John Wiens since 1975, the hotel seeks to maintain its historic charm while offering a full range of modern amenities and services. Guest rooms, decorated in both antique reproductions and more contemporary styles, are located in both the original 19th-century building and in a newer annex, the Prince of Wales Court. "Lovely restored building with two newer wings; our room in the newer part was small but comfortable, with good beds and a window that could be opened. Very clean but not 'luxe.' Our dinner was superb—my salmon entrée was delicious." *(Elizabeth Church)* "The bar serves an excellent hot apple toddy with some decidedly superior snacks. The food is well-regarded though pricey. There is an atmosphere of class about the entire hotel." *(HR)* "Our motel-like room was comfortable, but seemed ready for a bit of refurbishing." *(MA)*

Open All year.

Rooms 11 suites, 66 doubles, 27 singles—all with full private bath, telephone, radio, TV, air-conditioning. 70 with desk.

Facilities Restaurant, café, lounge with weekend entertainment, lobby, meeting rooms. Heated indoor pool, hot tub, platform tennis. Off-street parking.

Location Center of town. From Hwy. 55 turn right on Queen St. which becomes Picton St. Go 6 blocks to hotel.

Credit cards Amex, MC, Visa.

Rates Room only, $182–228 suite, $112–182 double, $106–172 single. Extra person, $12. Children under 2 free in parents' room. Summer Sunday packages. Alc lunch, $12–20; alc dinner, $30–50.

Extras Limited wheelchair access. Airport/station pickup by prior arrangement. Crib, babysitting. French, German spoken.

NORMANDALE

Union Hotel B&B ¢   *Tel: 519–426–5568*
Mailing address: Box 38, RR 1, Vittoria N0E 1W0

In the early 1800s, Normandale was a bustling community because of its iron foundry. The Union Hotel was built in the 1830s to provide food and lodging for farmers bringing the wood needed for charcoal and for sailors carrying ironware to markets in Kingston and Chicago. Although the iron ore ran out long ago, the hotel has survived in this quiet little town on the north shore of Lake Erie, and for many years had a reputation as an excellent restaurant. In November of 1989, it was bought by Debbie Karges, who has restored it as a B&B, furnishing it primarily with Victorian antiques. Rates include a breakfast reflective of the early 1800s, such as a baked omelet, eggs Normandale, lemon zephyrs, or oven-baked pancakes with maple syrup, all accompanied by fresh fruit and juice, and homemade breads and muffins. Debbie notes that "Normandale is a serene village of about 100 houses, surrounded by forested Crown Land ideal for hiking, bicycling, and cross-country skiing. The lake is across the road, in a park-like setting ideal for picnicking, swimming, or fishing."

"It is obvious that a great deal of care and thought has gone into the restoration and decoration of this inn. Breakfast was hearty and filling, served in a quiet, private atmosphere." *(KW)* "Charming hosts, lovely old hotel with beautiful antiques. Breakfast served at an old pine table. We were left in peace to read our papers and help ourselves to coffee. Very relaxing. Quiet little spot near Lake Erie." *(Wayne & Nancy Wright)* "Beautiful combination of Victorian decor with comfortable living." *(Jack & Joyce Sullivan)* "I felt pampered, by an obliging but not overbearing hostess." *(Marilyn Armstrong Penfold)*

Area for improvement: "While stronger lights were needed for reading, we learned that the owners were already searching out appropriate lamps to coordinate with the vintage decor, so I'm sure this will be corrected soon."

Open All year.
Rooms 3 doubles share two baths.
Facilities Breakfast room with woodstove, living room with library, games; 2 porches. Lake with beach nearby for swimming, fishing, boating. Hiking, bicycling, cross-country skiing nearby.
Location SW ONT. N shore of Lake Erie. 1¾ hrs. S of Toronto; 1 hr. E of London.
Restrictions No smoking. No children under 12.
Credit cards None accepted.
Rates B&B, $65 double, $35–50 single.

OTTAWA

A visit to Ottawa, the capital of Canada, should start with Parliament Hill, which offers a good view of this small and livable city with a population of only 300,000. Try and make it by 10 A.M. on a summer morning, to enjoy the Canadian version of the Changing of the Guard. If you're traveling with kids, another favorite is the nearby Royal Canadian Mint, to see money in the making. The city has a wonderful collection of museums to suit all interests, from the Museum of Science and Technology to the dramatic new National Gallery. The newest star in this galaxy is the Museum of Civilization, across the river in Hull, with outstanding galleries devoted to Canadian Indians and Inuits. Parks and recreational opportunities are plentiful; in warm weather, the city's miles of bicycle trails are a pleasure, and in winter, there's the Rideau Canal, which has been described as the world's longest skating rink. Call the Convention and Visitors Bureau for details; 613–237–5158 or 800–267–0450.

Albert House ¢   *Tel: 613–236–4479*
478 Albert Street, K1R 5B5   In Canada: 800–267–1982

Built in 1875 by noted Canadian architect Thomas Seaton Scott, this inn has a distinctive Victorian design, with double bay windows and a semi-circular porch roof that extends across the entire front of the house. It has been owned by John and Cathy Delroy since 1987, who report that their family also includes "two large but friendly dogs." Guests are invited to help themselves to coffee, fruit juice, cereal, and freshly baked muffins and croissants on the dining room sideboard; also offered are yogurt, pancakes, French toast, or eggs of your choice, accompanied by bacon or sausage, pan-fried potatoes, and six different kinds of bread for toast.

"The Albert House is a comfortable walk to the Parliament buildings, Supreme Court, Art Gallery, the Cultural Centre, Byward Market and good restaurants and shops. The wakeup service is convenient, and the rooms are comfortable, though not posh. There is a good selection of reading material available; both national and local newspapers are available every day for use of the guests. Our breakfast included excellent coffee, hot and cold cereal, fresh fruit, delicious breads and croissants fresh from the market. Upon arrival, John and Cathy provide you with your choice of cold drinks, a pleasant touch." *(Linda Cohen)* More reports welcome.

Open All year.
Rooms 14 doubles, 3 singles—all with private bath and/or shower, telephone, radio, TV, desk, air-conditioning.
Facilities Dining room, living room with fireplace, TV. Laundry facilities.
Location In Ottawa town center.
Restrictions Limited on-site parking; guests must leave keys with owners. Light sleepers should request rooms away from street. No children under 12.
Credit cards Amex, DC, Enroute, MC, Visa.
Rates B&B, $59–85 double, $49–75 single. Extra person, $10. 2-day minimum during high season.
Extras Some French spoken.

Cartier House Inn
46 Cartier Street, K2P 1J3
Tel: 613–236–4667

This turn-of-the-century brick Victorian mansion was once the home of Supreme Court Justice Thibodeau Rinfret. Although bordered by high-rise apartment buildings, the Cartier House was mercifully saved from the wrecker's ball, and was renovated in 1986 at a cost of over $1 million. The eclectic but elegant decor combines handsome fabrics—both period florals and contemporary abstracts—with new brass fixtures and Victorian, Georgian, and other antiques. Rates include a breakfast of fresh fruit and juice, cereals, whole-grain breads, and other home-baked goodies, served in the dining room or brought to your room with the morning paper. Evening turndown service, with bedtime chocolates, is among the other amenities.

"We were welcomed with refreshing raspberry soda by the attentive innkeeper. Our room was beautiful, the breakfasts relaxed, and the staff accommodating. When we asked about cross-country skiing, the innkeeper provided information on several nearby areas, as well as restaurants and other things to do. We had delightful discussions with him about poetry (his own and that of other Canadian poets), about Canadian culture and society, and about Ottawa." *(William Blauvelt & Lisa Barsky)*

"Friendly but professional atmosphere with quality service. Have experienced no problems with my room—cleanliness, lighting, and plumbing are all up to par." *(Dan Coffin)* "Helpful in every possible way. Very quiet." *(James Muir)* More comments please.

Open All year.
Rooms 3 suites, 8 doubles—all with full private bath, telephone, radio, TV, desk, fan. Suites with Jacuzzi.

Facilities Large breakfast room, lounge with library, fireplace; veranda, off-street parking. Rideau Canal for walking, jogging, bicycling nearby. 12 m to Gatineau Hills for downhill and cross-country skiing. Walking distance to Parliament Hill, Rideau Centre, museums, and Byward Market Sq.

Location NE Ont. Downtown. From Queensway (Hwy. 417), exit at Metcalfe St. and go N to Somerset St. West. Turn right on Somerset and go 2 blocks to inn at corner of Somerset and Cartier Sts.

Restrictions No smoking. Some traffic noise in corner room might disturb light sleepers. Children discouraged.

Credit cards Amex, DC, Enroute, MC, Visa.

Rates B&B, $129–144 suite, $104–124 double, $84–109 single. Extra person, $15. 10% senior discount. Restaurant, National Arts Centre packages; corporate, weekly rates Nov.–April.

Extras French spoken. Member, Relais du Silence.

Clarion Hotel Roxborough ¢ ♦ ✕

123 Metcalfe Street, K1P 5L9

Tel: 613–237–5171
In Canada: 800–458–6262
In USA: 800–CLARION

The Hotel Roxborough is an older hotel, with an imposing brick facade. Typical of hotels of its vintage, guest rooms are small and layouts basic. Recent renovations have added private bathrooms and contemporary furnishings. "The Roxborough was a pleasant hotel, quiet and well located within walking distance of Parliament Hill and other main attractions. Our room was small but clean, and the entire hotel was well-maintained. The complimentary breakfast was good and we received a free morning newspaper and overnight shoeshine." *(Muriel & David Green)*

Open All year.

Rooms 6 suites, 33 doubles, 107 singles—all with private bath and shower, telephone, radio, TV, desk, air-conditioning.

Facilities Dining room, TV room, lounge with music daily 5P.M.–9 P.M.

Location In center of town at corner of Metcalfe St. and Laurier West.

Restrictions Certain floors designated "non-smoking."

Credit cards Amex, DC, Discover, Enroute, MC, Visa.

Rates Room only, $105 suite, $54–68 double. Children under 18 free in parents' room. Continental breakfast, $5; full breakfast, $6.

Extras Crib, babysitting.

Gasthaus Switzerland ¢

89 Daly Avenue, K1N 6E6

Tel: 613–237–0335
800–267–8788

In 1984, Josef and Svetlana Sauter, newly emigrated from Switzerland, arrived in Ottawa and converted this sturdy brick and stone building into a little piece of Switzerland. Each cheery guest room has a queen-size futon mattress, kept cozy with a duvet; the duvet covers and curtains are all a bright red and white plaid, handmade by Svetlana.

"With bright, clean and well-appointed rooms, this inn has a quiet and comfortable elegance about it. The proprietors are gracious people, without being intrusive; they treat guests like friends." *(Dr. John Moss)*

"The Sauters are a charming couple who like to meet people and are available to help with any problem. They serve an extraordinary Swiss breakfast, featuring Birchermuesli, made with homemade yogurt with fresh fruits and raw oats, followed by hard-boiled eggs, Swiss cheese, homemade bread, and jam. The rooms are ample in size, well equipped, perfectly heated and clean; hot water is always in good supply." *(Ursula Lehmkuhl)*

"Well situated, close to the business and shopping center of Ottawa yet still a quiet location. Rooms have been refurbished, but maintain a cozy Swiss style." *(E. Ligteringen)*

Open All year.
Rooms 25 doubles—22 with private shower and/or bath, 4 with a maximum of 4 people sharing bath. All with telephone, TV, desk, air-conditioning. 1 with Jacuzzi.
Facilities Breakfast room, living room with TV/VCR, garden, off-street parking. Near Ottawa River for fishing, swimming, near Rideau Canal for ice skating. 15 min. to downhill, cross-country skiing. Limited off-street parking.
Location Downtown. From Queensway (Hwy. 417), take Nicholas Exit, turn right on Laurier Ave.; go left on Cumberland to inn at corner of Daly & Cumberland. From Hwy. 16, take Bronson N, Laurier E until Cumberland, turn left.
Restrictions No smoking. No children under 12.
Credit cards Enroute, MC, Visa.
Rates B&B, $78–88 suite, $68–88 double, $58–68 single. Extra person, $15.
Extras Serbo-Croatian, German, Rumanian, Russian, French spoken.

McGee's Inn
Tel: 613–237–6089
185 Daly Avenue, Sandy Hill, K1N 6E8

Once home to many of Canada's prime ministers and leaders, the fine houses of Daly Avenue declined lamentably as the 20th century progressed. In 1984, when Anne Schutte decided to restore the dilapidated 1886 home of John McGee—Canada's first clerk of the Privy Council—as a B&B, she received an exceptionally quick approval from local authorities. A major political convention would soon be in full swing, and beds were in short supply. Within a matter of a few months, the house received a new roof, eight bathrooms, and innumerable coats of paint and wallpaper. Its exterior stone-trimmed brick was chemically cleaned to show off its fine Victorian detailing. Inside, Anne, working with her mother, Mary Unger, decorated the rooms in soft tones of ivory, rose, and taupe, with English antiques and beautiful flowered fabrics. Rates include a full breakfast, with blueberry pancakes with Canadian maple syrup among the favorites.

"Service is impeccable, decor pleasing and original, service and personal appointments clean and tidy, completely up-to-date. It is a small, quiet place, and although parking is limited, it is safe and secure." *(Barbara Holmquest-Gotz)* "Charming, friendly hosts provide a good, ample breakfast and good service. Close to everything, especially for touring." *(Mrs. Albert Dennis, Jr.)*

"Our room was attractively furnished and outfitted with hair dryer, lotions, clock radio, and reading material. Our delicious breakfast was well prepared and served. The location is close to restaurants of all sorts yet the building is extremely quiet and devoid of noisy traffic." *(Joan Newstead)*

Open All year.
Rooms 2 suites, 12 doubles—10 with private shower and/or bath, 4 with maximum of 4 people sharing bath. All with telephone, radio, TV, desk, air-conditioning. Some with fireplace, refrigerator, or Jacuzzi.

Facilities Breakfast room with fireplace, parlor with piano. Near Rideau Canal for boating, skating.
Location Downtown, Sandy Hill area. At corner of Daly and Nelson Sts. Walking distance to Rideau Centre, Congress Centre, Ottawa University. From the Queensway (417), exit at Nicholas Ave. Turn right onto Laurier Ave. E, then left on Nelson St.
Restrictions No smoking. "Well-behaved children welcome."
Credit cards MC, Visa.
Rates B&B, $120 suite, $68–108 double, $62–102 single. Extra person, $15. 2-night holiday weekend minimum.
Extras French, Spanish spoken.

PORT HOPE

The Carlyle Inn ¢ ✕   *Tel: 416–885–8686*
86 John Street, O1A 2Z2

The Carlyle Inn, an Italianate Victorian building that once housed the local bank, was rescued from a long decline by David and Jeanne Henderson. In 1986 they opened a restaurant here, and after an 18-month restoration, began welcoming overnight guests as well. Rates include a hearty breakfast. Port Hope is a well-preserved Victorian town about one hour east of Toronto.

"Homey atmosphere. The Hendersons are extremely approachable and friendly—you can walk into the kitchen just to chat. The dining is fabulous as Dave has owned several restaurants. The location is downtown but quiet. They have tried to bring back the history of the old bank as much as possible." *(Denis & Carol Legros)*

Open All year.
Rooms 1 suite, 3 doubles, 1 single—all with private bath and/or shower, telephone, TV, air-conditioning. Suite with whirlpool tub.
Facilities Restaurant, lobby, conference room.
Location C Ont. 70 m E of Toronto, on Lake Ontario coast. Center of town. From Hwy. 401, go S on Hwy. 2 to Lakeshore/Ridout Rd. and turn right. Continue 3 blocks to John St. and turn right to inn on right.
Credit cards None accepted.
Rates B&B, $85 suite, $65–85 double, $60 single.

PORT STANLEY

Kettle Creek Inn ♦ ¢ ✕   *Tel: 519–782–3388*
Main Street, N0L 2A0

Squire Samuel Price built a sturdy two-story summer home for his family in 1849; in 1918 it was converted into an inn, and in 1983 the Kettle Creek Inn reopened, after extensive renovations, under the ownership of Gary and Jean Vedova. The guest rooms are highlighted by fluffy white duvets, and terry robes to wear en route to the shared baths. In 1990 the Vedovas added two guest houses that have more luxurious rooms, with en suite bathrooms. The inn's dining room has a good reputation; favorites include herbed shrimp, chicken with mushrooms and tarragon, and lamb with mustard and garlic. Sunday brunch is a popular meal, with specialties such as Brunch Wellington, a concoction of bacon, scrambled eggs, peppers, onions, spinach, and tomato, all wrapped in puff pastry and topped with hollandaise sauce.

In the early 1900s, Port Stanley was known as the "Coney Island of Canada," attracting thousands of summer visitors who arrived by rail and steamer; recent years have seen a revival of the town's appeal as a summer resort.

"Wonderful atmosphere in this refurbished inn located in an attractive Lake Erie fishing village. Several good fish restaurants, specializing in perch dinners, are nearby, along with a great beach and harbor. Excellent hostess/owner, charming bar and residents' lounge. Beautiful gardens with gazebo and water garden." *(Helen Nisbet)*

"A delightful escape from the urban hubbub. Rooms are small and spartan, yet surprisingly comfortable. Loved the large, elegant shared bath with sauna. Spent hours reading in library, garden, and gazebo. Good food! Owners and staff delightful." *(Jack Johnstone)*

Open All year.
Rooms 3 suites, 14 doubles, 1 single—8 with private bathroom, 6 with shared men's and women's bathrooms. All with desk, air-conditioning. 8 rooms in 2 guest house, with telephone, radio, TV, private entrance, balcony; 3 suites with whirlpool tub, gas fireplace.
Facilities Dining room, pub, living room with fireplace, library, sauna, patio, gazebo. Fishing, sailing, swimming, bicycling, ice fishing and ice-skating, cross-country skiing nearby.
Location SW ONT. 30 min. S of London, 141 m SW of Toronto, 125 m NE of Detroit, MI.
Restrictions No smoking in some guest rooms.
Credit cards Amex, MC, Visa.
Rates B&B, $125–150 suite, $60–90 double, $50–80 single. Extra adult, $10. Children free in parents' room. 15% gratuity suggested at guest's discretion. Senior discount midweek. Off-season MAP packages. Alc lunch, $5–10; alc dinner, $50–60.
Extras Wheelchair access. Crib, babysitting. Some French, some German spoken.

ST. JACOBS

Jakobstettel Guest House 🎋   *Tel: 519–664–2208*
16 Isabella Street, N0B 2N0

The Jakobstettel Guest House is a handsome, 90-year-old brick mansion, originally built for the owner of the village mill. It was converted to an inn in 1982, and is managed by Ella Brubacher. Rooms are attractively fitted out with reproduction furniture, although to some tastes, the rooms may seem overly "decorated" with matching everything. Collectors will be interested in the abundance of crafts and artisans in the area; there are over 90 shops, many of them in the converted mill. The millrace provides ideal skating in the winter months, covering a distance of 1½ miles.

"The Jakobstettel Guest House is an ideal place to stay for rest and relaxation. The bedrooms are large—all differently furnished. Comfortable armchairs, large windows with quiet vistas help to make one feel at once at home and relaxed. The appointments and bathrooms are spotlessly clean. An informal continental breakfast of home-cooked muffins, fruit, and cheese is provided; you help yourself from the kitchen. St. Jacobs is a small Mennonite town with much farming and local crafts." *(Geoffrey Steel)*

"Their slogan, 'where quiet can still be heard,' is very appropriate. Clean, quiet, wonderful hospitality. The coffee is always on and the cookie jar is always full!" (Marie Young) "Quiet little village with nice shops, restaurants, churches. Staff is extremely accommodating and friendly." *(Robert Boian)* "Great aromas come from the kitchen at breakfast and when late-night snacks are being prepared. We had the Blue Room and found it spacious and comfortable. The innkeepers were friendly and informative about local points of interest. Even on a rainy day the canal walk nearby is a good reason for a morning stroll." *(Janis Feron)*

Open All year.
Rooms 11 doubles, 1 single—all with private bath and/or shower, telephone, radio, desk, air-conditioning, fan. Some with balcony.
Facilities Living room/lounge, library, meeting room, deck, patio. Games, books, snacks. 5 acres with badminton, swimming pool, horseshoe pits, volleyball, bicycles, rose garden, tennis court, hiking, cross-country skiing. Fishing nearby.
Location S ONT, Waterloo County. 75 m W of Toronto. 2 blocks from center of town. From Hwy. 401, take Hwy. 8 W to Kitchener; take Conestoga Pkwy., follow Hwy. 86 N signs to St. Jacobs exit Regional Rd. 17. In St. Jacobs, turn right at mill and proceed to Isabella St.
Restrictions No smoking. Children over 6 preferred.
Credit cards Amex, MC, Visa.
Rates B&B, $100–150 double, $80–135 single. Extra person, $15. No tipping. Midweek corporate discount. By prior arrangement, for groups, prix fixe lunch, $10; dinner, $19.
Extras Babysitting can be arranged. Pennsylvania German spoken.

ST. MARYS

Westover Inn 🛏 ✗   *Tel: 519–284–2977*
300 Thomas Street, Box 280, N0M 2V0

Owners Robert and Eileen Steubing spent two years and almost $2 million dollars restoring the Westover to provide modern amenities in a Victorian atmosphere. The limestone exterior has gingerbread "icicles" dripping from the eaves, and inside, the leaded glass windows and carved wood embellishments have been handsomely restored. More simply styled are the rooms in the outbuildings that housed priests in training as foreign missionaries. A permanent legacy of the era when the estate was owned by the Roman Catholic Church is the shrine nearby that is always open to the public. A continental breakfast is served buffet-style, and the inn's restaurant offers regional cuisine, served by candlelight, and an extensive wine cellar.

"About twenty minutes drive from Stratford and the Shakespeare Festi-

275

val is the riverside town of St. Marys, with its well-preserved old stone buildings of 1830 to 1890 vintage. There are good shops and interesting walks. Westover is an old estate now converted to an inn, with the main lodge and dining room being the old residence. Our lodge, a two-room suite just behind the main house, was nicely furnished, quiet, and clean. We had a great buffet-style breakfast and an excellent dinner and pleasant evening." *(Steven Bond)*

Minor niggles: "Some rooms are quite small, and most bathrooms lack storage space."

Open All year.
Rooms 3 suites, 8 doubles—all with private bath and/or shower, air-conditioning. 2 suites, 3 rooms in 2 separate cottages. 1 suite with whirlpool tub.
Facilities Restaurant, living room, lobby, meeting rooms. 19 acres with swimming pool, jogging trails, gardens.
Location SW Ont. 15 m SW of Stratford. Go S on Hwy. 7 to Rte. 19 to town.
Credit cards Most major cards accepted.
Rates B&B, $170–207 suite, $89–105 double, $82–190 single. Extra person, $25. Children under 12 in parents' room, free; breakfast $7.
Extras Crib, $5.

STRATFORD

Located about 100 miles west of Toronto on the banks of the Avon River is the town of Stratford, home of the Stratford Theatre Festival. For 22 weeks a year, beginning in early May, performances are given in one or all of the three stages, ranging in size from the 2,200-seat Festival Theatre to the informal, theater-in-the-round Third Stage.

Information please: Additional recommendations for Stratford would be welcome. One possibility is the **Hazen House**, a well furnished B&B (129 Brunswick Street N5A 3L9; 519–271–5644).

Stone Maiden Inn   *Tel:* 519–271–7129
123 Church Street, N5A 2R3

Named for the carved stone figureheads that adorn the front hall, the Stone Maiden Inn provides a fresh, country atmosphere in a restored 1872 Victorian building. Built as a private residence, it was converted in the early 1900s into a railway hotel and then a boardinghouse. In what seems to be the usual course of events of many inns, it became run-down and dilapidated; in 1982 it was totally renovated to become once again an elegant hotel. Owners Barb and Len Woodward, who purchased the inn in 1989, have decorated the guest rooms with antiques, quilts, and wicker furnishings.

Rates include afternoon beverages on the veranda, coffee and tea available all day, and a breakfast buffet of meat, fried potatoes, an egg casserole, cereal, fruits, juice, toast and jams, and sliced tomatoes in season, served in the dining room or veranda.

"Our room, with canopied bed, whirlpool tub, and wall-to-wall carpeting was immaculate; early morning coffee was brought to our door. Len and Barb are gracious hosts who respected our privacy." *(CC, and others)* "Breakfast is my favorite meal, if done well, as it was here—nicely served, delicious and enjoyable. I particularly liked our table in the bay window overlooking the flowered side yard." *(Patricia Pitts)* "The warm, considerate innkeepers made us feel as if we were the most important people here. We are vegetarians, and they were happy to accommodate our breakfast preferences." *(Jaclyn & Bradley Ross)* "Beautiful heritage home, very quiet and relaxed. Menu differs every day, but all delicious. Quilts are on the beds, turned down at night with a chocolate and a 'sleep' quote on your pillow." *(Lorraine & Pete Krause)*

"Ideal location within walking distance to town and theaters." *(Jayne & Stuart Wallace)* "Wonderful attention to detail, from the ever-present refreshments to a welcome note and candy in our room." *(Robert Kain)* "All questions were answered eagerly, honestly, and graciously. The room was immaculate with towels and bedding changed daily." *(Eugene Swetin)* "Firm mattress, fully appointed bath with ample hot water and pressure, plus adequate storage for clothes and personal items." *(Carol Wyant)*

Open Mid-April to Dec.
Rooms 15 doubles—all with private bath, radio, air-conditioning, ceiling fan. Some with TV, desk, whirlpool tub, fireplace, refrigerator.
Facilities Dining room with fireplace, living room with fireplace, piano, stereo, library with books, parlor, veranda. Tennis, golf nearby.
Location S ONT. 80 m SW of Toronto. 120 m NE of Detroit. 2 blocks from downtown.
Restrictions Smoking permitted in parlor, guest rooms only. "Well-behaved children welcome."
Credit cards MC, Visa.
Rates B&B, $85–145 double. Extra person, $25. Theater, midweek packages. Off-season discounts. 2-night weekend minimum during July, Aug., Sept.
Extras Limited wheelchair access. Local airport/station pickup by prior arrangement. Babysitting.

TORONTO

With a population of 3 million, Toronto is Canada's largest city, offering visitors the advantages of a major metropolitan center with few of the usual accompanying urban problems. Set on Lake Ontario, less than 100 miles north of Buffalo, Toronto offers first-rate theaters, major league sports, and a variety of shops (especially at Eaton Centre) and ethnic restaurants. Top sightseeing attractions include the Art Gallery of Ontario, the Royal Ontario Museum, and the Ontario Science Center; when you're ready for some greenery, take the ferry to Toronto Island for strolling, swimming, and picnicking, along with a beautiful view of the city.

Weekend rates at most Toronto hotels offer substantial savings; be sure to request details when making reservations.

Also recommended: For budget travelers, *Jon Melnick* suggests **Burken Guest House** (322 Palmerston Blvd., M6G 2N6; 416–920–7842) "as a low cost alternative on a beautiful street. It is in a great neighborhood with excellent transportation—two trolley lines nearby. Three or four guest rooms share a bath, but there's a sink in each room. There is a nice breakfast on the porch (in summer), all for $65 double." This brick Victorian, with massive pillars supporting a double porch, is furnished with antiques, and accommodates only non-smokers.

With 379 rooms, the **Four Seasons** is too big for this guide, but is recommended by many as tops in the luxury hotel category (21 Avenue Road, M5R 2G1; 416–964–0411). Another possibility in the "grand luxe" class is the **King Edward Hotel** (416–863–9700 or 800–225–5843; 37 King Street East, M5C 1E9), a 315-room historic landmark hotel, recently restored to its turn-of-the-century elegance. The public rooms boast inlaid marble floors, a columned rotunda, and elaborately carved ceilings, while the well-appointed guest rooms have been redone in traditional decor; reader reports have been most positive.

Recommended nearby: We received a rave review of **Langdon Hall** (Rural Route 33, Cambridge N3H 4R8; 519–740–2100 or 416–338–8800) too late for a full write-up. "This recent addition to the Relais et Chateaux group is a splendid country house and property, less than an hour southwest of the Toronto airport. The Colonial Revival-style house was the retreat of John Jacob Astor's grand-daughter and the grand lawn, spectacular gardens and little walking trails allow you to indulge in a great fantasy of 'country living' with a definite English flair. The rooms are generally large, tasteful, with Oriental rugs and other accessories, most with working fireplace. All rooms in the 'Cloisters' (annex) have very cozy sitting areas and huge bathroom/dressing rooms. Beds have crisp linens and fluffy comforters, and robes are provided. The kitchen is one of the great attractions. Chef Nigel Didcock was trained in France at Troisgros, and he has made it one of the finest restaurants in Canada. Plenty of sitting areas, reading rooms, bar, private dining room, and outdoor seating made for a nice variety." *(LI)*

Information please: We need more reports on the **The Bradgate Arms** (54 Foxbar Road /Avenue Road at St. Clair, M4V 2G6; (416–968–1331 or 800–268–7171) listed in past editions. Created from several turn-of-the-century apartment buildings and three rambling old houses, the result is a 110-room luxury hotel containing a six-story covered atrium with trees, plants, and a fountain; a piano lounge; and traditionally furnished guest rooms. One reader liked its location, convenient to Toronto's restaurants and public transportation, its European-style lobby, and her comfortable, well-appointed room; another found the decor bland and the location in the residential Forest Hill district remote. Your opinions welcome.

Of interest nearby: Fifteen miles south of Toronto, on the lake, is the **Glenerin Inn** (1695 The Collegeway, Mississauga L5L 3S7; 416–828–6103), a rambling, 1927-vintage limestone mansion restored as an inn after years as a monastery. Austerity has given way to modern amenities and private bathrooms, and rates include a continental breakfast. The inn's restaurant, Thatcher's, presents creative variations of classic entrées, all of them named for British prime ministers; the Sir Winston Churchill is prime rib of beef with traditional Yorkshire pudding, of course, while the Harold MacMillan is a braised halibut in an orange sauce.

The **Philip Shaver House** (1034 Highway 53 West, RR 1, Ancaster
L9G 3K9; 416–648–5225), is located about 25 miles south of the Toronto.
The Shaver family was one of the first to settle in this area in the late
1700s; Philip Shaver, one of thirteen Shaver children, built this Georgian
house in 1835. The house remained in the same family until 1982, when
it was converted into an inn and restaurant. Many of the original furnishings have survived, including a spinning wheel. A full country breakfast
is included in the rates. Reports most welcome.

Camberley Club Hotel ¢   *Tel:* 416–947–9025
40 King Street West, Scotia Plaza, M5H 3Y2   800–866–ROOM

Scotia Plaza is a new complex combining shopping, business, and entertainment in both high-rise and underground buildings. The Camberley
Club, opened in 1990 under the management of Christopher Davies,
provides all-suite accommodations on the 28th and 29th floors of the
building. Guest rooms have traditional furnishings, terry robes, fresh
flowers, and thrice-daily maid service. Rates include continental breakfast,
afternoon tea, evening hors d'oeuvres and cocktails, and petit fours. Lunch
and dinner is available from the hotel kitchen via room service, with
selections of salads and sandwiches and entrées such as filet of trout,
grilled salmon steak, filet mignon, and a pasta special.

"You would never even know the Camberly, located on the 28th floor
of the Scotia Plaza in Toronto, was there except for a small sign in the
lobby. Check-in is a pleasure—the concierge will remember your name for
the rest of your stay. The rooms are luxurious without being ostentatious.
The bathroom had a very large whirlpool and my room had a magnificent
view of Toronto. The food was excellent, ranging from a breakfast of
pastries, cereals, and fruits, to outstanding dinner entrées, through efficient
room service." *(Ken Brooks Jr., and others)*

"Everyone at the Camberley made us feel special—even when we
needed directions to a toy store for my four-year-old daughter. Never
having used the Toronto subway, I found the hotel location perfect for
any destination. I felt very safe, even after dark." *(Stefanie Herrera)* "The
hotel is centrally located in downtown Toronto. Cocktails are served
every evening in an attractive lounge area. The service is what I really
appreciated; they placed a hot water bottle in my bed on a cold winter
night." *(Maria Sarli)* "Underground parking with easy access. Views from
the floor-to-ceiling dining room windows are spectacular at night." *(Miles
Browning)*

Areas for improvement: "More effective room-darkening shades. Better
bathroom lighting and counter space for make-up application."

Open All year.
Rooms 54 suites—all with full private bath & Jacuzzi, telephone, radio, TV/VCR,
desk, air-conditioning, fan.
Facilities Dining room, living room with TV/VCR, stereo, books, bar/lounge,
laundry facility. Underground parking.
Location Downtown Toronto. Intersection of King and Bay sts.
Restrictions Non-smoking rooms available.
Credit cards Amex, DC, Enroute, MC, Visa.
Rates B&B, $105–210 suite. Alc lunch, $15; alc dinner, $50.
Extras Wheelchair access. Airport/station pickup. Crib. French, Polish spoken.

TRENTON

The Smithrim House ¢ 👫   *Tel: 613–394–5001*
272 Dufferin Avenue, K8V 5G2

While many of innkeeper Dorothy Neufeld's guests are long-term tenants looking for permanent housing in the area, she looks forward to the variety brought by visitors just passing through. Her Craftsman-style home is eclectically furnished with comfortable sofas and chairs and brass accent pieces. Guest rooms have reproduction brass and cherry beds, with ruffled comforters and pillows. Included in the rates is a continental breakfast—served in the elegant dining room or enjoyed by the pool. For an extra $2.50, Dorothy will whip up some pancakes, French toast, or frittata.

"The owner and hostess, Mrs. Neufeld, went out of her way to accommodate me; she herself seemed to create the friendly, hospitable atmosphere that filled her house and affected her guests. I would recommend this inn to even the most demanding house guest." *(Eric Larsen)*

Open All year.
Rooms 3 doubles—with a maximum of 6 people sharing bath. All with radio, air-conditioning.
Facilities Dining room, living room with fireplace, TV, stereo; sunroom with TV, books. Garden with swimming pool. Golf, cross-country skiing, Lake Ontario for boating, fishing, swimming nearby. Downhill skiing, 5 m.
Location 100 miles E of Toronto. 10 min. walk from town center. Take Rte. 401 to Wooler Rd. (Exit 522); go S to Hwy. 2, E to Hwy. 33 (Dufferin).
Restrictions Traffic noise could disturb light sleepers. No smoking.
Credit cards None accepted.
Rates Full board, $75–85 double, $50–60 single. MAP, $65–75 double, $45–55 single. B&B, $45–55 double, $35–45 single. Extra person, $10. $6 discount for children. Murder Mystery packages. Prix fixe lunch, $5, dinner $10–15.
Extras Airport/station pickup. Housebroken pets welcome by prior arrangement. Babysitting.

WIARTON

Maplehurst B&B ¢   *Tel: 519–534–1210*
Frank Street, N0H 2T0

Set at the top of town, Maplehurst is a brick Victorian home overlooking Colpys Bay. Rates include a breakfast of croissants, eggs, ham, home fries, poached pears in yogurt and honey sauce, cereal, buttermilk and carrot muffins, juice, and coffee.

"Jim and Arlene Kibbler (and their 14-year-old dog, Beau) are delightful hosts. Our room with king-size bed was comfortable and beautifully decorated. The Kibblers provide a large breakfast at flexible hours, and offer a sitting room filled with video tapes for your evening entertainment. It's easy to feel at home here." *(Suzanne Burton)* More reports needed.

Open May 1–Feb. 28.
Rooms 3 doubles—1 with private bath, 2 sharing 1 bath.
Facilities Sitting room with fireplace, TV/VCR; veranda. Hiking, fishing, swimming pool, tennis, ice-skating, cross-country skiing nearby.
Location W ONT, Bruce Peninsula, between Lake Huron & Georgian Bay. 3 hrs. N of Toronto. Arriving in Wiarton, pass through gates and go down hill. Turn left at Frank St. to inn at top of hill across from Anglican Church at corner of Gould St.
Credit cards None accepted.
Rates B&B, $40–45, $35 single. Family rates.

Key to Abbreviations and Symbols

For complete information and explanations, please see the Introduction.

¢ Especially good value for overnight accommodation.
♦ Families welcome. Most (but not all) have cribs, baby-sitting, games, play equipment, and reduced rates for children.
✕ Meals served to public; reservations recommended or required.
♠ Tennis court and swimming pool or lake on the grounds. Golf usually on grounds or nearby.
Rates: Range from least expensive room in low season to most expensive room in peak season.
Room only: No meals included; European Plan (EP).
B&B: Bed and breakfast; includes breakfast, sometimes afternoon/ evening refreshment.
MAP: Modified American Plan; includes breakfast and dinner.
Full board: Three meals daily.
Alc lunch: À la carte lunch; average price of entrée plus nonalcoholic drink, tax, tip.
Alc dinner: Average price of three-course dinner, including half bottle of house wine, tax, tip.
Prix fixe dinner: Three- to five-course set dinner, excluding wine, tax, tip unless otherwise noted.
Extras: Noted if available. Always confirm in advance. Pets are not permitted unless specified; if you are allergic, ask for details; *most innkeepers have pets.*

Appendix

STATE AND PROVINCIAL TOURIST OFFICES

Listed here are the addresses and telephone numbers for the tourist offices of the Midwestern states covered in this book. When you write or call one of these offices, be sure to request a map of the state and a calendar of events. If you will be visiting a particular city or region, or if you have any special interests, be sure to specify this as well.

Illinois Bureau of Tourism
1000 Business Center Drive
Mt. Prospect, Illinois 60056
312–793–2094 or 800–223–0121 (out of state)

Indiana Tourism Development Division
1 North Capitol, Suite 700
Indianapolis, Indiana 46204–2288
317–232–8860 or 800–289–6646

Iowa Tourism Office
200 East Grand Avenue
Des Moines, Iowa 50309–2882
515–242–4705 or 800–635–7820

Kansas Department of Economic Development—Travel and Tourism Division
400 West 8th Street, Suite 500
Topeka, Kansas 66603
913–296–2009 or 800–252–6727 (within Kansas)

Michigan Travel Bureau
Department of Commerce
P.O. Box 30226
Lansing, Michigan 48909
517–373–1195 or 800–543–2 YES

Minnesota Tourist Information Center
375 Jackson Street
Farm Credit Service Building
250 Skyway Level
St. Paul, Minnesota 55101
612–296–5029 or 800–657–3700 (out of state) or 800–652–9747 (in Minnesota)

Missouri Division of Tourism
P.O. Box 1055
Jefferson City, Missouri 65102
314–751–4133

Nebraska Division of Travel and Tourism
P.O. Box 94666
Lincoln, Nebraska 68509
402–471–3796 or 800–228–4307 (out of state) or 800–742–7595 (within Nebraska)

North Dakota Tourism Promotion
Liberty Memorial Building
604 East Boulevard
Bismarck, North Dakota 58505
701–224–2525 or 800–472–2100 (within North Dakota) or 800–437–2077 (out of state)

Ohio Office of Travel & Tourism
600 West Spring Street
Columbus, Ohio 43216-0001
800–848–1300 or (800) 282–5393

South Dakota Division of Tourism
Capitol Lake Plaza
711 Wells Avenue
Pierre, South Dakota 57501
605–773–3301 or 800–952–2217 (within South Dakota) or 800–843–1930 (out of state)

Wisconsin Division of Tourism
P.O. Box 7970-B
123 W. Washington
Madison, Wisconsin 53707
608–266–2161 or 800–372–2737

(within Wisconsin and neighboring states) or 800–432–8747 (out of state)

Travel Arctic
Government of Northwest Territories
Yellowknife
Northwest Territories, Canada X1A 2L9
403–873–7200

Ontario Ministry of Tourism and Recreation
Customer Sales and Services
Queens Park
Toronto, Ontario, Canada M7A 2E5
416–965–4008 (within Canada) or 800–668–2746 (from continental U.S./Canada—except Yukon and the Northwest Territories)

MAPS

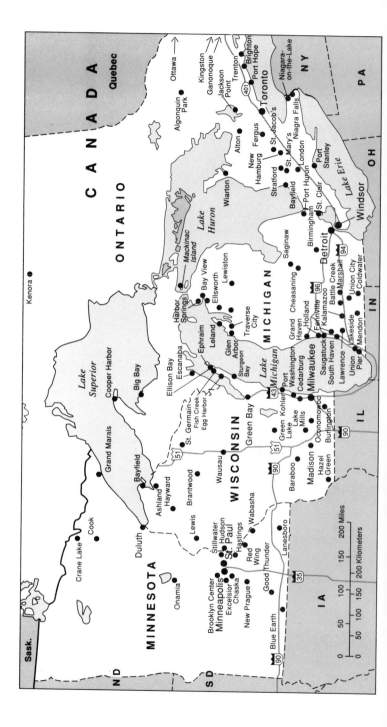

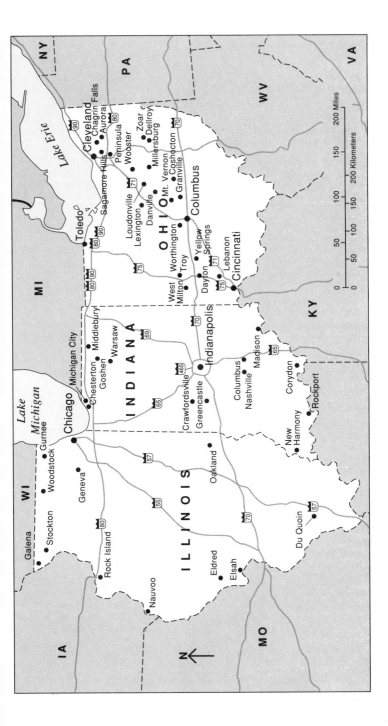

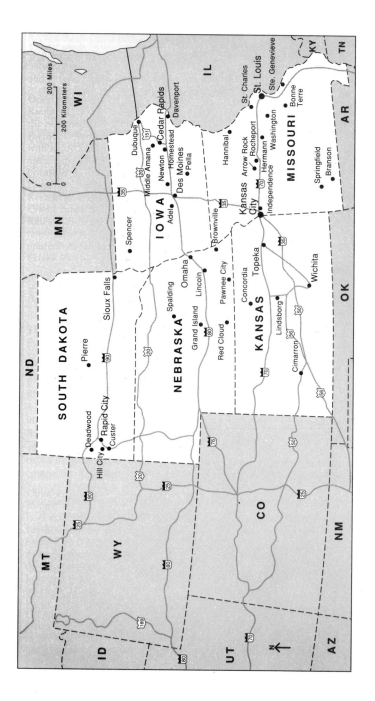

Index of Accommodations

Hotel/Inn Report Forms

The report forms on the following pages may be used to endorse or critique an existing entry or to nominate a hotel or inn that you feel deserves inclusion in next year's edition. Whichever you wish to do, don't feel you have to use our forms, or, if you do use them, don't feel you must restrict yourself to the space available. All nominations (each on a separate piece of paper, if possible) should include your name and address, the name and location of the hotel or inn, when you have stayed there, and for how long. A copy of the establishment's brochure is also helpful. Please report only on establishments you have visited in the last eighteen months, unless you are sure that standards have not dropped since your stay. Please be as specific as possible, and critical where appropriate, about the character of the building, the public rooms, the accommodations, the meals, the service, the nightlife, the grounds, and the general atmosphere of the inn and the attitude of its owners. Any comments you have about area restaurants and sights would also be most appreciated.

Don't feel you need to write at length. A report that merely verifies the accuracy of existing listings is extremely helpful, i.e., "Visited XYZ Inn and found it just as described." There is no need to bother with prices or with routine information about the number of rooms and facilities, although a sample brochure is very helpful for new recommendations. We obtain such details directly from the hotels selected. What we are eager to get from readers is information that is not accessible elsewhere.

On the other hand, don't apologize for writing a long report. Although space does not permit us to quote them in toto, the small details provided about furnishings, atmosphere, and cuisine can really make a description come alive, illuminating the special flavor of a particular inn or hotel. Remember that we will again be awarding free copies to our most helpful respondents—last year we mailed over 500 books.

Please note that we print only the names of respondents, never addresses. Those making negative observations are not identified. Although we must always have your full name and address, we will be happy to print your initials, or a pseudonym, if you prefer.

These report forms may also be used, if you wish, to recommend good hotels in Europe to our equivalent publication, *Europe's Wonderful Little Hotels & Inns* (published in Europe as *The Good Hotel Guide*). Reports should be sent to *Europe's Wonderful Little Hotels & Inns*, St. Martin's Press, 175 Fifth Avenue, New York, NY 10010; to P.O. Box 150, Riverside, CT 06878; or directly to *The Good Hotel Guide*, 61 Clarendon Road, London W11. Readers in the UK can send their letters postage-free to *The Good Hotel Guide*, Freepost, London W11 4 BR.

To: *America's Wonderful Little Hotels & Inns,*
    P.O. Box 150, Riverside, CT 06878.

Name of hotel_____

Address_____

Telephone_____

Date of most recent visit_____ Duration of visit_____

☐ New recommendation   ☐ Comment on existing entry

Please be as specific as possible about furnishings, atmosphere, service, and cuisine. If reporting on an existing entry, please tell us whether you thought it accurate, and whether you would return. Unless you tell us not to, we shall assume that we may publish your name in the next edition. Thank you very much for writing; use your own stationery if preferred:

I am not connected directly or indirectly with the management or owners.

I would stay here again if returning to the area.   ☐ yes   ☐ no

Signed_____

Name_____
                        (Please print)

Address_____
                        (Please print)

MW92